PENGUIN BOOKS

P9-EJI-049

ALL IN

Paula Broadwell has more than a decade of military service and over a decade and a half of work in counterterrorism and counterinsurgency. She is a research associate at Harvard University's Center for Public Leadership and a PhD candidate at the University of London. She graduated with honors from the United States Military Academy and earned an MA degree from the University of Denver and an MPA degree from Harvard's Kennedy School of Government. She lives with her husband and their two children in North Carolina.

Vernon Loeb is the metro editor at *The Washington Post*. In 2003, he embedded with the 101st Airborne Division under Petraeus's command in Iraq.

Praise for *All In*:

"*All In* provide[s] . . . a valuable perspective on how General Petraeus—the most successful U.S. general of his generation—approached the war in Afghanistan and other crucial junctures in his career. . . . [Broadwell's] account is dead-bang accurate. It is, in fact, probably the best depiction yet of General Petraeus's management style. . . . Many of the *All In* vignettes will have anyone familiar with General Petraeus nodding in recognition. . . . Even those most familiar with General Petraeus will learn something new here."
—*The Wall Street Journal*

"Paula Broadwell offers a fascinating account . . . present[ing] a work that is at once a partial biography, a study in Patraeus's particular brand of military leadership, and an examination of his command year in Afghanistan." —*The Houston Chronicle*

"[General Jack] Galvin said in an interview with Broadwell, 'live up to it all with the highest standards of integrity. You become part of a legend.' *All In* fits neatly into that."
—ABC News

"Broadwell's excellent biography portrays him as a modern exemplar of the soldier-scholar-statesman and one who has exerted a profound influence on the American military establishment."
—*Foreign Affairs*

"Broadwell traces in academic prose Petraeus's key role in drawing the Army's attention to counterinsurgency warfare before the wars in Iraq and Afghanistan."
—STLToday.com

"Audacious . . . with its on-the-ground reporting . . . the biography has already won praise from high places."
—*The Charlotte Observer*

"General Petraeus is one of the most important Americans of our time, in or out of uniform. This riveting insider's account of his life and education is at once instructive and inspiring."
—Tom Brokaw, anchor and managing editor, *NBC Nightly News*
and author of *The Greatest Generation*

"This majestic biography will set the standard for all future works about General Petraeus. With superb narrative skill, Broadwell simultaneously provides an intimate look at Petraeus the man, a fascinating account of modern warfare, and an elegant study of leadership."

—Doris Kearns Goodwin, Pulitzer Prize–winning author
of *No Ordinary Time* and *Team of Rivals*

"David Petraeus is, in the words of former Defense Secretary Robert Gates, 'the indispensable soldier/scholar of this era,' and make no mistake, this is no tranquil era in the history of the American military. Anyone seeking to understand the nature of American warfighting in the twenty-first century, how it is both like and utterly unlike that of any previous one, needs to understand Petraeus, his remarkable career, his thinking, and his character. *All In* is an excellent place to start. It is fascinating and insightful, informed by remarkable access to the man both on and off the battlefield, and stands as the first good biography of the most important general of our times." —Mark Bowden, author of *Black Hawk Down*

"*All In* vividly demonstrates the influence General David Petraeus has had on a whole generation of military officers—showing by the force of his personal example what it means to be tough, loyal, committed, and smart. Paula Broadwell takes readers into the briefing rooms and onto the battlefields to better understand the lessons and sacrifices of America's wars."

—Nathaniel Fick, *New York Times* bestselling author of *One Bullet Away*

"There have been several books written about parts of the career of David Petraeus, but this is the first one that could be called a biography of the most prominent American general since World War II. It is written with an insider's lively understanding of the workings of today's Army. I've known David Petraeus since he was a colonel and written two books in which he appeared, but I still learned a lot about him from this book. *All In* feels at times like we are sitting at his side in Afghanistan, reading his e-mails over his shoulder."

—Thomas E. Ricks, Pulitzer Prize–winning author of *Fiasco* and *The Gamble*

"Teddy Roosevelt once said that it is not enough to be intelligent; a leader must also be honest and fearless. In General David Petraeus (himself a T.R. fan), America has been fortunate to have a soldier-scholar who is all three. Paula Broadwell, soldier-scholar in her own right, tells the Petraeus story masterfully, providing especially rich detail and insight into his Afghanistan mission. This book helps us understand how Petraeus has become the living legend he is."

—David Gergen, director, Harvard Kennedy School Center for
Public Leadership, and author of *Eyewitness to Power*

"This is the best book yet on General David Petraeus, written by a remarkable former Army officer who spent months on the ground in Afghanistan herself. Paula Broadwell captures his basic tenets of counterinsurgency and basic approach to leadership—as well as Petraeus's personal qualities and character—in a highly readable and pithy fashion. No one gives a truer picture of the war, or of the finest general of this era and one of the greatest in modern American history."

—Michael O'Hanlon, senior fellow, the Brookings Institution, and
author of *The Wounded Giant* and *The Science of War*

ALL IN

THE EDUCATION OF
GENERAL DAVID PETRAEUS

PAULA BROADWELL

WITH VERNON LOEB

PENGUIN BOOKS

PENGUIN BOOKS

Published by the Penguin Group

Penguin Group (USA) Inc., 375 Hudson Street, New York, New York 10014, USA • Penguin Group
(Canada), 90 Eglinton Avenue East, Suite 700, Toronto, Ontario M4P 2Y3, Canada (a division of
Pearson Penguin Canada Inc.) • Penguin Books Ltd, 80 Strand, London WC2R 0RL, England •
Penguin Ireland, 25 St Stephen's Green, Dublin 2, Ireland (a division of Penguin Books Ltd) •
Penguin Group (Australia), 707 Collins Street, Melbourne, Victoria 3008, Australia (a division of
Pearson Australia Group Pty Ltd) • Penguin Books India Pvt Ltd, 11 Community Centre,
Panchsheel Park, New Delhi – 110 017, India • Penguin Group (NZ), 67 Apollo Drive, Rosedale,
Auckland 0632, New Zealand (a division of Pearson New Zealand Ltd) • Penguin Books (South
Africa), Rosebank Office Park, 181 Jan Smuts Avenue, Parktown North 2193, South Africa •
Penguin China, B7 Jiaming Center, 27 East Third Ring Road North, Chaoyang District,
Beijing 100020, China

Penguin Books Ltd, Registered Offices: 80 Strand, London WC2R 0RL, England

First published in The Penguin Press, a member of Penguin Group (USA) Inc. 2012
Published in Penguin Books 2012

1   3   5   7   9   10   8   6   4   2

Photograph credits appear on page 395.

THE LIBRARY OF CONGRESS HAS CATALOGED THE HARDCOVER EDITION AS FOLLOWS:

Broadwell, Paula.
All in : the education of General David Petraeus / Paula Broadwell with Vernon Loeb.
p.   cm.
Includes bibliographical references and index.
ISBN 978-1-59420-318-3 (hc)
ISBN 978-0-14-312299-9 (pbk.)
1. Petraeus, David Howell.   2. Generals—United States—Biography.   3. United States.
Army—Biography.   4. Iraq War, 2003—Biography.   I. Loeb, Vernon.   II. Title.
III. Title: Education of General David Petraeus.
E897.4.P48B76 2012   2011043881
355.0092—dc23
[B]

Printed in the United States of America
DESIGNED BY NICOLE LAROCHE

Map on pgs viii–ix by Jeffrey Ward

To my three favorite troopers,

Scott, Lucien and Landon Broadwell,

and to those who serve

To strive, to seek, to find, and not to yield.

—Alfred, Lord Tennyson, "Ulysses"

"This isn't double down, Mr. President. It's all in."

—General David Petraeus to President George W. Bush
in the Oval Office, January 23, 2007,
on the eve of the surge in Iraq

CONTENTS

Map of Afghanistan viii–ix
Acronyms and Abbreviations xiii
Cast of Characters xix
Preface xxvii

CHAPTER 1: **GROUND TRUTH** *1*

CHAPTER 2: **RESULTS, BOY** *29*

CHAPTER 3: **TRUE BELIEVERS** *57*

CHAPTER 4: **SCREAMING EAGLES** *83*

CHAPTER 5: **ANACONDA** *113*

CHAPTER 6: **CLEAR, HOLD AND BUILD** *145*

CHAPTER 7: **LINES OF OPERATION** *171*

CHAPTER 8: **WASHINGTON AND BACK** *199*

CHAPTER 9: **HIGH STAKES** *225*

CHAPTER 10: **TRANSITION** *255*

CHAPTER 11: **DRAWDOWN**   *291*

CHAPTER 12: **MASK OF COMMAND**   *311*

CHAPTER 13: **STILL ALL IN**   *339*

Acknowledgments   *359*
Appendix A: Counterinsurgency Guidance Letter   *365*
Appendix B: COMISAF's COIN Contracting Guidance   *369*
Appendix C: Anaconda Strategy   *371*
Appendix D: Engine of Change   *373*
Notes   *375*
Index   *383*

ACRONYMS AND ABBREVIATIONS

ABP   Afghan Border Police

A-CAAT   Afghan Counterinsurgency Advisory and Assistance Team

ALP   Afghan Local Police program

ANA   Afghan National Army

ANP   Afghan National Police

ANSF   Afghan National Security Forces

APRP   Afghan Peace and Reintegration Program

BCT   brigade combat team

CAAT   Counterinsurgency Advisory and Assistance Team

CENTCOM   U.S. Central Command

CERP   Commander's Emergency Response Program

CFSOCC-A   Combined Forces Special Operations Component Command–Afghanistan

CIA   Central Intelligence Agency

C-IED   counter–improvised explosive device

CIG   Commander's Initiatives Group

CINC   commander in chief

CJCS   Chairman of the Joint Chiefs of Staff

CJIATF   Combined Joint Interagency Task Force

CNAS   Center for a New American Security

CODEL   congressional delegation

COIN   counterinsurgency

COMISAF   Commander, International Security Assistance Force Afghanistan

CORDS   Civil Operations and Revolutionary Development Support

CPN   criminal patronage network

DHS   U.S. Department of Homeland Security

DOD   U.S. Department of Defense

EKIA   enemy killed in action

EOD   explosive ordnance disposal

FAO   foreign area officer

FATA   Federally Administered Tribal Areas (Pakistan)

FOB   forward operating base

GIRoA   Government of the Islamic Republic of Afghanistan

GMIC   Government Media and Information Center

GOVN   Government of the Republic of Vietnam

GPS   Global Positioning System

HASC   House Armed Services Committee

HQN	Haqqani network
ICG	International Crisis Group
IED	improvised explosive device
IJC	ISAF Joint Command
INL	Bureau of International Narcotics and Law Enforcement Affairs
ISAF	International Security Assistance Force
ISR	Intelligence, Surveillance and Reconnaissance
JRTC	Joint Readiness Training Center
JSOC	Joint Special Operations Command
KIA	killed in action
MEDEVAC	medical evacuation
MLRS	Multiple Launch Rocket System
MNSTC-I	Multi-National Security Transition Command–Iraq
MOI	Ministry of the Interior
MRAP	Mine-Resistant Ambush-Protected vehicle
NAC	North Atlantic Council
NATO	North Atlantic Treaty Organization
NCO	noncommissioned officer
NDS	National Directorate of Security (Afghan)
NGO	nongovernmental organization
NOFORN	no foreign nationals

NROLFSM   NATO Rule of Law Field Support Mission

NSA   National Security Agency

NSC   National Security Council

NSS   National Security Staff

NTC   National Training Center

NTM–A   NATO Training Mission–Afghanistan

ODA   (Special Forces) Operational Detachment Alpha

OP   observation post

OSD   Office of the Secretary of Defense

OTAN   Organisation du Traité de l'Atlantique Nord

PICC   Palace Information Coordination Center

PID   positive identification

POTUS   President of the United States

PRT   Provincial Reconstruction Team

PTDS   Persistent Threat Detection System

RC   Regional Command

ROLFF–A   Rule of Law Field Force–Afghanistan

SASC   Senate Armed Services Committee

SEAL   Sea, Air, Land teams

SHAPE   Supreme Headquarters Allied Powers Europe

SIGACTS   significant activities

SMU   Special Mission Unit

SOCOM   Special Operations Command

SOTF   Special Operations Task Force

SRAP   Special representative for Afghanistan and Pakistan

TBI   traumatic brain injury

TF   task force

UAV   unmanned aerial vehicle

UNAMA   United Nations Assistance Mission in Afghanistan

USAID   U.S. Agency for International Development

VTC   video teleconference

VSO   Village Stability Operations

WIA   wounded in action

CAST OF CHARACTERS

David M. Axelrod: White House senior adviser.

Joseph Biden: Vice president of the United States (January 2009–present).

Lieutenant General James Bucknall: ISAF deputy commanding general at ISAF headquarters.

Lieutenant General William B. Caldwell: Commander, NATO Training Mission–Afghanistan; commander, Combined Security Transition Command–Afghanistan (November 2009–present).

David Cameron: Prime minister of the United Kingdom.

Major General John F. Campbell: Commander, ISAF Regional Command East (June 2010–May 2011); 101st Airborne Division commander. Promoted to lieutenant general in September 2011.

Hillary Clinton: U.S. secretary of State (January 2009–present).

Ryan C. Crocker: Ambassador to Iraq during Petraeus's time there—his civil-military "wingman" in Iraq—and now ambassador to Afghanistan.

Karim Dad: Malik of Khosrow Sofla village in Arghandab District, Kandahar Province.

Ambassador Karl W. Eikenberry: U.S. ambassador to Afghanistan (April 2009–July 2011).

Rahm I. Emanuel: White House chief of staff (January 2009–October 2010).

Lieutenant Colonel David G. Fivecoat: One of Petraeus's protégés and his aide-de-camp in 2001–02 in Bosnia and during the 2003 invasion into Iraq. Commanded 3rd Battalion, 187th Infantry Regiment, 101st Airborne Division; deployed to Ghazni and Paktika provinces.

Lieutenant Colonel David S. Flynn: Commanded 1st Battalion, 320th Field Artillery Regiment, 101st Airborne Division; deployed in the Arghandab River Valley, Kandahar Province, during Operation Dragon Strike.

General (Retired) John R. (Jack) Galvin: Longtime mentor to Petraeus. Petraeus served as Galvin's aide-de-camp while he commanded the 24th Infantry Division, then served as Galvin's military assistant while he was supreme Allied commander in Europe.

Major Jim Gant: Special Forces operator whose paper *One Tribe at a Time: A Strategy for Success in Afghanistan* influenced Petraeus's thinking on the Afghan Local Police program.

Ambassador Simon Gass: NATO's senior civilian representative in Afghanistan (April 2011–present).

Robert Gates: U.S. secretary of Defense (December 2006–July 2011).

Senator Lindsey Graham (R–S.C.): Member of the Armed Services Committee and an Air Force Reserve colonel who has served multiple short drill periods in Iraq and Afghanistan working on law-of-armed-conflict issues.

Colonel Bill Hickman: Petraeus's executive officer in Afghanistan.

Richard Holbrooke: Special representative for Afghanistan and Pakistan, former U.S. ambassador to the UN.

Chief Warrant Officer Four Mark Howell: Head of Petraeus's personal security detachment (PSD).

Hamid Karzai: President of the Islamic Republic of Afghanistan.

General (Retired) Jack Keane: Mentor to Petraeus, former vice chief of staff of the Army.

David Kilcullen: Australian-American defense intellectual and COIN theorist, key adviser to Petraeus during the Iraq surge.

Ambassador Hans Klemm: Coordinating director of Rule of Law and Law Enforcement, U.S. Embassy, Kabul, Afghanistan (July 2010–present).

Peggy Knowlton: Petraeus's mother-in-law.

General William A. Knowlton: Petraeus's father-in-law, superintendent of West Point when Petraeus was a cadet there.

Senator Carl Levin (D–Mich.): Chairman of the Senate Armed Services Committee; ex-officio member of the Senate Select Committee on Intelligence.

Senator Joe Lieberman (Ind.–Conn.): Senior member of the Armed Services Committee.

Major Fernando Lujan: Adviser, ISAF Counterinsurgency Advisory and Assistance Team.

Lieutenant General (Retired) Douglas E. Lute: National Security Staff coordinator for Afghanistan-Pakistan policy.

Nouri al-Maliki: Prime minister of Iraq (May 2006–present).

Brigadier General Mark S. Martins: Commander, NATO Rule of Law Field Support Mission; commander, Rule of Law Field Support Mission–Afghanistan. Worked in Afghanistan in various roles in CJIATF-435 from October 2009 to September 2011.

Senator John McCain (R–Ariz.): Senior member of the Armed Services Committee; ex-officio member of the Senate Select Committee on Intelligence.

General (Retired) Stanley A. McChrystal: Commander of USFOR–A/ISAF (June 2010–June 2011).

General (Retired) David McKiernan: General McChrystal's predecessor, commander of ISAF from June 2008 to June 2009.

Brigadier General H. R. McMaster: Director of Combined Joint Interagency Task Force–Shafafiyat, author of *Dereliction of Duty*, Petraeus acolyte.

Colonel Mike Meese: ISAF deputy chief of staff (August 2010–July 2011), head of Social Sciences Department at West Point, Petraeus's peer at Princeton.

Brigadier General Scott Miller: Commander, Combined Forces Special Operations Component Command–Afghanistan (March 2009–June 2011).

Haji Shah Mohammed: Arghandab District governor during Operation Dragon Strike.

Saad Mohseni: Founder of Tolo TV and CEO of its parent organization, Moby Group.

Admiral Mike Mullen: Chairman of the Joint Chiefs of Staff (October 2007–September 2011).

Lieutenant Colonel (Retired) John Nagl: Counterinsurgency theorist and Petraeus acolyte. President of CNAS.

General Mohammad Naim: Kandahar's chief of the National Directorate of Security during Operation Dragon Strike.

Colonel (Retired) Keith Nightingale: Longtime mentor of Petraeus, who served under him in Vicenza, Italy, as a second lieutenant. Nightingale had commanded a company in the 1/75th Rangers when Petraeus first met him. He later served as a leader of the Iran Hostage Rescue Mission and the Grenada invasion and helped form the Army Ranger Regiment.

Barack Obama: President of the United States of America.

Michael O'Hanlon: Defense analyst at the Brookings Institution.

Lieutenant Colonel (Retired) Douglas Ollivant: Senior civilian adviser in Regional Command East for the Counterinsurgency Advisory and Assistance Team and former Army officer who worked closely with Petraeus during the surge in Iraq.

Mullah Mohammed Omar: Leader of the Afghan Taliban movement.

Colonel Bill Ostlund: One of Petraeus's platoon leaders when he commanded the 3rd Battalion, 187th Infantry Regiment, 101st Airborne Division.

Leon Panetta: Director of Central Intelligence (February 2009–June 2011), U.S. secretary of Defense (July 2011–present).

Anne Petraeus: The general's daughter.

Hollister "Holly" Knowlton Petraeus: Wife of General Petraeus.

Miriam Howell Petraeus: Petraeus's mother.

Sixtus Petraeus: Petraeus's father, a Dutch sea captain.

Stephen Petraeus: Petraeus's son, an infantry platoon leader in Wardak Province with the 173rd Airborne Brigade Combat Team.

Robert Pittman: Retired master sergeant who worked as an adviser for the Asymmetric Warfare Group. Died from wounds suffered in an attack in Kandahar Province on July 30, 2010, during the Battle for Bakersfield.

Anders Fogh Rasmussen: NATO secretary general.

Colonel Abdul Raziq: Key leader in the Afghan Border Police. Later would become interim Kandahar provincial chief of police after a Taliban assassination.

Lieutenant General David M. Rodriguez: Commander, ISAF Joint Command (March 2010–July 2011).

Donald Rumsfeld: U.S. secretary of Defense (November 1975–January 1977; January 2001–December 2006).

Mohammed Zia Salehi: Chief of administration for the Afghan National Security Council.

Ambassador Mark Sedwill: NATO's senior civilian representative in Afghanistan (February 2010–April 2011).

Captain Andrew Shaffer: One of Lieutenant Colonel Flynn's company commanders in the 1st Battalion, 320th Field Artillery Regiment, 101st Airborne Division.

Rear Admiral Gregory J. Smith: ISAF deputy chief of staff for communications (June 2009–February 2011).

Specialist Michael L. Stansbery: Soldier of the 1st Battalion, 320th Field Artillery Regiment, 101st Airborne Division, who died from wounds suffered in an IED attack on his unit in Kandahar Province on July 30, 2010, during the Battle for Bakersfield.

Sergeant Kyle B. Stout: Soldier of the 1st Battalion, 320th Field Artillery Regiment, 101st Airborne Division, who died from wounds suffered in an IED attack on his unit in Kandahar Province on July 30, 2010, during the Battle for Bakersfield.

Lieutenant Colonel J. B. Vowell: Commanded 2nd Battalion, 327th Infantry Regiment, 101st Airborne Division; deployed in Kunar Province, along the Pakistan border, during Operation Strong Eagle I.

General (Retired) Carl Vuono: Chief of staff of the Army (June 1987–June 1991). Petraeus served as Vuono's aide-de-camp and assistant executive officer during this time.

Haji Sayed Fazlullah Wahidi: Kunar provincial governor during Operation Strong Eagle.

Chris White: Petraeus's roommate at West Point.

PREFACE

first met General David H. Petraeus in the spring of 2006, when I was a graduate student at Harvard University's Kennedy School of Government. After two tours in Iraq, including command of the 101st Airborne Division during the 2003 invasion, he was visiting Harvard to speak about his experiences and a new counterinsurgency manual he was developing as the three-star commander of the Army's Combined Arms Center at Fort Leavenworth, Kansas. It would get its first real test run a year later, during the surge in Iraq, with Petraeus himself in command.

I was among the students invited by the school to meet with the general at a dinner afterward, because of my military background. I, too, was a West Point graduate, and I had been recalled to active duty three times to work on counterterrorism issues in the wake of the 9/11 attacks. I had since joined the Army Reserve and begun graduate studies with the intent of returning either to active duty or to the policy world. I introduced myself to then–Lieutenant General Petraeus and told him about my research interests; he gave me his card and offered to put me in touch with other researchers and service members working on the same issues. I later discovered that he was famous for this type of mentoring and networking, especially with aspiring soldier-scholars. He immediately responded to the e-mail, inviting me to bounce ideas off him. I took full advantage of his open-door policy to seek insight and share perspectives.

Soon after his visit to Cambridge, Petraeus assumed command of the Multi-National Force in Iraq and the plan to "surge" nearly thirty thousand additional U.S. forces to pull the country back from the brink of civil war. The focus of his command would be comprehensive civilian-military counter-insurgency operations—protection of the Iraqi population from insurgents' intimidation, coercion, violence and murder. To accomplish this task, he moved U.S. forces off big bases and into small outposts in the community. Violence escalated and casualties soared, forcing even advocates to question whether the surge would work. But living among the people paid dividends in trust, familiarity and better intelligence. By midsummer, with Petraeus also supporting reconciliation that would grow to include more than one hundred thousand former Sunni insurgents and Shia militia members, violence had started to fall. By the following summer, the country had stabilized and the surge forces had started coming home. Petraeus had believed the surge could work, and he had overseen its successful execution together with a team of U.S., coalition and Iraqi civilian and military partners.

In 2008, I began to pursue a Ph.D. in public policy and to conduct a case study of Petraeus's leadership. A few months into my research, General Petraeus, who was then leading Central Command, invited me to go for a run with him and his team along the Potomac River during one of his visits to Washington. I figured I could interview him while we ran. Soon I learned what Petraeus means when he says, "The only thing better than a little competition is a lot of competition!" My intent was to test him. I'd earned varsity letters in cross-country and indoor and outdoor track and finished at the top of my class for athletics at West Point; I wanted to see if he could keep stride during an interview. Instead it became a test for me. As we talked during the run from the Pentagon to the Washington Monument and back, Petraeus progressively increased the pace until the talk turned to heavy breathing and we reached a six-minute-per-mile pace. It was a signature Petraeus move. I think I passed the test, but I didn't bother to transcribe the interview. I later learned that, at the time, he was nearing the end of eight and a half weeks of radiation treatments for prostate cancer.

I intended for my dissertation to trace the key themes—education, experience and the role of key mentors—of Petraeus's intellectual development and to examine these principles in action over his career. But when President Obama put him in charge of the war in Afghanistan in the summer of 2010, I decided to meld my research with an on-the-ground account of his command in Kabul—his last military command, as it turned out. He would again become the face of a highly unpopular war, with a surge of 33,000 U.S. troops deploying. When his command was announced, Lieutenant General David Rodriguez, the operational commander in Afghanistan and the architect of the war plan, told his staff, "Now we're going to win." But the war was at a critical juncture, and many observers both inside and outside the U.S. military weren't so sure.

Petraeus had a year to make the gains in Afghanistan that the president would need in order to begin his promised drawdown of forces in July 2011. Every minute counted. He commanded from his fourteen-hundred-person headquarters in Kabul and traveled frequently throughout Afghanistan visiting the more than 150,000 soldiers from forty-nine nations, of which 100,000 were from the United States. By the fall he seemed to hit his stride. But every day in Afghanistan was hard, and no one was certain how it would end.

This was the story I would report across several months in Afghanistan, observing Petraeus and his team, embedding with combat units, and interviewing dozens of senior officials, officers, soldiers and Afghans. I spent time with infantry, artillery, Special Operations Forces and other military and civilian elements. I reported from the headquarters of the International Security Assistance Force in Kabul, the United Nations Assistance Mission in Afghanistan, and the U.S. Embassy. I flew by helicopter to the sandy desert of Helmand Province, the jagged mountains of the Hindu Kush in eastern Afghanistan and Kandahar's lush Arghandab River Valley. I broke bread with Afghan ministers, businessmen and barefoot villagers. I ate MREs and T-rations in the field with our soldiers, some of whom were my former peers or West Point classmates. I traveled with retired general Jack Keane on a theater-wide assessment in February, and I covered Petraeus's trips back to Washington for his testimony on the war before Congress, his drawdown discussions with the White House, his confirmation hearing to become director of the CIA and his last week in Kabul. Throughout, I had numerous interviews and innumerable e-mail exchanges with Petraeus and his inner circle.

Beyond the strategic focus on Petraeus, his intellectual journey and his larger initiatives, this book also chronicles the year of war at the tactical level through the eyes of three battalion commanders in the 101st Airborne Division (Air Assault)—the same division Petraeus had led during the 2003 invasion of Iraq. Lieutenant Colonel David Flynn commanded a repurposed artillery battalion, the "Top Guns," in the Arghandab River Valley, the Taliban's home terrain. Lieutenant Colonel J. B. Vowell led his No Slack battalion on large-scale air assaults into the mountains of Kunar Province, in eastern Afghanistan. And Lieutenant Colonel David Fivecoat, my West Point company mate and Petraeus's aide in Bosnia and during the invasion of Iraq, directed operations in Taliban-infested Ghazni Province in south-central Afghanistan. Finally, the experience of Major Fernando Lujan, a Special Forces officer and specially trained "Afghan Hand," stands as a cautionary tale about the limits of passion and expertise in the face of military bureaucracy. All of their stories are rich examples of leadership on the line.

History has yet to fully judge Petraeus's service in Iraq and Afghanistan, his impact on the U.S. military and his rank among America's wartime leaders. But there is no denying that he achieved a great deal during his thirty-seven-year Army career, not the least of which was regaining the strategic initiative in both wars that followed the terrorist attacks of September 11, 2001. His critics fault him for ambition and self-promotion. I will note in the pages that follow that he is driven and goal-oriented, but his energy, optimism and will to win stand out more for me than the qualities seized on by his critics. Serving, in his mind, is winning.

One of Petraeus's favorite quotes comes from Seneca, a first-century Roman philosopher: "Luck is what happens when preparation meets opportunity." This has been true for Petraeus at many turns; his greatest "luck," however, might have been the opportunity to lead the world's finest troopers over six and a half years of deployments since 9/11.

I've had some luck, too, with this endeavor, and I am grateful and wiser for the journey.

ALL IN

CHAPTER 1

GROUND TRUTH

General David H. Petraeus sat deep in thought as he made the short drive from the Pentagon to the White House. The next three hours could change the course of his life, the course of a war, maybe even the course of the nation. He hadn't a clue what was going to happen. The only comment he made to Chief Warrant Officer Four Mark Howell, his personal security officer since the surge in Iraq, was that he hoped General Stan McChrystal had survived his meeting with President Obama. McChrystal, the four-star commander of the war in Afghanistan, had been called back to Washington the previous day for comments he and his aides had made to a reporter from *Rolling Stone* that some thought came close to insubordination. On this hot and muggy Wednesday morning, June 23, 2010, McChrystal had reported to the White House an hour and a half before Petraeus. By the time Petraeus's black GMC Yukon Denali pulled up at the West Wing security gate, McChrystal had already come and gone. Howell and the rest of the general's inner circle knew they could be heading for Afghanistan if McChrystal had been fired. "We were in a state of denial," Howell said.

Once inside the White House, Petraeus went to a small office down the hall from the Situation Room to see his longtime friend Doug Lute, a retired Army lieutenant general who served as senior adviser and the National Security Council's coordinator for Afghanistan-Pakistan policy. As head of the U.S. Central Command (CENTCOM)—and McChrystal's boss—Petraeus was at the White House that morning for his once-a-month meeting with the president and his national security team on Afghanistan and Pakistan. He was disappointed about how the situation had unfolded for McChrystal and was concerned for a trusted colleague. They were old friends and battle-field comrades and had worked closely together over the past year on Afghanistan, the president's "war of necessity," after serving together for several years in Iraq. Afghanistan was at a critical juncture, politically and operationally. "How'd it go for Stan?" Petraeus asked Lute. Lute demurred. It was not a good sign. They made awkward small talk for a few minutes, waiting to head to the Situation Room. Then one of the president's assistants stuck his head in the door. "Has anyone seen General Petraeus?" he asked. "He's wanted up in the Oval."

Petraeus headed upstairs. As he entered the Oval Office, Robert Gates, the Defense secretary, and Hillary Clinton, the secretary of State, were coming out, along with other members of the president's national security team. Obama was alone. Petraeus knew then that Obama had just fired McChrystal without a replacement confirmed, hours before he likely would appear in the Rose Garden and explain his actions to the nation. He and Petraeus sat down together. Obama cut to the chase. "I am asking you, as your president and commander in chief, to take command of the mission in Afghanistan." Petraeus believed that for anyone in uniform, there is only one answer when a president asks such a question, and he said as much. Then, he responded, "Sir, it would be an honor." Petraeus could see the burden Obama and the nation faced at that moment. The discussion was sober and frank as they discussed the way ahead in Afghanistan. Obama explicitly told Petraeus to avoid clearing areas that his troops could not hold, and he reviewed the policy that had been announced at West Point the past December, including the plan to begin reducing surge forces in July 2011. Obama described his expectations of a military commander, and Petraeus pledged fealty to the civil-military hierarchy, assuring the president that he would also provide forthright military advice. When the general returned downstairs forty-five minutes later, he said to Howell, "Chief, get my wife on the phone."

Howell figured the die had been cast—McChrystal was out, Petraeus was in. Why else would he be calling his wife? But Howell noticed something about his boss. He thought he saw the same spark in Petraeus's eyes that he'd last seen when he was commanding the war in Iraq. "It's that undeniable look in sports where the player is in the zone and he says, 'Give me the ball, I want the ball,'" Howell said. He dialed Holly Petraeus's number, got her voice mail and handed the phone to the general, who left a simple message: *Watch the news at 1:30 for a presidential announcement—we'll be in the Rose Garden.* He asked Howell to send her a text message, too, gave him the phone and went inside the Situation Room just before noon.

Clinton, Gates and Admiral Mike Mullen, chairman of the Joint Chiefs of Staff, were there, waiting for Petraeus, and the president and Vice President Biden joined them after a few minutes. "This is a bad day; a sorrowful day," Obama said. Keeping McChrystal in command, he said, would have made it difficult to achieve unity of effort and maintain respect for the military. He acknowledged that replacing him might slow momentum in Afghanistan, though replacing him with Petraeus would mitigate that risk. He wanted no sniping in the press. They needed to be focused, as a team, on the way ahead.

Obama said he had had long conversations on the subject with Gates and Mullen, and now with General Petraeus. The best way forward, he told the room, was for Petraeus to step in as commander in Afghanistan. He noted that he had already committed additional troops to show that America would not allow al-Qaeda to return to Afghanistan. *We'll see next July if the strategy is working,* Obama said. *If not, we'll redesign it. It's important that we deliver a clear message about what we're trying to do,* he continued. *We have to acknowledge the real tension that exists between how long we stay and how much it costs.* There were rumors of tension with Petraeus, but Obama noted that he had asked Petraeus to meet with him and share his views candidly. *We've agreed to trust each other,* Obama said, *and to share assessments in private.* Vice President Biden added that it was the right decision, and a sad day, to let McChrystal go. But it would be an opportunity to clarify civil-military relations. The president said he would call Afghan president Hamid

Karzai, British prime minister David Cameron and the NATO secretary general, Anders Fogh Rasmussen, to let them know of his decision.

Obama walked out of the Oval Office and into the Rose Garden an hour later. Petraeus stood to his immediate left, flanked by Gates. Biden and Mullen stood to Obama's right.

"Today I accepted General Stanley McChrystal's resignation as commander of the International Security Assistance Force in Afghanistan," Obama began. "I did so with considerable regret, but also with certainty that it is the right thing for our mission in Afghanistan, for our military and for our country. I'm also pleased to nominate General David Petraeus to take command in Afghanistan, which will allow us to maintain the momentum and leadership that we need to succeed."

Obama said he was "extraordinarily grateful" that Petraeus had agreed to serve. It would be Petraeus's fifth overseas assignment since 2001—including some four years during three tours in Iraq—for a man who was possibly the most well-known general officer in America since Dwight D. Eisenhower. He'd already been deployed over five and a half years since 2001, managing to miss most of his son's time in high school—although Afghanistan would offer a reunion of sorts: Stephen Petraeus had recently graduated from MIT and was serving as an Army lieutenant in Afghanistan.

Holly's phone had been in her purse, on vibrate, while she attended a business luncheon at the Mayflower Hotel. "Chief, what's up?" she asked when she finally called Howell back. Howell explained the details. She was used to her husband being asked to serve the nation. She listened, then said simply, "Roger, Chief, thanks."

On the drive back to the Pentagon, Petraeus called Holly to update her and then called his executive officer, Colonel Bill Hickman, who was at the Pentagon. Petraeus told him to clear the schedule, except for two speeches the next evening in his hometown of Cornwall, New York—one for Purple Heart recipients and the other a commencement address at his old high school, marking the fortieth anniversary of his class's graduation. He scribbled a to-do list—start assembling a team, cancel future events, write an opening statement for a confirmation hearing, review rules of engagement, start drafting his first-day letter to the troopers in Afghanistan, develop a timeline. He paused, then started jotting down the names of all those he needed to call—Ambassador Richard Holbrooke, General McChrystal, Secretary Clinton, and Ambassador Ryan C. Crocker, his diplomatic partner in Iraq. He told Hickman to call Central Command's congressional liaison and line up meetings with members of the Senate Armed Services Committee for the following Monday, and to get his enlisted aide to start packing his bags back in Tampa. *And if you're willing to deploy one more time,* he told Hickman, *you're needed.* Hickman didn't hesitate. He would go to war with Petraeus again—for the fourth time since 2003. Petraeus turned to Howell and said they had to start preparing for his confirmation hearing the following week. He asked Howell if he was ready to go, too. "Might as well," Howell said. "We've spent more time together over the past three years than I've spent with my wife."

"I know, Chief," Petraeus agreed. "We have...."

THE WHITE HOUSE was full of skeptics—chief of staff Rahm I. Emanuel and senior adviser David M. Axelrod among them. They had come to see Petraeus as an inflexible commander who wanted as many troops as possible for Afghanistan and was never interested in giving the president options for fewer troops, despite clear requests for this during the 2009 Afghanistan policy review. They had suspicions that he was a Bush general, given his close personal relationship with the former president.

Petraeus also had his detractors in a military in which every service was fiercely committed to its own new high-tech weapons systems. None of them particularly benefited from Petraeus's advocacy of counterinsurgency, which didn't rely on new ships or tanks or fighter jets. Generals from the heavy Army built to defeat the Russians at the Fulda Gap thought his belief in counterinsurgency bordered on religious zeal. They were worried that he was taking the Army down a path that was diminishing its ability to fight a formidable opponent such as China. Others who had crossed paths with him during his relentless rise to the top saw him as an overly ambitious self-promoter.

But there was little doubt among most active and retired generals, and the American public, that he was a highly capable combat commander and arguably the Army's most influential general officer since World War II. In his first combat command, he had led the 101st Airborne Division during the 2003 invasion of Iraq with skill and determination. He then took the Screaming Eagles north to Mosul, where most observers credited him with successfully overseeing post-combat operations in northern Iraq for the rest of the year. The war in Iraq consumed six years of his life. After pacifying Mosul and returning briefly to the United States, he was soon back in Iraq, in charge of the effort to recruit, train and develop the Iraqi military. He returned to the States for fifteen months, overseeing the drafting of the Army/Marine Corps *Counterinsurgency Field Manual* and helping overhaul numerous aspects of the Army's preparation of leaders and units for deployment. He will be most remembered, however, for commanding the "surge" in Iraq in 2007, when the country was enveloped in violence and on the brink of civil war. The added troops, Petraeus's counterinsurgency strategy and a reconciliation effort he designed that convinced 100,000 Sunni and Shia insurgents to support the new Iraq all helped to stem the violence and salvage some measure of success for the Bush administration.

At Petraeus's change of command in Baghdad in the summer of 2008, Secretary Gates claimed that "history [would] regard Petraeus as one of the nation's great battle captains." Upon Petraeus's assumption of command of U.S. Central Command in October 2008, Gates offered that "he is the preeminent soldier-scholar-statesman of his generation, and precisely the man we need in this command at this time." Petraeus's success on the battlefield, his status as a military intellectual and his will to succeed allowed him to shape not only doctrine but also organizational design, training, education and leadership development in the Army and, in many respects, the broader military. He was clearly charting the Army's course for the kind of war the nation was fighting.

Obama had in one important way done Petraeus a huge favor, given the drama surrounding McChrystal's firing. Petraeus had always used his reputation to help capture the imagination of those he led. "Given what I was facing in Iraq and then Afghanistan," Petraeus reflected some months later, "I've had a certain affinity for leaders who have been given seemingly lost or at least very difficult causes." He thought of Grant in the Civil War, Matthew Ridgway in Korea and British field marshal William Slim, who led the Allied Forces' efforts to retake Burma in World War II, as described in his aptly titled autobiography, *Defeat Into Victory*. Nations had turned to them to help salvage critical war efforts. All three commanders came to execute the strategies they had helped design. Thanks to Obama, Petraeus was being asked to do the same, having already done so in Iraq under President Bush.

The following Tuesday, Petraeus testified before the Senate Armed Services Committee. Ostensibly there to be confirmed to his new post, Petraeus also had to defend the war effort and the time and commitment it would take to make progress in Afghanistan. He sat alone at a large rectangular witness table in the cavernous hearing room in the Dirksen Senate Office Building, across from the U.S. Capitol. His wife, Holly, sat in the first row of seats in the gallery, making her first appearance at one of her husband's confirmation hearings. Holly preferred to stay out of the public light, but she was there this day to show support and represent the sacrifice of military families—to "show the flag," she would later say. Petraeus wore his dress green uniform, with decorations on his left breast, the Ranger tab on his left shoulder and the patch of the 101st Airborne Division, the unit he'd commanded in combat in the early days in Iraq, on his right.

Senator Carl Levin, a Michigan Democrat, gaveled the hearing to order and thanked Petraeus for his "willingness, at the president's request . . . to take charge of the campaign in Afghanistan. We appreciate your sacrifice and that of your family." He acknowledged Holly's presence and thanked her for her commitment and sacrifice. Senator John McCain of Arizona, the committee's ranking Republican, also thanked Holly, adding, as a personal aside, "We think you made a wise decision more than thirty-four [*sic*] years ago to accept a blind date with a young cadet."

Hollister Knowlton was the daughter of the West Point superintendent, Lieutenant General William Knowlton, when she arrived one football weekend in the fall of 1973 and wound up attending the game with David Petraeus, a cadet who was the assistant brigade adjutant and who would graduate that spring in the top 5 percent of his class, a "star man." After an initial wariness passed, they quickly hit it off; they were married in the chapel on West Point's campus on July 6, 1974.

Beyond their warm reception for the general and his wife, McCain and his Republican colleagues were on a mission. They wanted to expose what they thought was the folly of Obama's July 2011 drawdown date. And they tried their hardest to create a rift between Petraeus, who was believed to be no fan of the July 2011 drawdown commitment but had publicly defended it, and the president, who considered it an imperative. Petraeus proved an elusive target.

"I am, needless to say, humbled and honored to have been nominated by the president to command the NATO International Security Assistance Force and U.S. forces in Afghanistan," Petraeus responded, reading from a prepared statement that he had written over the weekend and carefully vetted with his most trusted aides, including nonmilitary colleagues.

"As we take stock of the situation in Afghanistan, it is important to remember why we are there," he said. Petraeus took advantage of the bully pulpit to try to convey to the public why the mission mattered. "We should never forget that the 9/11 attacks were planned in southern Afghanistan and that the initial training of the attackers was carried out in camps in Afghanistan before the attackers moved on to Germany and then on to U.S. flight schools. It was of course in response to those attacks that a U.S.-led coalition entered Afghanistan in late 2001 and defeated al-Qaeda and the Taliban elements that allowed al-Qaeda to establish its headquarters and training camps in Afghanistan."

Petraeus had been watching international terrorist organizations since his days as the executive officer for the chairman of the Joint Chiefs of Staff in the 1990s. He understood the challenging battle against an extremist ideology. There was resignation among many policy makers that there would be no "victory" over extremists. Petraeus acknowledged as much when he noted that the ongoing conflicts were not ones that would be ended by "taking the hill, planting the flag, and going home to a victory parade." Rather, he saw the efforts in Afghanistan and elsewhere as elements in what was a long, tough fight against extremists who were ideologically committed to attacking the United States, its Western allies and even many of the governments in power in the Middle East. Afghanistan was a key location in this fight, a country that had been a sanctuary for al-Qaeda before and had to be sufficiently "hardened" to enable it to avoid becoming one again.

Petraeus knew that the president, as commander in chief, felt the burden of command for this war. He also knew how strongly the administration was committed to beginning the drawdown of forces in Afghanistan in July 2011. In an attempt to preempt the Republican assault on Obama's pending drawdown of forces a year hence, Petraeus tried to make it clear that he and Obama were in synch, something he felt was important for the Republicans—and Obama's wary aides—to hear. "I was part of the process that helped formulate the president's strategy for Afghanistan, and I support and agree with his new policy," he said. This was a delicate issue, since it was known that the White House had not fully embraced the advice that he, McChrystal, Mullen and Gates had offered the previous fall. But he knew what he needed to do to support a policy decision after it had been made. "During [the policy's] development, I offered my forthright military advice, and I have assured the president that I will do the same as we conduct assessments over the course of the months ahead. He in turn assured me that he expects and wants me to provide that character of advice."

His assessment of the conditions in Afghanistan was sober. He worried about insurgent sanctuaries in Pakistan, corruption in the Afghan government and Taliban strongholds in Kandahar Province. "There is no question that levels of violence in Afghanistan have increased significantly over the last several years. Moreover, the Taliban and their affiliates had, until this year, steadily been expanding the areas they control and influence. This year, however, ISAF has achieved progress in several locations." Petraeus went on to describe the main effort in Helmand Province, a Taliban stronghold in southwestern Afghanistan, while admitting that it had been two steps forward, one back in many locations.

To Petraeus, a sign of progress earlier in the spring had been his ability to walk through markets in Marjah with the district governor. The area had been Taliban-infested just six months prior, with only four market shops open. By summer there were dozens of shops, and the displaced population was returning home. With heavy fighting ongoing and casualties mounting, however, it was hard to convey the feeling of progress he had witnessed. To him it was a bit of *Fingerspitzengefühl*—the German word for "fingertip feel." Though he knew he had a lot to learn about the country, he had been devouring intelligence on operations and threats in Afghanistan daily for nearly two years, which had helped him understand the way the campaign was heading. It was hard to convince Congress of progress by describing what his *Fingerspitzengefühl* told him, however, so he talked about the slowly expanding security bubbles and the successful operations by Special Forces that General McChrystal had increased with Petraeus's support at Central Command. There was only so much he could say in an unclassified forum, but he had been able to meet with nearly all the senators on the committee prior to the hearing, and he had shared classified assessments with them in those sessions.

With a glance over his shoulder, he concluded his remarks by thanking his wife, seated behind him. "As you noted, Mr. Chairman, my wife, Holly, is here with me today," he said. "She is a symbol of the strength and dedication of families around the globe who wait at home for their loved ones while they're engaged in critical work in Afghanistan, Iraq and elsewhere. She has hung tough while I've been deployed for over five and a half years since 9/11. So have untold other spouses, children and loved ones as their troopers have deployed and continued to raise their right hands time and time again. Clearly, our families are the unsung heroes of the long campaigns on which we have been embarked over the past decade."

He closed with a flourish. "One of America's greatest presidents, Teddy

Roosevelt, once observed that far and away the best prize that life has to offer is the chance to work hard at work worth doing. There are currently nearly 140,000 coalition troopers and over 235,000 Afghan security force members engaged in hard work very much worth doing in Afghanistan," Petraeus said. "If I am confirmed by the Senate, it will be a great privilege to soldier with them in that hard work that is so worth doing in that country."

Petraeus had spent hours preparing for this testimony and, beyond the Republican attempt to attack Obama, was not anticipating tough questions from either side. He'd been in this seat many times before. He also commanded the high ground. Both Obama and his Republican opponents were committed to salvaging the war effort in Afghanistan, if not prevailing outright.

Levin began the questioning. "General, you've commented on these questions in your testimony, and I want to ask them again to get very clear, direct answers to them. Two fundamental elements of the Afghanistan strategy that the president announced in December 2009 are, first, a surge of thirty thousand additional U.S. troops by the end of the summer to help regain the initiative and, second, the setting of a July 2011 date for the beginning of the reduction in our combat presence in Afghanistan, with the pace of a reasonable drawdown to be determined by the circumstances at that time. Do you agree with the president's policy?"

"I do," Petraeus said.

"Do you agree that the setting of that July 2011 date to begin reductions signals urgency to Afghan leaders that they must more and more take responsibility for their country's security, which is important for success of the mission in Afghanistan?"

"I do," Petraeus said.

But McCain, who went next in the questioning, was undeterred.

"General, at any time during the deliberations that the military shared with the president when he went through the decision-making process, was there a recommendation from you or anyone in the military that we set a date of July 2011?"

"There was not," Petraeus said.

"There was not by any military person that you know of?"

"Not that I'm aware of," Petraeus said.

McCain appeared to have found a way to cleave the general from the president, but Petraeus had merely stated a fact, not a point of policy disagreement. Senator Lindsey Graham, the South Carolina Republican and a reserve military colonel, continued the assault.

Hadn't Vice President Joseph Biden, Graham asked, been quoted as saying, "Come July we're going to begin to leave in large numbers—you can bet on it"?

Petraeus tried to answer, but Graham, pressing his point, cut him off twice. Finally, Petraeus explained that Biden had expressed his full support of the administration's Afghan policy during a National Security Council meeting immediately after Obama tapped him to command the war. What's more, Petraeus said, Defense secretary Gates had recently told Congress in testimony that he'd never heard Biden say that—and neither had Petraeus.

As he told Senator Jack Reed, the Rhode Island Democrat, who asked him at another point in the hearing about Obama's planned drawdown in July 2011: "Let me be very clear, if I could, Senator. Not only did I say that I supported it, I said that I agreed with it. This is, again, an agreement that was made back . . . in the fall of last year, based on projections about conditions that we hoped we'd obtain, that we were going to strive to achieve in Afghanistan a full year from now. So that was . . . an 18-month or more projection at that time."

Petraeus had defended Obama's announced troop drawdown in July 2011. It was the president's policy decision, which trumped whatever desires Petraeus may have had for more troops on the ground. He accepted that as a soldier. He took orders from the commander in chief, and, after proffering his best advice, it was his job to execute them. But he was firm that all decisions about how many troops to withdraw and where to deploy those that remained had to be made with the goal of preserving hard-fought gains at the village, district and province levels so that momentum would not swing back to the Taliban. He noted that the president had stressed in announcing the policy that decisions on the pace of the drawdown would be conditions-based.

Throughout his testimony, Petraeus played his political, as well as military, role; he also executed the four tasks he felt strategic leaders had to perform. Regarding the first—getting the big ideas right—he described the fundamentals of a comprehensive civil-military counterinsurgency campaign, which he had employed in Iraq and pushed continually in Afghanistan. "You must capitalize on every capability that is out there—host nation, U.S., international, whatever it may be. That's what this takes: everything from the very hard-edged, targeted Special Mission Unit operations to the reintegration of 'reconcilables' to conventional forces expanding their security zones," he said.

Petraeus repeated the word "relentless" and repeatedly stressed the importance of the United States' "will" to win, underscoring the second task of a strategic leader: effectively communicating the big ideas. "This is a test of wills. And again, the enemy has to know that we have the will to prevail."

To the third task of a strategic leader—overseeing the implementation of the big ideas—he promised, once he arrived in country, to review the Tactical Directive and the rules of engagement, which were seen as too restrictive by many soldiers on the ground. "I want to assure the mothers and fathers of those fighting in Afghanistan that I see it as a moral imperative to bring all assets to bear to protect our men and women in uniform and the Afghan security forces with whom ISAF troopers are fighting shoulder to shoulder," he said. "Those on the ground must have all the support they need when they are in a tough situation."

To accomplish the fourth task—capturing best practices and lessons and cycling them back through the system to help refine the big ideas—he noted that he already had his favorite think-tank analysts, academics and military experts packing their bags, and that he was in communication with commanders and key staff officers on the ground in Afghanistan.

The tasks of strategic leadership he described had been the keys to the success of the "surge" that pulled Iraq back from the brink of civil war in

2007. His three tours in Iraq enabled him to speak with confidence about another important concept—achieving unity of effort among all participants—
as he prepared to take command yet again: "We know, in fact, that we can
achieve such unity of effort because we've done it before." But as Petraeus
himself had said on many occasions, Afghanistan was not Iraq. Indeed, Afghanistan, in some ways, made Iraq look simple.

"You certainly can't take lessons learned in Iraq and just apply them in a
rote manner in Afghanistan," Petraeus told Senator Mark Udall, the Colorado Democrat. "They have to be applied with a keen understanding of the
situation on the ground, village by village, valley by valley. All counterinsurgency is local, as they say."

He created a sense of measured optimism as he noted that the arrival in
Afghanistan of the final surge brigade (nicknamed Currahee) from the 101st
Airborne Division was scheduled for September. He concluded:

> The combination of all these initiatives is intended to slowly but
> surely establish the foundation of security that can allow the develop-
> ment of viable local political structures, enable the improvement of
> basic services, and help Afghan leaders and local governance achieve
> legitimacy and greater support.... While relentless pursuit of the Tal-
> iban will be critical in Kandahar and elsewhere, we know from Iraq
> and other counterinsurgency experiences that we cannot kill or cap-
> ture our way out of an industrial-strength insurgency like that in Af-
> ghanistan. Clearly, as many insurgents and citizens as possible need
> to be convinced to become part of the solution rather than a continu-
> ing part of the problem.

As the confirmation hearing concluded, Democratic and Republican
senators effusively praised their new commander in Afghanistan. Senator
Saxby Chambliss, a Republican from Georgia, gave Petraeus credit for defending not only America but the entire globe. "Thanks to you, thanks to
your family, for the great commitment that you continue to make to protect
America, as well as literally the whole world." One of his longtime mentors,

Keith Nightingale, a retired Army colonel, called the hearing a coronation—and it worried Nightingale greatly. Obama's decision to nominate Petraeus to succeed McChrystal, Nightingale said, was brilliant. If Petraeus could pull a rabbit out of the hat in Afghanistan, so much the better. If he couldn't, Obama would be able to say he'd done all that he could by appointing America's best general to command the campaign—and blame Petraeus. How their relationship would evolve was anyone's guess.

There remained great skepticism about the United States' ability to succeed in Afghanistan. Many analysts, particularly those in the Democratic Party and the Obama administration, doubted whether the United States, struggling economically and beset by record budget deficits, could continue spending $100 billion a year on the war in Afghanistan—borrowed money—for the amount of time it would take Petraeus's counterinsurgency strategy to succeed. Few believed that would happen anywhere close to the July 2011 drawdown date. Many also argued that the initial rationale for war in Afghanistan—driving out al-Qaeda—no longer existed, since the terrorist organization had long since left Afghanistan and regrouped in the tribal areas of Pakistan, as well as in Yemen, East Africa and Iraq. Pakistan's covert role in supporting the Taliban remained deeply troubling and had the potential to undermine whatever progress Petraeus's forces made on the ground in Afghanistan. And many saw the government of President Hamid Karzai as deeply corrupt and inept, hardly a force around which to win hearts and minds.

Indeed, some analysts in Washington argued that, as a strategy, counterinsurgency wasn't really applicable, because Afghanistan was not a country with a central government beset by a repressive insurgency, but rather one in the midst of a civil war with multiple ethnic and sectarian parties vying for power. Many believed that international intervention in Afghanistan was a hindrance to the development of effective government in Afghanistan, not a catalyst for creating it, and that counterinsurgency was the problem, triggering a surge of suicide terrorists reacting to foreign military occupation. Richard N. Haass, president of the Council on Foreign Relations and a reported centrist Republican, summed up the policy angst in a cover story in

Newsweek that hit the newsstands shortly after Petraeus arrived in Afghanistan. The headline: "We're Not Winning. It's Not Worth It. Here's How to Draw Down in Afghanistan."

The next night, following Petraeus's confirmation hearing, Vice President Biden flew to MacDill Air Force Base, in Tampa, the home of Central Command headquarters, to have dinner with Petraeus and his wife as a show of support. One of Petraeus's aides called it "the last supper." Petraeus had been confirmed unanimously in a 99–0 vote by the Senate that day, and he departed for Afghanistan the next morning.

VILLAGE BY VILLAGE, valley by valley, Afghanistan is one of the most forbidding, inhospitable places on earth to fight a major war. The soaring, snow-capped Hindu Kush range bisects the country, which is about the size of Texas, running from its eastern border with Pakistan to its western border with Iran. The average altitude is 14,000 feet, with some peaks reaching 25,000 feet. The hazards and hardships of fighting there were first brought home in the early days of the global war on terror, when seven service members died on a freezing mountain called Takur Ghar in March 2002. It was the largest combat loss of life in a single day since eighteen soldiers had died during the Black Hawk Down battle in Mogadishu, Somalia, in 1993. But by July 2010, the heaviest fighting had shifted to the lush terrain around the southern city of Kandahar, where canals, mud walls, vineyards and dirt roads had all been intricately seeded with deadly improvised explosive devices (IEDs)—roadside bombs by a fancier name. They were by far the biggest killers of American troops and their NATO allies.

"Every tiny piece of terrain out here exacts a terrible price," Army Special Forces officer Major Fernando Lujan wrote to his former students at West Point [members of the "Long Gray Line"], who themselves would soon be serving in Afghanistan. "You just hope that commanders will learn quickly to pay only once. Don't clear what you can't hold. The Taliban will reclaim it before you finish walking or driving back to your base and lay IEDs along the way you came." It is axiomatic in counterinsurgency warfare that land taken but not held becomes a victory for the insurgents. Once the insurgents return, the population feels abandoned. Lujan, starting a three-year tour rotation between Afghanistan and an Afghan-related billet in the United States, had just returned from an advisory mission with U.S. and Afghan units in the lush Arghandab River Valley, outside Kandahar, where Soviet forces staged their last offensive before withdrawing in defeat in 1989. His letter to his students captured the war Petraeus was about to inherit.

Lujan described the "worst IED threat I have ever seen in my life" and said that the "insurgents have figured out how to make caveman-simple, pressure plate or command wire devices against which all our technology is worthless. We're seeing a reverse evolution in tactics, and they're deadly effective." Lujan foreshadowed the fighting that was to come in the Arghandab District of Kandahar Province in the fall.

By the time he wrote the cadets, Lujan was speaking Dari, sporting a heavy beard and wearing an Afghan uniform. Lujan had gone native in his role, melding his background and training as a Special Forces and foreign-area officer. He loved what he was able to do and figured that if he died in Afghanistan, it would have been for a worthwhile cause.

Lujan, as a member of the Counterinsurgency Advisory and Assistance Team (CAAT), was part of Petraeus's team of "directed telescopes," and Petraeus would come to greatly value his insights. The directed telescope concept, once employed by Napoleon, is a process by which a senior commander uses aides or trusted advisers, often junior officers, to focus on issues beyond his sights, thus helping the commander expand his knowledge of the battlefield. As such, the CAAT was a group of current and former military officers, heavy on Special Operations experience and Ph.D.s, created a year earlier by McChrystal to help develop ideas to enable troopers on the ground to shift their primary mission from killing the enemy to protecting the population. Working out of the regional commands and circulating from combat base to combat base, CAAT members would gather periodically in Kabul and brief commanders, a practice that would be continued—and encouraged—by Petraeus, whose need for information never seemed to be satisfied.

The CAAT is not to be confused with Petraeus's Commander's Initiatives

Group (CIG). If the CAAT was an external brain trust, the CIG was an internal one, operating within Petraeus's command headquarters as a team of trusted action officers, all with advanced degrees and most with time in Afghanistan, focused on issues of particular and immediate importance to the general—preparation of briefings for important visitors and for video teleconferences (VTC) with Washington and Brussels, provision of talking points for meetings with Karzai, help with issues at Central Command and the Pentagon and drafting responses to urgent requests for help from the regional commanders. What Petraeus prized in the CIG, and on the staff, was brains, judgment and a great work ethic. Rank was often immaterial. Petraeus also had a coterie of former subordinates and colleagues with whom he kept in touch via e-mail as part of a "virtual CIG." He considered himself a "relentless" communicator, both for getting his message out and for vacuuming information up.

Petraeus also depended on another group of "directed telescopes"—the academic experts, outside mentors and think-tankers he brought in to provide yet another set of eyes to help him sort out various issues. While Petraeus considered Lujan and other CAAT members to be important directed telescopes, he also asked former officers, such as his mentor, retired Army general Jack Keane, and defense intellectuals, such as Frederick W. Kagan of the American Enterprise Institute and his wife, Kim, founder of the Institute for the Study of War, to travel the country and gather information and insights from the field. Though some in the field did not take kindly to their probing, the insights they brought back supplemented those provided by the normal chain of command and various staff officers and were crucial for Petraeus's understanding of the effectiveness of the campaign in Afghanistan.

Just as Lujan provided insights to Petraeus, he also counseled his former students by e-mail. "This is the land of old school, light infantry style, small unit patrolling—walking 5-10 km cross country in 110 degree heat," he wrote to them. "The enemy is aggressive, and not afraid of direct, violent, short-range combat. . . . There are villages out here that are literally completely deserted, populated only by Taliban and foreign fighters, rigged with some of the most complex IED arrays ever witnessed in modern warfare. Leave them be. Focus your resources on places you can make a difference. Disrupt the enemy when required to support your campaign or to gain some space and time. Strike at his networks—but don't fixate on him."

Just weeks before Obama nominated Petraeus to be his new commander in Afghanistan, the war there had become America's longest. It had been eight years and nine months since fighting began in Afghanistan on October 7, 2001, less than a month after the 9/11 terrorist attacks on New York and Washington. The Vietnam War had lasted eight years and eight months, from the passage of the Gulf of Tonkin resolution in Congress, on August 7, 1964, to the final withdrawal of American ground forces in March 1973. Almost nine years of fighting and more than one thousand dead in Afghanistan had produced little in the way of security. The fighting was fierce. In July 2010, more American service members were killed—fifty-eight—than in any other month of the war. By the end of August, when troop fatalities for the year reached 359, 2010 had already become the bloodiest year of the long campaign. Civilian casualties—deaths and injuries—were also surging, up 31 percent in the first six months over the same period a year earlier, the United Nations Assistance Mission in Afghanistan reported. The UN attributed nearly three-quarters of those casualties to the Taliban and other "anti-government elements" and noted two ominous trends behind their attacks: more increasingly sophisticated IEDs and a 95 percent increase in assassinations and executions, all aimed at keeping Afghans from cooperating with the Americans and their NATO allies.

The Taliban had spread to all but one of the country's thirty-four provinces. Just four years earlier, they had been active in only four. Conditions in the countryside had become so dangerous that aid workers could safely travel in only 30 percent of Afghanistan's 368 districts, according to the UN, and a group called the Afghan NGO Safety Office said the country had become more dangerous than in any year since the war began. Part of the Taliban's surge had apparently come in response to an American plan, announced the prior year, to concentrate on 80 of those 368 districts, mostly in the east and south, where the Taliban were concentrated. The Taliban simply moved to where the Americans were not. That the Taliban were still around at all in significant numbers spoke to how the war in Afghanistan had been "under-resourced" since the beginning of the U.S. intervention, as Petraeus would frequently note. In fact, when McChrystal had arrived in Afghanistan and conducted his review in the summer of 2009, it became readily apparent to him that more forces were necessary to begin to meet the objectives the administration had laid out. At Central Command headquarters, Petraeus agreed with this assessment and supported McChrystal's desire for more troops, as did Secretary Gates and Admiral Mullen, the chairman of the Joint Chiefs of Staff.

It wasn't until May 2010 that troop strength in Afghanistan surpassed the number of troops in Iraq—and this was only after the number in Iraq had been reduced significantly. Even so, the 100,000 U.S. forces in Afghanistan would be some 65,000 less than the U.S. high-water mark during the surge in Iraq. But the issue was more than just numbers of troops; Petraeus thought everything that was needed to win had been slighted in Afghanistan—Special Forces, intelligence systems, civil engineers, State Department analysts, trainers for Afghan troops, contract-management specialists. He recognized the irony: As commander in Iraq, he had fought for every resource possible—and had received most of what he requested. But that had deprived the commanders in Afghanistan and other conflict areas of what they needed from the military's robust but still finite resource pool. Now Petraeus would have to fight the bureaucracy to acquire those resources for his new battlefield. Thankfully, he recognized, Mullen and Gates supported his requests.

Having increased troop strength in Afghanistan from 32,800 to 69,000 in his first year in office, Obama announced on December 1, 2009, in a speech to cadets at West Point, that he had acted on a recommendation from the military and Gates and decided to add another 30,000 troops—the last of which would not arrive in the country until late August 2010, several weeks after Petraeus had arrived in theater, as it happened. But by July 2011, Obama said, a drawdown would begin at a pace based on conditions on the ground.

The new surge of troops added momentum to the campaign, which continued to make incremental progress. Militarily, the Taliban had for months been suffering heavy casualties, both from Special Operations Forces, in targeted raids aimed at killing leaders, and from conventional forces conducting clearance operations in ever greater numbers. U.S. and NATO forces had killed numerous Taliban shadow governors and wrested control from the Taliban of a number of safe havens, although Petraeus was clearly concerned about the insurgents' ability to seek refuge and regroup across the border in Pakistan. Before his demise at the hands of *Rolling Stone,* McChrystal in 2009 had succeeded in creating three new three-star military commands— one to train Afghan forces, which was meeting its goals, the second to serve as the operational commander in Afghanistan and the third to oversee U.S. detainee operations, reform Afghanistan's prisons and focus on improving the Afghan legal system. The overall result of the additional forces and other resources was that, by midsummer, in 124 key districts, the military reported deterioration in seven but progress in seventeen.

For Petraeus, the uneasy situation in Marjah, a former Taliban stronghold in Helmand Province where U.S. Marines had fought hard in February and March, provided the best window into what immediately awaited his command in Kandahar, birthplace of the Taliban. The battle for Marjah, Operation Moshtarak, had been the largest military operation in Afghanistan since the initial assaults that toppled the Taliban in 2001. Until that sector was cleared, no real progress could be made throughout the rest of Helmand Province. But it was hardly a battle of opposing armies. The American-led forces cleared the constellation of poor villages house by house, encountering pockets of resistance and a welter of IEDs. Thousands of Afghans fled or cowered in their homes. By the time the fighting was over, two weeks later, eight Marines, two Afghan soldiers and an Afghan police officer had lost their lives. U.S. military officials immediately promised to deliver a new "government in a box" to speed the delivery of services to villagers and brought back Haji Abdul Zahir from Germany as Marjah's governor.

But on the eve of Petraeus's arrival in July, Zahir was fired for incompetence. Effective local government remained an elusive goal, and Marjah remained a difficult place for U.S. forces. Part of the problem might have been overpromising on governance when the real accomplishment had been purely military, eliminating the Taliban stronghold and staging area. But the damage was done, and even Ambassador Richard Holbrooke, the American special representative for Afghanistan and Pakistan, was ambivalent. "It's not accurate to say Marjah's a failure, and it's premature to say Marjah's a success," he observed. The box that was supposed to have contained the district government was derided by many commentators as having been empty.

At his confirmation hearing before the Armed Services Committee, Petraeus described Marjah as having been the "nexus" of the Taliban and the illegal narcotics industry. He noted that "the enemy has fought back as we have taken away his sanctuaries. . . . Nothing has been easy in those operations, but six months ago we could not have walked through the market in Marjah, as I was able to do with the district governor there two months ago." Unspoken was Petraeus's sense that McChrystal's command had overpromised in Marjah and paid a price publicly when holding the critical town in Helmand became far more difficult than people had been led to expect. Petraeus knew that the strongholds around Kandahar, if anything, would be even more difficult to seize and hold, to say nothing of the difficulty of fighting in the harsh high altitudes of the forbidding Hindu Kush to the east along the Pakistan border. Indeed, the markets in Marjah had become dangerous places again since his visit, and the Taliban worked hard at intimidating— and, at times, executing—those who cooperated with the Americans. Insurgents, who easily blended into the population, enjoyed relative freedom of movement.

The slow progress in Marjah did not bode well for what had always been envisioned as the follow-on phase of Operation Moshtarak: the assault on Kandahar city, to the east of Helmand Province. If Marjah was mainly a military target and had been effectively neutralized, Kandahar was far more. The stronghold of the Taliban movement, Kandahar city and the difficult surrounding terrain would have to be cleared militarily by ISAF and Afghan forces and then pacified and governed effectively by local Afghans if Petraeus was to be able to achieve real success on the ground.

PETRAEUS'S SO-CALLED COINdinistas—counterinsurgency acolytes throughout the military establishment—were ready to report what they saw in Afghanistan, problems as well as successes, because they wanted him to know what he was getting himself into. Petraeus had learned from experience that he needed his followers to help him assess the situation, refine plans, establish measures and metrics they all understood and then execute the plan.

There were several overarching problems. The Afghan government was incredibly corrupt. Moreover, many Afghan military units couldn't, or wouldn't, fight. Some of the NATO allies weren't much better. And some U.S. Army units were clearly better than others when it came to conducting counterinsurgency operations, which could be hard to grasp for a nineteen-year-old who had joined the Army for the thrill of full-on combat. The frank assessments started pouring in less than an hour after Obama announced that he had nominated Petraeus to replace McChrystal as commander of the war in Afghanistan. First came a two-sentence e-mail from Douglas Ollivant, a former Army officer with a Ph.D. in political science, now serving as the senior civilian adviser for the CAAT in the eastern command sector in Afghanistan. Ollivant had worked closely with Petraeus during the surge in Iraq, when he was a lieutenant colonel: "Let me know what I can do. I guess I work for you again."

Petraeus responded: "Top 10 insights/recommendations welcome, Doug. Thx!" Ollivant's ideas about locating troops among the people and pushing decision making down to the battalion level became important tenets in Petraeus's campaign in Iraq. When Ollivant got to the city in the fall of 2006, he was charged with drawing up a plan for securing Baghdad. One of his bosses at the time was then–Brigadier General John F. Campbell, assistant division commander of the unit commanding the Baghdad area. Not only was Ollivant working for Petraeus again in Afghanistan, he was also once again working for Campbell, who was commander of both the 101st Airborne

Division and the Regional Command East, which covered the eastern provinces and the mountainous border.

In Iraq, Petraeus had encouraged Ollivant, five ranks beneath him, to bypass the normal chain of command and communicate directly with him. "You're a very bright guy, and these are exceptional times. We're going to get one last shot at this, and we need to make it really count—and you're the planner for the main effort," Petraeus wrote to him in an e-mail as the Iraq surge was commencing, emphasizing the importance of the citizens of Baghdad—"the human terrain"—as the most important terrain. "We're putting it all on the line and we need to be cognizant of that. It's not business as usual, as I'm sure you know."

Ollivant, like Petraeus, was a soldier-scholar. He had the intellect and analytical skills to develop a theoretical framework for combat strategy. The two men also shared a passion for the art of soldiering. Ollivant had argued in an article in 2006, written with 1st Lieutenant Eric D. Chewning, that a combat battalion had to master all the skills necessary to mount successful counterinsurgency operations. The essay won a competition Petraeus sponsored that year as he headed up the effort to produce a new Army/Marine Corps counterinsurgency manual at Fort Leavenworth, Kansas. Soon enough, both men were back in Iraq putting their ideas into practice during the surge.

The list of top ten insights Ollivant e-mailed Petraeus in 2010 amounted to a withering critique of what the commander would soon be inheriting in Afghanistan in the International Security Assistance Force (ISAF). The ISAF Joint Command (IJC), an operational command headed by Army lieutenant general David M. Rodriguez that was charged with coordinating all operations involving U.S., NATO and Afghan troops, was, he asserted, "structurally dysfunctional," lacking the means to coordinate its activities with civilians who report to the U.S. Embassy. This was not a reflection on Rodriguez, Ollivant said, and he recommended that Petraeus make Rodriguez his deputy for maneuver. He also said the IJC had designated too many "key terrain districts" in the eastern command sector and was likely to make progress in ten at best. "You taught me well—'underpromise; overdeliver.' We have violated that principle here."

He recommended rethinking the military's emphasis on Kandahar, in the south, and placing greater focus on the east. He also said he had "serious misgivings" about efforts to recruit and train the Afghan police, which he did not think would yield significant results by the announced drawdown in July 2011. "As I think you know well, the dirty secret on Iraq is that we never did really fix the police—we just made the Army good enough that no one noticed," he wrote. "I maintain we would be much better off focusing on training the Afghan Army (we know how to train armies—we are one!) . . . The bottom line is that resources poured into the police effort (in general— exceptions abound) are not going to pay off by Summer 2011. If that date no longer carries meaning, then that changes things."

He said a revised Tactical Directive from the commander was desperately needed, given the "palpable" sense of isolation troops feel from senior commanders.

Ollivant also noted the difficulties involved in asking young officers and their enlisted men to execute effective counterinsurgency operations, and he advocated pushing more support assets down to the company level, as he had in Iraq. Captains and lieutenants commanding these desolate outposts need human and technical intelligence assets, civil affairs support, even help running psychological operations. "There's just too much to expect a 24-29-year-old with limited life experience to accomplish," he wrote, explaining that they need assistance in partnering with Afghan units and help from more senior field-grade officers.

Finally, Ollivant told Petraeus that his forces needed to focus on improving the quality of local government, which ideally should mean the assignment of more foreign-service officers from the State Department to help knit local officials into the national government structure, with its provincial and district governors, which President Karzai controlled.

The place where effective government in Afghanistan happens, Ollivant explained in a subsequent e-mail to Petraeus, is at the district level, where power held locally by tribes, subtribes and clans can be merged with ministries and divisions of the national government. "It may be the closest thing to an overall decisive point that we have," Ollivant wrote. When this melding of local and national happens and a Kabul-appointed governor meets a traditional council of elders, he added, "all relevant and legitimate interests can be at least acknowledged, if not always accommodated."

Petraeus always found Ollivant's input thought-provoking, though he disagreed with his conclusion that they had failed to fix the police in Iraq. Petraeus thought the Iraqi police had made significant strides—albeit after Ollivant had redeployed to the United States. But he did agree with Ollivant on a great deal, including that more foreign-service officers were needed to help translate military gains into better local governance. He had already advocated, in fact—together with Ambassador Karl Eikenberry in Kabul—for more diplomats and other civilian experts, but the State Department had yet to provide them in the full numbers needed. Although Eikenberry had expressed concern over the lack of civilian support for the tremendous military effort that would be expended to secure and rebuild villages, his superiors in Washington were slow to respond. "Sending additional combat brigades will require tens of billions of dollars annually for years to come, costs not detailed in DOD charts," Eikenberry wrote in a cable several months later. "Yet an Embassy request this summer for a $2 billion increase in our budget for development and governance was analyzed and debated in great detail, only to be rejected."

AS HE PREPARED to head to Afghanistan, Petraeus viewed the campaign in simple terms. The key to victory lay in protecting the indigenous population, not just in killing the enemy. That was the insight Petraeus stressed over and over. Killing the enemy was certainly part of his counterinsurgency doctrine—a key part. But he knew only too well that, without the support of the Afghan people, you could never kill your way out of an insurgency.

Petraeus had repeatedly warned—at Central Command, in the press and behind closed doors in the various policy reviews over the previous two years—that he never thought the situation in Afghanistan could be "turned" as quickly as U.S. efforts were able to help turn Iraq. The conditions were different. But President Obama was firm on July 2011 as the date by which he would begin to draw down the American surge forces. Nobody expected to create a Western democracy overnight in Afghanistan, nor was the president asking Petraeus for that. But he wanted Petraeus to create the conditions for an end state that was tolerable: an Afghanistan that could secure and govern itself sufficiently to avoid once again becoming a safe haven for al-Qaeda. Petraeus had one year.

CHAPTER 2

RESULTS, BOY

P etraeus looked out the aircraft window and saw the barren, brown Hindu Kush Mountains, outside Kabul. He felt a twinge of anticipation for the imminent landing, even though it was a familiar view. He had traveled to Afghanistan nearly a dozen times as CENTCOM commander over the past two years, and he had been here once before that, on a special assessment mission for Defense secretary Donald Rumsfeld in 2005. He knew the challenges below, having worked with General McChrystal on the plan to commit significant resources to the neglected and troubled theater. Those challenges were now his to master.

His plane landed in Kabul at dusk on July 2, 2010. The smell of burning garbage lingered in the air. The shadows were long as the sun set on a warm, dry evening. U.S. ambassador Karl Eikenberry, Ambassador Mark Sedwill, NATO's senior civilian representative in Afghanistan, and Petraeus alighted together from a blue-and-white C-40 with UNITED STATES OF AMERICA emblazoned on the fuselage. Petraeus encouraged his civilian counterparts to exit the plane first. Accompanied by aides and security officers, they walked briskly to three Black Hawk helicopters, their rotors whirling, to take them to the headquarters of the International Security Assistance Force, a five-minute flight away.

Despite the six-hour-and-forty-five-minute flight from NATO headquarters in Brussels, Petraeus was all energy the next morning when he met with Rear Admiral Greg Smith, deputy chief of staff for communications. Smith, who had been one of Petraeus's media gurus during the surge in Iraq, and then served with him at Central Command, recorded no fewer than seventeen directives from Petraeus in his small five-by-seven-inch notebook. "Just need to keep pushing out little stories, most won't make the news, but they do add up," said one of Smith's notations. "Get with bureau chiefs, new sheriff in town," said others. Petraeus was in an information war. Everything coming out of his mouth and the ISAF press office was likely to be "parsed" by the press, he concluded. It was critical to get the narrative correct, because that would be the key to buying time. The last note Petraeus emphasized to Smith: It would be essential to strive once again to be "first with the truth."

An advance team from CENTCOM had arrived a few days earlier to outfit Petraeus's quarters: a warren of Conex containers, four in all, that the troops called his "hooch." The first eight-by-twenty-foot Conex included a stationary exercise bike, a flat-screen TV and three large printers; the next one housed his desk, with three computers and considerable communications equipment: secure and unsecure telephones, VTC capability, and all the other technology needed to keep up with events—and the ticking clocks—in Washington and Kabul and the capitals of up to forty-nine nations contributing to the NATO-directed coalition. The third was his bedroom, which consisted of a single bed, an old mattress, two small lockers and an attached bathroom with a tiny shower. And the fourth was home to his enlisted aide. It was a stark contrast to the villa in which he'd lived in Baghdad—rumored to have been Saddam's mother's—or the new quarters he and his wife had moved into in Tampa just one month earlier.

In his first "stand-up" briefing at 7:30 the following morning, Petraeus promised a review of the Tactical Directive, a document that provided detailed guidelines on the use of force in combat that had been issued exactly a year earlier—and had been strictly enforced—by his predecessor, the now-cashiered McChrystal. The document stressed the need to protect the Afghan people and called for limiting the use of close air support and artillery against residential compounds. "We must avoid the trap of winning tactical victories—but suffering strategic defeats—by causing civilian casualties or excessive damage and thus alienating the people," it read.

This Tactical Directive had proved problematic. The *Rolling Stone* article that led to McChrystal's downfall scorched the general and his aides, caricaturing them as testosterone-addled frat boys as they insulted Obama, Biden, Holbrooke, Eikenberry and even Karzai, with whom McChrystal reportedly got along famously. But the article's lengthiest passage described McChrystal's meeting with a group of soldiers at an outpost near Kandahar who believed that his Tactical Directive and severe restrictions on the use of airpower were tying their hands and getting them killed.

At ISAF headquarters in Kabul, looking out over forty staff officers seated before him at two horseshoe-shaped tables in the Situational Awareness Room, Petraeus said he understood the troopers' message. "There is no question about our commitment to reducing civilian loss of life, which is a moral imperative I absolutely support," he said, repeating the words he'd used during his Senate confirmation. "There is, however, concern in the ranks and in some of our nations about how we have applied the Tactical Directive, and they must be addressed." Petraeus explained that he would rely on his operational commander, Lieutenant General David M. Rodriguez, to make recommendations. There was, Petraeus observed, "a clear moral imperative to make sure we are fully supporting our troopers in combat. This debate is not about changing the rules of engagement; it is about implementing the Tactical Directive in a way that gives soldiers in trouble the support they need while doing everything possible to protect the Afghan people."

Petraeus would rely heavily on Rodriguez to oversee military operations. Rodriguez had spent more time in Afghanistan and knew the country better, down to the village level, than any other general in theater. Tall and rumpled, Rodriguez had first arrived in Afghanistan in 2007, as a division commander, just as the Taliban were reemerging as a potent insurgency. He then became Defense secretary Gates's senior military assistant, until Gates sent him back to Afghanistan as McChrystal's deputy in the summer of 2009. Part of that assignment involved standing up the new ISAF Joint

Command to unify NATO, U.S. and Afghan forces. Rodriguez was also the principal architect of the operational-level campaign plan Petraeus was inheriting. Rodriguez and McChrystal had been classmates at West Point and remained close friends. McChrystal considered Rodriguez "the best combat leader I have ever known."

Rodriguez identified ninety of four-hundred-plus districts in Afghanistan—population centers, markets, transportation nodes and agricultural centers—which would have to be controlled to turn back the Taliban. A principal focus was the capital region, around Kabul, home to one-fifth of the Afghan population and one of the safest places in Afghanistan, with the security zone expanding south and east against fierce Taliban resistance in some areas. The focus in northern Afghanistan was the Baghlan-Kunduz corridor, a densely populated region along two main commercial arteries. The western parts of the country remained relatively stable, and Herat, in Herat Province, to the far northwest, was a bustling city, largely free of violence, although there were periodic attacks. The Taliban strongholds were to the southwest, in Helmand Province, to the south, in Kandahar, and in the eastern provinces that lay on the routes from Pakistan's rugged tribal areas to Kabul.

Helmand had been Rodriguez's first thrust in March 2010. It was considered home to the illegal narcotics industry in fertile southern Afghanistan that fueled the Taliban insurgency. Now that central Helmand Province had largely been cleared, Petraeus would command the next thrust, focused on Kandahar and its surrounding districts, the birthplace of the Taliban movement. Once the Taliban had been rooted out there, Petraeus would turn his focus in late 2010 to the east and the mountainous terrain along the Pakistan border, the country's most difficult terrain in both human and physical terms. There, an earlier strategy for holding desolate mountain valleys with a far-flung network of combat outposts had been largely abandoned. It had given way to more targeted operations aimed at shutting down insurgents' "rat lines" across the border and establishing a layered defense against those insurgents who did manage to get through.

Petraeus had begun his remarks to the staff at ISAF headquarters with a laudatory reference to McChrystal. "I am delighted to be here, but I am not delighted to be here under the circumstances," he said. "I admire what General McChrystal achieved in terms of input and output and will take much of his work forward." But he knew that McChrystal's Tactical Directive wasn't the only issue that needed to be addressed, as he'd been hearing from people like Doug Ollivant even before he left Washington. One of his first acts as commander of the war in Afghanistan came that morning when he announced that checking e-mail or surfing the Web during the morning brief—a practice McChrystal not only tolerated but practiced himself on three laptops at a time—was unacceptable. With that, a clicking chorus of more than sixty closing laptops filled the room.

Comparisons between Petraeus and McChrystal were inevitable. Both men, lean if not slightly gaunt, were famously fit and ran religiously. Both were West Point graduates and prodigious readers. Both attracted loyal followings among ambitious young officers. Both were open to new ideas and popular with reporters. But lost on many in Washington was the reality—soon to be apparent to those on the ground in Afghanistan—that there was a new strategic force loosed in Kabul: Petraeus's will.

"RESULTS, BOY!" his father used to say. He was not interested in excuses. The preternaturally gifted young David Petraeus delivered. Whether it was by winning the newspaper boy delivery contest as an adolescent, scoring the winning goal in a critical high school soccer game, or becoming the head of the ecumenical religious youth groups in Cornwall, New York, just seven miles from West Point, Petraeus displayed his drive early. The "no-excuses" attitude Sixtus Petraeus displayed with his son came from his own experience as an officer on a Dutch ship and then as the captain of a U.S. Merchant Marine ship in World War II. Sixtus allowed little room for error in the younger Petraeus's performance in school, in sports, or at home, in part because of these high standards. A desire to please his father would, in great part, shape Petraeus's desire to excel. His father was an austere perfectionist who would do anything for his son but who dispensed his affection in the form of "gruff love," as Petraeus describes it. Still, he respected his father and relished hearing stories of his time in the military.

Petraeus's father had been at sea with a Dutch ship when Germany invaded Holland in May of 1940. According to Petraeus's only sibling, his older sister, Carol, their father's ship had just arrived in New York City when he received the news that the Netherlands had been overrun. There was no way he could return to Holland. He found himself and his crew welcomed in New York at a soldiers-and-sailors event in a local auditorium in the Seamen's Church Institute. One of the event coordinators he met was the petite and pretty Miriam Howell, a librarian who had attended Oberlin College, in Ohio. Sixtus and Miriam were married in April 1941 in the Ocean Avenue Congregational Church, in Brooklyn, New York. Soon after, Sixtus and most of his shipmates signed on with the U.S. Merchant Marine, and ultimately he became a U.S. citizen.

Born near Rotterdam, Sixtus and his family were originally from the Friesland area, in the northern part of Holland. This area was distinct from the country's eleven other provinces, with its own dialect, its dense agricultural production and its heavy presence of windmills. "I'm not Dutch; I'm Friesian," Sixtus would sternly tell his new friends in the community, in his thick accent.

On his mother's side, David Petraeus was English. Miriam Howell's great-great-great-grandfather was a lord of Westbury Manor, where his son, Miriam's great-great-grandfather Edward Howell, was born in 1584. Edward Howell's family emigrated to New England as part of the "Great Migration" of the English Puritans, landing in Lynn, Massachusetts, in the 1630s.

After gaining his citizenship, Sixtus quickly found a new home. The U.S. Merchant Marine was desperate for experienced sailors. It was losing sailors faster than they could be generated. With his experience and English skills, Sixtus was promoted in the subsequent years and quickly rose in rank, eventually becoming a captain in 1945. He was one of a corps of decorated Merchant Mariners whom the Russians would later recognize with a medal of achievement—in part for having survived a convoy to Murmansk, an extremely dangerous mission in which numerous ships typically were sunk by German U-boats operating from Norwegian fjords.

After the war, Sixtus and Miriam moved to Cornwall-on-Hudson, a "Norman Rockwell community" along the Hudson River with a little white church and steeple on the village's Main Street. The two were active in their church, paid cash for everything they bought, including their house, and kept a low profile in local politics.

Sixtus's career at sea meant that he and Miriam, a town librarian, wouldn't have children until later. Carol was born in 1947, David in 1952. Their simple life in Cornwall consisted of few faraway adventures but plenty of East Coast ski trips (Sixtus remained a member of a downhill ski club into his seventies), camping trips in local state parks, and trips to historical sites in New England—visiting Concord and Walden Pond and beyond and reading excerpts from history books and relevant literature along the way. The Petraeuses' backyard had ropes for climbing, a pull-up bar, a baseball backstop, a basketball hoop and various sports equipment; there were always soccer balls and baseball bats lying around. The simple two-story, one-and-a-half bathroom, four-bedroom house was rich with books and newspapers. Petraeus's mother was, at times, overly attentive and prone to worrying, but she adored her children and, as a librarian and a lover of Charles Dickens and other classics, took great care in Petraeus's intellectual development. Miriam wanted her son to go to Oberlin College, where she and all her cousins had received their degrees. But for a boy growing up seven miles from West Point, the allure of the U.S. Military Academy was irresistible.

Petraeus's soccer coach had been captain of the West Point team, and his math teacher had taught at the academy. The director of admissions lived right around the corner—Petraeus delivered his newspaper. During high school, Petraeus dated the daughter of an Air Force officer in the town and was influenced by her father's demeanor. It was almost preordained that he would become a cadet.

David Petraeus got in the family car with his parents on July 1, 1970, and drove the seven miles from Cornwall to West Point for "R-Day," reception day for the incoming class of new cadets. He was assigned to Company C-1, "Charging Charlie."

Although known as fun-loving by his peers, Petraeus was also driven to excel. His roommate, Chris White, had decided to pursue the pre-med track, one of the most demanding academic programs at West Point, which gave medical-school scholarships to around ten top graduates. The hypercompetitive Petraeus decided to join him—not so much because he wanted to be a doctor, he later realized, but because he found the competition irresistible. "It was the Mount Everest of academic tracks," he recalled. Petraeus rarely stayed up past the 11:30 P.M. lights-out curfew; the pace of the West Point day, which for him included competing on the intercollegiate soccer and ski teams, rendered him exhausted and in bed by lights-out.

By the time he was a firstie, as seniors are called, Petraeus had risen to the top 5 percent of his class based on his performance in leadership, athletics and academics—the three areas in which cadets are ranked against their peers. He and White, his roommate again during the last semester of firstie year, were known as the most focused students in their company. "I think every cadet questions the discipline at West Point at one time or another during his years here," Cadet Petraeus said at the time, grinning. "But in the long run the imposed discipline brings out self-discipline in each cadet, and I think that's very beneficial."

While White remained intent on becoming a doctor, Petraeus realized that what he really wanted to do "was to lead folks in service, to serve in the essence of the military organization, that of a combat infantry unit." He would impose discipline on himself to be the best in the infantry, and he later told his former girlfriend from Cornwall, Ellen Smitchger, that he "wanted to lead the Army" someday.

This inspiration to join the infantry came in part from a favorite West Point expression: "Much of the history we teach was made by people we taught." Many of those heroes he had studied in his military history classes—MacArthur, Eisenhower, Ridgway and Galvin among them—came from the infantry. Infantrymen often rose to the top of the Army. At the time his class selected their branch choice and assignment, he knew he wanted to earn a Ranger tab, become an Airborne trooper and serve abroad. He knew his place at the top of the class would allow him to begin his career on the most likely path to the top. In time, Petraeus would be first in his Ranger School class and would command multiple airborne units.

White was prophetic in the description he wrote of Petraeus for the 1974 West Point yearbook, using the nickname that had stuck with Petraeus since Little League: "Peaches came to the Mil Acad with high ambitions, but unlike most, he accomplished his goals. A striver to the Max, Dave was always 'going for it' in sport, academics, leadership, even his social life. This attitude will surely lead to success in the future, Army or otherwise."

The reference to his social life was a nod to his engagement to Hollister Knowlton, the daughter of West Point's superintendent, a military intellectual who had distinguished himself on the battlefield in World War II and Vietnam. In the fall of 1973, "Holly" Knowlton was a senior at Dickinson College, a beautiful, smart and witty young woman who wrote her senior honors dissertation on François Mauriac, a French novelist who had been awarded the Nobel Prize. On a visit to West Point one football weekend, a friend of the family hoped to fix her up with a certain cadet to take her to the game. But when he was otherwise engaged, a call was placed to the cadet brigade headquarters to find a replacement, the assistant brigade adjutant on duty: David Petraeus. Not knowing who his blind date was, he agreed to take on this potentially sensitive mission. Soon, the two would find themselves commuting to each other's colleges whenever time allowed, sometimes braving fierce New York snowstorms to spend time together. Petraeus would sneak in the side door of the superintendent's home aside the Plain, the academy's parade field, to visit Holly when she made the trip back to West Point. Both maintained their first priorities of graduating at the top of their classes, and both did: Petraeus graduated fortieth in his class, a "star man," signifying top 5 percent, cadet captain and varsity letterman, while Holly was summa cum laude and Phi Beta Kappa, with honors in both French and English. The two were married on July 6, 1974, at the Cadet Chapel on West Point's campus a month after Petraeus received his commission from Lieutenant General Knowlton as a 2nd lieutenant in the infantry.

David's roots stood in sharp contrast to his bride's patrician-military up-bringing. To Petraeus, the stature of Holly's family was intoxicating. He loved becoming a part of it. Holly's well-connected and accomplished grand-parents had a large compound in West Springfield, New Hampshire, with a boathouse on a nearby lake that they would visit often. Holly's father, Lieu-tenant General Knowlton, came from a prominent and well-to-do Massa-chusetts family and had graduated seventh in his class at West Point. He fought in four campaigns during World War II, beginning in Normandy. In the last weeks of the war, he was awarded a Silver Star for leading a recon-naissance mission deep behind German lines to make one of the first con-tacts with the Soviet forces north of Berlin. After the war, as the Cold War lines hardened, he was one of a handful of officers selected to help General Eisenhower establish the new NATO headquarters in Paris. Knowlton later served two years under General Westmoreland in Vietnam, where he vis-ited every province as a senior official in the Civil Operations and Revolu-tionary Development Support program and commanded combat forces in the Mekong Delta. When he returned to the Pentagon, Knowlton pushed to conduct a serious investigation of the My Lai massacre. Promoted to three stars at West Point, he retired three tours later as a four-star general. He would become Petraeus's "military father," according to Knowlton's wife, Peggy. Petraeus would be their "fourth son," and General Knowlton would pass on to him tales of his fights against the Nazis and the Vietcong after Petraeus had proven himself as a cadet.

Petraeus was eager to fight and win the kinds of wars Knowlton described during dinners at the superintendent's house, Quarters 100—one of the most distinctive buildings at West Point. Sitting at the long rectangular dinner table in the historic supe's house was an honor afforded to the academy's rising stars. The dinner was always a cut above the mess hall. Petraeus's early interest in the topic of "uncomfortable wars" began at West Point—at these dinners. There were no mandatory classes on counterinsurgency warfare at West Point at that time.

Life at the academy generally shielded cadets from the antiwar sentiment that prevailed at the time, and Knowlton tried to inculcate in the cadets the virtues of the profession of arms, even while the Army was approaching its post-Vietnam nadir. In his oral history, Knowlton later reflected that he was the "commander of a stockade surrounded by attacking Indians."

Knowlton served as the academy's forty-ninth superintendent. He was involuntarily ordered to West Point on twenty-four hours' notice by Westmoreland after the departure of Major General Sam Koster, whose record was tainted because of his association with My Lai. Westmoreland wanted Knowlton to establish some "consistency" and improve communications between the Pentagon and the nation's oldest military academy, especially as the Army began to resurrect itself after the morass of Vietnam. The rapid turnover in superintendents and the frequent personality clashes between them and the Army chiefs of staff had not been healthy for the Corps of Cadets; Westmoreland thought that if Knowlton stayed for four years, he could help stabilize important leadership initiatives in this time of transition for the academy. Westmoreland himself had served as superintendent and had a soft spot for the Corps and a burning interest in everything that went on at West Point.

Knowlton was determined to run West Point differently from his predecessors. From the time he arrived, he would write long memorandums to the Pentagon, sometimes every day. In the memos, he didn't ask for permission to conduct affairs the way he saw fit. Rather, he explained the critical issues facing the school and described how he planned to deal with them. Petraeus began drafting the same sort of "commander's update" for his boss when he was in Bosnia and carried the tradition with him to Iraq, Central Command and Afghanistan.

Knowlton buffered the cadets from the negativity surrounding Vietnam in part by sharing stories about his own positive experiences there. The Civil Operations and Revolutionary Development Support (CORDS) initiative was the main U.S. pacification program. The mission of CORDS was three-fold: providing security for the local population, destroying insurgent infra-structure and building Vietnamese government capacity—and doing all of this on a scale large enough to be decisive. These concepts would later be-come part of Petraeus's strategy for the surge in Iraq.

While on Westmoreland's staff, Knowlton had made it a goal to visit as many of the districts in Vietnam as he could, to gather local knowledge and perspectives from the detachment teams. He went into the countryside to show the interest of the central government in the life of his teams and the people in the area. These teams would gather "atmospherics" and then initi-ate locally requested projects to improve standards of living, which included building medical facilities, schools and bridges. This level of understanding of local socioeconomic factors helped Knowlton to establish the Hamlet Evaluation System, an initiative to capture metrics for levels of security throughout the sub-provincial geographic areas.

But metrics in counterinsurgency are messy, as both Knowlton and Petraeus learned in their respective military commands.

WHEN HE ARRIVED IN Afghanistan, Petraeus, who had gone on to study advanced economics and international relations at Princeton, devoured statistics and data to help him understand the state of the war. He also knew that a commander could improve "situational awareness" and his under-standing of the circumstances in various locations by reaching out to those in the field. He'd been schooled in techniques for achieving situational awareness by Knowlton and other early mentors, and now he worked to gain it by dint of his own eighteen-hour days, part of which he spent communicat-ing directly with soldiers, scholars and journalists in the field, in locations ranging from the desolate outposts in Kunar and Nuristan provinces, on the Pakistan border in northeastern Afghanistan, to the main fighting effort in Helmand and Kandahar provinces, to the southwest.

He was painfully aware that he didn't know Afghanistan nearly as well as he had known Iraq when he assumed command of the surge in Baghdad in

2007. Others noticed it as well. In Iraq, he had already had nearly two and a half years on the ground when he arrived to command the surge. He'd had an inner circle team that was familiar with Iraq, too. This was, by contrast, his entry-level position in Afghanistan. He'd visited the country many times but he'd never lived there. Other than his military aide, no one on the small team he brought with him from Central Command had deployment experience there, either: not his executive officer, Commander's Initiatives Group director, personal security detachment commander or personal public affairs officer. Petraeus valued their loyalty and their ability to interpret his vision more than their specific expertise. They would all gain that in time, he thought, and in the interim they would rely on the subordinate commanders and the personal and headquarters staff with Afghan experience whom he had inherited and would also reach out to his "directed telescopes."

In the meantime, he set out immediately to build what were perhaps his two most critical relationships. The first was with Ambassador Eikenberry, with whom there had long been some professional tension with the military in Kabul. Eikenberry had been in the news most recently for feuding with McChrystal. The second was with President Karzai, whom Petraeus had met a number of times in person in Kabul and Washington and with whom he had communicated periodically by telephone from the States.

Petraeus had more than a little in common with Eikenberry, a retired Army lieutenant general who had graduated from West Point and Ranger School. They weren't close friends, but they weren't rivals, much less enemies. Petraeus had worked well with Eikenberry in past years, and he respected Eikenberry's long service in, and knowledge of, Afghanistan. One Petraeus aide said the two men were determined to work together and put the past civil-military tensions behind them. Petraeus had invited Eikenberry to fly into Kabul from NATO headquarters, in Belgium, with the team. "It's about creating a culture of teamwork," the aide recalled. "He was setting a tone: We're going to work *together*.'"

After Eikenberry's cables critical of Karzai were leaked in 2009, Eikenberry became the focus of complaints from Karzai. The Afghan president would repeatedly bring up the cables and also Eikenberry's supposed interference with the presidential elections in 2009 with visiting officials, including Petraeus, over the course of the next year. Although Petraeus and the ISAF staff had a good partnership with the embassy, Petraeus found that Karzai's visceral reaction to Eikenberry prevented the general from operating the way he had with Ambassador Crocker in Baghdad. There, Petraeus and Crocker attended all meetings with Iraq's Prime Minister Maliki together to present a united front. Ultimately, Petraeus stopped including Eikenberry in most of his personal meetings with Karzai because of the unhelpful atmosphere generated by his presence, according to Petracus's aides. Over time, Petraeus found that one-on-one meetings with Karzai were the most productive.

At the embassy's Fourth of July celebration on July 3, the day before he officially took command, Petraeus sought to set the right tone as he made remarks to the assembled employees and Afghan guests. "Cooperation is not optional," he stated firmly. "Civilian and military, Afghan and international, we are part of one team with one mission. . . . And I know that you all share the unshakable commitment to teamwork that Ambassador Eikenberry and I share. This is a tough mission. There is nothing easy about it. But working together, we can achieve progress, and we can achieve our mutual objectives." Petraeus's first meeting with Karzai took place that afternoon at the Presidential Palace. Eikenberry and Ambassador Sedwill attended, as did a number of key Afghan ministers. It did not go particularly well.

Petraeus's top priority was winning Karzai's approval for what was considered a critical program for creating village police forces across the country, with U.S. Special Forces training an initial cadre of ten thousand who would be paid about $120 a month. The Afghan Local Police (ALP), as these village policemen would come to be called, were seen as playing a potentially critical role in keeping the Taliban from coming back to villages that had been cleared by U.S., NATO and Afghan troops—and could thus be decisive in the long term. What was most important about the Afghan Local Police, as the last line of indigenous defense, was that these units would exist at the village level. The members of the Afghan National Security Forces who made up the first lines of defense consisted of two separate forces, the Afghan National Army (ANA) and the Afghan National Police (ANP). The army was the larger of the two, having grown from 97,000 in November 2009, when the "train and equip" mission first became a NATO command under Lieutenant General William Caldwell, to more than 144,000 by October 2010. Caldwell's goal was to build the Afghan army to 164,000 by the fall of 2011. In most operations, the Afghan National Army fought side by side with U.S. and NATO forces. The Afghan National Police, which patrolled more at the district and provincial level, numbered about 114,000. Caldwell hoped an additional 20,000 police could be recruited, trained and equipped in the coming year. The Afghan National Police focused on keeping the peace and fighting crime. Unlike the Afghan Local Police, who would focus on village defense and early warning, the Afghan National Police had the power to arrest and detain insurgents and criminal suspects.

The growth of the ALP, the ANA and the ANP would greatly improve what Petraeus thought of as "COIN math": the ratio of counterinsurgents to population. To achieve the numbers recommended in his field manual, he had to alter the coalition ratio of 1 counterinsurgent to 90 Afghans to the 1:20 the manual prescribed. But recruiting, training and equipping the Afghan National Army and the Afghan National Police could happen only so quickly, especially given a literacy rate for recruits of only 14 percent and a desertion-and-casualty rate for Army recruits of about 25 percent per year.

Training Afghan Local Police detachments furthered relationships that Special Forces A-Teams had been building in villages by living among the people, learning their ways, helping with basic needs like medical care and clean water and eventually winning their trust. These efforts were officially known as Village Stability Operations, a top-priority program begun by U.S. Special Operations commanders in 2009 under McChrystal in areas where there were no other coalition or Afghan forces. The idea was to support military operations conducted by conventional forces by establishing Special Forces teams in areas the insurgents might occupy after being cleared from more populated areas. Special Forces would train and equip local villagers to provide for their own defense, and those secured areas would, ideally, grow toward other cleared areas in the theater and form a chain-link fence of security. The goal had been to expand to twenty-five villages. But if Karzai could be persuaded to support the Afghan Local Police program, Special Forces could accelerate their focus from Village Stability Operations to building and mentoring these new village police detachments. Petraeus, meanwhile, was simultaneously working on initiatives to take insurgents off the battlefield through such efforts as the Afghanistan Peace and Reintegration Program as well as through targeted raids conducted by Special Operations elements.

The cumulative effect of all the factors in the complex equation, Petraeus hoped, would result in fewer insurgents and more friendly forces. And the Afghan Local Police held considerable promise. Petraeus had been led by some Afghan security officials to believe that Karzai was fully supportive. But the meeting with Karzai at the Presidential Palace quickly degenerated when the Afghan leader began voicing his concern that the local police forces could quickly become out-of-control militias.

So began Petraeus's courtship of Karzai, with whom he would meet no fewer than thirty times in July. The initial discussion was officially termed a "forthright" airing of issues and concerns on both sides. Petraeus, however, had come with clear rules of engagement, developed in Iraq, for dealing with heads of state. They did not include public criticism. As he had done for the most part with Iraq's Prime Minister Maliki, Petraeus planned to take Karzai's commitments at face value, repeat them publicly as praise and, having done so, work to make them happen through Karzai's government. As he had with Maliki, Petraeus repeatedly noted that Karzai was the leader of a sovereign nation. He remained sensitive to Karzai's resentment of foreign troops in his country. "You literally do have to walk a mile in his shoes pretty often, and have a degree of understanding," Petraeus noted. "I'm not saying you necessarily have to empathize fully, but you do have to understand. Again, keep in mind that most issues here are not black or white; they are varying shades of gray."

The security initiatives, however, could be solidified only if various components of the rule of law could be improved. Before Petraeus had even arrived in Kabul, he and Eikenberry had devised a civil-military structure to direct and oversee creation of a functioning justice system in Afghanistan. Afghanistan needed judges, prosecutors, defense attorneys, courtrooms, jails and administrative staffs to help address corruption and lawlessness in the countryside. Despite nine years of war and effort, the United States had never taken on this gargantuan task, which Petraeus, from his command in Iraq, knew was essential if progress was to be made. Districts without judges were among the mostly hotly contested by the insurgents, who filled the void with their own brand of ruthless Islamist justice. This area was, Petraeus often noted, one in which the Taliban could compete with the government.

The overall "rule of law" effort was to be headed by a diplomat of ambassadorial rank, Hans Klemm, and overseen on the military side by Vice Admiral Bob Harward, assisted by an Army brigadier general who was going to lead a command titled "Rule of Law Field Force–Afghanistan." Petraeus knew precisely who he wanted to handle this latter assignment: Brigadier General Mark S. Martins, one of the Army's top lawyers and a man whose credentials, intellect and force of personality rivaled Petraeus's own. While Petraeus and many of those in his inner circle were new to Afghanistan, Martins had already been there a year, serving first as interim commander and then deputy commander of Joint Task Force 4-35, a group McChrystal had created in the fall of 2009 to oversee U.S. detainee operations after realizing that Afghanistan's prison system had become an out-of-control breeding ground for the insurgency. Not only did Taliban leaders plot attacks from inside the Afghan prison walls, but the prisons, with their lack of due process, helped create future insurgents.

Petraeus first met Martins in 1991, when Petraeus was a battalion commander in the 101st Airborne Division and Martins was one of the division's military attorneys. Drawn to each other by mutual intensity—Martins was in Petraeus's class as a runner—Petraeus considered Martins a "once-in-a-generation" officer, and Martins looked up to Petraeus as a mentor. Martins had been Petraeus's top lawyer and legal adviser during the surge in Iraq, when they worked to establish legal "green zones" there to enable secure administration of justice. Building on his work in rule-of-law issues,

Martins would work to establish "green zones"—secure areas for law and justice in Afghanistan—beginning with the Chel Zeena Criminal Investigative Center, adjacent to Kandahar's largest detention facility, Sarposa prison.

Petraeus formally assumed command at NATO headquarters on the Fourth of July. "As each of you knows well, we are engaged in a tough fight," he said during a ceremony at NATO headquarters. "After years of war, we have arrived at a critical moment. . . . We are engaged in a contest of wills. Our enemies are doing all that they can to undermine the confidence of the Afghan people. . . . In answer, we must demonstrate to the people and to the Taliban that Afghan and ISAF forces are here to safeguard the Afghan people, and that we are in this to win. That is our clear objective."

The following morning, during his stand-up briefing at ISAF headquarters, Petraeus hammered away at the most important counterinsurgency principle of all, protecting the people. "The big idea today, which applies at every level of this command, is the importance of engagement with the local population ranking alongside the importance of our kinetic activity," he said. "All commanders at every level are to be prepared to brief me on their interaction with the locals, the impact this is having, and how you will further develop local relations with key players and the mass of the local population." He repeated that cooperation was not an option; he talked about an "enduring commitment" to success in Afghanistan, and he again stated, "We are here to win." But this time, he explained what that meant. "Winning in COIN is not planting the flag at the top of the hill," he said. "Winning is making progress."

Later that afternoon, Petraeus took his message to his local partners, speaking in highly personal terms at a ceremony honoring noncommissioned officers in the Afghan National Army. "Your leadership matters to your troopers and the people of Afghanistan," he told the attendees. "When I think of the value of senior noncommissioned officers, in fact, I often recall a bit of guidance my Dutch sea captain father shared with me when I was young: 'It's results, boy, results.' And every commanding officer knows that getting results is what senior NCOs do best. . . . You get results." In the margin of his speech, Petraeus scrawled: "As this conference stresses, leadership is best provided by example," a point he made to the Afghan senior NCOs as well.

Petraeus believed his presence at a conference of Afghan NCOs could help develop leaders who might determine whether their units succeeded or failed on the battlefield. Petraeus's instinct as a commander was to seek to be at a point where he could best understand what his unit was engaged in. In conventional military operations, this location, the "point of decision," was typically where the fighting was heaviest. But in the kind of irregular warfare he faced, Petraeus thought the point of decision was less obvious. It might be in negotiations over an "awakening moment," as he learned in 2007 while engaging with local Iraqi tribal leaders willing to stand up to al-Qaeda in order to establish security in their communities, or at a field command post where all of the information from a highly distributed operation comes together, or even on Capitol Hill, when explaining the situation in a particular mission.

At this moment, addressing this group of Afghan sergeants major was important to ultimate organizational success. In the U.S. military, the NCO corps was regarded as the "backbone" of the Army, and Petraeus felt these Afghans could play that role here as well. He believed in motivating them by example and behaved as though the amount of energy and commitment he personally poured into that event—and every moment—was a critical factor in the war.

"You have to believe in what you're doing, in what you're arguing for, especially when you're in a position where your decisions involve people giving their lives for a cause and for the country," Petraeus later shared.

The morning stand-up was a venue Petraeus used not just to receive various updates but also to communicate his priorities and decentralize his network, although some saw in it Petraeus's penchant for micromanagement. Petraeus entered the briefing room at 7:29 A.M. on July 5, his third full day in Afghanistan, nodding to those he knew. "In the spirit of General McChrystal, I will flatten the network as far as possible, then go one level lower," he noted at one point in the session. He was trying to teach. The message was apt as he spoke to a disparate audience during the secure video teleconference. It included officers at all the subordinate and regional commands in Afghanistan, and also representatives at the U.S. Embassy, numerous Afghan element locations, various NATO headquarters, CENTCOM headquarters in Tampa, the Joint Staff in the Pentagon and a handful of other locations.

That morning, Petraeus had three big ideas to share. The first was that the military couldn't fight and win this war alone; civilian counterparts, Afghans as well as international, were critical. Civil-military tensions ran high at the tactical level, where civilians who headed Provincial Reconstruction Teams held the same rank as the military task-force commander in an area of operations, such as Lieutenant Colonel David G. Fivecoat, who had served as Petraeus's aide in Bosnia and during the invasion of Iraq in 2003, and was now in Paktika Province, in eastern Afghanistan, commanding Petraeus's old battalion in the 101st Airborne Division. Petraeus wanted the big ideas to filter down to that level, so while the brief progressed each morning, Petraeus's ISAF deputy chief of staff, Colonel Mike Meese, distilled the brief into succinct notes that were then posted on the secure internet and distributed down to battalion level. Commanders like Fivecoat could have a daily dose of their overall commander's intent to ensure they understood the campaign priorities and theater trends as they carried out tactical operations. Echoing his message throughout the chain of command was vital, Petraeus believed.

The second big idea was worth emphasizing after nine years of war: "We are," Petraeus said, "here to win." That, in Petraeus's mind, was why Obama had picked him. "The president didn't send me here to make a hasty retreat," he said. Petraeus was resolute with the president, though he hadn't made any demands when he agreed to accept the job. But the unspoken understanding was that the president would support him.

The third idea fell right in line with that affirmation. "We need to communicate that we have an enduring commitment here, but the nature of this enduring commitment will change over time as we transition authority to the Afghans," he explained. He was careful to point out that nuanced language was critical. "We are not transferring; we are transitioning. This supports the concept that we are not 'pulling out' but we are 'thinning out.'" He would repeat the three big ideas to his staff and on battlefield circulations.

Questions about metrics and progress had been raised for months in Kabul, Brussels and Washington. Petraeus's answer was to emphasize, again, that "winning is making progress. Clearly we are making progress. Obviously, within this, there are successes and failures, which you have to reconcile and then address in a nuanced way. For example, violence is going up, and that is not good, but it is due in part to our increased tempo of operations and the conduct of operations in an enemy stronghold. We are also making a lot of inputs into many areas, and these are important because they will enable the outputs that we are ultimately focused on. Therefore, when engaging on the subject of 'Are we winning?' think clearly about what you are saying and the clarity that you must achieve."

Petraeus also wanted to communicate that idea of winning to his Afghan partners, some of whom had grown weary of NATO after years of war, death and destruction. Beyond conveying that message, Petraeus also issued his first apology to Afghan forces that day, after a NATO helicopter gunship mistook an Afghan National Army patrol in the Andar District of Ghazni Province for insurgents and unleashed a barrage of missiles, killing five and wounding two. Petraeus offered his personal condolences to the families of the dead troops. It would become a common refrain, even as Petraeus's disciplined approach brought down the number of civilians mistakenly killed by U.S. and NATO forces. His apology was accompanied in that day's headlines with Britain's announcement that one thousand British troops would turn over the Sangin District, in Helmand Province, where they had sustained heavy casualties, to U.S. forces. The *Independent* in London said British forces had been engaged in "the fiercest fighting the British Army has seen since the Second World War."

Petraeus made his first battlefield circulation the next day, visiting Canadian brigadier general Jon Vance, NATO commander in Kandahar, at a recently constructed checkpoint designed to help keep the Taliban from moving in and out of the city. His battlefield circulation to visit Canadians in the Taliban stronghold of Kandahar was designed to send a message: The alliance will not be deterred. Beyond the symbolism, he saw with his own eyes that the heavily fortified checkpoint, manned round the clock, would have a deterrent effect on insurgents, as long as the searches were conducted thoroughly and respectfully. As always, he felt it important for a commander to capture the ground truth at times by seeing it for himself.

Petraeus had worked hard while at Central Command to continue to engage the Canadians, who had announced earlier that year the end of their mission in Afghanistan to be in the summer 2011. As challenging as the coalition politics of the then–forty-seven nations were, Petraeus considered the coalition to be hugely important and wanted support from all the coalition-contributing countries for as long as he could keep it. Though "coalition maintenance" took considerable time, Petraeus subscribed to Churchill's observation that the only thing worse than allies was not having any.

In subsequent days, Petraeus paid his first visit to the 101st Airborne and its commander, Major General John Campbell. Campbell not only led the 101st Airborne Division but also served as commander of ISAF's Regional Command East, a region that encompassed fourteen provinces, seven million people and four hundred tribes across 46,000 square miles, an area roughly the size of Pennsylvania. Having graduated from West Point in 1979, five years after Petraeus, Campbell was the archetypal Army commander in the post-9/11 era. He had already commanded a combat brigade of the 82nd Airborne in Afghanistan—the same one Petraeus had commanded—and he had distinguished himself in Iraq as one of the individuals most responsible for implementing the Baghdad Security Plan during the surge in 2007. Barring a serious misstep, he was already considered a likely future four-star general: Ranger-qualified, with time in Special Forces, he had also taught military science at the University of California, Davis, and served as deputy director of regional operations at the Pentagon for the chairman of the Joint Chiefs of Staff.

Petraeus arrived on a tough day for his old division. The 101st had lost two soldiers earlier in the day, Sergeant Shaun M. Mittler, of Austin, Texas, and Specialist Carlos J. Negron, of Fort Myers, Florida, in separate Taliban attacks. Two days earlier, Private First Class Anthony W. Simmons, of Talla-hassee, had died in yet another attack. At least eight other U.S. service members had been killed in RC East since Petraeus took command, bringing the total number of dead in Afghanistan since late 2001 to 1,079. It was, Pe-traeus said, a "lick 'em tomorrow" day for the 101st Airborne.

The reference was to a quote from Major General Ulysses S. Grant, one of Petraeus's military heroes, that helped sustain him during his darkest hours in command in Iraq during the surge. In an interview, Petraeus re-called the Battle of Shiloh: In April 1862, after one of the bloodiest single days of fighting in the nation's history, Grant repaired to a wooden cabin seeking shelter from the rain. Both sides had hunkered down for the night. Grant saw that surgeons were using the shelter as an operating room. Am-putated arms and legs lay on the bloody floor. The cries of the wounded were all around him. He went back outside and took cover under a tree, chewing on an unlit cigar. His favorite subordinate commander, Major General Wil-liam Tecumseh Sherman, found him there. "Well, Grant," Sherman said. "We've had the devil's own day, haven't we?" "Yep," Grant replied. "Lick 'em tomorrow, though."

"Needless to say, that's the toughest part of command by far," Petraeus told a friend that evening, referring to the 101st's casualties in Afghanistan, "and it never gets easier." Always in the back of his mind was the fact that his only son, who was leading an infantry platoon in Afghanistan in a unit at-tached to the 101st and engaged in intense combat, could become a casualty as well.

During the visit, Campbell arranged a meeting via VTC between Petraeus and the division's brigade commanders deployed in southern and eastern Afghanistan. As Campbell recalled, "Right away—that day—Petraeus was resolving and addressing issues we brought up. That's just how he operates. I'd get a response back that night or the next day: *Bam,* he took care of it. That's the power he brings to this effort," Campbell said.

Privately, many in Petraeus's inner circle harbored concerns about whether the general, despite his lifelong emphasis on physical fitness, could keep up the pace. "He isn't twenty-five anymore," one of Petraeus's mentors said. "He knows he has been given the challenge of his life—can he manage this with detachment and balance?" But there was no letting up. Petraeus's jam-packed schedule, since the day he arrived in Kabul, most often featured twenty meetings, briefings, appearances and visits a day; it typically began at 5:30 A.M., when the general, pedaling his exercise bike, read his morning intelligence brief. His aide and his executive officer knew to fill each minute with something productive. There was no time to spare.

By the tenth day of his command, Petraeus had met with Karzai for the seventh time on creating the Afghan Local Police. By then, Petraeus had helped his Afghan partners address the concerns that Karzai and other Afghan leaders had harbored, and ultimately Karzai assumed the role of championing the initiative and leading the Afghan debate (with Petraeus privately admiring how Karzai had initially represented the concerns of others as his own before guiding the push to final approval of a program Petraeus suspected Karzai had wanted for years). Karzai's government announced the following day that it had approved creation of the local police. The deal came after the security ministers and Petraeus agreed to a proposal that would ensure the ALP would report to district police chiefs and be paid by Karzai's Interior Ministry, thereby guaranteeing central control and reducing the risks of the elements being warlord militias. The agreement called for as many as ten thousand to be trained by U.S. Special Forces and Afghan National Police, many of whom would be focused in the south, where the insurgency was strongest. Petraeus publicly lauded the accomplishment and saw the development, achieved in less than two weeks, as one that could potentially affect the outcome of the war.

The same morning, Petraeus had begun his stand-up by projecting a painting by Frederic Remington, *The Stampede,* on the wall of the briefing room, saying it was symbolic of the challenges they faced in Afghanistan. He had taken the idea from his mentor General Jack Galvin, who had used the painting when Petraeus was his aide in the 1980s. Petraeus had also used it as a tool during his command in Iraq. "I use this painting to convey what it is we do," he told his staff officers, explaining the metaphor.

I use this image to tell you that I am comfortable with semi-chaotic situations. The picture depicts an outrider galloping at full tilt over rough terrain at the height of a violent storm while steering a willful mount and guiding a sometimes frightened and unthinking herd of cattle to its destination. It represents getting the job done despite the challenges. The terrain is rocky, the wind is in their faces and it is raining sideways. Some of these cattle will get out ahead of us—that's fine, we will catch up. Some cattle will fall behind and we will have to circle back and get them—that's fine, we will bring them on. We must be comfortable with this environment of uncertainty, challenge, risk, danger and competing agendas. We need to accept it. But we need to do more than simply hang on to the saddle. We must master our mount and we must flourish in the apparent chaos. I am comfortable with this. It is a privilege to be part of the Kabul stampede—kick on.

AFTER A MONTH in Afghanistan, Petraeus issued his updated Tactical Directive, a statement of war-fighting policy, to the 150,000 U.S. and NATO forces under his command. Stressing a "disciplined use of force," the unclassified portions of the directive provided his guidance and intent for following the rules of battlefield engagement. In practical terms, the document governed the use of what Petraeus had called, during his confirmation hearing, "large, casualty-producing devices"—bombs, close air support, attack helicopters. The biggest single change in his update was stated unequivocally in its first paragraph: "Subordinate commanders are not authorized to further restrict this guidance without my approval." His conclusion was that the problem lay not so much with McChrystal's directive but with subordinate commanders who had added conditions that made it more difficult for U.S. and NATO forces to fight—in essence, restricting units beyond McChrystal's intent.

But Petraeus also sought greater clarity. Where the prior directive had instructed "leaders at all levels to scrutinize and limit the use of force like close air support against residential compounds and other locations likely to produce civilian casualties in accordance with this guidance," Petraeus's said: "Prior to the use of fires, the commander approving the strike must determine that no civilians are present. If unable to assess the risk of civilian presence, fires are prohibited." The only exception: protecting the lives of ISAF or Afghan forces.

Petraeus's directive called to mind the observation by F. Scott Fitzgerald: "The test of a first-rate intelligence is the ability to hold two opposed ideas in the mind at the same time, and still retain the ability to function." The directive required commanders to do everything humanly possible both to protect Afghan civilians, which typically meant not firing, while also protecting those in uniform, which often meant firing full bore.

To help alleviate that tension, Petraeus stated unequivocally in the new Tactical Directive that he wanted ISAF troops to partner with Afghan forces on "every operation." "Partnering is how we operate," the directive states. "Some civilian casualties result from a misunderstanding or ignorance of local customs and behaviors. No individuals are more attuned to the Afghan culture than our Afghan partners."

The key difference between the old and new directives, in Petraeus's mind, was the provision that prohibited subordinate commanders from issuing more restrictive conditions, such as limiting the use of attack helicopters and close air support. "It was the *application* of the last Tactical Directive that created some of the mythology that we had restricted the dropping of bombs," Petraeus said. As a matter of fact, Petraeus had no qualms about dropping bombs—albeit when and where appropriate. The number of bombs dropped in Iraq under Petraeus's command increased dramatically during the surge in 2007, just as the tempo of Special Operations raids there had—and that tempo was increasing on his watch in Afghanistan as well. The *Counterinsurgency Field Manual* he produced in 2006 at Fort Leavenworth, between tours in Iraq, "doesn't say that the best weapons don't shoot," he said. "It says *sometimes* the best weapons don't shoot. Sometimes the best weapons do shoot." Still, the new Tactical Directive was quite clear: "*Every Afghan civilian death diminishes our cause. If we use excessive force or* operate contrary to our counterinsurgency principles, tactical victories may prove to be strategic setbacks."

In any event, the bitter complaining by troops who felt their hands had been tied ceased after Petraeus issued his update.

AT ISAF HEADQUARTERS on the morning of August 15, Petraeus and his staff geared up to begin doing press engagements again, after Petraeus, following the precedent he'd set in Iraq, had eschewed such activities in his first month in Afghanistan. NBC's David Gregory, the first to arrive, called him "easily America's most famous warrior" at the start of the broadcast and asked him during a lengthy interview whether he would ever run for president. "I am not a politician and I will never be, and I say that with absolute conviction," Petraeus said, paraphrasing Sherman's famous response to a similar question.

"No way, nohow?" Gregory asked.

"No way, nohow," said Petraeus.

Since arriving in Afghanistan, he had spoken again and again during his stand-ups about the need for skillful media interplay, mindful of what one of his heroes, T. E. Lawrence, said in 1920: "The printing press is the greatest weapon in the armory of the modern commander."

As he sat down with Gregory, Petraeus repeated a point he had made during a stand-up back in early July: "We're making progress, and progress is winning." His performance was measured. "I think it's incumbent upon us to show greater progress . . . really just began this spring."

Petraeus said that he and General McChrystal had spent the past year and a half getting "the inputs" right. By the end of the month, when the final brigade from the 101st Airborne had arrived, the number of U.S. forces in Afghanistan would be three times what it had been at the beginning of 2009. Now the real fight could begin.

CHAPTER 3

TRUE BELIEVERS

America's involvement in Afghanistan since the fall of 2001 had been a colossal missed opportunity. The brilliant combination of U.S. Special Operations Forces, the Central Intelligence Agency, Afghan Northern Alliance fighters, and American airpower that toppled the Taliban in three months was squandered when the United States marched headlong into Iraq in early 2003. The war there diverted troops, airpower, technology, and focus from Afghanistan, where U.S. and NATO forces were far too few in number to stop an insurgency that had returned with a vengeance by 2006. The reemergence of al-Qaeda, the Taliban and other insurgent fighters was by no means inevitable, if America and its NATO allies had capitalized on the Taliban's swift demise and brought enough soldiers to Afghanistan to protect the people and rebuild the nation, beginning at the village and provincial level. But that was never to be. By the time McChrystal's predecessor, General David McKiernan, took command of the war in Afghanistan in the spring of 2008, the United States had only 33,000 military personnel in the country—and only about a third of them were fulfilling combat missions. Despite the success of counterinsurgency tactics in Iraq, where U.S. forces moved off large bases to live with the people, in Afghanistan most U.S. forces remained on heavily fortified bases and a limited number of outposts. Protecting the Afghan people, rooting out corruption and fostering competent government were not priorities they could execute.

The "light footprint" mandated by then–Defense secretary Donald Rumsfeld for the first five years of the war reflected Rumsfeld's preference—critics would call it a prejudice—for speed, agility and precision instead of a heavy, massed force. The Powell Doctrine of overwhelming force was an outdated Cold War imperative that, in Rumsfeld's mind, was no longer necessary in an age of proxy forces, smart bombs and armed drones that could find and kill the enemy without any troops at all. The stunning speed with which small numbers of Special Forces and CIA operatives, working in tandem with Afghan warlords, had dispatched the Taliban the first time around only served to confirm and validate Rumsfeld's notions. Indeed, Rumsfeld imposed a "force cap" in Afghanistan in 2001 and 2002.

His preference for a lighter force also contributed to the downward spiral in Iraq, where U.S. forces invaded with fewer troops than most generals, including Petraeus, thought advisable. While the invasion force easily toppled Saddam Hussein's regime, the Bush administration did not have enough personnel to either secure the nation or contain the sectarian violence that brought the country to the brink of civil war in late 2006. In both wars, Petraeus was called on to command "surges" that finally addressed troop shortfalls and made progress possible.

With Iraq on the brink of civil war in 2006, Afghanistan also increasingly faced a "perfect storm of political upheaval." Effective and honest government was largely absent; Pakistan had emerged as a sanctuary for the Taliban, al-Qaeda and other insurgent groups, and Islamist fervor had enabled the Taliban to recruit villagers alienated by the corrupt central government in Kabul. By the time McChrystal took command of the war in the summer of 2009 and began implementing the tactics spelled out in Petraeus's *Counterinsurgency Field Manual*, it was almost too late. The insurgency had spread to virtually every province in Afghanistan, with civilian fatalities, suicide bombings, attacks and assassinations all surging. McChrystal recognized that he lacked sufficient forces to root out the Taliban, secure the border with Pakistan and hold the villages that had been cleared.

Though he also would not have all the forces he'd have liked, Petraeus wouldn't have that problem to the same extent. When he replaced McChrystal in July, nearly all of the new surge forces were in country. They would work closely with Afghans at the district level and even the village level in the key districts identified in Rodriguez's campaign plan.

Petraeus issued counterinsurgency guidance to all the forces in Afghanistan in early August—the twenty-four commandments to accompany "King David's Bible," the *Counterinsurgency Field Manual*. The four-page document was not your run-of-the-mill memo from the commander. One had to wonder what Afghanistan might have looked like, eight years after September 11, 2001, had these tactics been carried out from the beginning.

SECURE AND SERVE THE POPULATION. The decisive terrain is the human terrain. The people are the center of gravity. Only by providing them security and earning their trust and confidence can the Afghan government and ISAF prevail.

LIVE WITH THE PEOPLE. We can't commute to the fight. Position joint bases and combat outposts as close to those we're seeking to secure as feasible. Decide on locations with input from our partners and after consultation with local citizens and informed by intelligence and security assessments.

PURSUE THE ENEMY RELENTLESSLY. Together with our Afghan partners, get your teeth into the insurgents and don't let go. When the extremists fight, make them pay. Seek out and eliminate those who threaten the population. Don't let them intimidate the innocent. Target the whole network, not just individuals.

WALK. Stop by, don't drive by. Patrol on foot whenever possible and engage the population. Take off your sunglasses. Situational awareness can only be gained by interacting face-to-face, not separated by ballistic glass or Oakleys.

BE FIRST WITH THE TRUTH. Beat the insurgents and malign actors to the headlines. Preempt rumors. Get accurate information to the chain of command, to Afghan leaders, to the people, and to the press as soon as possible. Integrity is critical to this fight. Avoid spinning, and don't try to "dress up" an ugly situation. Acknowledge setbacks and failures, including civilian casualties, and then state how we'll respond and what we've learned.

LIVE OUR VALUES. Stay true to the values we hold dear. This is what distinguishes us from our enemies. We are engaged in a tough endeavor. It is often brutal, physically demanding, and frustrating. All of us experience moments of anger, but we must not give in to dark impulses or tolerate unacceptable actions by others.

These imperatives and others were neatly distilled in the *Counterinsurgency Field Manual* of 2006, the first revision of Army counterinsurgency doctrine since Field Circular 100-20, a slim low-intensity-conflict manual from 1986 that had survived the systematic purge of everything the Army had learned about counterinsurgency warfare after Vietnam. The new manual Petraeus produced as commander of the Combined Arms Center at Fort Leavenworth was downloaded 1.5 million times in the first month following its release via the Web by the Army in December 2006. The University of Chicago Press then released it in book form, which was favorably reviewed on the cover of the *New York Times Book Review*. Former lieutenant colonel John A. Nagl, a Petraeus acolyte, wrote in a foreword to the book version that at the start of the Iraq War in 2003, most conventional Army officers knew more about the Civil War than they did about counterinsurgency. But by the time Petraeus assumed command in Afghanistan seven years later, this was no longer true, thanks to many hard-learned lessons in Iraq, Petraeus's work at Leavenworth in 2006, and success with the counterinsurgency doctrine during the surge in Iraq in 2007 and 2008.

While it was certainly true that U.S. forces hadn't fought a successful counterinsurgency during the first seven or eight years of the war in Afghanistan, due to the focus of troops and resources being in Iraq, McChrystal had been working to implement a counterinsurgency campaign for a year prior to Petraeus's arrival. And many of the U.S. forces serving in Afghanistan— especially the officers commanding units—had prior counterinsurgency experience in Afghanistan or Iraq. Petraeus's counterinsurgency guidance bore some parallels to the guidance he'd issued in Iraq in 2007, but it had also been modified to reflect the challenges in Afghanistan.

Petraeus first issued the points on July 27, only to uncharacteristically pull the document back almost immediately. When he reissued it five days later, he explained that it was his first update, slightly revised based on feedback he had received from "Afghan partners," "elders" and Special Forces teams in Herat Province's Zerkoh Valley. "I welcome further feedback," Petraeus wrote. Most of the changes softened the document's tough stand on corruption by stressing the need to cooperate with NATO's Afghan partners.

HELP CONFRONT THE CULTURE OF IMPUNITY. The Taliban are not the only enemy of the people. The people are also threatened by inadequate governance, corruption, and abuse of power—recruiters for the Taliban. President Karzai has forthrightly committed to combat these threats. Work with our Afghan partners to help turn his words into reality and to help our partners protect the people from malign actors as well as from terrorists.

Only two words were added to the earlier release: "Help" in front of "confront the culture of impunity"—meaning that this was something U.S. forces could do only in partnership with the Afghans—and "forthrightly," to highlight Karzai's commitment to combating corruption. Petraeus hoped to see Karzai assume a leadership role in that important effort.

BE A GOOD GUEST. Treat the Afghan people and their property with respect. Think about how we drive, how we patrol, how we relate to

people, and how we help the community. View our actions through
the eyes of the Afghans and, together with our partners, consult with
elders before pursuing new initiatives and operations.

This final sentence was refined from the earlier version, which had included two sentences that read: "View your actions through the eyes of the
Afghans. Alienating Afghan civilians sows the seeds of our defeat."

PETRAEUS WASTED LITTLE TIME implementing the Afghan Local Police
program he'd won approval for shortly after his arrival in July. His enthusiasm was based in part on a paper written by Special Forces major Jim Gant,
entitled *One Tribe at a Time: A Strategy for Success in Afghanistan*. Petraeus
made it required reading for leaders in Afghanistan. If you believed what
Gant was saying, as Petraeus did, you could believe that success in Afghanistan was possible, that Afghan hearts and minds could, indeed, be won.

The son of a middle school principal in Las Cruces, New Mexico, Gant
sported tattoos of Achilles and Chinese characters that say FEAR NO MAN on
his right arm. He carried three times as much ammunition as he needed for
a mission and had been called "Lawrence of Afghanistan." Not all of his peers
and superiors thought so highly of him, but "Lawrence of Iraq" (a title Petraeus had earned for his four years there) embraced Gant's ideas.

Gant's story in Afghanistan began with a six-man Special Forces team,
Operational Detachment Alpha 316, part of the Army's 3rd Special Forces
Group, in Kunar and Helmand provinces in 2003 and 2004. Gant and his
cohort dropped out of a helicopter in Kunar, in northeast Afghanistan on
the Pakistan border, in the middle of the night with a mission to kill the Taliban and other "anti-coalition" fighters. After fighting their way out of an
ambush by hostile forces armed with rocket-propelled grenades (RPGs),
they ended up in a village called Mangwal, whose tribe was led by a malik
(chief) named Noorafzhal. Gant spent hours with him, explaining what this
small band of Americans was doing there to fight the Taliban and al-Qaeda.
When Noorafzhal explained to the American that he was involved in a dis-

pute with a subtribe that had taken land that did not belong to them, Gant said his team, which had grown to eight, would fight with the malik's eight village warriors if necessary. "With that, a relationship was born," Gant writes. "We talked for hours, discussing what next steps to take. Then, out of the blue, the malik leaned over and told my interpreter to tell me that he had not been completely honest, that he had not eight, but 80 warriors." Later, after more talk and more tea, the malik looked Gant in the eye and said, "'Commander Jim, I have 800 warriors and they are at your disposal. You only need to ask and they will be yours.'"

Afghan villagers in some areas would resist any form of outside interference, Gant realized, be it from a foreign power or the central government in Kabul. The only form of governance that mattered was tribal. "We saw firsthand the depth and power of the existing (though initially invisible to us) tribal defense system," Gant wrote, referring to the tribal army he found at his disposal. "And we grasped the absolute necessity of working with and bonding with the tribal leader—man-to-man, warrior-to-warrior."

Gant's conclusion: "The enemy thinks he can wait us out. However, we can turn time into an ally if we engage and partner with the tribes and, most importantly, demonstrate our commitment to them. Once they believe that we share the same objectives and are not leaving, they will support us and fight alongside us." It was a common theme in counterinsurgency theory, and for Petraeus, who also believed that all counterinsurgency operations were local, understanding politics at the tribal level was key for a successful transition.

AFTER WEST POINT, Petraeus's interest in counterinsurgency only deepened when, as a newlywed and newly minted 2nd lieutenant, he headed to Vicenza, Italy. He was assigned to the 1st Battalion, 509th Airborne Battalion Combat Team. In those days of the "hollow Army," still recovering from Vietnam, the 509th was an elite unit, the first choice of the top-ranking graduates from West Point. It fell under the headquarters at the Southern European Task Force, whose primary mission was to oversee the security and transfer in wartime of tactical nuclear weapons based in Italy, Greece and Turkey, and that focus meant that the higher headquarters generally left the 509th to its own devices. Many of the unit's captains and above had Vietnam combat experience. One of them was a "Plankholder cadre" member of the 1/75th Rangers, a major named Keith Nightingale. Petraeus admired his irreverent, cocky spirit. Nightingale would become a mentor for life.

"The first time I met him, I knew he was different and unique," said Nightingale, who later would help develop what evolved into the Joint Special Operations Command. He would also play a key role in planning the ill-fated Iran Hostage Rescue Mission that ended when aircraft failed in the desert en route to Tehran in April 1980. "I said in an evaluation report that this man has the potential to be the chief of staff of the Army. The colonel running our higher headquarters said, 'You can't say this.' But I said, 'It's true,'" Nightingale recalled. "He already was a cut above everybody else." His skills were such that, even as a young lieutenant, he ran certain aspects of the unit during the tenure of a very hands-off battalion commander. Nightingale liked to think that he taught Petraeus to never take no for an answer— and to understand that there's an exception to every rule.

The 509th presented Petraeus with ample opportunity to train with NATO forces, and he did so in Belgium, Italy, the United Kingdom, Germany, France and Turkey. On a training mission in France to compete for French Jump Wings, he learned about Marcel Bigeard, a legendary French general and paratrooper who had been captured during the siege of Dien Bien Phu, in Vietnam. Upon Bigeard's release, he went back to France, regrouped with his men and, employing the lessons they had learned fighting the Viet Minh, attempted to pacify the Casbah in Algeria. Bigeard was the inspiration for Lieutenant Colonel Pierre Raspeguy in Jean Larteguy's 1963 novel *The Centurions*. Petraeus read the book as a captain and admired what it had to say about leadership and the cohesion of successful fighting units. Petraeus later wrote to Bigeard, beginning a correspondence that would continue intermittently until Bigeard's death in the summer of 2010, three weeks after Petraeus took command in Afghanistan. By then Bigeard had acknowledged Petraeus's accomplishment in Iraq and addressed him as a peer.

After his tour in Italy, Petraeus attended the Armor Officer Advanced Course, following which he was assigned to the 24th Infantry Division (Mechanized) at Fort Stewart, Georgia. He and McChrystal served briefly together there as captains. Both had their eye on assignments with the elite 1st Ranger Battalion, a unit formed in the mid-1970s as part of a chief of staff of the Army initiative implemented by Nightingale and others to build a unit of exceptionally high standards and training readiness. Petraeus so distinguished himself in the 24th as a company commander that he was selected to serve as the aide-de-camp to the incoming division commander, then–Major General Jack Galvin, who would become his most important mentor.

Galvin was an intellectual force in the American military who, like Knowlton, came from Massachusetts and was an archetypal soldier-scholar. Commissioned in the infantry from West Point in 1954, Galvin came of age in Vietnam and was among a key group of officers who helped rebuild the Army in the 1980s. When Galvin arrived at Fort Stewart and assumed command of the 24th Infantry Division, he found that Petraeus had managed to anticipate all of the first tasks Galvin would need done—and accomplished them in advance. Petraeus's chagrin over giving up a battalion operations job in the division, however, was not completely muted.

Sensing this, Galvin assured Petraeus that the insights he would gain would contribute to his personal development like no other assignment. Galvin took Petraeus on trips throughout the United States as he oversaw division training—to include maneuver exercises at Eglin Air Force Base, in Florida and Fort Bliss, Texas, as well as a major international exercise called "Bright Star" in Egypt, which was designed as preparation for a potential ground war should the Soviets invade Iran. In all, Galvin and Petraeus had thirty-five trips together in twelve months. "Help me expand my impact," Galvin instructed Petraeus, expecting the young officer to be not just his eyes and ears but a surrogate voice as well. In turn, Petraeus inspired

Galvin, according to Galvin's unpublished memoirs and their exchange of letters. Galvin considered him an intellectual "sounding board" with "sharp and often original perspectives." Galvin's associates thought Petraeus was a "bit of a tonic" and source of energy for the senior officer. Petraeus took notes as Galvin schooled the division's senior officers in the importance of military history, the concept of "chain training," the conduct of heavy/light force operations and soldier-scholar skills. They even discussed the history of aides-de-camp, which Galvin, slightly tongue in cheek, said he thought was "glorious."

Galvin also schooled Petraeus on a concept he called "the big M," which stood for individual mystique or mythology. "'When the going gets hard, we need a leader to pull us together,'" he remembered telling Petraeus. "'Through your mythology, people create you. Set the example. It doesn't have to be flamboyant, like Patton and his pistols always seen driving to the front. Ridgway and his grenades. Grant with his cigar. They want you to be bigger than you are, so they magnify you. They laud you to everyone. Live up to it all with the highest standards of integrity. You become part of a legend.'"

Galvin gave Petraeus a signed print of Remington's *Stampede* as a farewell gift to symbolize the chaos surrounding the transformation of the under-strength 24th Infantry Division into a trained and ready mechanized infantry unit that became part of the nation's new Rapid Deployment Force. The print—and its symbolism—would accompany Petraeus throughout his career.

Galvin was also instrumental in convincing Petraeus to go to graduate school, which took Petraeus, his wife and their first baby, Anne, to Princeton in the fall of 1984, where he began work on a master's degree—and ultimately a Ph.D.—at the Woodrow Wilson School of Public and International Affairs. There, Petraeus sought out the tutelage and mentorship of Professor Richard Ullman, known for his common sense and realistic liberalism in foreign policy. He would push Petraeus intellectually. During work on his doctoral dissertation, which he completed in 1987, Petraeus taught at West Point's Social Sciences department. His son, Stephen, was born during this academic hiatus, just miles from his father's birthplace, and four years after the birth of the Petraeuses' daughter, Anne, who was born during the general's year at the Command and General Staff College at Fort Leavenworth.

Petraeus's growing interest in Vietnam—the subject of his doctoral research—and counterinsurgency were evident in a letter he wrote to Galvin in August 1985 from West Point. "I think the next big debate will be about counterinsurgency operations—whether the U.S. should get involved in them, and if so, how," he wrote. "One of the sub-debates will undoubtedly be over whether the Army is capable of developing forces suited for counterinsurgency operations."

The following summer, Galvin invited him to spend time with him at the Southern Command headquarters, in Panama, which Galvin led as a newly promoted four-star general. Petraeus was thrilled and offered some research prospects—to compare and contrast the differences between the intervention in Vietnam and the U.S. military's activities in Central America, or perhaps a look at the efforts of military and civilian officials to coordinate their activities. "These efforts," Petraeus observed, "seem a good example of political-military integration, something that, as you know, many in the military would rather avoid, preferring instead to worry only about 'purely military matters' and wanting to be left alone in pursuing them. Those instincts are, of course, contrary to what must be done in fighting low intensity conflict. Civil-military integration efforts also seem to be an example of success in spite of the system, rather than because of it."

The theater for which Galvin's Southern Command was responsible encompassed Central and South America, and it was defined by multiple Communist insurgencies, which Petraeus found fascinating. He traveled with Galvin throughout Panama and to Honduras and El Salvador, where U.S. trainers were helping the Salvadoran army defeat Communist guerrillas. Although brief, the time was formative for Petraeus, who had known only garrison and field training to that point. "This has been a tremendous experience," Petraeus wrote to a colleague from Princeton in July 1986. "When I showed up at the house [of the Mil Group Commander in El Salvador]—his wife greeted me, ushered me to the guest wing . . . and handed me a loaded

MP-5 submachine gun to keep me company.... I [later] asked a Salvadoran soldier if he'd seen much combat. 'Not much,' he said, matter-of-factly; 'I've only been in about 85 firefights.'"

At the end of the summer, Galvin sent a note to the head of the Social Sciences department, thanking him for releasing his favorite protégé: "Dave did not try to wear my stars while here, but rather helped me to wear them more effectively. I told him to help and expand my impact and he did that—without ruffling feathers. In fact, his enthusiasm, dedication, and pleasant personality proved infectious to others in the command group."

Petraeus sent a note to Galvin from West Point upon his return in July 1986. "To really make an impact on Army thinking about small wars," Petraeus reflected, "you need to institutionalize your ideas. That requires, of course, that you get your ideas/concepts into doctrinal manuals." Petraeus proposed that Galvin encourage his staff to produce a new version of a field circular on low-intensity conflict. He thought it could evolve into a replacement for a "rather poor" field manual on the subject drafted in the early eighties. A quality field manual on this type of warfare, he said, presciently, "could be very valuable in coming years."

Petraeus continued to immerse himself in the study of Vietnam and low-intensity conflict, reflecting in the same letter to Galvin on a particular book that had captured his interests, Andrew Krepinevich's *The Army and Vietnam*. In it, Krepinevich argued that the Army had not gotten its campaign strategy right, that it had focused too much on the "big war"—large units conducting search-and-destroy operations—when it should have put more emphasis on the "smaller war": small elements living with and securing the people and helping develop host-nation capacity to secure and govern themselves. Petraeus thought Krepinevich's book was "the best there is" and later used it to inform the *Counterinsurgency Field Manual*. "Maybe we should marry Andy's book and Harry Summers' *On Strategy* (which, as you know, criticizes our preoccupation with the insurgency)," he wrote to Galvin. "The two together might have provided a solution—though I occasionally wonder if there was anything we could have done to 'win' in Vietnam given the obvious domestic unwillingness to stay for the long haul and given the absence of a 'Vietnamese Duarte,'" Petraeus concluded, referring to José Napoleón Duarte, the Salvadoran leader with whom the American military successfully worked to demobilize and reintegrate the guerrillas there.

Petraeus completed his Princeton Ph.D. thesis, *The American Military and the Lessons of Vietnam: A Study of American Influence and the Use of Force in the Post-Vietnam Era,* in 1987. He concluded that, contrary to stereotypes, military officials in the wake of Vietnam had not been as hawkish as their civilian counterparts. He based this on an examination of historical case studies between Korea and Vietnam, a discussion of the Vietnam legacy and finally a review of the post-Vietnam military interventions—eleven in all—through the mid-eighties.

He found that from 1973 to 1986, military decision makers tended toward a more cautious approach than the president's most hawkish principal civilian advisers in their advice on whether to commit troops. In his research, he highlighted the conclusions of Samuel Huntington, who, in *The Soldier and the State,* his seminal work on the history of the military profession and civil-military relations up to World War II and then from 1940 through the mid-1950s, found that military officials had been cautious professionals. As for the future, he offered three conclusions. First, small wars were more likely on the threat horizon than nuclear or other large-scale ground wars. Second, the military needed to be prepared, even if it was unlikely that decision makers would advise intervention. And third, that it was wiser, when possible, to use small teams of advisers than massive troop deployments to assist countries engaged in a counterinsurgency campaign, a conclusion he drew from his experience in Latin America.

But in assessing the failure in Vietnam, rather than pinning the blame on civilian leaders or reporters (as was in vogue among those in uniform at the time), he concluded, like Krepinevich, that the Army had fought the war in the wrong way. Instead of strategies like search-and-destroy, Army commanders would have been much better off with tactics that fell under the heading of counterinsurgency.

When his studies at Princeton and his teaching at West Point came to an end, Major Petraeus again joined his mentor General Galvin, who was to become the Supreme Allied Commander for Europe, at the Supreme Head-quarters Allied Powers Europe (SHAPE), in Belgium. There were nearly 250,000 U.S. forces in Europe at that time, the vast majority of them stationed in West Germany. It was key terrain for, and the focus of, the U.S. military. Petraeus agreed to serve as Galvin's military assistant under two conditions: first, that he could travel with Galvin and hear his boss deliver the speeches that Petraeus had drafted, and second, that he could be assigned to a tactical unit in Europe after a year as a speechwriter. He'd been away from troopers for five years and was anxious to return to the field.

In the meantime, he took lessons in NATO leadership. "The boss continues to amaze me even now," Petraeus wrote to his mentor from the 509th, Nightingale, in January 1988. "As long as I've known him, [Galvin] has always, within a few months of taking command, initiated some project that proved to be truly visionary in terms of how important it later became. Here . . . it's the NATO posture related to the intermediate nuclear forces agreement."

The most important lesson Petraeus took, however, was one on civil-military relations and the responsibility of senior leaders in the wake of a policy decision. In a speech by Galvin one year after assuming command, he noted that inheriting the decision to accept the Nuclear Force Agreement constituted a "marching order" and meant that "it was then time for the military to move on, unless we felt we could not carry out the mission under the new arrangements"—meaning after the elimination of the intermediate-range missiles that were the first line of nuclear deterrence in Europe at the time.

PETRAEUS REJOINED the infantry as a battalion operations officer in the 1st Brigade of the 3rd Infantry Division (Mechanized), based in Schweinfurt, Germany. After a year there, which included the largest force-on-force exercise in NATO history, he was selected to become the brigade's operations officer. He loved everything about large-scale maneuver warfare exercises and mechanized force training, Petraeus wrote in a letter to Keith Nightingale in the winter of 1988, with the exception of the relatively scripted conduct of live-fire training exercises. While he sought to increase the realism through variety in the scenarios, the predictability in such exercises would bother him for years.

But overall, Petraeus enjoyed his new post enormously. He and Holly liked living in a small German village with their two young children, and Petraeus relished his position as brigade operations officer. Then the phone rang. General Carl Vuono, the Army chief of staff, wanted him to fly to Washington immediately to interview for a job as his aide-de-camp. The Army chief of staff had heard about Petraeus from his current aide and had vetted Petraeus through Knowlton and Galvin. He was impressed with what he heard: conscientious, outgoing, smart, full of fresh ideas, positive. Vuono could deal with the rumors about the young officer's ambitiousness if Petraeus would perform. "If the definition of a ticket puncher is a guy who seeks the hard job," Vuono said, "well, then I want an Army of ticket punchers!" These would be Vuono's last two years on active duty, and he wanted a top aide. "I needed the best," Vuono said.

Petraeus was intrigued by the prospect but torn about leaving troops, until Galvin called him to counsel him on the opportunity. Petraeus responded in a letter: "As I mentioned, I'm torn over the prospect of leaving troops so soon, moving again, . . . etc. I had been concerned about your reaction to whichever decision I made on the aide job: if I fought the job, I was concerned you'd think I was putting career or family concerns ahead of the Army." Back in Washington, Petraeus met the gruff Vuono for the first time. Vuono wanted to know how he felt about the job. Petraeus said he was in a "win-win" situation. "If I become your aide, I'll learn a lot," he said. "If you don't hire me, I'll still be the brigade S3, which I'd prefer!"

"I wouldn't want you if you really wanted the job," Vuono replied. "Report in three weeks."

By August 1989, Petraeus had moved his family to Washington for his new vantage point at the highest level of the Army. Petraeus traveled the world with Vuono. A few months into the job, the first Bush administration launched Operation Just Cause in Panama to apprehend the nation's outlaw strongman, Manuel Noriega. The mission was to protect citizens in Panama, ensure safe operation of the Panama Canal and support democratic institutions there. It was the most complex "contingency deployment" since Vietnam. "Commanders responsible had the opportunity to plan the fight and then fight the plan," Vuono said in a January 1990 speech that Petraeus helped refine.

In between the Panama invasion and the deployment that began after the Iraqi invasion of Kuwait, in August 1990, Vuono focused on preparing the Army for a full spectrum of future threats on the battlefield. The night before he was due to deliver an important "white paper" to a Defense Writers Group breakfast and subsequently across the entire Army, Vuono handed Petraeus the latest draft, noting that it still needed work. Petraeus pulled an all-nighter with Vuono's speechwriters to refine the document, which laid out Vuono's six imperatives for a "trained and ready" Army. Efforts like this endeared Petraeus to his superiors. He was able to provide strategic and operational recommendations, understand the thinking of his superiors and help them convey their ideas more persuasively.

Petraeus watched Vuono manage a highly complex plan to support the deployment of forces for what ultimately became the 1991 Gulf War. Vuono took him on three trips to the Gulf during that period and brought him to meetings with General Norman Schwarzkopf and the team at Central Command headquarters in Riyadh, which oversaw Operations Desert Shield and then Desert Storm. Petraeus desperately wanted to deploy to the Gulf and tried to get Vuono to release him. But the last thing Vuono was willing to do with the nation at war was give up his right hand.

After the war, Petraeus wrote a memo for Vuono outlining what he thought were shortcomings in the Army's basic mechanized infantry battalion, including insufficient dismounted infantry training, headquarters companies that were too large and anti-tank companies that sucked up too many resources for what they provided. Vuono had Petraeus write a memo for him to sign and ordered the Army staff to conduct a review.

Vuono also came to value his young aide as a motivator. Petraeus once lectured him at the end of a long and exhausting day that he simply had to be at his best during a speaking engagement that night in Louisville. "'Chief, I know you're tired; we're all tired,'" Vuono remembers Petraeus telling him. "'I know you gave six speeches already today and flew across the country. But that group tonight—they don't know you gave six speeches. They don't know where you've been today. They just know you're the chief of staff of the Army. This is the one and only time that they will ever hear a CSA.'" Vuono got it. "I said, 'All right, let's go,'" he recalled. "I gave a helluva speech!"

As Petraeus began to mentally prepare himself for a return to the infantry, he watched as Vuono focused on building a "trained and ready" Army. Vuono believed in developing key themes and ideas and, through relentless communication, he drilled them into every engagement. Petraeus's concept of four tasks of strategic leadership—get the big ideas right, communicate them effectively, aggressively oversee their uniform implementation, and create a feedback loop to measure progress and refine the big ideas—evolved directly from Vuono.

To improve training for low-intensity conflict, Vuono directed a colonel named Jack Keane, a barrel-chested Irishman and paratrooper from New York City with a master's degree in philosophy, to develop a new training center for light infantry that had been established at Fort Chaffee, Louisiana, the Joint Readiness Training Center. Keane, who had served as a platoon leader in Vietnam, found himself among a small group of Army leaders who had concluded by the late 1980s that the future of warfare, with the Cold War coming to a close, would most likely involve low-intensity conflict—peacekeeping and counterinsurgency operations. Keane would retire as the four-star Army vice chief of staff and go on, in retirement, to play a key role in advocating for the surge in Iraq.

Petraeus first met Keane on one of Vuono's trips to the new training center at Fort Polk. Keane quickly realized he could gain valuable insights on Vuono's thinking from his young aide. "He was respectful to people more senior than him, but not intimidated and not arrogant," Keane said of Petraeus. "We immediately had a visceral connection," Keane said. Petraeus's time in Central America with Galvin had cemented his belief that small wars were the threat of the future. The new training center Keane had established for Vuono would be the proving ground for important new light infantry tactics in an Army that for decades had focused on armor and mechanized infantry for its conventional warfare readiness. Keane would soon become a key Petraeus mentor as well.

As Vuono's tenure as chief came to a close in July 1991, Petraeus eagerly awaited release of a new list of lieutenant colonels selected for battalion command. He had his eye on a unit in the 101st Airborne Division. It had just returned from Iraq, where its soldiers had helped cut off a Republican Guard unit's retreat into Kuwait.

DURING PETRAEUS'S PRESS engagements in Afghanistan in mid-August 2010, reporters pressed him on his feelings about the drawdown scheduled for the following July. During his *Meet the Press* interview, Petraeus noted that the extent of the drawdown would be based on conditions on the ground and not be any kind of precipitous pullout. When Petraeus was asked whether he could foresee telling the president next July that conditions did not allow for a drawdown, he responded that it was not inconceivable, noting that the plan, however, was clear and that the intent certainly was to execute it.

Defense secretary Robert Gates took a somewhat different line the following day in Washington, saying in an interview that there was no question in anyone's mind that at least a modest drawdown would begin in July 2011. Representative Jane Harman, the California Democrat, and Michael O'Hanlon, a moderate Democrat and defense analyst at the Brookings Institution, took Gates's argument one step further, calling for Obama to explicitly state how many troops could come out in July 2011. This would assuage fears that the war was unending while demonstrating that the drawdown would not be precipitous. Reducing troop strength from 100,000 to 80,000 by the end of 2011 struck them as reasonable. But Petraeus, from his command of the surge in Iraq, knew that counterinsurgency operations required boots on the ground, and lots of them and that making commitments to draw down a specific number 18 months hence was unwise. No one was better at holding and solidifying gains at the district and village level than American soldiers, and he was reluctant to make promises or predictions so far in advance about the number of Americans that might be sent home.

Part of the sensitivity stemmed from Obama's televised address to the nation on August 31, in which he announced the end of combat operations in Iraq after seven and a half years. Petraeus and his aides were listening for a strong statement of resolve from the president on Afghanistan. They got the resolve they were hoping for—*and* an unambiguous commitment to draw down forces the following July. "Now, as we approach our tenth year of combat in Afghanistan, there are those who are understandably asking tough questions about our mission there," the president said from the Oval Office.

But we must never lose sight of what's at stake. As we speak, al-Qaeda continues to plot against us, and its leadership remains anchored in the border region of Afghanistan and Pakistan. We will disrupt, dismantle and defeat al-Qaeda, while preventing Afghanistan from again serving as a base for terrorists. And because of our drawdown in Iraq, we are now able to apply the resources necessary to go on offense. In fact, over the last nineteen months, nearly a dozen al-Qaeda leaders— and hundreds of al-Qaeda's extremist allies—have been killed or captured around the world.

Within Afghanistan, I have ordered the deployment of additional troops who—under the command of General David Petraeus—are fighting to break the Taliban's momentum. As with the surge in Iraq, these forces will be in place for a limited time to provide space for the Afghans to build their capacity and secure their own future. But, as was the case in Iraq, we cannot do for Afghans what they must ultimately do for themselves. That's why we are training Afghan Security Forces and supporting a political resolution to Afghanistan's problems. . . . The pace of our troop reductions will be determined by conditions on the ground, and our support for Afghanistan will endure. But make no mistake: This transition will begin—because openended war serves neither our interests nor the Afghan people's.

The Afghans would also ultimately be responsible for another force fueling the Taliban's resurgence: the corruption in Hamid Karzai's government. On the eve of Obama's speech, the story broke that Karzai had fired one of the most senior prosecutors in Afghanistan, Fazel Ahmed Faqiryar, for refusing to back away from corruption investigations involving senior members of Karzai's government. Faqiryar's staff had been probing seventeen of Karzai's cabinet members, five provincial governors and three ambassadors. Compounding the problem was the inconvenient coincidence that one of those officials under investigation, Mohammed Zia Salehi, chief of administration for Afghanistan's National Security Council, had reportedly been on the CIA's payroll for years.

Karzai's government was considered one of the world's most corrupt, and Karzai's seeming inability to address that challenge was fueling deep concern inside the Obama administration about the worthiness of its Afghan partner. In early August, Karzai ordered an investigation of two units the United States had established to stop Afghan officials from smuggling millions out of the country and building mansions in the United Arab Emirates. Karzai ordered the probes following the arrest of Salehi, one of his senior aides, for allegedly soliciting bribes to help block a corruption investigation of a financial firm. Salehi called Karzai from jail and was freed. Shortly after Petraeus's arrival in early July, a nonprofit group called Integrity Watch Afghanistan reported survey results showing that corruption had doubled since 2006, presumably in direct proportion to the amount of money flowing into the country, with an estimated $1 billion in bribes paid in 2009 alone. The survey was based on interviews with 6,500 Afghans. One in seven said they had experienced bribery in their daily lives, and one in four families reported that they had been forced to pay bribes to receive government services.

Petraeus adopted a long-term approach to the urgent concern of corruption, viewing it as a cultural issue that it would take a generation or more to overcome. Other U.S. leaders were not so patient. Just a year earlier, Ambassador Eikenberry had warned President Obama against sending more troops because of corruption. But Petraeus thought improvement was possible, and he knew just the officer to lead the effort. On the day in late June that Obama asked him to take command in Afghanistan, Petraeus had already decided to take Brigadier General H.R. McMaster with him.

A rugby player with a Ph.D. in history from the University of North Carolina at Chapel Hill, McMaster was a charismatic, freethinking officer who had demonstrated the potential of classical counterinsurgency doctrine in Tal Afar, in northern Iraq in 2005, long before COIN became the Army's dominant approach during the surge in 2007. McMaster instinctively preached respect for the Iraqi people and dispersed his troops in small outposts throughout the city. McMaster was the kind of officer who would embrace one particular Petraeus mantra, the final imperative in the recently issued counterinsurgency guidance:

EXERCISE INITIATIVE. In the absence of guidance or orders, figure out what the orders should have been and execute them aggressively.

McMaster would lead what would become the Combined Joint Inter-Agency Task Force–Shafafiyat. *Shafafiyat* means "transparency" in Pashto and Dari. In keeping with the desire to be respectful and not publicly confront the Afghan government and the penchant of some to steal large quantities of American aid, McMaster would, by design, do most of his work behind closed doors.

His first task was the drafting of his counterinsurgency contracting guidance, which Petraeus refined and issued on September 8. This was their attempt to bring discipline and principle to the awarding of contracts. The clearly stated one-sentence imperatives were reminiscent of the counterinsurgency guidance Petraeus had issued earlier:

Hire Afghans first, buy Afghan products, and build Afghan capacity. Know those with whom we are contracting. Consult and involve local leaders. Act. Get the story out.

The corruption problem was one of enormous magnitude. A report released that October found that between 2002 and 2010, the United States alone had provided nearly $55.7 billion in reconstruction funding without having established a comprehensive U.S. strategy for fighting corruption in Afghanistan. By that point, the amount spent on the reconstruction of Afghanistan exceeded the amount spent on reconstruction in Iraq. While Congress had required the Pentagon, the State Department and the U.S. Agency for International Development to create a common database to keep track of contractors' compensation, they didn't really know how to use it. Nor could they tell auditors which contracts, cooperative agreements and grants were spent on reconstruction and which ones were spent on support for U.S. troops and other activities. In fiscal years 2007, 2008 and 2009 alone, more than $17.7 billion had been designated for 6,900 contractors. Many of the contractors had not kept their ends of the bargain. For instance, when the U.S. Army Corps of Engineers awarded a $5.9 million contract for building six Afghan National Police (ANP) headquarters in Helmand and Kandahar provinces, payments were made to Afghan contractors despite project delays and shoddy construction. Oversight of the project was so lax that U.S. taxpayers would probably have to foot another $1 million—17 percent of the contract value—to complete the headquarters.

These shortcomings by U.S. officials paled in comparison with the deficiencies of their Afghan partners. In Nangarhar Province, the United States invested $100 million in 2009. The report concluded that "the province does not have the capacity to independently manage development funds, lacks a functioning development planning process, and is unable to sustain completed projects." It also voiced "growing concern that some companies hired to provide security, supplies, and reconstruction work have been siphoning off money to fund the Taliban and criminal groups." One of the groups identified and subsequently suspended and debarred was Watan Risk Management, an Afghan private security contractor that the special inspector general found "had been funneling large sums of money to insurgents." The firm was headed by two of Karzai's cousins, Ahmed Rateb Popal and Rashid Popal. In all, auditors reported eighty-one ongoing investigations, including problems at the Kabul Bank, as well as the export of large amounts of cash through the Kabul airport. American bureaucrats had done business the only way they knew how, with almost no understanding of Afghan culture or appreciation of what Afghan businessmen were capable of accomplishing.

Petraeus expected all civilian and military personnel involved with contracting, especially commanders, to support qualified Afghan partners, to dedicate additional personnel to contract oversight, and to take action against corrupt businesses that were impeding the mission. Contracting was a weapon every bit as potent as direct fire. "Commanders must know what contracting activity is occurring in their battle space and who benefits from those contracts," Petraeus's contracting guidance stated. "Integrate contracting into intelligence, plans and operations to exert positive influence and to better accomplish our campaign objectives."

Petraeus wanted McMaster's anticorruption team to design a plan that would help Afghan partners define, penetrate, prosecute and ultimately undo the culture of corruption that defined the Afghan political system. It was a tall order for McMaster, one much more difficult than pacifying Tal Afar, in northern Iraq, the signal achievement of his regiment there. Corruption was so endemic in Afghanistan that it was taken for granted, like the noisy, dusty streets in Kabul and the cold, hard winter that sets in over much of the country. McMaster's team attacked its mission with a planning timeline that began in early September, a cache of PowerPoint briefings and, ultimately, a plan that pinpointed political patronage networks dominated by the Afghan elite, including some officials at the highest levels of Karzai's government.

McMaster's nickname in his new job was the Henchman, but at five feet eight inches, with a shiny bald head and a forehead that creased with intensity when he briefed, he came across as a Southern Baptist preacher, bubbling with energy and enthusiasm. His team, an assemblage of anticorruption experts from the military, the State Department and contractors, was determined to come up with fresh new approaches.

One afternoon in late September, McMaster went to Tolo TV, in Kabul. Tolo had helped to force Karzai's transparency during the Afghan presidential election and in other issues through its newscasts and public broadcast messages. McMaster had come with a couple of lieutenant colonels to meet with the producers of an anticorruption campaign the U.S. military was funding on radio, TV, posters and billboards.

McMaster met Saad Mohseni, founder of Tolo TV and CEO of its parent organization, Moby Group. Mohseni, who felt equally comfortable in Washington, Sydney, Kabul or Dubai, was no great friend of Karzai. He had partnered for years with USAID to pursue various transparency initiatives. Mohseni was the son of an Afghan diplomat who had been raised abroad. He cared about his country, and he had also found a way to make money there. It wasn't entirely clear how pristine his own record was; however, McMaster recognized the leverage Mohseni's partnership could provide for Shafafiyat. And he knew Mohseni was savvy in the ways of Afghan politics. Mohseni played devil's advocate for McMaster's plan.

"If there's no political will in Afghanistan to indict and prosecute, what do you do about that?" Mohseni asked.

"Well, it's an issue of influence, you know, exhorting the government to do more," McMaster said.

"Is that your only option?" Mohseni asked.

"No, there are a lot of options," McMaster said. "A lot of the problem is related directly to our money, how our money flows into the system. So that's something over which we have a great deal of control: who gets the international community's money, and our money in particular."

"But that doesn't really work, you know that," Mohseni said.

"You mean because somebody will capture that contract from someone—"

"Or they can get the money from the Iranians, or someone else, or they could utilize drug money; they operate in that gray zone."

Mohseni was too smart to accept McMaster's simplistic formulation and was taking him to a deeper understanding of the situation in Afghanistan, where issues were rarely as they seemed on the surface. McMaster's education had begun to enter the graduate level.

In early October, McMaster presided over a review of Task Force Shafafiyat's work in a briefing room at ISAF headquarters that was packed with four dozen interagency representatives from NATO, the State Department, the Drug Enforcement Administration and other agencies with a stake in the anticorruption effort. McMaster was blunt in his opening remarks, noting that "there has not been one historical record of a case of corruption being solved by an outside party exclusively."

"We've been engaging with Afghan leaders, and civil society, and framing the problem from an Afghan perspective as best we can," he said, adding that "many of the leaders with whom we're engaging . . . are kind of complicit in the problem set we're dealing with." McMaster's goal was to find the "islands of integrity" among Afghan officials and publicly reward them. There was a general perception that the ministries of Defense and Interior were fairly clean. But the truth, one of McMaster's deputies said, was that the Ministry of Defense "steals money mainly from us," whereas the Ministry of the Interior "steals mainly from the Afghan people." McMaster knew his effort would entail dealing with at least minimally corrupt Afghans to meet his objectives. It was the best he could hope for to achieve Petraeus's goals.

McMaster turned the briefing over to Lieutenant Colonel Joel Rayburn, a Ph.D. whom Petraeus called his "designated thinker" while they were in Iraq and at Central Command together. Rayburn began with the group's conclusion that corruption in Afghanistan stemmed primarily from "criminal patronage networks," but he added that a great many "reform-minded" Afghans had also been identified in senior government positions. The U.S. military and the broader international community had to begin by cleaning up their own houses so they weren't, in Rayburn's words, "doing harm" with all the money they were dumping in the country. Then they needed to make sure their Afghan counterparts understood "the severity of the problem so that, to the extent that it's possible, they internalize the threat to themselves and to the future of their state."

One problem, McMaster interjected, had been a tendency to respond reactively to corrupt practices instead of attacking them preemptively by presenting Afghan officials with hard evidence. "Do we understand what the vision for anticorruption efforts is for key Afghan leaders?" he asked. "Have we asked them that question? Have we determined what common ground we have, what we can work on together?"

One of those seated around the long rectangular table was David Kilcullen, an Australian-American defense intellectual and counterinsurgency expert who had become a key adviser to Petraeus during the surge in Iraq. Like McMaster, he was not shy about saying what he thought. He had come to Petraeus's attention in 2006 after writing an essay, "Twenty-Eight Articles: Fundamentals of Company-Level Counterinsurgency," that went one better than T. E. Lawrence's "Twenty-Seven Articles" about fighting in the Middle East in 1917.

"It's a little too complicated," Kilcullen said after listening to the briefing for about half an hour. "You're making it seem too linear." To succeed, he said, they would have to deal with all the layers of corruption, beginning with the Afghans. But this would include the United States, coalition country governments and the international community, all of which contributed to the problem. All were accomplices in one way or another.

"Yeah, that's right," McMaster agreed. "There's no way this is conducive to any centralized form of action. It just has to allow the various organizations that are engaging on this issue to take initiative and deal with a common understanding of the problem." That included a very large cast of players, and no one had attempted to orchestrate the initiative in a comprehensive manner before McMaster and his Shafafiyat effort.

McMaster's prescription followed Petraeus's management fundamentals. Getting those fundamentals right in Afghanistan, though, would be the challenge of a lifetime.

CHAPTER 4

SCREAMING EAGLES

Petraeus had a special affection for the 101st Airborne Division, the Screaming Eagles. The storied unit had been severely tested in Europe in World War II, and in Vietnam and Iraq. Afghanistan would do the same.

After the division's creation, in August 1942, its paratroopers were among the first to land in occupied France in the early hours of D-Day, June 6, 1944. Months later, it would participate in the airborne landings in Holland that began the liberation of that country. In December, the division refused to surrender when surrounded by Germans at Bastogne, Belgium, during the Battle of the Bulge. The acting commander famously responded to a German ultimatum with a single word: "Nuts!" During the Division's seven-year deployment in Vietnam, in 1969, the 3rd Battalion, 187th Infantry Regiment—the Rakkasans—fought their way up Hamburger Hill in one of the toughest battles of the Vietnam War, suffering heavy losses: 329 men killed and wounded. The battalion's nickname, however, went all the way back to the World War II occupation of Japan, where the local people called the unit's paratroopers "Rakkasans," Japanese for "falling-down umbrella."

In 1991, as part of Operation Desert Storm in Iraq, the Rakkasans conducted an air assault and cut off Iraqi Republican Guard units fleeing Kuwait and heading back into Iraq. Several months later, Lieutenant Colonel David Petraeus took command of the 3rd Battalion, 187th Infantry Regiment, the first essential step up the ladder in the career of any future four-star general. Twelve years later, he commanded the 101st Airborne during the 2003 invasion of Iraq. It was Petraeus's first combat command. He led the division through battles in Najaf, Karbala and Hillah on the way to Baghdad. But it was in Mosul after the invasion that Petraeus and the division's members distinguished themselves most, achieving early progress through their ability to conduct nation-building and counterinsurgency operations, pacifying their area in northern Iraq during their charge of it while other sectors spiraled into violence.

Once the division's 4th Brigade Combat Team arrived in Afghanistan in August as the final unit in Obama's surge, nearly the entire 101st Division was deployed together for the first time since Petraeus led the Screaming Eagles to Baghdad. The 4th Brigade, known as the "Currahees"—the word means "stands alone" in Cherokee—would join the 1st Brigade Combat Team, nicknamed Bastogne, and the 3rd Brigade Combat Team, the "Rakkasans," in the war's eastern sector. The division's 2nd Brigade Combat Team, nicknamed "Strike," had been sent to southern Afghanistan to clear the area west of Kandahar city as part of Operation Dragon Strike. Thousands of soldiers from the Strike Brigade, teamed with units from the Afghan National Army, pushed into the Zhari District west of Kandadar city in mid-September, searching booby-trapped villages for Taliban insurgents. Beyond its tactical significance, the area was of considerable symbolic importance: The Taliban movement was established in a village in the district called Sangsar in 1994 when a cleric named Mullah Mohammed Omar ordered the hanging of a local warlord who had raped two young girls. Dragon Strike was the first major military operation the Americans had mounted since the Marines cleared Marjah, to the west in Helmand Province, in February.

Petraeus and his team knew that the PR blitz that heralded that Marine operation had backfired after the fight in Marjah became far harder and longer than the U.S. command had imagined. Operation Dragon Strike wouldn't be formally announced for a week, even though hard fighting had been under way in the area for months. Dragon Strike was the largest operation mounted in the nine-year-old war and the third and final phase of a broader push to clear Kandahar Province, called Operation Hamkari, from the Dari word for "cooperation." Phase one had begun in the early summer to increase security in Kandahar, the most important city in southern Afghanistan, with a population of more than 500,000. Phase two began in late July with the clearing of the Arghandab River Valley, north of the city. The lush terrain of the Arghandab, with its vineyards, pomegranate groves and marijuana fields, provided the perfect cover for Taliban fighters to ambush U.S. forces with AK-47s and rocket-propelled grenades and then melt back into the villages.

Phase three was Operation Dragon Strike, which included attacks on Taliban positions along Highway 1 and in the Zhari District, west of the city. And phase four, in October and November, would involve clearing the Taliban out of Zangabad, Mushan and Talukan, in the Panjwai District southwest of the city. Control Zhari, Arghandab and Panjwai and the flow of insurgents into Kandahar would be considerably reduced.

By American historical standards, the fighting in Afghanistan seemed an order of magnitude smaller. U.S. battle deaths in the summer, while the highest by far since the war began in 2001, had peaked at 58 in July and then declined to 54 in August, then to 30 in September, before rising to 47 in October with the initiation of the new offensives. But those numbers were deceptive and did not capture the vicious nature of the fight in Afghanistan, particularly in the south, where the terrain was riddled with thousands of IEDs. The homemade weapons came in all shapes and sizes—some detonated by pressure plates, others by command wires, still others by remote control. The crude bombs maimed soldiers horribly, blowing off arms and legs, filling torsos with shrapnel and scrambling brains with such concussive force that large numbers of troops were left suffering from the misunderstood and difficult-to-diagnose war wound called traumatic brain injury. Others suffered silently from post-traumatic stress disorder. In some ways, the better measure of the savage nature of the combat in Afghanistan, particularly in the south, was battlefield injuries, which were running about ten times the number killed. In June, 539 U.S. troops were wounded, the highest monthly total since the war began. The number increased to 606 in July and 608 in August and hardly tapered off as summer gave way to fall and Operation Dragon Strike, with 590 U.S. troops injured in September and 578 in October.

On Petraeus's first visit to Kandahar in July, where coalition loss of life and limb were highest, he asked the 101st's Strike Brigade Combat Team commander, Colonel Art Kandarian, "What do you need to succeed?" Kandarian asked for M58 Mine Clearing Line Charge for breaching capability, Military Working Dogs to sniff out IEDs, and interpreters. Petraeus immediately relayed these requirements directly to Secretary of Defense Gates. "I know that Petraeus personally took these on and without his personal efforts I am certain the requests would not have been filled," Kandarian recalled. On Petraeus's second visit, in August, Kandarian gathered his battalion commanders for a discussion with Petraeus. At the end of the meeting, Petraeus asked everyone to leave the room so that he could spend a few minutes alone with Kandarian, who had suffered the largest combat losses of any brigade commander in the division. "How are *you* doing, Art?" Petraeus asked point-blank, sensing the colonel's emotional struggles and looking him in the eye. No one carried the weight of losing soldiers in battle, the "heavy rucksack" feeling, like a commander. "It was clear to me that he was a 'commander's commander,'" Kandarian observed, noting that Petraeus had made five visits to his unit alone over the year and also called routinely to check on the commander and Strike's progress.

Even before Dragon Strike officially commenced, targeted Special Operations raids and initial clearing operations in Kandahar had started to show early gains. The situation was improving, but Petraeus didn't want to declare success prematurely. He was keenly aware of how the United States had overpromised in Marjah. He addressed this phenomenon in his counterinsurgency guidance: "MANAGE EXPECTATIONS. Avoid premature declarations of success. Note what has been accomplished and what still needs to be done. Strive to under-promise and over-deliver."

"We need to be careful announcing dates of upcoming operations and what we expect to achieve by a certain date," Petraeus said during his stand-up a week before the soft launch of Dragon Strike. "One of the lessons learned from operations in central Helmand was to be careful on what we announce." He struck the same theme in his stand-up three days later. "We will not tell the enemy in advance of our intentions," he said. "In my dealings with the press I have restricted myself to stating that operations have started and resisted the temptation to state when we will have achieved success. Do not amp up expectations about Kandahar: no specifics, no dates. A deliberate campaign has begun, and events will unfold."

There were numerous fierce firefights, but the Taliban were more difficult to find when troopers from the Strike Brigade showed up before dawn in villages in Zhari, many of which were largely abandoned. Many of the insurgents had melted back into society. The massed force, backed by A-10 attack jets and Kiowa and Apache helicopters, tipped off the Taliban better than any press conference ever could, but this was fine with Petraeus. The objective was clearing the area of enemy and forcing them to displace from long-held command-and-control nodes and IED-manufacturing sites, not killing every last one of them.

WHILE MUCH OF THE 101st's 2nd Strike Brigade was moving across the Zhari District, west of Kandahar city, in September, Lieutenant Colonel Dave Flynn's unit, the 1st Battalion of the 320th Field Artillery Regiment, remained in the Arghandab River Valley, northwest of Kandahar city, clearing villages of Taliban fighters and the hundreds of IEDs they had left behind.

The Arghandab River Valley had historically been a very tough area. Previous units there had suffered tragic losses, and Flynn's soldiers had been in an intense fight since the moment they had arrived in late June. Nine years after the 9/11 terrorist attacks, Flynn was a typical Army commander, experienced and skilled in conducting counterinsurgency operations after multiple tours in combat. Intense and athletic, with piercing blue eyes, Flynn was an artilleryman by training. He grew up outside Boston in suburban Norwood, a Red Sox fan, but attended Clemson University, in South Carolina. His father, a Korean War veteran and retired Army sergeant major, convinced him to join the ROTC in college. Flynn had served in Kandahar from

2004 to 2005, when his artillery unit from the 25th Infantry Division performed what he called a "provisional" infantry role. He remembered that tour as "the good years," the period before the Taliban had regrouped. He deployed to Iraq with the 25th Infantry Division in 2006 and 2007, serving in Kirkuk with an artillery unit again repurposed to perform infantry tasks. They called themselves "infantillary."

When he took command of the battalion at Fort Campbell in 2009, Flynn was initially told that his unit would deploy to Iraq. Flynn spent six months with his soldiers reacquiring artillery skills, only to shift gears and focus for the next nine months on training in infantry tactics before deploying to Afghanistan in late spring 2010. "I'm not downplaying the concern the Army has about the erosion of artillery skills, but I believe you do what you must do now to win," Flynn said. "There will be time to re-train." Artillery battalions made sense as an integral component of an Army brigade designed to fight the Cold War, when U.S. war planners contemplated epic battles between large, mechanized forces that included massive artillery duels. Converting artillerymen to infantrymen able to fight small-arms engagements and interact with people at the village level made the 1st Battalion, 320th Artillery Regiment, the "Top Guns," relevant to the kind of war the nation had been fighting since 9/11. This transformation was difficult, but Flynn believed it was possible.

The readiness of his troops became an issue in one of the first battles they fought as they patrolled jointly in the Arghandab River Valley with combatsavvy soldiers they would soon be replacing from the 2nd Battalion of the 508th Parachute Infantry, 82nd Airborne Division. With temperatures over 100 degrees and extremely high humidity, the paratroopers from the 82nd led an assault on Taliban positions through an orchard on July 11, only to stop when some of Flynn's soldiers passed out with extreme heat fatigue. The problem became so acute that helicopters had to be called in to evacuate the troops. When the Black Hawks arrived with reinforcements, they took withering fire as soldiers loaded their incapacitated comrades aboard.

After the remaining soldiers in the orchard, under heavy fire, were finally able to return to the compound where the patrol had begun hours earlier, tensions ran high. Squad leaders from the 82nd clashed with officers from the 101st. "You're not putting my guys at risk anymore," Staff Sergeant Christopher Gerhart, of the 82nd Airborne, told 2nd Lieutenant Zak Pantaleo, from the 101st. "You dudes need to think about my guys, who have been out here for eleven fucking months." Meanwhile, Flynn directed a complex helicopter assault to fly reinforcements to the scene, and he arrived at the compound with a dismounted patrol a short while later. He was struck by the acrimony of the sergeants from the 82nd Airborne toward his soldiers of the 101st. He made it clear that their attitude was unacceptable among American soldiers. He then organized the movement of both units from the battlefield and personally led his reinforcements back to their base on foot.

Given his previous tours in Afghanistan and Iraq, Flynn was an experienced counterinsurgent. He arrived in Afghanistan as part of the 2010 surge with a nuanced understanding of Petraeus's tactical approach. He bought in to the mission, and he was prepared to adjust tactics as the mission dictated.

Staff Sergeant Gerhart was later quoted in the press as saying that the soldiers from Flynn's artillery unit "weren't prepared physically, mentally, and tactically." But in February, when Flynn had learned that his unit would be deployed in the Arghandab River Valley, he had intensified its training on dismounted infantry operations. He could have argued that they should have deployed as an artillery unit, but, having served previously in Kandahar, he knew they would contribute much more as infantrymen—and they'd likely end up performing infantry missions regardless. "As artillerymen, I fully recognize that we could not attain the expertise and experience of our Army's premier infantry units," Flynn noted. "But at the same time I knew we could prepare our men to be better than the Taliban, and we are. . . . We studied the area for six months and had access to the 82nd's classified reports. We knew the terrain, the people and the enemy. We studied the 82nd's tactics and rehearsed them at Fort Campbell before we deployed. The curve is certainly steep. The weather, the vegetation, terrain and a wily enemy all made this a tough fight but not one we didn't expect." Flynn noted that his unit had mounted a "no-notice air assault" to evacuate the soldiers with heatstroke, something very few could pull off without training. "We all have three, four or five deployments to Iraq and Afghanistan and would not put a unit in a position for which it was unprepared," he said.

The fighting only grew more intense for his soldiers. On July 30, they began a carefully choreographed operation to clear a group of buildings long controlled by the Taliban outside the town of Jelawur. The buildings, which the Americans called Objective Bakersfield, occupied an important intersection of two major roads that connected four U.S. combat outposts. An eerie calm fell over Bakersfield as the first of Flynn's soldiers arrived at first light. Flynn, accompanied by members of his battalion staff and his personal security detail, set out on foot toward Bakersfield shortly before 8:00 A.M., following a convoy of engineers who were clearing the route of IEDs. But as Flynn approached, an IED detonated and the Taliban opened up with a barrage of small-arms fire. Then another IED went off and Flynn saw Specialist Michael L. Stansbery, 21, of Mt. Juliet, Tennessee, down on the road, injured by the blast. It had ripped his torso in half. A huge cloud of smoke hung in the air. Captain Andrew Shaffer, one of Flynn's commanders, remembered how, at that moment, time seemed to slow to an agonizing crawl. "Medic!" he heard someone shout. Radios crackled with reports of small-arms firing coming from the south.

Minutes later, yet another IED exploded, leaving two of Flynn's sergeants bloodied and dazed. Then he saw Sergeant Kyle B. Stout, 25, of Texarkana, Texas, in the choking black smoke, gravely wounded on the road. His face was frozen, mouth open. There was a blank look on his face. Three limbs were gone. Shaffer knelt beside him and forced a tourniquet over exposed bone and pulled it tight on flaps of skin and muscle. He remembered thinking how strange it was that Stout wasn't bleeding—his body was "shunting," instinctively cutting off blood flow to its extremities in a last-ditch effort to protect its vital organs. Flynn knelt by his side and tried to talk him back to consciousness. A call went out for medevac. A Black Hawk helicopter soon landed in a field fifty meters to the northeast and evacuated Stansbery and Stout from the battlefield.

Flynn huddled with commanders near one of the simple buildings at Bakersfield to consolidate and reorganize to continue the assault. When he walked the north side of his unit's perimeter, he felt another IED shake the battlefield, detonating thirty-five meters away, on ground he'd just walked across. At least two more soldiers had been wounded. Flynn regrouped again with commanders, calling for reinforcements from battalion headquarters in what had by now become a battalion-level engagement. With small-arms fire coming from three sides of the battlefield, Flynn set up a command post in the hay-filled building. Then a report came over the radio of another casualty, sixty meters to the west. By the time Flynn got to Robert Pittman, a retired master sergeant working as an adviser for the Asymmetric Warfare Group, Pittman was conscious but unresponsive. Blood trickled from his ear. His eyes were open but unresponsive. He had been a tower of strength for the soldiers. "Mr. Pittman, can you hear me?" a soldier asked. Pittman could not speak, but he blinked his eyes. He'd been hit by gunfire.

After what seemed like an eternity, a medevac helicopter approached— and Flynn's men opened up with all the fire they had to provide cover. The shooting was insanely loud. A team of soldiers dashed toward the Black Hawk with Pittman and loaded him on board in hopes that he could be saved. Rotor wash cleared the landing zone of debris as the helicopter lifted off. Minutes later, Flynn grabbed Shaffer. "Drew," he said. "We can't shoot like that. We've got friendlies eighteen hundred meters in that direction." He was concerned about the volume of fire at Command Outpost Nolen.

"Yes, sir," Shaffer said, feeling almost lost.

He and Flynn learned later, as the fighting raged and they maneuvered soldiers across the battlefield, that Stansbery, Stout and Pittman had died of the wounds they suffered in the opening moments of the battle. It soon became clear to them how important this simple crossing was to the enemy. The fighting continued for five days before Flynn's soldiers finally cleared the objective.

Flynn called Pittman's wife, Melissa, on the battle's first day, after her husband's death had been confirmed. He remembered it as an exceedingly difficult conversation. Except for a short article in the 2nd Brigade Combat Team's monthly publication, *Heart Beat*, the Battle for Bakersfield made not a single headline and received not a word of press coverage. It was typical of the grinding combat in Kandahar that almost never rose to conventional force-on-force battle. Regardless, the Arghandab was, as Flynn observed, a "hellacious" place to fight.

A few days later, at ISAF headquarters in Kabul, Petraeus described the ongoing effort in Kandahar during his morning stand-up. "The important part about Kandahar is that it is a very comprehensive approach," he said. "Months ago we began targeting Taliban in Kandahar through Special Forces operations. We continue with this, and the tempo of these highly effective strikes builds. Now we have thickening of conventional forces, and that will also continue and will become more visible in the weeks and months ahead . . . as will the eventual addition of Afghan Local Police elements. All of this is following an established timeline. In sum: This is how a COIN operation is conducted; it is not a conventional operation with a D-Day—we need to push this message."

Whatever weaknesses Flynn's forces had coming into the fight in the Arghandab River Valley in July, they had overcome them by late August, having pushed farther into Taliban country than the 82nd before them ever had. "The fight here has been intense and almost exclusively dismounted in the densely vegetated river valley," Flynn said. "The enemy in our area was estimated to number 150 strong. . . . We have conducted two major offensive operations that have by and large routed the enemy from this area. We now own the villages that have long been Taliban sanctuary."

Soon after, in Babur, a village long controlled by the Taliban, Flynn met with village elders and told them they needed to choose whether they wanted to live under the Taliban or under the government. His sense was that the villagers hated the Taliban but were deathly afraid of them, having watched them assassinate those who cooperated with the government and the Americans. His subordinate commanders started holding weekly *shuras* [councils, generally of elders] with elders in the area, using a "cash for work" program that paid five hundred afghani (about ten dollars) a day to clean canals, refurbish mosques and fix roads.

In early October, Flynn and other U.S. commanders devised a final plan for clearing the remaining Taliban out of the Arghandab River Valley with the help of Haji Shah Mohammed, the district governor; General Mohammad Naim, Kandahar's chief of the National Directorate of Security, the country's equivalent of the FBI; and Colonel Abdul Raziq, a charismatic leader of the Afghan Border Police. Flynn's Top Guns had seized significant terrain and villages south of the Manarah Canal, on the west side of the Arghandab River, but had yet to clear eight villages north of the canal, including Tarok Kolache, Charqolba Sofla and Khosrow Sofla. General Naim had grown up in Khosrow Sofla, and Flynn had become close with Karim Dad, the village's chief, or malik. Flynn nodded in agreement as General Naim explained that Khosrow Sofla and Charqolba Sofla had become hubs of Taliban activity and major bomb-making centers and they had to be cleared.

Colonel Raziq struck Flynn as a brash young Afghan, dressed in upper-class Pashtun garb—off-white dress, Kandahari hat and loafers. A profile in *Harper's* in 2009 had described Raziq as a corrupt warlord protecting the opium trade along the border and working closely with U.S. and NATO commanders, who tolerated his corruption because he was brutally effective, with his three-thousand-man command, at helping keep the peace in Kandahar Province. "I have been fighting in the area we are discussing for the past hundred days," Flynn said, describing a plan to clear and hold Tarok Kolache following a raid by U.S. Special Operations Forces so that Raziq's Afghan forces and U.S. Special Forces could clear Khosrow Sofla, Charqolba Sofla and Lower Babur. Raziq looked at Flynn and asked, "You've been fighting in Arghandab for a hundred days?" With a flamboyant wave of his index finger, he added, "I will clear all of Arghandab in one day." It was all Flynn could do to restrain himself. But Raziq would prove to be an effective tactical leader in the days ahead.

Flynn began the work of clearing the Arghandab with directed strikes by lethal rockets from a Multiple-Launch Rocket System (MLRS) on a ten-ton truck. In Afghanistan, those weapons had supported the U.S. military's Joint Special Operations Command (JSOC) exclusively until 2010, when they were also allocated for support to conventional force-clearing operations. The JSOC controls the military's most skilled and highly classified units: the Army's Delta Force, the Navy's SEAL Team 6, and the Air Force's 24th Special

Tactics Squadron, in addition to the Army's 75th Ranger Regiment and the 160th Special Operations Aviation Regiment. These were the units conducting night raids across the country, directed by a Special Operations command center at Bagram Air Base.

Flynn's strikes targeted two compounds in Khosrow Sofla that the insurgents were using to manufacture homemade explosives. A short time later, a London tabloid, the *Daily Mail,* published a story in which Flynn was quoted as telling villagers that if they did not tell him where IEDs had been buried in Khosrow Sofla, he would wipe the village off the face of the earth. But the reporters weren't at Flynn's meeting with villagers, who in fact were told that the Americans would have no choice but to destroy compounds from the air if they were unable to determine where they had been laced with explosives. The villagers no longer lived in Khosrow Sofla and knew they would never be able to return unless the village was somehow cleared of bombs.

After the rocket strikes, Flynn maintained "persistent" surveillance of the village using video from a Predator drone to assess battle damage and capture "patterns of life" in Khosrow Sofla, if any remained. From his command center, he watched six men walking through the rubble of the damaged homes. Flynn thought they looked angry as they walked quickly around the village. Stopping at various places, they might have been planting new IEDs. Although the six were not carrying weapons, Flynn could have killed them with Hellfire missiles from the Predator under the rules of engagement. But he gave them the benefit of the doubt, knowing U.S. forces would take the village within seventy-two hours and could kill or capture them then if they were still around.

Planning continued the following day as Flynn coordinated with U.S. Special Operations Forces in the clearance operation, which had been given the code name Eagle Claw 1. Special Operations Forces, with Afghan commandos, were planning additional air assaults on two villages north of Khosrow Sofla, Tarok Kolache and Khosrow Olya. Captain Shaffer, the Top Gun company commander who had been fighting in Tarok Kolache since July, knew which compounds to hit. He was a proponent of destroying as much as possible from the air, with good reason: His unit had suffered three traumatic casualties there over the past two weeks. Flynn told the Special Operations Forces that he had five or six compounds he wanted destroyed but that they should try to preserve as much of the village as possible so residents could eventually move back in. The Special Operations Forces coordinated with Flynn because it was his area of operations, but they were the ones who would implement. As Flynn went to sleep for a couple of hours before the next morning's attack into Tarok Kolache, he told his executive officer, Major Tom Burrell, that he was not in favor of destroying more compounds in the village if they didn't need to. But at 2:00 A.M., Burrell woke him up and told him that the Special Operations Forces wanted to destroy the entire village because it had been thoroughly laced with all kinds of bombs and explosives. Like Captain Shaffer's men, the Special Operations Forces had suffered numerous IED casualties over the summer in the villages of the Arghandab. Flynn was convinced, and unleashed a thunderous display of firepower on Tarok Kolache, rattling the countryside for miles around.

When B-1 bombers began dropping two-ton bombs on the village, the earth shook and the windows and walls rattled in Flynn's command center, less than two kilometers west of the village. Flynn's staff listened to the radios as American Special Operations Forces landed by helicopter and began their assault. Almost immediately, one of the assault force soldiers stepped on an IED. It malfunctioned—and prepared the Special Operations Forces for what was to come. As they cleared the village, they discovered IEDs, jugs of homemade explosives and fifty-gallon drums of explosives in the homes—house-borne IEDs. Raziq's Afghan Border Police forces did not arrive until the next day. They fought alongside the teams that went to Charqolba Sofla and Khosrow Sofla.

Some months later, the blogosphere erupted with complaints that Flynn, with Petraeus's full support, had reverted to Vietnam tactics—destroying villages in order to save them. But Flynn believed that Tarok Kolache had been destroyed when the Taliban drove out all of its residents and seeded its fields and compounds with explosives. When Captain Shaffer's soldiers fanned out across the village at first light on October 7, the compounds—and the bombs—were gone.

By the end of October, Flynn's battalion had lost seven soldiers and had awarded eighty-three Purple Hearts. Three-quarters of those wounded had been hit by IEDs. Fourteen soldiers lost a limb or been so gravely wounded that their lives would forever be changed. Four had lost both their legs. Flynn was firm in his belief that they had achieved important results. "There's no space for the Taliban to return to this district during the spring," Flynn said. "This war either ends at the negotiation table or when the people unite and collectively reject the Taliban."

One reporter accused Flynn of war crimes and violation of the Geneva Convention for approving the air strike on Tarok Kolache. Yet many of the villages in his area of operations had been abandoned for two or three years, according to the village maliks. Like many villages in the area, Khosrow Sofla was an insurgent safe haven, a weapons factory used to build and export munitions throughout the south. Decades ago, the Soviets had failed to take this terrain from the mujahideen. Until the American troop surge and Flynn's unit's arrival, coalition forces had not been able to push forward from Jelawur beyond a second canal. The fall offensive and mass of troops, enablers and close air support finally shifted the balance. But it came at a tragic cost, inscribed on a card neatly folded in Flynn's battledress pocket—the names of his seven men killed and the fourteen who had suffered life-changing injuries.

Flynn approved precision strikes on Khosrow Sofla the same night Tarok Kolache was razed. He intended to take back the village, a key terrain feature on the Arghandab River, from the insurgents. The targets were acquired through a sophisticated reconnaissance aircraft that could detect homemade explosive materials the size of raisins.

After striking several of the Taliban IED depots, Colonel Raziq's four hundred ABP, aided by U.S. Special Forces, were tasked to clear Charqolba Sofla and other villages in the Arghandab. Though locals accused Raziq's men of mistreatment, their U.S. Special Forces liaison team saw no such actions; moreover, there was no doubt they were effective in convincing the local population to show them where the deadly IEDs were located along the approaches to the villages. They cleared numerous key areas in a single day, according to the Special Forces team that partnered with Raziq. Raziq's men and the Special Forces had discovered dozens of IEDs and opened the way for Flynn's forces and the local population to gain access to Charqolba Sofla.

The Border Police then withdrew, and the task to finish clearing the village was handed off to one of Flynn's platoons. The unit employed bombsniffing dog teams, EOD specialists, minesweepers and local sources in a painstaking process that took two weeks, at the cost of two additional soldiers wounded, before they could declare the village safe and start to rebuild.

Flynn was intent on preventing the Taliban's return and clearing Khosrow Sofla so that the villagers could move back. Always in his mind was that the villages needed villagers to return, and that he needed to help equip them with the capacity to secure their own villages in the future. Within days of the attacks, Flynn rallied the displaced villagers and explained that he needed help in finding the IEDs. "I implored them to ask the Taliban where the IEDs were or else I would have no other choice but to use lethal means to remove the IEDs. I told them I didn't want any more of my soldiers to get blown up, nor did I want the locals to get hurt either. They agreed to consider my request."

One week later, the village malik came to Flynn's operating base and relayed that all the IEDs were gone. Flynn and his men went through the village and verified it. "No dozers. No mass punishment. They were already punished by the Taliban," Flynn said with a cracked voice.

A HUNDRED AND TWENTY-FIVE miles northeast of the Arghandab River Valley, in the high steppe of east Ghazni Province, Lieutenant Colonel David Fivecoat rolled out of Forward Operating Base Andar with his five-vehicle convoy. When he was a captain in 2003, Fivecoat had served as Petraeus's aide during the invasion of Iraq and got as good a view as anyone of the general as a combat commander. Back in the United States, Fivecoat oversaw the writing of *Field Manual 3-24.2: Tactics in Counterinsurgency* in 2008 and 2009, the tactical-level companion for Petraeus's COIN manual.

Now Fivecoat was commanding the 3rd Battalion, 187th Infantry Regiment of the 101st Airborne Division—the Rakkasans. The Rakkasans had extensive combat experience in Afghanistan and Iraq since General Petraeus had led the battalion between 1993 and 1995. The unit was extremely proud of its combat history in every engagement since World War II.

When the remainder of the surge forces arrived in September, including the 101st's Currahee brigade, the 4th Brigade Combat Team, Fivecoat's battalion completed a move from Paktika to the far more troubled terrain of eastern Ghazni. Although NATO forces had maintained some presence in Ghazni since 2001, it had been only intermittently patrolled for the past two years, primarily by Polish troops, and, given the lack of permanent presence, they had a mixed record of success before the Rakkasans arrived. That summer, the Regional Command East commander, Major General Campbell, had recognized that it was time to do something about the Taliban's growing infestation in the area. In choosing which of his battalions to move to the challenging terrain, Campbell asked Fivecoat if it would make more sense to send Fivecoat's unit or a newly arrived Currahee battalion of the 4th Brigade Combat Team into the Taliban-controlled area. Fivecoat said it would be easier for his battalion to go, because he could capitalize on his unit's combat experience to deal with fighting in a new area. The move was exhausting, but Fivecoat and the Iron Rakkasans completed the transition within a few weeks.

Campbell and Fivecoat had served together when Campbell was a brigade commander in the 82nd Airborne Division and Fivecoat was one of his company commanders. Campbell had taken an interest in Fivecoat's career ever since, supporting his assignment as an aide to Petraeus in Bosnia in 2001. Fivecoat appreciated how Campbell had listened to his position on why it made more sense for the Rakkasans to move to Ghazni.

Soon the battalion's units were occupying the terrain where Nir Rosen, an American journalist, had embedded with the Taliban in 2008 to write an article in *Rolling Stone* that Fivecoat would come to assign to his officers as mandatory reading, "How We Lost the War We Won." "Until recently, Ghazni, like much of central Afghanistan, was considered reasonably safe," Rosen writes. "But now the province, located 100 miles south of the capital, has fallen to the Taliban. Foreigners who venture to Ghazni often wind up kidnapped or killed. In defiance of the central government, the Taliban governor in the province issues separate ID cards and passports for the Taliban regime, the Islamic Emirate of Afghanistan. Farmers increasingly turn to the Taliban, not the American-backed authorities, for adjudication of land disputes." By some estimates, the resurgent Taliban ran as many as twenty-eight schools, arbitrated land and property disputes in Islamic courts, levied taxes and occasionally assassinated those they thought were collaborating with the Americans. Their fighting force was thought to number around 400 insurgents, with active support from about 4,000 of the district's 150,000 people. The government cause was not helped when, in 2005, a number of corrupt local power brokers won elections and began brutalizing and stealing and making the Taliban look good by comparison. Meanwhile, it was apparent that Pakistan had provided at least some of the money, arms and matériel support for the Taliban's resurgence in the area.

On September 16, the same day Operation Dragon Strike kicked off down in Kandahar, Sergeant William Bickers, a Rakkasan mortarman from Cincinnati, took a bullet in the arm when insurgents attacked a foot patrol he was leading in the Andar District with AK-47s and rocket-propelled grenades. Campbell awarded him the Purple Heart and a Combat Infantryman Badge in the hospital a couple of days later, then watched as Bickers's platoon leader reenlisted him for another two years. In late September, Fivecoat's soldiers from C Company were attacked during a patrol in the Andar District. They were in enough trouble to call in Apache helicopters, the lethal gunships armed with 30-mm chain guns and Hellfire missiles. No matter how good the intelligence seemed, or how clearly fighters on rooftops were visible to the pilots, however, it was hard for the Apaches to be too discriminating once they started shooting. This particular battle was a case in point. Devoid of any larger significance, it left four Afghan civilians dead, including two small children, and three wounded. Fivecoat would later hold a *shura* with village elders and personally apologize.

Just two days after the civilians were killed, Fivecoat's men rolled out of their base camp in seven-ton $600,000 Mine-Resistant Ambush-Protected vehicles (MRAPs)—five in a row, as was the norm when the commander departed the outpost. They were heading for Combat Outpost Deh Yak, in Taliban-infested eastern Ghazni Province. The Iron Rakkasans had spent the first five months of their tour in neighboring Paktika Province, where contact with the enemy was sporadic. But the Andar and Deh Yak districts of eastern Ghazni were altogether different, infested with Taliban, whose influence was to be felt everywhere Fivecoat went but whose foot soldiers were elusive and almost never seen, in part because the local population helped to facilitate their movement and, Fivecoat had come to realize, in part because the local population produced many of them. The central government in Kabul had provided almost no meaningful governance there since the initial American victory in 2001.

The convoy passed a team of mine-clearing vehicles from the South Carolina National Guard that was working the route around the base, which was the size of a football field. The guardsmen's job was to clear the roads around the outpost so the infantry teams could go out on missions and Afghans could travel with some degree of safety.

The convoy drove through several tiny suburbs—fewer than a dozen houses made of sandstone and pieces of wood. Donkeys and goats walked in the road. Fivecoat waved at everyone, but only a few waved back; most often the locals didn't even look up. "What do you expect after years of our presence here?" Fivecoat said. "Wait," said a sarcastic trooper. "They used to throw rocks at us, so isn't their ambivalence a sign of progress?"

By any standard, Fivecoat was an expert in counterinsurgency operations, having served in the third of five surge brigades in Iraq that succeeded in pacifying the Mada'in Qada region of southeastern Baghdad Province, which was beset at the outset of the surge with Sunni and Shia insurgencies.

A West Point graduate who grew up in Delaware, Ohio, he wrote a lengthy paper on this experience in which he examined the counterinsurgency practices of Roger Trinquier, a legendary French colonel who had served in Indochina and Algeria, to examine which of Trinquier's practices were pertinent to the mission in Iraq. His answer: all of them except torture, which Trinquier had condoned. "As it was for Trinquier and his foes in Algeria," Fivecoat wrote, "the goal for both the insurgent and the counterinsurgent in Iraq is to 'control the population.'" His brigade in Iraq used six "lines of effort" to do that—security, transition, governance, rule of law, economics and communications.

Having served as Petraeus's aide during the invasion of Iraq in March 2003, Fivecoat didn't hesitate to send his old boss some unsolicited advice when Petraeus took command in July. "Come in, conduct a 30-day on the ground assessment, say the situation is much worse than imagined (but hard is not hopeless), and then take the gloves off for 6 months," Fivecoat counseled, looking ahead to the review planned by the Obama administration around Christmas. "There was a lot of killing for the first six months of the surge in Iraq—you could call it compellence theory. The December assessment will be bad because you will have a lot of units, a lot of violence and it won't taper off until November due to the weather."

Now, in the convoy to Deh Yak, Fivecoat pulled into a new combat outpost commanded by Captain Josh Powers. A graduate of the Virginia Military Institute, Powers exuded a deep grasp of counterinsurgency doctrine and its application in Afghanistan. He had already been awarded a Purple Heart for injuries suffered in an IED attack over the summer. Powers and Fivecoat stood on top of a lookout tower that was under construction and surveyed the landscape. Having attended a village wedding earlier in the day, Powers understood the value of building rapport with the locals to gain credibility, develop sources and filter the reconcilables from the irreconcilables. Members of his company had been welcomed into the tribal wedding with open arms, even though they'd come with odd gifts—cases of Coca-Cola. But he had not had the same luck with his Afghan National Army partners, who were supposed to be collocated with them at the new outpost.

The Afghan army refused to help build the outpost and refused to live in tents on the compound until the barracks were complete. Powers carried on without them.

As Fivecoat and Powers talked about the challenges he faced, the captain pointed out the roads where Taliban often rode by on their motorcycles. He pointed to the village where the district center was located and discussed the fact that his outpost was not directly in the village but instead had been positioned out on the plain, in full vantage from some nearby hills. Since the mission was to protect the population, he questioned the selection of the terrain he now occupied. Eventually they would turn the outpost over to their Afghan National Army partners; they, too, would be vulnerable to the surrounding high ground and a little too far from the village to rapidly respond. But someone higher than both of them had selected the outpost location.

From Powers's outpost, Fivecoat and his convoy headed to the district center, a few miles away. It was an old building, painted swimming-pool blue, situated on a barren hilltop overlooking a tiny village below. The district sub-governor apparently didn't spend much time there, preferring to stay in Ghazni city with the provincial governor instead. There was more going on at the provincial level, and he had been threatened by insurgents at his own headquarters.

About a quarter-mile away, there was a walled-in complex known as a *qalat*. The walls were made of sand and water and were in place to keep people and their animals in, and wild animals out. Two women walked down the main village road in full black burkas, with two children in long, brightly colored gowns, bright red and patriot blue, walking with them. There were solar-panel streetlights, which USAID had funded, on the road where the women walked, but all of the solar panels had been stripped from them. The terrain was barren and brown, though Fivecoat said it was once a lush and fertile green land according to research the Army had done.

On the trip back to FOB Andar, the driver of Fivecoat's MRAP said at one point, "We've crossed the point of no return, sir." That simply meant that if an accident requiring a medevac occurred, the convoy would continue on to Andar rather than head back to the district center. Everyone in the MRAP remained quiet. Once back at Andar, Fivecoat was told that one of the mine-clearing trucks from the South Carolina Guard had hit a mine, killing a soldier whose son happened to be in Fivecoat's battalion. The unit chaplain came into Fivecoat's office and explained that the mine-detection vehicle had flipped onto the guardsman, killing him instantly. It was after midnight, and Fivecoat was starting to focus on a raid planned for 5:00 that morning. A theater policy allowed any next of kin to escort the body of a relative back to the United States. The chaplain told Fivecoat that he was going to go and wake the soldier and get him on the next helicopter out, at 2:00 A.M., with his father's body. Fivecoat didn't flinch, thankful to have the chaplain attend to this tragic bit of daily business. Fivecoat had lost two soldiers so far, fewer than his compatriots in the south but still hard losses. War was tough, he said, without elaborating, but his eyes showed the burden behind the mask. Deaths represented a statistic in Washington but a face to him and his fellow commanders. The civilians killed a few days earlier in the Apache attack were still on his mind. Two children had died, and Fivecoat had gone into town to apologize to the grieving family and pay reparations. Fivecoat's voice cracked as he talked about the incident—he had a one-year-old of his own. But a moment later the stoic had returned.

He seemed weary of war, no longer certain that taking the gloves off and fighting hard, as he'd advised Petraeus back in July, would be enough. "There's gotta be some sort of game changer," he said. "We'll keep doing COIN, all day long, but it's hard to see payoffs," he lamented. "And we can continue to fight, but there's . . . to use the Vietnam analogy, there's no light at the end of the tunnel. We're all in, but I'm not sure the Afghans are all in. You can even see it in the senior Afghan leaders as they're all getting their houses in Dubai and carting a whole bunch of our cash out of the country."

Having served as Petraeus's aide as the 101st pushed from Kuwait into Baghdad and all the way up to Mosul in March 2003, he knew the general was perfectly capable of skepticism. He had been there in southern Iraq when

Petraeus famously asked, after recognizing the challenges that lay ahead, "Tell me how this ends?" But he also knew that if there was anyone now who had a sense of how this war in Afghanistan would end, it was Petraeus. How would Petraeus counsel him now? Fivecoat knew there was no need. "Petraeus, in his relentlessly positive way, would say, you know, keep pushing it every day, trying to do as much as you can."

LIEUTENANT COLONEL David Petraeus's special relationship with the 101st Airborne Division began in mid-1991 when he became commander of the 3rd Battalion, 187th Infantry Regiment, Brigadier General Jack Keane was the assistant division commander for operations and already seen as next in line to assume command of the 101st Airborne, the "Screaming Eagles."

The Rakkasans' 3rd Battalion had recently returned from the Gulf War in Iraq, where it had cut off a Republican Guard retreat to Kuwait as part of a massive air assault by the brigade of which it was part. But by all accounts, it was not quite a "high-performing unit" when Petraeus took over. Most of its soldiers had never encountered anyone quite like their intense, lean, physical-fitness-fanatic battalion commander. Inspiring his men to achieve "iron" fitness was Petraeus's top priority, an appropriate one for an air-assault infantry battalion. In an effort to create a "culture of hardness," Petraeus developed the "Iron Rakkasan" fitness competition and challenged his men to compete and beat his score. Nobody did during his two years of command, during which the battalion became officially known as the Iron Rakkasans.

A month after he assumed command of the Rakkasans, Petraeus was in the field walking with a unit while observing a live-fire maneuver exercise when a soldier sprinting out of a bunker tripped and accidentally discharged his M16 rifle. The shot hit Petraeus in the chest and left a massive exit wound in his back. Brigadier General Keane was by his side watching the exercise when Petraeus went down. "He's been shot—get the damn medic over here!" Keane shouted.

Blood came oozing out of Petraeus's back. Captain Fred Johnson, the company commander, shouted orders to halt the exercise and called medics to the scene. They ripped off Petraeus's battledress blouse and went to work. Keane held Petraeus in his arms and watched the color draining from his face.

"Dave, I want you to stay with us," Keane told Petraeus. Petraeus gripped Keane's hand in answer.

In a matter of minutes, Petraeus was evacuated by a Black Hawk medevac aircraft to the post hospital, where a chest tube was inserted, and then flown on to Vanderbilt University Medical Center, in Tennessee, with Keane at his side. An experienced surgeon named Bill Frist—who would later become a Republican senator from Tennessee and Senate majority leader—sliced through Petraeus's latissimus dorsi muscle to conduct thoracic surgery and cauterize an artery that had been nicked. Petraeus had nearly bled to death internally.

Holly had just finished taking her children and one of her daughter's friends to the movies near Fort Campbell. A friend contacted by medical officials broke the news to her after tracking her down. "Sit down, Holly," she said. "The good news is that he will live. The bad news is that he has been shot. The fact is that we need to go to the hospital." Holly said nothing.

But Petraeus soon turned his recovery into a competition to see how fast he could return to command. Doctors on at least one occasion had to order him to cool it. He was back in record time. He gave the soldier who had accidentally shot him a chance to redeem himself—by attending Ranger School. Twenty-seven days after the accident, Petraeus was back in the field, with his rucksack over one shoulder while the other shoulder healed, for a massive deployment and air-assault exercise at Fort Bragg, North Carolina. Keane later reflected that it was Petraeus's drive and spirit that captured Keane's attention.

Petraeus had followed General Vuono's example of the imperative of developing key themes and stressing them on every possible occasion. Petraeus's themes for the unit remained consistent over the years. First was physical fitness: An infantryman in an air-assault unit needed to view his body as the "ultimate weapon." Next, he demanded discipline—military bearing and self-control. He required everyone to get "high and tight" hair-cuts, button the top button of their combat jackets in the field and camou-flage their faces to a specific standard. It was all a part of his endeavor to shape the culture. Then he stressed, in order, small-unit training and live-fire exercises, Ranger training and air-assault operations. No one was more competitive. "Life is a competitive endeavor," he would remind them.

Even the skeptics had to admit after a year that Petraeus had taken an average unit and made it the best in the division. He stressed training. He stressed winning. By the end of his tour, the Iron Rakkasan *battalion* had more Ranger School–qualified soldiers than any other *brigade* in the divi-sion. A memorandum from one of Petraeus's subordinates summed up the driven Petraeus. "Without a doubt, we are doing some of the most complex and exacting training on post . . . but, this training has come at a price . . . many in the battalion question . . . if the late hours and weekends away from home were really worth it." Petraeus expected others to keep up the high standard he set for himself. The memorandum continued, "More than any commander I know of, you have taken a keen and proactive interest in the development of the battalion's officer corps. Even if some officers do not recognize how your emphasis on certain professional skills may apply to their careers, you must continue to stress them." "The challenge," Petraeus recalled, "was changing the culture without alienating those who really didn't embrace it fully."

He was more than a taskmaster. He believed in mentoring, and being mentored. He believed strongly in earned redemption. When West Point called him and asked him whether he would be willing to rehabilitate a cadet who'd been kicked out of the academy for an honor violation, Petraeus agreed—and challenged the soldier to complete a series of the infantry's most demanding schools, including the Air Assault and Ranger courses, and the trooper succeeded, ultimately returning to West Point and graduating.

Keane became division commander just after the conclusion of Petrae-us's two years in command of the Iron Rakkasans. The two had bonded after the shooting. Keane promptly made Petraeus the division's chief of operations, plans and training—the perfect preparation for his future command of the division itself. "He was hands down the best battalion commander I had observed," Keane said. "He had confidence. His knowledge about the job and what needed to be done was superior to others'. He had a sense of himself and what he brought to the job. He had a vision of where he would take the battalion."

UNLIKE FIVECOAT and Flynn, Lieutenant Colonel J. B. Vowell, another 101st Airborne battalion commander, fought a mountain war. In the early-morning light on June 27—four days after Obama tapped Petraeus as his new commander in Afghanistan—units from Vowell's 2nd Battalion, 327th Infantry Regiment staged a large-scale air-assault operation in the mountains above the village of Daridam, in mountainous Kunar Province, along the Pakistan border. They were part of the 101st's Bastogne Brigade. Twin-rotor Chinook helicopters dropped their ramps and deposited hundreds of soldiers across a series of overlook positions on the mountainside that enabled them to see movement in the valley below. They dug in with heavy machine guns, surrounded by sandbags, expecting to be attacked by Taliban fighters in the valley below.

Vowell's battalion was nicknamed "No Slack," having been deployed for seven straight years during the Vietnam War, the longest of any battalion. Vowell, 41, was an Army brat whose father had been awarded a Silver Star as a company commander in Vietnam, went to college at the University of Alabama, fully intending to become a doctor. But he took a military science class, fell in with ROTC, and realized during an all-night training exercise that leading men in combat was his calling. He typified the experience level common in the Army after nearly a decade of war following the September 11 terror attacks. He had already served in Afghanistan from 2004 to 2005 and in Iraq from 2006 to 2007 during the surge, when he briefed Petraeus at the start of the campaign. He had never forgotten how Petraeus, at the start of the Iraq surge, told his battalion staff that they were there to se-cure the people and win, not just transition to Iraqi forces and race for the exits.

Schooled in Petraeus's counterinsurgency doctrine, Vowell knew that this large-scale air assault, code-named Operation Strong Eagle I, was un-orthodox. Counterinsurgency was all about small footprints, not large of-fensive operations—though some of the latter were needed, as in Kandahar and Helmand. But Vowell had come to realize that the Taliban were a far more formidable force in Kunar Province than anyone had expected. Indeed, Vowell had lost eight soldiers during his first month in Afghanistan in a se-ries of savage attacks and ambushes. The only way he could help build an effective provincial government in Kunar was to clear this valley of what he estimated to be three hundred Taliban fighters. He had told his men to dig in with heavy weaponry because he expected a ferocious assault. He didn't have to wait long.

Within hours after the battalion's troopers assumed their positions, the Taliban opened up with a withering barrage. Vowell's scout platoon leader, Captain Kevin Mott, was shot in the head at his position along the southern mountain. The impact threw him down the mountainside. His platoon fought off a determined series of enemy attacks intended to capture him. Barely conscious, Mott had managed to crawl to a rock outcropping and hun-ker down. Air Force pararescue jumpers were ultimately able to get him out. They also grabbed Mott's radio operator, who had been hit in the body armor that protected his chest. Both were to make full recoveries. The next thirteen hours would be filled with frantic calls for medevacs, artillery, mortars, close air support and resupply.

Vowell had intended to oversee setting the conditions for the battle from a Black Hawk helicopter overhead, directing Apache and Kiowa attack heli-copters, reconnaissance drones and radio-jamming technology. He was planning to land once his soldiers started their push down into the valley. But as the Taliban unleashed simultaneous attacks on his positions, Vowell realized the mountainous terrain was making it impossible for his units to talk to one another. He decided to stay aloft in the Black Hawk in order to maintain full communications. He would return to Asadabad and refuel every two hours for the battle's duration. He desperately wanted to be down on the ground, in the fight. But he knew that if he landed, he would lose control of the bigger picture. His men spent the rest of the day fighting down the mountain and seizing the town. They killed more than 150 insurgents. Vowell lost two sergeants and watched as numerous soldiers were wounded in a battle that raged for hours at maximum intensity in 120-degree heat. It was the No Slack battalion's largest fight since Vietnam: Seven hundred U.S. and Afghan soldiers had assaulted nearly three hundred entrenched Taliban fighters—and won. "Finally, someone has done something good!" Fazlullah Wahidi, the district governor, told Vowell after the smoke had cleared. Nothing like this had happened in Kunar in decades. The Soviets tried but had dozens annihilated in the same valley Vowell's men had just claimed.

Strong Eagle I was the battalion's turning point after losing so many soldiers during its first month. With it, they had regained the initiative and driven the enemy from a key stronghold. Now that they had the momentum, Vowell became convinced that his men should go farther into the Ghaki Valley to the town of Chinar and hunt down remaining insurgents. He convinced Major General Campbell and his brigade commander, Colonel Andrew Poppas, to support Operation Strong Eagle II. The 101st Airborne Division (Air Assault) was well trained and equipped for just this type of full-scale air assault. The division had six dozen Apache gunships and squadrons of Black Hawk and Chinook helicopters that could fly four thousand soldiers more than one hundred miles in six hours. But when the operation launched in the dead of night, the No Slack soldiers encountered nothing but silence. There were no insurgents left to attack them. In talking to locals after the sun rose, Vowell was told over and over that the enemy was gone from the area. He realized he now had a chance to begin successful counterinsurgency operations with villagers, even start reconciliation efforts. Over the coming weeks, twenty insurgent fighters presented themselves to Governor Wahidi and said they were done fighting.

Major General Campbell and his adviser from the Counterinsurgency Advisory and Assistance Team, Doug Ollivant, had briefed Vowell on a strategy they had developed for reinforcing three key district centers with combat outposts. Vowell and Ollivant were friends from the Army's School of Advanced Military Studies. Vowell considered Campbell the best the Army had to offer, a general willing to listen to subordinates and support them with both sage advice and real freedom to command. Even so, Vowell thought this defensive strategy Campbell and Ollivant were pushing was misguided. None of the district centers were under attack, Vowell argued, and putting platoons in each of them would only invite Taliban attacks and send the message that Afghan political autonomy was a fiction. Campbell backed off. But he told Vowell that, having won the point, he almost had to guarantee success. Vowell thought he could pull it off.

Petraeus arrived one late-summer morning at Vowell's command center. He wanted a rundown on Operations Strong Eagle I and II. He stayed for eight hours. Vowell remembered feeling the morale of his men almost palpably surge during the visit. The atmosphere, he said later, was positively charged. It had seemed to Vowell that McChrystal had worked hard to hold U.S. forces back with his constant emphasis on limiting civilian casualties. Petraeus, on the other hand, came in and confirmed Vowell's mantra that the stability component of counterinsurgency operations couldn't begin until the security component had been pursued—i.e., until the Taliban had been cleared and the area was secure, just as had been done in Iraq. Petraeus told Vowell's troops that the Afghan military would eventually take over the mission but needed time to develop, and that Kunar Province would always be contentious. He also said that he enjoyed a positive relationship with the Pakistani military, which Vowell himself had already discovered locally. Vowel and Petraeus visited two district governors and the provincial governor, then traveled to Combat Outpost Monti, where Petraeus pinned medals on those who had distinguished themselves during Operations Strong Eagle I and II. He also knew the names of all nine soldiers in A Company who had been killed during No Slack's first six weeks in Afghanistan. He gathered the company in an orange grove on the base and told them how proud of them he was. It was clear from their eyes that the men were still hurting; Petraeus had come at the right time.

THE FINAL BRIGADE FROM the 101st Airborne, its 4th Brigade Combat Team, arrived in Afghanistan in late summer 2010. The Currahees assumed bases and outposts along the Pakistan border in mountainous Paktika Province, about 100 miles south of Kabul. Two provinces and about 150 miles separated the Currahees in Paktika from the Bastogne Brigade in Vowell's battalion, in Kunar Province to the northeast. The largest combat operations had been concentrated in Kandahar and Helmand provinces, in the south. Petraeus had been worried about the situation in these mountainous provinces along the Pakistan border from the moment he set foot in Kabul. "The challenges from the sanctuaries in a neighboring country are a bit more concerning than even I had thought at Central Command," he observed that summer.

In the dead of night on October 30, at a desolate six-man observation post in Paktika Province, James Platt, a private first class in the 2nd Battalion of the 4th Brigade Combat Team, reported to his sergeant, Donald Starks: "I see movement." Within moments, they were under attack from three sides by thirty insurgents, so close the Americans could hear them talking. The attackers briefly commandeered the Americans' MRAP and knew enough about it to shine one of the vehicle's spotlights on them. Starks led a counterattack, firing on the insurgents with a machine gun, rendering the MRAP unusable and blowing up his own ammunition dump with a hand grenade. He soon realized that two of his men were wounded and he broke contact with the enemy, leading his men 500 meters back down the mountain to the main base, Combat Outpost Margah, firing and calling in "danger-close" indirect fire on the enemy as they scrambled down the rocks.

Margah itself was now under fierce attack. One hundred and twenty insurgents from Arab countries and Chechnya and fighters from the brutal Haqqani network of Afghan and Pakistani insurgents opened fire on the sixty Americans and their Afghan National Army partners at the outpost with machine guns, rocket-propelled grenades and mortars. "We had multiple indicators an attack like this was going to happen in that area in an attempt to gain victory before the end of the fighting season, and our combined Afghan and coalition forces were ready for them," Campbell later related. Around Margah, there were four separate "direct-fire and attack-helicopter-engagement areas" established in locations where the insurgents had surrounded the outpost's perimeter, hoping to breach the wire. Campbell later reported that more than ninety insurgents lay dead on the battlefield when the fighting was over, along with two wounded attackers, who were evacuated for medical care. "To put it bluntly . . . the insurgents failed miserably," Campbell assessed, crediting artillery support, attack aviation, Air Force aircraft and "the dogged determination of soldiers in a fight."

Campbell went to Combat Outpost Margah on Veterans Day with Petraeus, who pinned the Silver Star medal on Sergeant Starks, the fire-team leader for C Company, 2nd Battalion, 4th Brigade Combat Team. "Starks was like just about all our true heroes, characteristically humble and full of praise for his buddies, while noting that he was just doing what they'd have done—and did do, in some cases—for him," Petraeus said later. "A wonderful American. What a night they had!"

CHAPTER 5

ANACONDA

With U.S. forces turning the tide on the dangerous terrain in Kandahar Province's Arghandab, Zhari and Panjwai districts, in late September Petraeus suddenly faced a new assault from Washington. Bob Woodward's latest book, *Obama's Wars,* had sent shock waves to Kabul. An officer in Petraeus's internal think tank, the Commander's Initiatives Group, fired off an e-mail to its members, alerting the team to a story in the *Washington Post* that summarized the book's details. "There are," the officer wrote, "a few quotations in this article, previewing Woodward's book, that are somewhat 'rollingstone-esque'—touching on several officials, and the Boss is mentioned here a few times," he relayed, making a clear reference to the *Rolling Stone* article that had toppled McChrystal. He mentioned one that jumped out: "During a flight in May, after a glass of wine, Petraeus told his own staffers that the administration was 'fucking with the wrong guy.'"

The heart of Woodward's book was a detailed look at the Obama administration's lengthy strategic review of Afghanistan and Pakistan policy that took place throughout the fall of 2009, with McChrystal commanding the war in Afghanistan and Petraeus, his boss, heading the military's powerful Central Command, based in Tampa. Obama wanted alternatives to endless, costly war and nation building in Afghanistan. Vice President Biden advocated a strategy he called "counterterrorism plus" that would have focused mainly on hunting down al-Qaeda's leaders in Pakistan and Afghanistan, as opposed to far more extensive counterinsurgency operations.

Woodward chronicles the administration's frustration over what he described as seeming resistance by top military leaders—McChrystal, Petraeus and Admiral Michael G. Mullen, chairman of the Joint Chiefs of Staff, all supported by Defense secretary Gates—to present anything other than plans calling for 40,000 to 80,000 more troops to implement a robust counterinsurgency strategy. Moreover, at every turn that fall, according to Woodward, the military had sought to limit Obama's options. In turn, Petraeus, McChrystal and Mullen felt they were simply urging enough troops to defeat al-Qaeda and the Taliban. "Does the president want to win or lose?" they reportedly asked each other, believing they were forthrightly laying out what was required to achieve the objectives established by the president—and ultimately convincing the president they were right.

Obama had, after all, campaigned on ending the Iraq War and concentrating on Afghanistan, which he described as the neglected conflict that should have been the nation's priority all along. Upon taking office in early 2009, Obama gave Bruce Riedel, a respected former CIA analyst who had worked on his campaign, sixty days to produce a strategy for Afghanistan and Pakistan. Obama embraced Riedel's recommendations and ordered the deployment of the 17,000 additional troops that had been requested by the commander in Afghanistan, General David McKiernan. "These soldiers and Marines will take the fight to the Taliban in the south and the east and give us a greater capacity to partner with Afghan security forces and to go after insurgents along the border," the president announced in March 2009. An additional 4,000 troops, Obama said, would also go to Afghanistan to train Afghan security forces. "There is an uncompromising core of the Taliban," the president said. "They must be met with force, and they must be defeated." There were, at the time, only 38,350 U.S. troops in Afghanistan. This was far below the troop-to-civilian ratio that the *Counterinsurgency Field Manual* stated was necessary for a successful counterinsurgency campaign—which would have required some 450,000 coalition and Afghan troops for the thirty million Afghans, though Petraeus would routinely note that not all areas needed anywhere near such densities. The insurgency was most serious in about half of Afghanistan, with pockets in the rest. There would never, it was clear, be that many troops, but commanders were mindful of the doctrine when they developed recommendations for force levels.

Less than two months after the new strategy and deployments were announced, Gates fired McKiernan, on the job not quite a year, and replaced him with McChrystal, the vaunted former commander of the Joint Special Operations Command who was then serving as Mullen's trusted deputy, as director of the Joint Staff at the Pentagon. Gates and Mullen felt strongly that McKiernan needed to be replaced with a new leader. Petraeus concurred, and they all had the utmost confidence in McChrystal, who had led JSOC forces in executing devastating counterterrorist operations in Iraq and Afghanistan for more than five years.

At his confirmation hearing on June 2, 2009, before the Senate Armed Services Committee, McChrystal observed that the key resource was people, and he noted that the 21,000 additional troops would all be on the ground by October. "You might properly ask if that is enough," McChrystal observed. "I don't know. It may be some time before I do." Jim Jones, a former Marine general serving as Obama's national security adviser, was miffed that McChrystal already seemed to be asking for more troops. But Jones and Obama agreed to Gates's recommendation that the Pentagon give McChrystal sixty days to conduct his own assessment of conditions on the ground.

Meanwhile, in mid-July, Jones sent the Pentagon a long-awaited Strategic Implementation Plan that defined the terms of the Riedel strategy and mapped out a series of metrics for measuring success in Afghanistan. The document preceded the review and guided McChrystal's implementation of the new strategy based on the Riedel review; it also provided guidance that would aid in his assessment. Jones had accepted a suggestion from Gates that the document should state that the goal was to "defeat" the Taliban, although the original White House draft had merely said "disrupt." The distinction was enormous to Mullen, Petraeus and McChrystal. As McChrystal later noted in an interview, he had not planned on asking for more troops when he began his assessment. But he quickly found that conditions in Afghanistan were far worse than he had anticipated, and as he dug into Jones's Strategic Implementation Plan document, he began to wrestle with what it would take to *defeat* the Taliban. It was clear to him early on that he didn't have nearly the forces needed to accomplish that task.

Over the course of the summer and into the fall, McChrystal assessed the situation on the ground and then worked on calculating how many brigades he would need to clear pieces of key terrain and how fast new Afghan troops could reasonably be made ready. He came to the conclusion that at least another 40,000 U.S. troops—in addition to the 21,000 already committed by Obama—would be needed, and that was still with a significant level of risk. In fact, more forces would be desirable if the president wanted to reduce the level of risk to mission accomplishment. "We were trying just to be as clear as we could on what we absolutely believed was the best military advice, which we owed the POTUS," McChrystal later recalled. But in hindsight, he acknowledged that his recommendation quickly "became more political than I expected. So we were kind of playing catch-up in appreciating that."

Meanwhile, Petraeus, Mullen and McChrystal and their staffs continued to carefully review the Strategic Implementation Plan. "There was the real work to determine what the new policy statement meant in operational terms," Petraeus later noted. "We got it, started tearing it apart and studying it, and it looked pretty good." What they didn't realize at the time was that some key aides in the White House apparently weren't aware that Jones had issued the Strategic Implementation Plan that called for "defeating" the Taliban. As a planner who supported Petraeus later observed, "All we were repeating during the subsequent policy review was what was in the promulgating order, and yet we didn't initially realize they were going to completely re-look the whole thing." In fact, at the time they received the order, planners at Central Command and in Afghanistan were not initially anticipating a full-fledged White House review of Afghan policy that would consume the entire fall.

During the subsequent policy review process, Petraeus quickly realized how politically charged McChrystal's request for 40,000 additional troops was becoming, and how divided the White House and Obama's national security team were over the appropriate course of action in Afghanistan. Before the process had begun, Petraeus had made his view clear in an interview with columnist Michael Gerson, whose piece appeared in early September in the *Washington Post*. Repeating what Mullen had stated in an open hearing on Capitol Hill the day prior to his interview, Petraeus told Gerson that accomplishing the objectives that had been established would require a "fully resourced, comprehensive counterinsurgency campaign." Continuing, he noted, with characteristic nuance, "I don't think anyone can guarantee that it will work out even if we apply a lot more resources. But it won't work if we don't.... [T]he Taliban have sanctuaries in Afghanistan. You can't take out sanctuaries with Predator strikes. We have to regain the initiative. We have to get ahead of this, to arrest the downward spiral, to [regain the] momentum."

The column reportedly angered White House aides who felt Petraeus was "prejudging a presidential decision," even though he was merely restating what Mullen had told the Senate Armed Services Committee the day before his interview, when the chairman stated that he supported "a properly resourced, classically pursued counterinsurgency effort"—and noted that that "probably means more forces." The rift between Petraeus, McChrystal, Mullen and Gates and a White House contingent led by Vice President Biden, who favored a narrower counterterrorist strategy, would only grow as the fall progressed.

Less than a week later, Woodward broke the story of McChrystal's classified assessment of the conditions in Afghanistan on the front page of the *Washington Post*, noting that the general had concluded that the United States' military effort in Afghanistan would fail without a significant troop buildup—though he had yet to finalize the numbers of additional forces needed. The leak ratcheted up the pressure on the White House to act. The final straw came when McChrystal, having been cautioned ahead of time, gave a speech in London on October 1 in which he insisted that only his counterinsurgency program could bring about success in Afghanistan. The White House wasn't pleased. But McChrystal, Petraeus and Mullen ultimately stood by the request for 40,000 more troops as the only way to make progress in Afghanistan. They saw this as providing forthright military advice, but all recognized that public statements early on, before they understood the implications of the policy review, had created tension between those in the White House and those in uniform. Petraeus and Mullen took key lessons from the experience and would apply them in the review of the situation in Afghanistan in December 2010 and then in June 2011, during the preparation for discussions over the pace of the drawdown of the surge forces.

Throughout the fall policy review, the military leaders had the support of Gates and Secretary of State Hillary Clinton. Clinton's views drew, in part, from her long-standing professional friendship with retired general Jack Keane that began when she was a senator from New York and Keane was vice chief of staff of the Army. Keane, who had also been an important advocate for the surge in Iraq, believed strongly that a robust and comprehensive counterinsurgency approach in Afghanistan was the only way to assure success, and Clinton was persuaded by McChrystal and Petraeus's logic.

But even with Gates and Clinton behind McChrystal, Petraeus and Mullen, Biden and some other key members of the White House staff resented what they felt was an unrelenting push for more troops. The group reportedly included Rahm Emanuel, Obama's chief of staff; David Axelrod, a senior adviser and key campaign strategist; Denis McDonough, a campaign adviser who became chief of the National Security Council staff; Tom Donilon, deputy national security adviser, who was close to Biden and had also worked on the campaign; and Doug Lute, a retired Army lieutenant general who served as senior adviser and the NSC's coordinator for Afghanistan-Pakistan policy. Lute, Petraeus and McChrystal had all attended West Point at the same time. Petraeus graduated in 1974, Lute in 1975 and McChrystal in 1976. Lute had overseen combat operations in Iraq and Afghanistan as director of operations for Central Command from 2004 to 2006, and he later joined the Bush White House as the so-called war czar during the surge in Iraq. He was reportedly not enthusiastic about the troop demands being jointly pressed by the military and Gates, who remained resolute about the need for more forces. Meanwhile, the Joint Chiefs' vice chairman, General James "Hoss"

Cartwright, resisted the call by McChrystal and Petraeus for 40,000 more troops. Cartwright wanted to develop a "hybrid option" that required only 20,000 additional troops. His plan, similar to that favored by Biden, was a more limited mission of hunting down the Taliban insurgents and training the Afghan police and army to take over. Mullen was furious when Cartwright presented the option during a meeting that Mullen missed due to travel, noting that no other serious military figure believed such an option was the least bit feasible for achieving the objectives in the current strategy document. In fact, a Mullen-hosted war game had shown that approach to be inadequate.

Like McChrystal and Mullen, Petraeus argued that he was merely recommending a force level needed to protect the nation's strategic interests—and achieve the president's stated objectives. "We truly didn't try to box them in," he told a friend a year later in his office at ISAF headquarters in Kabul. "I was disappointed when folks thought that. Yeah, we were all in league; we supported what we thought was the militarily sensible approach. It was an interesting period. Folks say we didn't give them options. We gave them options. We gave an eighty-thousand option, a sixty-thousand option, and a forty-thousand option, and we provided associated levels of risk to accomplish the mission for each option. And we said that below forty thousand you can't accomplish the mission. You couldn't do it with twenty thousand, so there was no way we could recommend something like that."

Obama ultimately agreed to 30,000 additional troops, with an additional 10 percent authorization for Gates, should that be needed for critical unanticipated requirements, and with a pledge to ensure generation of the rest of the needed 40,000 from other troop-contributing nations. But he also then insisted that Mullen, Petraeus, McChrystal and Gates agree to a secret six-page "terms sheet" that stated: "This approach is not fully resourced counterinsurgency or nation building, but a narrower approach tied more tightly to the core goal of disrupting, dismantling and eventually defeating al Qaeda and preventing al Qaeda's return to safe havens in Afghanistan or Pakistan." Gates and the military had not only seen the terms before they were asked to agree to them; they had provided input to those from the Pentagon who were helping the White House craft them. What Obama personally added at the last minute, Pentagon officials later shared, was the provision that a drawdown of forces would begin in July 2011. "As we learned in the Oval Office on Sunday evening the night before the policy was to be announced, it was take it or leave it," one participant later told an assistant. Gates, Mullen, Petraeus, McChrystal and the others "took it."

Obama announced the outcome of the review in a speech at West Point on December 1, 2009. In a huge auditorium filled with cadets in simple gray uniforms, Petraeus looked up from the front row alongside Mullen, Gates, Clinton and retired Army general Eric Shinseki, the secretary of Veterans Affairs. The president explained his decision: "As commander in chief, I have determined that it is in our vital national interest to send an additional thirty thousand U.S. troops to Afghanistan. After eighteen months, our troops will begin to come home. These are the resources that we need to seize the initiative, while building the Afghan capacity that can allow for a responsible transition of our forces out of Afghanistan."

Petraeus had flown to West Point with the president on *Air Force One*. It was the most time the two had spent together in such an informal environment. The president had requested that Petraeus travel with him, so Petraeus flew back to Washington from Tampa on short notice for the second time in two days. The show of solidarity was important, and it meant a great deal to Petraeus. Still, key members of the White House staff remained wary of Petraeus's stature and motives. In the fall of 2009, in fact, he and others involved in the review process reportedly had been warned by the White House not to speak to the press about the review, guidance he followed so diligently that journalist Thomas Ricks described one of Petraeus's presentations that fall as "Dave Does Dull." (Petraeus noted to his public affairs officer that it had taken great skill to be dull in such a charged atmosphere.)

There were other tensions, too. In early May 2010, Petraeus had been quoted in a story by the Associated Press as saying that Faisal Shahzad, who had attempted to detonate a bomb in New York's Times Square, was a "lone wolf." The AP's story made it appear as though he were contradicting statements by others in the Obama administration that Shahzad had been trained by the Pakistani Taliban. He had been misquoted, and the AP later put out a corrected version quoting him as saying that Shahzad was a lone wolf *who was inspired by militants in Pakistan but didn't necessarily have contact with them.* But the damage was done. Petraeus asked his spokesman, Colonel Erik Gunhus, to draft a short press release to correct the misimpression and directed Gunhus to inform the White House. But Gunhus was told by the White House not to issue the release and to let the matter blow over. It came up a few days later, when Petraeus and his staff were on a plane together. The general joined Gunhus and other officers in the rear cabin and had a rare glass of wine during the flight. "As the plane roared to its next destination," Woodward later wrote, "Gunhus noted that the White House still had a tendency to leave Petraeus twisting in the wind. 'They knock you down every chance they get,' Gunhus said. 'They're fucking with the wrong guy,' Petraeus responded."

There were eight people on the plane with Petraeus that day. One of them was Woodward's source. Petraeus later expressed his displeasure to all of them for betraying his confidence. He later surmised, with disappointment, that it was a field-grade officer on the trip who had been a loyal adviser for nearly five years. But Petraeus knew that he was ultimately responsible for making the intemperate remark, even if he assumed he was making it in private. When the comment turned up in Woodward's book, Petraeus—known for his accessibility and skillful press relations—felt himself pulling back. As he counseled subordinates in subsequent talks on leadership, someone is always watching. As had long ago become clear to him, very little was private in his life anymore. The scrutiny was enormous, and Petraeus tightened the mask of command further.

A long line of critics, including Woodward, had also remarked on Petraeus's "endless campaign of self-promotion." This has been a common refrain of those inside the military who viewed Petraeus with suspicion, or envy. He had become a target of such criticism earlier in his career because of his repeated assignments as an aide to powerful four-star generals—Galvin, Vuono and, from 1997 to 1999, General Hugh Shelton, chairman of the

Joint Chiefs. What few acknowledged was that four-star generals hired aides for their ability, not their political skills. Even detractors generally conceded that Petraeus's ability was off the charts.

Meanwhile, Petraeus's relationship with the president, beginning with the West Point trip, had markedly changed by the fall of 2010. The infighting between Obama's generals and his White House aides the previous fall, Petraeus thought, had been overtaken by events. Three months into his own command in Afghanistan, Petraeus was confident that Obama would not have picked him to replace McChrystal if he hadn't trusted him. It was inconceivable to Petraeus that Obama would pick someone regarded as an "outsider" to take charge of the most important national security initiative of his presidency. "If you're going to fire one guy, you better get another guy in there in whom people have confidence," Petraeus later said to a confidant. Though he'd have less direct contact with Obama than he did with Bush during the Iraq War, Petraeus had access and was now Obama's guy.

By September 2010, there were already indications coming out of the Obama White House that there had been a "mind meld" between the president and his most famous general. Petraeus thought he and his staff had been as loyal to the White House as was possible. He and his team had made a lot of sacrifices to assume command of the war on a moment's notice. He felt a deep sense of disappointment when he was told that there were some on the White House staff who doubted his loyalty to Obama. The battle with the rest of the White House would have to remain just under the surface.

PETRAEUS NOW COMMANDED the surge he, McChrystal, Mullen and Gates had argued for the previous fall. While he counseled caution in his morning stand-ups at ISAF headquarters and told the dozens of officers gathered for the morning briefing that progress would be slow in coming, his own approach was anything but cautious. He found ways to augment units with civilian intelligence personnel that would not count against formal troop ceilings. He "amped up" Special Operations night raids aimed at Taliban leaders, pushed hard to create Afghan Local Police across the country and carefully monitored conventional forces as they moved into the "hold and build" phases of counterinsurgency after their hard summer of fighting.

But Petraeus found Afghanistan, in some ways, more complex than Iraq, though the levels of violence were certainly far less. "Afghanistan is so dynamic at the moment that it is actually very difficult to track everything going on—and it is almost impossible to track if you are looking in from the outside," he observed to a friend at the time. "The fact is that in Iraq we had more forces, a smaller population to secure, and easier terrain than we are faced with in Afghanistan. Afghanistan has many more challenges than Iraq, although there is not the colossal level of violence that we faced in Iraq. Even in Iraq, it took us months to see progress, prove progress and then solidify the progress. What does this tell us about Afghanistan? Progress will take time."

Afghanistan was also a rural insurgency, as opposed to the urban insurgency in Iraq, and many inside the Beltway did not understand that the operation required a different approach. The decentralized nature of the government and the disconnect between officials in Kabul and people in the rural areas—more than 75 percent of the population—made every effort more challenging. Though Petraeus pushed for troops to implement all lines of effort—security, governance and development—security was obviously the first priority. It was difficult to build roads, repair mosques, open medical clinics and schools and foster economic development in areas still filled with Taliban, or where the villagers favored the insurgents over either the occupying force or corrupt, inept government officials.

In counterinsurgency doctrine, governance and development follow security gains, but troops should be setting the conditions for those activities within the concept of an increased security presence. Petraeus pursued progress on all fronts: attacking top- and midlevel Taliban commanders with Special Forces, cleaning out Taliban safe havens with conventional forces, developing the Afghan military and police, working with civilian partners to build the capability of the Afghan government, reconciling with Taliban elements tired of fighting and supporting Afghan initiatives to reintegrate those willing to switch sides. "All of this will accumulate over time," he told his staff. "Over time, imperceptibly, we will see improvement—but it will be like watching grass grow."

He'd honed this ability to attack multiple fronts most notably during his first assignment in a chaotic foreign capital, Port-au-Prince, Haiti.

WHEN HE LEFT THE 101st Airborne in mid-1994, after a year as the division's operations officer, Petraeus requested to spend his War College year as a fellow at Georgetown University. Shortly after he began the fellowship, the Clinton administration precipitated a showdown with General Raoul Cédras, the military strongman in Haiti, and forced his departure, deploying 20,000 U.S. troops to oversee the reinstallation of Jean-Bertrand Aristide, the elected president who had been overthrown by the military junta. Over the course of the fall and winter, the United States planned to reduce its contribution and build up forces from other countries to enable handing off the mission to a UN force of 6,000 military and more than 300 civilians.

Petraeus, not coincidentally, picked Haiti as his research topic at Georgetown, looking to get involved helping the National Security Council staff in this diplomatic and military initiative. He soon accompanied deputy secretary of State Strobe Talbott to a five-hour White House deputies meeting on the situation in Haiti, which he found very stimulating. When he bumped into a colonel he'd known on Vuono's staff who was looking for a few good officers to help set up and run the new UN task force, Petraeus jumped at the chance. He had, in fact, sought the fellowship in part to be able to deploy if the opportunity arose. When the UN force commander relieved his operations chief, Petraeus was selected for that critical position.

He landed in Port-au-Prince in February, sixty days before the UN was scheduled to take over, and he helped build the task force from scratch. There was no headquarters. There were no procedures. Petraeus had very little help and slept most nights of his four-month deployment on a cot stored behind the projector screen in a briefing room. When he finally heard he'd been given a permanent headquarters for the task force, he visited the facility and found it lacking. "For starters, there was no roof and there was no floor, also no communications, furniture or electricity," he later observed drily. Fortunately, he had just finished running a combat division ten times larger than the UN task force. His growing team had the operations center up and running by the time the UN assumed the mission.

Though he didn't know it at the time, setting up the task force, planning and directing operations, helping to train Haitian police and overseeing improvements to the Haitian judicial and prison systems served as a primer for a similar challenge he would face on his second tour in Iraq, when he had to create a new command to recruit, train, equip, advise and build infrastructure for the Iraqi military and police.

In Haiti, sleeping on his cot, running in the morning with Motorola radios in both hands, Petraeus immediately impressed his bosses and colleagues with his capacity for work and his ability to move back and forth between international diplomacy, security operations, nation building and infrastructure repairs. In mid-February, one week after arriving, he briefed Aristide, Deputy Secretary Talbott and other senior officials from the Clinton administration on the UN force's structure. Ten days later, after updating Aristide on conditions across the country, he jumped in his Toyota 4Runner and drove out to Port-au-Prince's main prison, where inmates were rioting and burning everything in sight. Petraeus and a group of military police galvanized the Haitian guards and regained control of the facility. Digging into the situation later, he discovered that many of the prisoners were still being detained after serving their full terms. He thought of them as "the people who time forgot." He and his team set out to help the Haitians regain control and improve conditions in the jail.

Petraeus realized that the task force's soldiers would need clear rules of engagement about intervening in Haitian-on-Haitian violence, remembering an earlier episode when U.S. forces—lacking such rules—stood by and watched as a riot erupted and Haitians killed each other. A document Petraeus wrote setting forth the rules of engagement, dated March 31, 1995, foreshadows the counterinsurgency guidance he would issue shortly after his arrival in Kabul. The list of nine bullet points began: "1. Treat all persons with dignity and respect."

While there was no insurgency in Haiti, there might well have been. Criminals robbed, terrorized and killed their countrymen. To respond, Petraeus recommended to the force commander that units base their troops out among the remote villages, which was a significant change to the previous U.S. practice of deploying conventional forces only in the country's two biggest cities.

In peacekeeping, as in counterinsurgency, Petraeus saw the people as the center of gravity. He worked closely with civilian aid groups, attempted to build up the Haitian police, staged raids to arrest fugitive leaders of paramilitary groups and started committing U.S. funds for desperately needed capital improvement projects. He also helped organize the voter registration process, a pillar of nation building. After he was told in a briefing that the process was ready to begin in five days, he visited a warehouse where registration supplies were being assembled and found "sheer chaos." He went to the U.S. helicopter battalion and asked if he could clear out its hangar so that the team could spread the election materials out on the floor. It was raining hard every afternoon during that season, and there was no other place to do it. The pilots moved their birds. Petraeus and the team helped move and organize the materials and then supported their movement to sites throughout Haiti. Registration was completed on schedule.

"Haiti was a great civil-military experience, a wonderful learning experience in terms of what nation building is all about, especially in a country that was one of the three poorest in the world at that time," Petraeus later reflected. He also noted that serving in an international coalition was an invaluable experience. The largest international coalition (in terms of countries) ever assembled awaited him in Kabul. "It's very easy in these kinds of missions, where the U.S. is so dominant, just to dominate, and yet that isn't the right course," he observed. "It's about keeping everybody with you. It's about making sure that the Nepalese battalion is as satisfied as the United States contingent."

His Haiti experience would prepare him well for many aspects of Bosnia, Iraq and Afghanistan. Yet while the country resembled a war zone, it hadn't counted as a combat tour. He would have to wait eight more years for a combat patch on his right shoulder.

His next assignment awaited upon his return to the United States in June 1995: command of the 1st Brigade of the 82nd Airborne Division at Fort Bragg, North Carolina. Only the best and the brightest—those officers with the potential to make general—became combat brigade commanders in the Army. Petraeus would be replacing another star, Colonel John Abizaid. He couldn't take command soon enough.

While both men shared superb reputations and similar beliefs about the Army's need to prevail in low-intensity conflicts and counterinsurgencies, their styles were strikingly different. Abizaid was loose and more laid-back. Petraeus was intense, competitive and highly structured. While Abizaid was happy to relax over a beer with his men after a maneuver, Petraeus wanted to conduct an after-action review—and then challenge everyone to a run— and then have a beer.

As an outsider who had never served in the 82nd before, Petraeus faced jealousy from some of his peers there—and elsewhere in the Army—who had served in combat in Panama or the Gulf with the division.

Petraeus's battalion commanders were aware of his intense competitive streak and his preference for a "systems approach." But at Bragg, Petraeus demonstrated that he'd learned to build a team rather than compete with the team. Five of his six infantry battalion commanders would become general officers, one would earn two stars (currently commanding the 82nd Airborne Division), two of them would become three-star generals, and another would earn four stars. All would serve in Iraq with Petraeus.

Commanding the "Devil Brigade," Petraeus's command and leadership style flowered, according to Lieutenant Colonel Kevin Petit, one of the brigade's company commanders at the time. He remembers Petraeus's first meeting with all field-grade officers. "He held it in the chapel in Fort Bragg," said Petit, who now refers to Petraeus as "Doc" in honor of his Ph.D. "Doc, I learned, never misses an opportunity to layer messages, both verbal and nonverbal. He proceeded to give his command philosophy, what was important to him. He began to question us tactically: 'What is the maximum effective range of the machine gun?' 'What are the three types of defensive wire?' It was a message that this was a level he wanted us to study. It is the paradox of rank that platoon leaders talk strategy and colonels and generals talk squads/platoons. So he established that this was the level at which we were expected to be experts."

Petraeus also established a new convention for training at the time. He felt live-fire exercises were too scripted. "I want to tell you about what I call Walk and Shoot University," Petraeus told his brigade's officers. "Army troopers do not have the skills we need to manage unscripted scenarios employing live fires, much less on a real-world deployment." The typical exercise that employed mortars and artillery, as well as attack helicopters and close air support, was highly prescribed and was of limited training value.

Petraeus set out to change that. As Petit recalled, "We cleared into the impact area lanes in which we would walk and call live fire on objectives around us and in front of us, a huge departure from the very static, linear training we had done previously," recalled Petit. "We responded in part because we broke rules to do it and we felt we were 'special' and clearly training with realism that no one else had to date." Petraeus had actually gotten the required waivers, but no unit had done so in such an aggressive manner before.

Petraeus's focus on tactical expertise to outthink the enemy surfaced again in brigade command. The Joint Readiness Training Center, the Army's light-infantry training grounds, which Keane had done so much to develop, included a scenario not unlike the urban warfare Petraeus would later see in Iraq—with civilian role players, suicide bombers and IEDs.

In the scenario, when Petraeus's units came upon the enemy, the so-called opposing force, on the outskirts of the city, they were unprepared and asleep. The town's defenses were not complete, and some of the enemy were still installing wire and pickets and barriers. The opposing force, Petraeus correctly deduced, had made a timeline of their own, based upon an 0500 attack, which Petraeus's brigade had published. "Sir, you had me fooled right up to the moment I was crossing the wire into the objective," Petit recalled. Petraeus looked at him and replied, "We defined the rules, then when the enemy defined their rules, we just changed ours." Petit found it unprecedented that he would pull one over on the enemy—and his own troops—to create favorable conditions for the team to win. "You and the Devils continue to do better than I've ever seen it done," e-mailed Brigadier General John Vines, the 82nd's assistant division commander for operations in March 1997.

After two years in command of the brigade, Petraeus headed up the East Coast yet again, for another tour at the Pentagon. This time it was General Hugh Shelton, chairman of the Joint Chiefs of Staff, requesting that Petraeus serve as his personal executive assistant. Petraeus had already seen the way the Pentagon functioned through the eyes of General Vuono, a service chief. Now he would come to understand the building from the all-important "joint" vantage point, in which all four military services worked, planned supported operations together—and, sometimes, fought with each other.

Working for Shelton, Petraeus gained exposure to civil-military relations at the highest levels. He had a superb vantage point from which to view the workings of the Clinton administration, the National Security Council and senior decision making. Petraeus also interacted daily with counterparts in the secretary of Defense's office, on the National Security Council staff, and at the State Department. Given Shelton's background as the commander of the Special Operations Command, Petraeus learned at the foot of a boss who thought about the balance between conventional and Special Operations Forces in a different way than the infantry officers with whom Petraeus had previously served. Contingency operations during his time with Shelton included the Iraq no-fly zones (northern and southern), the peacekeeping operation and war criminal hunt in Bosnia, counterterrorist operations focused on Osama bin Laden, kinetic strikes in Iraq after Saddam Hussein thumbed his nose at the international community and, in Shelton's second year, the Kosovo Air Campaign.

Petraeus then headed back to Fort Bragg to pin on his first star and serve as the 82nd's assistant division commander for operations. During a year full of training and contingency deployments, the 82nd would also send Petraeus to join the "general-of-the-month club" in Kuwait, where he led the Combined Joint Task Force–Kuwait (Operation Desert Spring)—a rotating contingent of three thousand soldiers in place for a month with the mission of deterring Saddam Hussein, assuring regional allies and supporting U.S. combined forces operations in theater.

Petraeus's last tour at Fort Bragg was as chief of staff for the XVIII Airborne Corps, the 82nd's parent organization. On the side, he enjoyed his addiction—skydiving with the Golden Knights, the Army's parachute team and other skydivers, until disaster struck: Petraeus's parachute lost air on a late turn and he crashed to the ground, leaving him with a fractured pelvis. Fortunately for Petraeus, his boss, Lieutenant General Dan McNeill, allowed him to work from home. McNeill knew Petraeus's capabilities and fitness, having had Petraeus as his assistant division commander when McNeill commanded the 82nd Airborne, and he was not about to lose him.

Petraeus asked the doctors to allow him to go swimming to speed his recovery and maintain a level of fitness. "No, absolutely not," replied his physician. "You'll displace your pelvis; you know you're just held together with screws and plates that need to solidify." Petraeus strapped a pull buoy between his legs and got in the pool anyhow. Keane, by now the Army's vice chief of staff, warned him against any more free-falling parachuting. "You give me a division and I'll stop skydiving," Petraeus half-joked. He would give up free-fall skydiving, but within nine months he was back to running and static-line parachuting, as well as simulated free fall in Fort Bragg's wind tunnel.

Near the end of his tour as corps chief of staff, in the late spring of 2001, Petraeus was the corps's representative at a conference hosted by the Army's John F. Kennedy Special Warfare Center at Fort Bragg. The question the conference addressed was whether Army Green Berets should continue to emphasize training of and working with host-nation forces or instead focus more on kinetic tasks like targeted raids. The events of 9/11 would put an end to the debate. Within months of the conference, the Green Berets would be very much back in business with the tasks that had long been their forte, including riding horses into combat in northern Afghanistan.

The debate prompted Petraeus to think hard about his upcoming deployment to Bosnia, where he would work extensively with various types of Special Operations Forces. The experience served him well later in Iraq—and Afghanistan.

THE NIGHT RAIDS IN Afghanistan during the fall of 2010 were largely the domain of the Joint Special Operations Command—and much more sophisticated than those Petraeus had participated in back in Bosnia. Petraeus had picked up the playbook for these operations from McChrystal, a Special Operations legend who had served as Petraeus's JSOC commander in Iraq during the surge in 2007.

In his morning briefings, Petraeus repeatedly stressed the performance of Special Operations Forces and their mandate to kill and capture Taliban leaders in night raids predicated on pinpoint intelligence—often communications intercepts, but also intelligence from human sources and imagery from unmanned aerial vehicles and tower-mounted optics. "Today's report on our nighttime raids again underscores that we must properly recognize the extraordinary courage of our small units and individual troopers who go out night after night into harm's way," he said in a stand-up in late September. "These operations are having a critical effect and must not be seen as 'just another day at the office.' This is extraordinary work which must be recognized appropriately." Special Operations Forces were devastating the insurgent networks, and Petraeus wanted their work to spread. They were a key component in expanding the security bubbles in much of the country.

A ninety-day summary that coincided roughly with Petraeus's first three months in command broke down the "accumulated effects" of Special Operations Forces into two categories, "kinetic" and "non-kinetic." There were 2,795 "kinetic" operations that resulted in the death or capture of 285 high-value insurgent leaders. An additional 889 insurgents were killed, and 2,084 midlevel insurgents were captured. On the "non-kinetic" side, Special Operations Forces carried out 1,823 population-centric operations.

The night raid operations were largely the business of secret "black" Special Operations Forces. Army Delta Force commandos and select Navy SEALs and Army Rangers are specially trained to capture high-value targets with great precision under the most difficult circumstances, including entrance to heavily guarded compounds.

Night raids in Afghanistan relied on tactical intelligence used to identify insurgent leaders and their precise locations. The National Security Agency and other units engaged in intercepting cell-phone, radio and Internet communications had made enormous strides since 9/11 in the speed with which they could process communications, determine exact locations and deliver data to Special Operations Forces. The proliferation of unmanned aerial vehicles with sophisticated optics provided real-time full-motion video, and human sources and other forms of intelligence provided important information as well. In some cases, night raids could now be planned and executed in a matter of minutes. In others, the intelligence picture would come together more slowly and required days, or even weeks, of careful surveillance, matched against signals intercepts, imagery and human intelligence. Virtually all the U.S. special-mission-unit night raids carried out on Petraeus's watch—about three hundred a month—were conducted in partnership with Afghan special-mission elements, highly trained and superbly equipped. Commanders at the Special Operations center at Bagram Air Base typically watched the raids in real time through various video feeds, including infrared video streamed by intelligence drones.

Night raids proved highly effective in eliminating mid- and high-level Taliban leaders, who seemed incapable of staying off the communications grid for long. They also became a significant source of intelligence, since most of the targets of these "kinetic" raids were captured without a single shot fired, so that they could be interrogated and, in some cases, turned. Yet some Afghan citizens despised the night raids, because it was terrifying to have American and Afghan commandos breaking down the doors of neighbors' houses in the dead of night. In certain cases, until Petraeus directed changes to the conduct of the raids, men were carted off in handcuffs without any explanation to the locals at all. On occasion, when the raids went wrong and Special Operations Forces found themselves under attack, innocent civilians were caught in the crossfire and killed.

To mitigate these effects, district governors were informed of and even invited to accompany the SOF elements on operations as often as was possible. The missions often began with helicopter insertions, leaving troops to walk the final leg—anywhere from half a mile to five or even ten miles—to their targets. The raids could go one of two ways: The Afghan special operators would do "callouts" in an attempt to get the insurgent out on the street so they didn't have to do a forced entry, or the forces could enter a compound by either blowing off the door or knocking it down. In each case, ISAF paid for damage to any facilities. Sometimes, Special Operations soldiers waited days near the target, stealthily watching and developing "pattern of life" analysis to supplement the intelligence, surveillance and reconnaissance assets they'd focused on the target location before the operation. Once they had eyes on the target, they executed a rapid entry and got in and out in a matter of minutes. Typically, Special Operations Forces were used against "high-value" commanders whose capture would disrupt insurgent operations and, often, yield valuable intelligence.

PETRAEUS FELT HE HAD a good grasp that fall on operations in Helmand and Kandahar provinces and elsewhere in the south, where troops were continuing to expand their footprint and connect growing secure areas. In the east, he pushed Campbell to focus on hammering insurgent networks, building on recent momentum and still working hard to improve his understanding of that area. He thought he had a reasonable feel for conditions in western Afghanistan, where the battlespace was relatively calm, and he had a clear sense that ISAF needed to do more in Baghlan and Kunduz, in the north, where ISAF had increased its force levels and operational tempo, to some effect. But for now, the priorities had to remain in the south and southwest, the traditional Taliban strongholds.

The surge had increased the ratio of troops to civilians in these areas, and the numbers reflected both the priority placed on the south and the still relative economy of force, given the number of soldiers required for a comprehensive counterinsurgency campaign. There was one ISAF soldier for every nineteen Afghans in Helmand Province and one for every thirty-three Afghans in Kandahar, the two provinces where forces had been concentrated to clear the Taliban from its strongholds. But in the mountain provinces of the east, where three of the four brigade combat teams from the 101st Airborne were fighting, the ratio was one to ninety-one Afghan citizens. In the northern provinces, the ratio was just one to 192.

As certain as Petraeus was about the ability of U.S. and Canadian forces to clear key areas in Kandahar, he knew the "hold" phase, when gains were consolidated, would likely be more challenging. Progress in the hold phase, to a considerable degree, depended upon establishment of effective local governance and local security, which the nascent but growing Afghan army—meeting its recruitment goals but beset by high AWOL rates—did not yet have enough troops to help provide. There was also still much work to do at the village level, coaxing villagers to return; rebuilding their homes, bazaars and mosques; and recruiting and training enough Afghan Local Police capable of standing up to the Taliban once they returned after the winter. Petraeus expected the enemy to fight back and try to regain ground that was important to them tactically and symbolically. "We will be staying in these areas to resist them, and that is new," Petraeus said. "We will not know the true impact of these operations until next year. . . . Ultimately, when you take away their safe havens, they will fight to come back."

He preached caution to his staff when it came to "chest pounding" about successes in Kandahar. He wanted his officers even to avoid claims of "cautious optimism" as they dealt with the media. Stick to the facts, he advised; just state them and let members of the press draw their own conclusions. But with a heavier conventional-troop presence and active operations

across Kandahar Province, many of the Taliban had beat a tactical retreat—
to redoubts across the border in Pakistan, where they were beyond the
reach of American forces. A headline on the front page of the *New York
Times*, "Coalition Routs Taliban in Southern Afghanistan," triggered a
counterattack by members of the antiwar class in Washington. Some saw
the article as evidence of how skilled Petraeus was at spinning reporters.
He responded that the *Times* piece had caught him by surprise and noted
that it was written by a woman who had spent years in Afghanistan and
was known as a hard-edged reporter.

Doug Ollivant was circumspect about whether U.S. forces had, indeed,
devastated the Taliban around Kandahar. "We just don't know," he said. "It's
like the blind men with the elephant. We don't know if what we are seeing is
the start of a trend or an anomaly. Be very, very careful." The Pakistan safe
havens, he knew, kept Petraeus from being able to attack "the Afghan insurgency at its root." U.S., coalition and Afghan forces controlled much ground
that had previously belonged to the Taliban. But if a single factor could undo
Petraeus's counterinsurgency doctrine, it was the sanctuaries in Pakistan.

For all the caution he counseled his officers to use when dealing with
the media, Petraeus was constantly engaged. While he never talked about
winning, he often moved the narrative by communicating, via e-mail, with
numerous reporters and columnists, sometimes on the record but also
on background, which, as was customary, was not attributed directly to
him. He also opened his fighting units up to hosting embedded journalists, because he knew that the easiest way to win over even the most hard-
bitten reporters was to have them spend time with U.S. forces, especially
ones in combat.

Beyond the success of Operation Dragon Strike in Kandahar, media reports also appeared regarding nascent peace talks. Petraeus shared with the
Washington Post what senior Afghan officials had told him: that "several
very senior Taliban leaders" had reached out to the Afghan government. But
Petraeus cautioned that this overture "certainly would not rise to the level
of being called negotiations." Privately, he wasn't sure that some of the secret talks—those set to take place in the Maldives and in a Gulf state, in

particular—were yet all that significant, seeing some of them more as "reconciliation tourism." Consequently, Petraeus struck a cautionary note with the *Post* similar to the one he used during his stand-ups. "Should these reports of Taliban holding peace talks with [the Afghan government] prove true, we cannot expect any favorable outcome for some time," he told his staff one morning in mid-October. "Additionally, the Taliban do not speak with one voice, and these talks will create strains within the Taliban senior leadership as they try and work out who is talking to whom. If talks are occurring, then I am not surprised, given the enormous pressure we are placing on the network: This pressure will only increase over the months ahead. Finally, do not make more of these talks than there is—it is more speculation than fact at this time."

Seeing the gains by conventional forces, coupled with the successful night raids by Special Operations Forces, some speculated that Petraeus had shifted strategy away from McChrystal's counterinsurgency approach. A story line emerged that Petraeus was moving away from classic counterinsurgency tactics in favor of the ironfisted night raids and greater reliance on air strikes, which increased dramatically during his tenure. Some in the media speculated that he was trying to bomb the Taliban to the negotiating table. Others speculated that Petraeus realized that counterinsurgency alone wasn't working, as Taliban influence spread to areas that had been peaceful. Petraeus continued to explain that a comprehensive counterinsurgency approach *included* counterterrorism strikes as well as all the other lines of operation in the overall strategy, but the nuance was lost on many journalists.

Michael O'Hanlon, a defense analyst at the Brookings Institution and a confidant for Petraeus and McChrystal, cited a paradox in comparing the commands of the two men. "I would underscore that there was more continuity than change," O'Hanlon later shared. "What I noticed was their shift in public relations strategy: Petraeus was willing to talk about killing bad guys more than McChrystal." McChrystal had largely been responsible for pushing for the increase in Special Operations Forces and associated enablers early in his command—with support by Petraeus at Central

Command—but he was reticent to announce it in the press. Petraeus was eager that fall to discuss progress, and the Special Operations Forces efforts were among those that seemed to indicate progress. He would later regret somewhat having raised the profile of night raids, but he was eager to share an indicator, and Special Operations Forces were the moneymakers at the time.

When Colonel Gunhus sent Petraeus a blog post by *Time*'s Joe Klein citing this pivot from counterinsurgency to a more violent strain of counterterrorism, the general was "exercised," Gunhus relayed, using Petraeus's expression for "irritated." Petraeus told Rear Admiral Greg Smith, his chief of strategic communications, to tell Klein and David Ignatius of the *Washington Post,* who had made a similar point in a column, that they had completely missed what was going on. He hadn't just increased counterterrorist force operations—he'd increased everything! His war strategy was a *comprehensive* civil-military campaign without silver bullets. Progress required all civilian and military efforts working in concert, albeit in different combinations, depending upon where in the country they were based.

The following morning in his stand-up, Petraeus was still perturbed. "The key point to stress is that we are doing more of *everything*. We have certainly increased the tempo of SOF operations. We have also increased the clear-hold-and-build operations conducted by conventional forces. We have increased our training effort with the ANSF, local security initiatives, and reconciliation and reintegration," Petraeus stated. "We've also increased support to local governance and development, increased information operations and so on." Petraeus called the overall approach "the Anaconda strategy," the same title he'd used to describe the comprehensive counterinsurgency approach in Iraq during the surge there, but modified for Afghanistan.

Petraeus first publicly unveiled a PowerPoint slide depicting the Anaconda strategy in Iraq before the Senate Armed Services Committee in September 2007. He had been refining it ever since. The diagram, which Petraeus routinely showed to staff and visiting delegations in Afghanistan, depicts seven central thrusts simultaneously aimed at the enemy. Named after the giant snake that squeezes its prey to death, the Anaconda strategy for Iraq was designed to squeeze the life out of al-Qaeda in Iraq and Sunni insurgents, as well as the Shia militia extremists. In Afghanistan in the summer of 2010, it featured seven categories of activity: kinetic operations, politics, intelligence, detainee operations, information operations, international engagement and non-kinetics, by which Petraeus meant programs for jobs, education, rule of law and development. Only one of the seven—kinetic operations—involved predominantly military action. McMaster's anticorruption task force was part of the "politics" thrust. Martins's Rule of Law Field Force fell under the heading of "detainee operations."

"If it appears on the Anaconda slide, then it has been ramped up," Petraeus would say during briefings, aiming a laser pointer at the Anaconda diagram. His seven categories were broken down into twenty-six tasks. The general might have been the only person on his staff capable of tracking them all at the same time amid the chaos of war.

Petraeus's reliance on "kinetics" for dealing with the "uncertainty, challenge, risk, danger and competing agendas" in Afghanistan came straight from Iraq, where he relentlessly attacked al-Qaeda and other extremists through night raids during the surge as his forces conducted large operations to clear AQ from safe havens. But, as in Afghanistan, Petraeus oversaw increases in clear-hold-and-build operations, as well as initiatives to negotiate with Sunni and Shia militants willing to lay down their arms and work with the Americans. Petraeus's focus on "protecting the people" did not imply a reticence in the use of force; as he would put it, he was just against *counterproductive* use of force. Indeed, he had always been firm that his counterinsurgency tactics include ironfisted counterterrorist operations by counterterrorist forces. The counterinsurgency guidance he issued on August 1 made it clear that killing the enemy was very much part of the plan:

PURSUE THE ENEMY RELENTLESSLY. Together with our Afghan partners, get our teeth into the insurgents and don't let go. When the extremists fight, make them pay. Seek out and eliminate those who threaten the population. Don't let them intimidate the innocent. Target the whole network, not just individuals.

FIGHT HARD AND FIGHT WITH DISCIPLINE. Hunt the enemy aggressively, but use only the firepower needed to win a fight. We can't win without fighting, but we also cannot kill or capture our way to victory. Moreover, if we kill civilians or damage their property in the course of our operations, we will create more enemies than our operations eliminate. That's exactly what the Taliban want. Don't fall into their trap. We must continue our efforts to reduce civilian casualties to an absolute minimum.

Petraeus mentor General Jack Keane came away from a two-week visit in October with an appreciation of the Anaconda strategy—and its architect. "What you have in Petraeus is a guy who has an enormous capacity level," Keane said. "And he has touched every aspect of this very quickly. He operates at the strategic level in terms of diplomacy, operates at the operational level to understand the entire framework of the war, and then he understands its tactical implications. He can do that back and forth. That's rare in a general officer."

Ever since he had landed in Kabul, Petraeus had been focused on July 2011 as the start of the drawdown. He knew he needed as much time as possible to execute his counterinsurgency strategy and he knew the Afghans were concerned about that date. Quietly, imperceptibly, he and his diplomatic partners began working to support a growing NATO and White House initiative to shift the focus at an upcoming NATO conference on Afghanistan in Lisbon from the beginning of the drawdown in July 2011 to formal approval of a plan for handing over the mission of securing the country to Afghan forces by the end of 2014, effectively buying another three and a half years to succeed.

There was no media blitz to promote the shift in focus to 2014, only quiet one-on-one conversations with ambassadors in Kabul and visiting defense ministers and heads of government. When they stopped in Kabul, each received a full-dress briefing from Petraeus and his diplomatic partner, Ambassador Mark Sedwill, NATO's senior civilian representative, on what they would hear at Lisbon.

Petraeus was pleased that he would be able to report progress at Lisbon. "But the overarching narrative that is important to stress," he explained during his November 6 stand-up, "is that this progress is fragile and reversible. This progress has been the product of a lot of hard fighting, and it will take more hard fighting to solidify it. Not only should we physically be prepared for the spring, but we need to be rhetorically and emotionally ready as well. The Taliban will be back with reinforcements. We will need to be ready—it isn't going to be an easy ride to 2014."

Petraeus knew that keeping the NATO coalition together meant giving members hope that there was an end in sight, and it meant putting time on the clock to achieve progress by moving the goalpost to 2014. Coalition management would dominate Petraeus's portfolio throughout the fall of 2010.

As the media in Washington began reporting in mid-November that the Obama administration was changing focus from the July 2011 drawdown to the transition to Afghan forces by the end of 2014, like-minded senators traveling to Afghanistan also emphasized the shift. "We're not going anywhere," Senator Joe Lieberman told the press in Kabul. "In fact, the better date to think about is the end of 2014." Back in Washington a week before the Lisbon conference, Senator Lindsey Graham said that "2014 is the right date to talk about. That's when Karzai suggests that Afghans will be in the lead, and I'm very pleased to hear President Obama talk about 2014."

But Karzai never made anything, including extending the American commitment to Afghanistan, easy. In late October, he admitted he'd been taking bags full of cash from an Iranian emissary. But that uproar paled in comparison with that triggered by an interview Karzai gave the *Washington Post* on the eve of the Lisbon summit in which he called for the United States to end night raids by Special Operations Forces and reduce its military footprint in Afghanistan. Petraeus was stunned.

Privately, Petraeus said that Karzai's statement put him in an untenable position. He immediately made his displeasure known at a meeting with

Ashraf Ghani, the Afghan official in charge of planning the military transition to Afghan forces. He never quite threatened to resign, but he made it clear how serious the situation was. In fact, he found what Karzai had done hard to understand. "I had a good chat with Ashraf and various ministers," Petraeus said in an e-mail to a colleague a day later. "I'll see President Karzai tomorrow and remind him in detail what we've been doing in each and every area. . . . Will be a good session. Just need to stay even/logical/firm." He struck a similar chord in a note he wrote to his mentor Keith Nightingale: "Spending an hour one-on-one with Pres K tomorrow, and we'll be fine. We all have the same goals, it just takes time to get there—and we've been addressing each of his issues for a bit now, and I'll remind him of that." When Nightingale made a despairing reference to the July 2011 drawdown, Petraeus allayed his fears. "Fear not on July 2011," he wrote, explaining the shift that had taken place. "In fact, as the Washington Post editorial page editor noted, the end of 2014 is the new 2011."

Despite the controversy over his remarks, Karzai promised Petraeus a united front, and he delivered in Lisbon. Once the conference began, Petraeus briefed NATO ministers on his plan for "Inteqal." From the Dari word for "transition," this was the classified plan to transfer power to Afghan forces in certain areas as early as the spring of 2011, with the final transition coming at the end of December 2014. President Obama used the conference to state publicly for the first time that he expected U.S. forces would complete major combat operations in the country by the end of 2014. "We aligned our approach on the way forward in Afghanistan, particularly on a transition to full Afghan lead that will begin in early 2011 and will conclude in 2014," Obama said at a wrap-up press conference.

Obama was blunt when it came to Karzai's recent criticism of night raids and the U.S. military presence. "If we're putting in big resources, if we're ponying up billions of dollars, if the expectation is that our troops are going to be there to help secure the countryside and ensure that President Karzai can continue to build and develop his country, then he's got to also pay attention to our concerns as well. . . . He's got to understand that I've got a bunch of young men and women from small towns and big cities all across America who are in a foreign country being shot at and having to traverse terrain filled with IEDs, and they need to protect themselves. And so if we're setting things up where they're just sitting ducks for the Taliban, that's not an acceptable answer either."

Asked whether he thought the current military strategy was working and would enable him to withdraw a significant number of forces by July 2011, Obama said to the press that it was.

You have fewer areas of Afghanistan under Taliban control. You have the Taliban on the defensive in a number of areas that were their strongholds. We have met or exceeded our targets in terms of recruitment of Afghan security forces. And our assessments are that the performance of Afghan security forces has improved significantly.

So thanks to the hard work of people like Dave Petraeus and Mark Sedwill and others, and obviously the incredible sacrifices of the troops on the ground from the ISAF forces, we are in a better place now than we were a year ago. As a consequence, I'm confident that we are going to be able to execute our transition starting in July of next year.

And General Petraeus is, in fact, in the process now of planning and mapping out where are those areas where we feel there's enough security that we can begin thinning out troops in those areas, where are areas that need further reinforcements as certain areas get thinned out—so that we can continually consolidate the security gains and then backfill it with the effective civilian improvements that are going to be needed.

So we have made progress. The key is to make sure that we don't stand still but we keep accelerating that progress, that we build on it.

Obama had embraced the shift in emphasis well before Lisbon, which seemed to indicate that he and Petraeus had reached a new level of trust in their relationship. Petraeus refused to talk about any aspect of his conversations with the president. For a man who enjoyed dealing with reporters and cultivated e-mail relationships with dozens of them, this was a do-not-enter zone. Obama was the second president for whom he had fought a war. It was no secret that he and Bush had become close personally. But Petraeus was sensitive to the fact that some Democrats saw him as Bush's general. He wasn't a politician and never would be, and he wanted it clear to all that he was as capable of serving a Democrat as he was of serving a Republican. That didn't mean tailoring his advice to fit the president's political agenda—the previous fall's strategic debate over troop levels in Afghanistan had made that clear. But he believed in service—to the nation and to the president. Asked a few days after Lisbon how he had managed to move the president to focusing on December 2014 instead of July 2011, Petraeus wouldn't take the bait. "I think, frankly," he said, "that all the leaders came to see the logic of December 2014."

CHAPTER 6

CLEAR, HOLD AND BUILD

After fighting hard all summer and fall, Lieutenant Colonel David Flynn's repurposed artillery battalion plunged headlong into village reconstruction. The fighting season had given way to a kind of winter hibernation when the Taliban receded to regroup for spring offensives. After six months in Afghanistan, Flynn knew the winter would give him a chance to consolidate his hold on the villages he had cleared in the Arghandab River Valley and expand the growing security bubble—or face a resurgent Taliban in several months. He was determined to rebuild the villages his forces had devastated, including Tarok Kolache, which had been largely abandoned but so heavily seeded with homemade bombs and explosives that Flynn's only option had been to call in a B-1 bomber air strike. He lobbied for reconstruction assistance from his commanders, the local Provincial Reconstruction Team and anyone else who would listen, mindful that these villages could be held only with the support of villagers. The same troops that had clashed in early July with battle-hardened paratroopers from the 82nd Airborne had by now pushed deep into terrain the Taliban had held since 2007. Seven of Flynn's soldiers had been killed in action, and eighty-three had been wounded, many catastrophically—the military's term for multiple amputations. Two-thirds of the battlefield casualties had been caused by improvised explosive devices. Flynn figured that his men had seen more than two hundred IEDs in one area of operations alone, a two-by-six-kilometer area on the west side of the Arghandab River. That broke down to more than forty roadside bombs per square mile of terrain.

TO THE EAST, in the mountains and valleys of Kunar Province, Lieutenant Colonel Vowell faced the same threat. On his way to visit C Company at Combat Outpost Penich one morning, his patrol tripped a large improvised explosive device. As Vowell scrambled out of his vehicle, he knew the roadside bomb had been detonated by a "command wire." He helped his men out of the vehicle that had been hit and then ran into the open plowed field by the roadside. As he ran, he was looking for wire. He didn't see it, but instinct told him to press across the field toward a grouping of mud homes. His radio operator and another soldier joined him. Instantly, a man shot up in the field about 300 yards away and started running. Vowell yelled at him to stop in Pashto and in English. But he kept running. The Americans chased him for forty minutes before losing him. They did find the command wire—all 500 yards of it—buried in the dirt all the way to the road.

Vowell repeated the trip three days later, determined to make it to Penich. This time, he had his team dismount early and cross the fields with large copper rods plowing the dirt, hoping to pull up command wires and their IEDs. As they walked the mile and a half through the fields, Vowell had his vehicles pull up behind them. As the team was about to get back in the vehicles, they came under very heavy machine-gun and rocket-propelled-grenade fire. A dozen RPGs sailed around them, and a hail of bullets rained down on them.

Sergeant Major Tony Perry, Vowell's operations NCO, was hit in his right ankle by an RPG. After his men moved him to cover behind a building wall, Vowell started applying a tourniquet. A medic took over, allowing Vowell to take tactical command of the patrol. He watched his men perform with what he remembered thinking was incredible skill and valor. One talked Kiowa helicopter gunships onto enemy positions. Another directed bombing by two F-15s that arrived on station almost instantaneously. Vowell wanted to counterattack with the insurgents in the open. But with Perry in precarious condition, Vowell ordered his men to break contact. He started organizing a medevac landing zone. By the time the helicopter arrived to take Perry out, men from C Company had arrived as reinforcements. When the battle was over, Vowell and his men walked to the enemy's ambush positions. He could not believe the dense piles of spent brass bullet casings all around them. He had chosen a tough line of work.

SECRETARY OF DEFENSE Robert Gates landed at Bagram Air Base at noon on December 7. The Defense secretary's traveling party immediately boarded helicopters and flew to Forward Operating Base Joyce, in Kunar Province, to visit Vowell's battalion. Attacks on FOB Joyce had increased 200 percent over the past year. "Every single day in this valley, we are either dropping bombs or shooting Hellfire missiles, because this is a very, very kinetic fight," said Major General John Campbell, commander of the 101st Airborne and Vowell's boss, during a visit to Kunar. "Out here we're fighting the Taliban and a few al-Qaeda, but probably the most dangerous enemy we face is the Haqqani network, because they have sanctuary in Pakistan. We should make no bones about that fact, because they go back and forth across the border at will." It was a sobering visit.

That night, Gates met privately with Petraeus, his partner now in two troubled wars. It had been a year since Obama committed to a troop surge in his address at West Point, and Petraeus had once again succeeded in creating a new momentum, including progress in Kandahar and Helmand, even if conditions on the ground at places like FOB Joyce remained violent and dangerous. Gates said progress in the war was exceeding his expectations. But he had difficult news to relay to Petraeus about the one job in the military in which Petraeus was interested—chairman of the Joint Chiefs of Staff. Forget about it, Gates said. It wasn't happening. Petraeus's mind whirled, even though, as he'd told a close friend, he'd had distinctly mixed feelings about the position. Nonetheless, being told it was out of the question stung.

He wasn't nearly ready to retire. But, according to a Pentagon official and one of Petraeus's confidants, the jobs Gates mentioned—chief of staff of the

Army or NATO's supreme commander in Europe—while very important and prestigious, no longer held the allure they once had for Petraeus. He wanted to stay more directly engaged in the fight against al-Qaeda and the extremists who threatened the United States and its allies—the effort to which he had devoted virtually the entire past decade. As always, he was intrigued by the prospect of something new. What about the CIA? he asked. Petraeus knew how important the agency was in fighting terrorism and told Gates he thought he could contribute as its director. In fact, he had been thinking about it for some time. Gates was enthusiastic. He had served as the agency's director after a long career with the agency. He thought Petraeus would be a superb choice to replace Leon Panetta, who likely would be a candidate to replace Gates as Defense secretary the following summer. While they had no sense of this at the time, their conversation would come to influence both the arc of the war in Afghanistan, which Petraeus would leave sooner than he wanted, and that of the ongoing war against al-Qaeda and other Islamist terror groups, which Petraeus wanted to help prosecute as director of the CIA. Gates took that option back to the White House and, according to one of Gates's aides, relayed to Petraeus that the president had been intrigued by the idea. Petraeus never said anything about this to anyone on his team until after decisions were made months later; and though he and Gates periodically revisited the idea, Petraeus wouldn't discuss it face-to-face with Obama until he returned to Washington for testimony in March.

PETRAEUS'S INTEREST in the CIA would not have surprised Andy Milani. It was summer 2001 in Sarajevo. Milani was a lieutenant colonel, a Delta Force aviator who was serving in Bosnia as the chief of staff of a Joint Special Operations Command task force hunting war criminals. It was the largest deployment of Special Mission Unit forces anywhere in the world. Petraeus and Milani had met at a pre-deployment briefing at Fort Bragg while Petraeus was in his final months there. Protective by nature in a highly classified world, Milani did not know exactly what to make of Petraeus, a newly minted brigadier general who'd started hanging around Milani's operations center. Petraeus had arrived in late June 2001 as assistant chief of staff for operations for NATO's Stabilization Force in Bosnia. He had convinced a young captain who had served in his brigade in the 82nd Airborne, David Fivecoat, to deploy to Bosnia and serve as his aide. He also recruited Lieutenant Colonel Mike Meese, a permanent professor at West Point's Department of Social Sciences and the son of former attorney general Edwin Meese, to join his team. Meese would later join Petraeus in Iraq in 2003 and again during the surge in 2007 and 2008, and then deploy for a year to Afghanistan when Petraeus assumed command there in July 2010.

Petraeus's fascination with counterinsurgency made him curious about peacekeeping. In Bosnia, he would become immersed in the Multi-Year Road Map, a blueprint for managing civil-military, governance and development-oriented operations whose concepts and structure would prove useful for Petraeus when he found himself as a virtual potentate in Mosul for much of 2003. He worked closely with the EU, the Office of the High Representative and UN officials—his first in-depth exposure to such agencies.

Petraeus also found himself drawn to Milani's Special Mission Unit task force, the only one in the peacekeeping theater carrying out operations aimed at war criminals of the Bosnian civil war. Prior to each of the task force's operations, Petraeus would sit in on Milani's briefings, take notes on targeting and ask provocative questions, according to joint task force members. Even though he wasn't in the Special Operations chain of command, Petraeus was responsible for ensuring the Stabilization Force's support of the task force operations, as well as the operations of other nations' special operations forces that were conducting war criminal–hunt operations. By the late summer, Petraeus was designated the deputy commander of the "forward" task force in Bosnia as well.

Petraeus didn't care that Milani was two grades below him. He saw that Milani's Special Mission Unit operators—from multiple government agencies and military services—had capability, expertise and energy. "One day I put him on a helicopter and dressed him up [in civilian attire] and a ball cap," Milani explained. The team flew over steep gorges, five-thousand-foot mountains and sheer cliffs and beautiful rivers to destinations unknown.

"We jumped in a van with blacked-out windows and you could just tell he was like a kid in a candy store." They met with intelligence collectors and sources and visited safe houses that enabled surveillance of war criminals. Petraeus started going on nighttime "house call" missions with the task force. He also asked Lieutenant Colonel Sean Mulholland, an Army Special Forces officer, if he could go out with his men on their night raids, which typically went down around 2:00 A.M. "It's probably too dangerous," Mulholland said. "I'd like to go anyway," Petraeus insisted.

Bosnia marked the first time Special Mission Units and Special Forces would share the high-value targeting mission. Petraeus would often wait outside in a vehicle as a house was surrounded and the area secured, then he would emerge wearing no body armor and deliver a letter from the Stabilization Force commander to the individual of interest. The night raids were designed to send a signal to or detain and interrogate those known to be aiding and abetting war criminals; the tactical intelligence often gathered in the wake of such operations would lead to the next target.

At the top of the task force's list was Dr. Radovan Karadzic, a Bosnian Serb politician wanted for war crimes against Bosnian Muslims and Croats, in his infamous pink house in the town of Pale, cradled in the Bosnian mountains in a Bosnian Serb area within the French sector. But the French were initially resistant to U.S. activity in their area. General John B. Sylvester, the NATO Stabilization Force commander and now also the commander of the forward Joint Special Operations Task Force, cleared Petraeus and Milani to work with the French to coordinate their activities. At one point, the task force's intelligence analysts tried to recruit Karadzic's driver and had a pitch letter delivered to his home. But the driver thought he was being set up and immediately contacted the Serbian government, which in turn contacted the U.S. Embassy. The operation had been blown, and the task force suffered a major embarrassment. The setback strained relations between task force officers and CIA operatives, who told the agency's director, George Tenet, that they had opposed the operation, even though the CIA had participated. Petraeus understood that the Special Operations–CIA relationship had a long way to go. Still, he found the hunt for war criminals an intellectually challenging and exciting mission.

But the Special Mission Unit focus in Bosnia would soon shift to counterterrorism after the September 11, 2001, terror attacks, which ultimately led to vastly improved cooperation and intelligence sharing. Within two weeks, a Joint Interagency Task Force–Counterterrorism was created, combining military, law enforcement, intelligence and diplomatic resources in Bosnia for the first time. In addition to his other peacekeeping duties, Petraeus became its deputy commander, again reporting to Sylvester, who was designated commander of this task force as well.

Bosnia had long been a transit area for foreign Islamist fighters, in part because the Bosnian Muslims had been desperate for assistance to counter the Serb nationalists who were conducting ethnic cleansing during the civil war in the early 1990s. Some of them continued to facilitate extremist activities through Bosnia in support of former fighters for al-Qaeda. From its inception, the Joint Interagency Task Force included Special Operations personnel and representatives from the FBI and the Defense Intelligence Agency and analysts and interpreters from the National Security Agency. Two weeks after 9/11, the Joint Interagency Task Force used CIA intelligence to plan a raid on an Egyptian and a Jordanian hiding out in the Hollywood Hotel in Sarajevo. "We flipped the switch and went from hunting war criminals to looking for al-Qaeda," explained Milani.

During a pre-brief on the operation, Petraeus leaned over, raised his brow and asked Milani, "So, could this be a career moment?" Milani responded, "What does that mean, sir? A high-risk moment where we might lose our careers?" Milani laughed. "I'd say 'Roger,' sir; that's the world I live in." Petraeus liked his attitude. The operation began at the hotel with Special Operations soldiers carrying suitcases as part of their cover—empty suitcases, which they could use to conduct tactical exploitation of materials in the room. They captured their targets, but not without a fight. They eventually threw the two men, Al-Halim Hassam Khafagi and Hamed Abdel Rahim al-Jamal, into the back of a van, wrapped in sheets. Petraeus and Milani came out to meet the soldiers upon their return, opened the doors and saw the sheets were covered with blood. Petraeus was concerned. One of the two had sustained a concussion. But neither was seriously injured. Interrogations and computers seized in the raid ultimately helped lead them to three Egyptians, one Jordanian and five Pakistanis.

The operation marked a turning point for joint interagency operations, especially relations between the Special Operations community and the CIA. After the Hollywood Hotel raid, the combined team conducted operations that led to the arrest of terrorists and individuals linked to nongovernmental organizations suspected of links to terrorist organizations. One of them, Benevolence International Foundation, a Chicago-based religious organization, was using its tax-exempt status as a charity to raise funds for transnational terrorists. At its offices in Bosnia, the Joint Interagency Task Force uncovered documents that established direct communication between Benevolence and an al-Qaeda lieutenant, which the FBI used to put Benevolence International Foundation's leader behind bars in Chicago on perjury charges. By August 2002, according to one of its analysts, Captain Jeanne Hull, "intelligence and open-source reporting indicated that some armed groups were looking to avoid Bosnia rather than use it."

While Special Mission Unit teams continued to pursue war criminals, their main mission became counterterrorism. It was a formative period for Petraeus that built on his peacekeeping experiences in Haiti and his time on General Shelton's staff, where he had first been exposed to the mission in Bosnia and the Special Mission Units there. Because of his time in Bosnia, he better understood the importance of "unity of effort," working at both the strategic and tactical levels with U.S. and coalition military and civilian partners, international organizations, foreign embassies and host-nation officials. He worked to merge the combined efforts of Special Mission Units and Special Forces teams on the war-criminal and counterterrorism missions, and he learned from the intelligence-gathering techniques the Special Mission Units used to locate high-value targets. The interagency task force that he helped establish to pursue terrorist suspects would be a blueprint he would again use in Iraq and in Afghanistan. Perhaps most important, he carried with him a blueprint for a Multi-Year Road Map for the comprehensive nation building he had first experienced in Haiti and now implemented in war-torn Bosnia. He left Bosnia in 2002 after learning that he would be promoted to major general and given the job of his dreams, commander of the 101st Airborne Division. Word at Fort Campbell, Kentucky, was that the Screaming Eagles were ticketed for Iraq.

IN AFGHANISTAN, Petraeus cherished his time in the field with units from the 101st Airborne. On December 20, he flew to Kandahar to visit Flynn's battalion, touching down in a Black Hawk helicopter in a barren brown field near the site where the Battle of Bakersfield had been fought in July. Flynn led the general to a bridge where his men had fought the days-long battle. Flynn asked Petraeus to pin a Silver Star on the chest of Sergeant First Class Kyle Lyon, an Army meteorologist by training who had led a platoon through the Battle of Bakersfield. Petraeus promised he would look into Lyon's request to reclassify as an infantryman. He awarded medals to seven other soldiers as well, noting that the opportunities to recognize heroic troopers were among his greatest pleasures. Flynn had given Petraeus the basic facts of the fighting that had taken place as they walked to the bridge from the landing zone, and Petraeus repeated them verbatim in his remarks to the troops. Flynn was impressed by his memory and thought the personal remarks he had made to each soldier were eloquent.

After the ceremony, Flynn led Petraeus and the members of his traveling party inside Combat Outpost Stout, where he briefed them on his battalion's tactical operations and reconstruction efforts. Flynn explained that they measured success by counting the number of farmers working in fields, the willingness of potential informants to be recruited, and the number of villagers willing to take part in "cash for work" programs and various other indicators. Flynn's converted artillerymen were conducting the kind of intensive counterinsurgency operations normally performed by the infantry and Special Forces. Petraeus later told Major General James Terry, commander of the Regional Command South in Afghanistan, that he wanted a similar approach followed in the south.

Flynn shared other insights as well. He understood Petraeus's intent—the Afghan Local Police were intended to promote local security and supplement the growing Afghan security forces, including uniformed and border police. Adding the Afghan Local Police to the mix would help achieve something closer to the 1-to-20 troop-to-population ratio prescribed in U.S. Army counterinsurgency doctrine, when both ISAF and Afghan forces were included. A similar bottom-up defense initiative in Iraq, the Sons of Iraq, had been one of the tipping points for greatly improved security. Could it work in Afghanistan? Could conventional forces assume part of this training mission? Special Operations forces promoting the Village Stability Operations were spread thin as it was. Petraeus had asked his Counterinsurgency Advisory and Assistance Team (CAAT) to study whether conventional forces were up to the task. Flynn clearly thought that they were.

Petraeus listened intently to Flynn's briefing, which gave him a snapshot of what his unit had achieved in their seven months in country and an analysis of the enemy. Flynn described his current lines of effort, including efforts to promote local governance and development. Petraeus said the Taliban senior leadership was concerned by the expansion and effectiveness of the ALP, which he felt would have real impact on the Taliban's popular support, communications and safe havens. He still hoped that the ALP would spread like a chain-link fence across key terrain districts that lacked sufficient numbers of soldiers and police.

Petraeus continually reiterated the value of, and his aspirations for, the ALP initiative at his morning stand-up briefings. He had asked Brigadier General Scott Miller, the commanding general of Combined Forces Special Operations Component Command–Afghanistan, to update him weekly on its expansion as the initiative was being implemented by Miller's Special Forces detachments. Miller's command was cautious about other efforts to train and equip local police, in part because of the importance of maintaining ties to the Ministry of the Interior and control over the dispersal of weapons—tasks that his teams explicitly oversaw. Miller, however, recognized that conventional forces had to take part in order to achieve the desired ratio of troops to villagers. There simply weren't enough Special Forces detachments to do the job at the pace that was necessary to halt the insurgency's momentum.

After Flynn's briefing, the entourage set off on foot to Tarok Kolache so that Petraeus could see the development there for himself. Flynn was worried that he wouldn't see anyone he knew, after emphasizing his close relations with villagers during the briefing. But the first man they ran into was Abdul Baqi, a homeowner eager to see his house rebuilt. He greeted Flynn warmly. Soon there were others, including village maliks who told Petraeus that they didn't want Flynn to leave. At one point, as a small crowd gathered at the site of the demolished Tarok Kolache mosque, Petraeus discussed the need for reconstruction so that villagers could once again live in peace and prosperity. Mark Howell, the security chief who accompanied Petraeus, knew how much Petraeus enjoyed visiting these onetime Taliban strongholds. "I saw a light in the boss's eyes I saw in Baghdad after the Battle of Sadr City in March '08," Howell recalled. "The light that said, 'I've got you now, and there's more where that came from.' Joe Taliban has an interesting winter ahead of him, and those that are left standing come April may be a little more open-minded." Major General Terry later passed a quote from Petraeus to Flynn: "Best day that I've had since I've been in Afghanistan."

That night, after Petraeus returned to ISAF headquarters in Kabul, Major Fernando Lujan briefed the commanding general. Lujan had seen Flynn's battalion during their initial operations back in July, when he and his colleagues from the Counterinsurgency Advisory and Assistance Team embedded with Flynn's unit. But tonight's topic wasn't Flynn or his troops. It was the future of the CAAT itself. At the start of his tour back in July, Lujan had been assigned by the CAAT's commander, Colonel Joe Felter, to build a team that could take the CAAT concept inside the Afghan military, which would at some point be inheriting the war from the Americans and their NATO partners. Lujan was well suited to create an Afghan CAAT, or A-CAAT. In addition to being a Special Forces officer, he was in a special program created by the chairman of the Joint Chiefs of Staff called the "Afghan Hands." Those in it trained in either Dari or Pashto and spent three years rotating back and forth between Afghan-related billets in Afghanistan and the United States. All of this was designed to build language fluency, cultural expertise and country knowledge. The A-CAAT took shape almost coincidentally, when Lujan was joined in Kandahar by two other Afghan Hands who also spoke Dari, an infantry officer and a Defense Department contractor. They spent the fall on eight combat embeds advising Afghan forces on best counterinsurgency practices.

In a conference room at ISAF headquarters filled with Petraeus aides and three Special Forces colonels, Lujan said the vision he and Felter shared was for the A-CAAT, over time, to essentially supersede the CAAT and become an increasingly important contribution to the campaign as ISAF forces thinned out and turned the war over to the Afghan troops. But the only way to expand the A-CAAT so that it had three separate regional teams, in the south, southwest and east regional commands, Lujan argued, was for the U.S. Special Operations Command (SOCOM) to assume responsibility and provide staffing. Only with SOCOM support could enough Afghan Hands be assigned to carry on the mission. By the summer of 2011—when the drawdown of U.S. forces would begin—Lujan envisioned having five A-CAATs—one for each regional command. While Lujan and Felter had heard that the Special Forces colonels were there to try to keep the Afghan Hands out of the A-CAAT expansion, they kept their mouths shut after Petraeus responded enthusiastically to the A-CAAT expansion. "'We need command-track guys for these Afghan Hands billets, not guys who didn't have any career options,'" Lujan later quoted Petraeus as saying. "You need the best."

Petraeus promised Felter and Lujan that the CAAT would remain based at ISAF headquarters, in close proximity with Petraeus and his staff. "'As long as I am COMISAF, you will always report directly to me,'" Lujan remembered him saying. "That will never change." Lujan said in an e-mail he fired off to his CAAT brethren back in Kandahar when the briefing was over, "We literally got every single thing we asked for. We are hereby institutionalized.

Expect big influx of resources and people over the next few months. We have the charter to create a new paradigm out here."

"We'll do everything possible to ensure the CAAT remains a relevant and effective asset both now and in the years ahead," Felter wrote to Petraeus. "It's really a privilege to serve with this great group and for us to have the chance to support you and ISAF at this critical time in the fight." Petraeus responded later that night: "Actually Joe, I thank you. In truth, my 'direction and guidance' were pretty fuzzy! The idea was to allow for max initiative. But my support should have been very clear. The CAAT is a true force multiplier, and it's been great to see what you and the team have done to develop it. Thanks for all that you've done!"

Three days later, Flynn convened a meeting between his staff and representatives from the U.S. Agency for International Development and Afghan government agencies to discuss the rebuilding of Tarok Kolache. He estimated that the cost to replace the buildings and compensate the farmers for the revenue lost from pomegranate sales would total well over $500,000. As they had walked days earlier in Tarok Kolache around the bulldozed site, Petraeus had directed him to spend what was needed; if he had to, "spend a million," the ceiling allocated for funds through a program called CERP, for Commander's Emergency Response Program. "Blame the CERP ceiling restrictions on that darned former Central Command commander," Petraeus joked, referring to himself in his old job as head of Central Command. Petraeus and Flynn felt a deep obligation to rebuild what had been damaged or destroyed. Construction of a new mosque was scheduled to begin in late December. Shortly thereafter, landowners would be paid for assisting in the reconstruction of the village. Building—or, in this case, rebuilding—was by far the hardest stage of the clear-hold-and-build process.

At the same time that his unit engaged in the rebuilding of Tarok Kolache, Flynn had begun talks with villagers from Charqolba Olya on establishing an ALP force there, the site of one of three nascent ALP units in his area. Charqolba Olya had previously been infiltrated by the Taliban, and the villagers had been displaced to Kandahar city and other nearby villages by the time Flynn's unit had arrived in the Arghandab River Valley in June. By January, villagers were starting to move back into their homes. Flynn's team was helping to rebuild damaged properties, and he was eager to help them defend what they rebuilt.

One challenge Flynn faced was the territorial feeling that the Special Operations community had about its Village Stability Operations, the forerunner of the ALP program. Many Special Forces soldiers felt conventional units were simply unqualified and incapable of working closely with villagers to win their trust and build a local security apparatus. Flynn agreed that it took mature soldiers to run an ALP program and thought conventional forces had to be selective in choosing the right leaders to do it. He knew conventional forces had been successful in raising indigenous forces in Vietnam and in Iraq. Also, conventional forces had a green light from Petraeus to launch ALP initiatives in accordance with guidelines he established.

Providing the local citizens with arms, however, also proved to be a complicating factor. The Afghan government understandably feared that they were arming warlords and militias to face off with each other and the central government in Kabul. Petraeus issued guidance saying that U.S. forces must not arm the ALPs; the weapons had to come from the Ministry of Interior as part of the official ALP program. This was among the guidelines established with Karzai. But the program was not always as agile as needed, and weapons were very important to the Afghans. Flynn tried to talk to some of his villagers about community watch and reporting on Taliban activity, and the first response they always gave was, "I need a weapon." Afghanistan was awash in AK-47s, RPGs and other weaponry, and with heavily armed insurgents marauding across the countryside, a local security force member's power emanated from the barrel of a gun. It was that simple.

Compensation for the ALP was also an issue. At Nagahan, the first place in the Arghandab where an ALP was established, the Afghan Ministry of the Interior had yet to start paying the new ALP members by January, which left the A-Team, a Special Forces unit of twelve soldiers, responsible for the payroll. In working to develop an ALP unit in Charqolba Olya, Flynn found that offering ALP members only 60 percent of what a member of the Afghan National Police earned was "a show stopper." All the bureaucratic delays in Nagahan related to pay and weapons could doom the effort in Charqolba and keep Flynn from having a coherent force in place by the time the Taliban came back in the spring.

In late December, Flynn's soldiers intercepted a conversation that said a lot about the state of affairs in the Arghandab River Valley. "The Americans in this area are very brave and they are everywhere!" said one Taliban fighter. "Don't worry," replied his comrade. "It will be okay when our friends all come back."

Flynn thought there was only a small number of Taliban fighters left in the entire Arghandab, perhaps as few as ten or twelve. They were conducting limited and infrequent harassing attacks to determine where their fighters would be able to maneuver in the spring. They would probably not return in earnest until after the leaves were back on the trees in March, at the earliest. The enemy knew how to take advantage of the cover and concealment that the pomegranate fields and their foliage provided. Significant numbers probably wouldn't be encountered, Flynn thought, until late May or June, if they came back at all. Flynn's soldiers had seen some freshly planted IEDs among the dozens of older ones and removed them from the battlefield during the early winter months. The few Taliban who remained were also trying to intimidate the population and dissuade them from supporting the government or the coalition. They targeted, in particular, the village maliks. It was a classic counterinsurgency struggle.

Flynn considered himself fortunate to have a good working relationship with CIA officers in his area of operations. He met with them biweekly in what was by far the closest relationship he had had with the agency in three overseas deployments. At one point, Flynn hosted the base chief and some of his officers for an overnight stay at his battalion headquarters. In late December, Flynn's battalion hosted a medical clinic for a team of indigenous Afghan doctors working for the CIA. Without appearing to be connected to the United States, the doctors treated more than four hundred villagers in two days. The CIA was also responsible for introducing Flynn to one of his primary Afghan contacts, Inayatullah, a former checkpoint commander in the Afghan military who'd served in Kandahar the first time Flynn was deployed there in 2004.

Flynn had also recently befriended Issa Mohammed, a native of Charqolba Olya who had moved to Kandahar about ten years earlier. He was the appointed malik of Charqolba Olya and was the brother of the district police chief, which made him an important figure in the establishment of the ALP in the village. Mohammed, a member of the Alokozai tribe, was part of the tribe's effort to reassert itself in the Arghandab River Valley. The Alokozai had dominated the district historically, but the tribe's influence and role in the Kandahar government had waned since 2002. Other tribes in the district, the Sayeeds, Kakar and Ghilzai, had been friendlier to the Taliban and had helped them gain a foothold in the district.

Issa Mohammed arrived on New Year's morning with six of his villagers, ready to start the ALP unit. Inayatullah was absent, attending another meeting elsewhere. Flynn got a commitment from one of Mohammed's men, Shah Mamood, and another villager, Sherullah, to lead the effort. Flynn walked into the dimly lit *shura* room at Forward Operating Base Terra Nova with all seven Afghans already seated on the red cushions spread around the floor. He moved to Mohammed first and offered his best Pashto greeting and proceeded around the circle to offer a customary greeting and handshake. Flynn was always struck by the pleasant manner in which Afghans offered greetings no matter what the circumstances. Two nights earlier, Flynn and his men had sat through a *shura* in the village of Babur that was led by the malik there to make peace after a village brawl. Before him were five bloodied villagers who had beaten each other with shovels and picks over wood cut during a cash-for-work project. The dispute was resolved when the younger men approached the malik and kissed his hand. The malik then kissed each man on the head, and calm was restored after two hours of arguing and wrangling.

Building an ALP unit in Charqolba was an interesting proposition, since no one was left living there at the time. It had been totally abandoned even prior to the Americans' arrival in the Arghandab River Valley in June. Flynn's soldiers had captured the village from the Taliban in mid-August. A walk through the village in January left no question about the battle that had taken place there: The adobe-like buildings were riddled with bullet holes, large craters existed where mortar fire had landed, crumbled mud homes looked like kicked-over sandcastles, and torn pieces of uniform from soldiers who had lost their lives there still littered some trees and bushes.

Issa explained that there had been three mosques in Charqolba, but members of only one were participating in the ALP. Flynn promised to work through the local Afghan government to make sure they would be rewarded with a new mosque for their effort. After more discussion, Flynn said they could practice with the Americans' weapons until they could legally procure their own.

But the Afghans continued to express concerns about the people of nearby Jelawur, which the Alokozai describe as a place that was welcoming to the Taliban. Flynn told them that he was relying on them to tell him who was good and who was bad. They told Flynn that U.S. forces shouldn't interfere when they detained a suspect. It was no secret that the Afghan National Police beat their detainees and treated them in ways that were unacceptable by U.S. standards. Flynn did not tolerate such beatings if he observed them, and he told the Afghans he thought it was counterproductive, but he also knew that prisoner abuse in Afghanistan would not end on his watch. When the session ended, Flynn felt optimistic that a local security force in Charqolba Olya might actually be established. This wasn't the textbook process—but there really was no textbook for ALP yet, just guidelines, and he knew that the chain of command was comfortable with those at his level exercising initiative within the guidelines.

As Flynn and his men worked to rebuild the villages in the Arghandab River Valley, a commission appointed by President Karzai reported in mid-January that fighting in and around Kandahar the previous fall had resulted in $100 million in damage to homes and farms. Petraeus mobilized an effort to get the facts out, having walked through villages in the Arghandab River Valley with Flynn and through the other districts with other commanders. He had seen for himself both the damage and the enormous amount of reconstruction under way. At his morning command briefing at

ISAF headquarters in Kabul, Petraeus said that roads were being rebuilt and thousands of trees had been planted, with tens of thousands more to be planted in the weeks ahead. Flynn felt that the homes he and other commanders had ordered destroyed needed to be destroyed: They had been abandoned and wired with what he called an "ingenious array of bombs" that were hidden in the door frames, windows and floors and that prevented the original inhabitants from returning; they made conventional clearing operations nearly impossible or too costly to risk. He was "more than outraged" that comments from an Afghan government spokesman had reinforced the impression that U.S. forces had heavily damaged properties without repairing or replacing the damage. A representative of the ISAF Joint Command noted that photos had been taken of every building or home that had been destroyed, to show that troops were not engaged in the wholesale destruction of villages. A database had also been created, detailing all compensation that had been paid.

Petraeus ordered up a "constant drumbeat" of stories out of the southern regional command regarding the compensation efforts. "I want to drown out the stories of property damage," he said, "with the truth of what we have done, and will be done, regarding this issue," he said. At his briefing the following morning, Petraeus remained agitated at officials around Karzai. "I have walked the ground there," he said. "None of them have. We need to be applauded, not criticized, for our efforts" to repair the damage done. He wanted to make sure this issue was discussed at the next meeting of Karzai's National Security Council. "This is an open wound for me," he said. "Warn them: if they put salt on it," he cautioned, he would get "exercised."

The Afghan report claiming $100 million in property damage also set off a brief eruption in the blogosphere. Joshua Foust, a fellow at the American Security Project and a PBS columnist who previously worked in the intelligence community, revisited Flynn's decision in October to level Tarok Kolache in a post called "The Unforgivable Horror of Village Razing." He cited the inaccurate *Daily Mail* story quoting Flynn as telling villagers in Khosrow Sofla that if they did not tell him where IEDs had been buried, he would wipe the village off the face of the earth. He argued that bombing villages in Kandahar Province as a means of ridding them of IEDs and home-made explosives violated Article 33 of the Geneva Convention. Foust also questioned whether Flynn was circumventing oversight by the Afghan Ministry of the Interior by independently choosing members of the Afghan Local Police detachment in Charqolba Olya. He wondered whether Flynn and other U.S. commanders should have involved Afghan colonel Abdul Raziq in the clearing of Khosrow Sofla and other villages in early October. By supporting warlords such as Raziq, Aikins had written in the *Harper's* story, "the ISAF has come to be associated, in the minds of many Afghans, with their criminality and abuses. 'We're doing the Taliban's work for them,' said one international official with years of experience in counternarcotics here."

Flynn, however, had never set out to destroy villages with bombs and missiles—especially not those of the residents with whom he had become close. But in the case of Tarok Kolache and Khosrow Sofla, destroying the villages really was the only way to safely disarm the invisible and countless IEDs that terrorized the population and would have maimed any forces trying to clear them. Flynn also noted that, as far as the Afghan Local Police detachment in Charqolba Olya was concerned, members were being vetted through the Ministry of the Interior and had yet to receive weapons. Moreover, he noted, "Farmers are moving to their fields by the hundreds since the clearing operation, as opposed to handfuls when Tarok Kolache was a Taliban sanctuary. Our cash-for-work employment of the locals is in the hundreds, up from zero. Village-level shura attendance is on the rise." By winter's end, the mosque in Tarok Kolache was nearly completed and fifteen homes were under construction in the village. Renovations to the mosque in Khosrow Sofla were almost completed, and a new mosque in Charqolba Oyla, where training of the Afghan Local Police unit continued, was 80 percent finished.

But despite all the progress, Afghanistan could break a commander's heart when he least expected it. As Flynn sat buried in paperwork in his office on the evening of January 21, his phone rang. It was Akmal, his Afghan interpreter, calling. "Sir, I've got some bad news.

"I just got a call from Karim Dad's nephew, and he said Karim Dad is dead," Akmal said. "Somebody killed him outside his home thirty minutes ago." Flynn was saddened but not surprised. Karim Dad, the malik for the village of Khosrow Sofla, had told Flynn several times that the Taliban had threatened him. After Flynn was forced to call in the bombing strikes on Khosrow Sofla, decimating about half of the abandoned village, his relationship with Karim Dad had grown stronger. He recalled a conversation outside his village in which Karim Dad told him, "There are people who are trying to kill me, but I don't care. I am not afraid of them and will continue to work with you to fix our village." Karim Dad said the Taliban had moved into the village several years ago and turned it into their base of operations. He had been happy to see the Taliban routed from his village.

The following day, Flynn went to see Niaz Mohammed, the district police chief, at his office. Niaz invited him in to drink chai and discuss the ALP detachment being formed in the village of Lowy Manarah. Niaz told Flynn many times that he was worried that his brother, Issa, would be killed. He thought Issa was too careless when he went to visit the area and the village. Flynn brought up the killing of Karim Dad. "Karim Dad is one of our cousins, and we are all very sad today," Niaz Mohammed said. "I know who did this and would like your help in finding the killer. He must be killed. There is no other way to deal with these people." Flynn told Niaz he had his full support, although Flynn clearly preferred capture. "Once we capture him, he'll have to go to trial," Flynn said. Niaz clearly was not interested in capture.

Niaz cut his conversation with Flynn short and said he and his aides were all headed to Jelawur to attend Karim Dad's funeral. Flynn considered Karim Dad a friend and felt partly responsible for his death. "Do you think it would be a good thing or a bad thing if I attended the funeral?" he asked Niaz.

"I think it would be a good thing. You can follow us and go with me," he said. Flynn had never attended an Afghan funeral and was concerned about the cultural sensitivities associated with his presence. Flynn stripped off all his body armor, helmet and ammunition and wore only a pistol under his shirt. He wanted his presence to be as low-key as possible.

The funeral took place outside in the desert, about a mile north of the gardens of Khosrow Sofla, between Jelawur and Durie. There were hundreds of people milling about. Graves were marked by mounds of stones, some with ornate strips of cloth hanging from tree branches dug into the ground next to the graves. Karim Dad's body lay on a straw-thatched bed next to his open grave. It was lowered into a grave, and the Afghans began covering his body with earth. Akmal told Flynn he did not think it would be a good idea for him to take part, so Flynn sat and watched, wanting in some way to pay his respects, beyond just his presence.

The loss of Karim Dad was a significant blow to Flynn's efforts to rebuild Khosrow Sofla and other villages in the district. If the Taliban had killed Karim Dad, Flynn feared he might have been in the midst of a terror campaign against all government leaders in the area, a foreboding sign of the fight to come in the spring. Only time would tell.

WHILE FLYNN'S TOP GUNS braced for the spring fighting season in the Arghandab, Lieutenant Colonel David Fivecoat's Iron Rakkasans had already rotated home to Kentucky, their fight over. Fivecoat remained behind in Afghanistan, waiting to turn over the Andar and Deh Yak districts of eastern Ghazni Province to the 2nd Battalion, 2nd Infantry Regiment. His change-of-command speech on February 8 was hardly a declaration of victory. "It has been my distinct privilege to lead the Iron Rakkasans here in Andar and Deh Yak for the past seven months as we tried to improve the security situation, forge friendships with our Afghan and coalition partners and defeat the insurgency. It has been a tough struggle, but I believe the task force and our Afghan and ISAF partners have made a difference in the lives of the people of eastern Ghazni."

The numbers compiled by the Rakkasans told one story: 1,600 patrols, seven air assaults, a hundred insurgents killed or captured, thirty-three weapons caches seized and destroyed. His men had provided basic government services in both districts, fixing potholes and opening schools. But polling data compiled by the Afghan government in Ghazni Province told a different story and suggested a standoff at best: 48 percent of those living in the province believed foreign forces do not help the people, 28 percent believed them to be incompetent, and another 11 percent believed that the foreign forces do not bring peace, especially in unsafe areas, which translated to twelve of the province's eighteen districts. Nearly a quarter of the people in Ghazni supported the Taliban, a percentage that was behind only Kandahar, Helmand and Nuristan. In the Deh Yak District, where Fivecoat had traveled in September in the heavily armored convoy, 40 percent believed what the Taliban were saying. At one point, during a clearing operation in the town of Bashi, his troops had discovered an accurate terrain model of Forward Operating Base Andar, his headquarters. It had bothered him to think that the Afghans working on the base might be spies for the Taliban.

Ghazni had been in the neglected eastern region, third in order of priority for resources behind Helmand and Kandahar. The move from Paktika to Ghazni had forced Fivecoat's men to start over midway through their tour, which made it difficult to develop local sources and fully understand what was happening. Fivecoat's task force was also placed under the command of a Polish brigade in Ghazni that did not have the enablers of a U.S. brigade and thus had a difficult time executing some of the counterinsurgency tactics favored by Petraeus. The Poles could maneuver and coordinate artillery, small arms and air support, but they lacked robust staff capacity, intelligence collection and analytic training. Moreover, their development capacity, construction management and contracting capabilities were virtually nonexistent, according to those on a Provincial Reconstruction Team in the area. But Fivecoat knew the importance Petraeus placed on the presence of NATO allies on the battlefield, and the Poles and all of the allies were steadily improving along the way—a benefit of coalition warfare. Whatever the Poles' organizational limitations as counterinsurgents, their spirit and the fact that they and thousands of other NATO forces were fighting side by side with Americans and Afghans brought strategic legitimacy to their cause, which was critical, given the view much of the rest of the world had of America years into its wars in Iraq and Afghanistan.

In any event, Fivecoat had enough experience in counterinsurgency—in both Iraq and Afghanistan—to take initiative. He did need intelligence, and he lucked out with a cooperative Afghan partner in the National Directorate of Security. He also had a West Point classmate who happened to be the lead intelligence officer in Campbell's eastern regional command. She took care to provide the additional intelligence assets and analysis. He understood that the tactics were all about protecting the people, whose lives he was able to touch with development projects, health care and security. But even with daily interaction with villagers, his classmate's intelligence reports, insights from interrogations, and captured documents and photos, Fivecoat still found the enemy network and its sources of funding opaque.

In an article for *Infantry* magazine, Fivecoat and three of his captains wrote that they faced "a strong and determined enemy in Ghazni Province" who had attacked the Rakkasans 420 times, or an average of 2.3 attacks per day. In November, Fivecoat began using a Persistent Threat Detection System—a blimp—in his fight against the Taliban. Equipped with video and infrared sensors, the helium-filled blimp could provide twenty-four-hour surveillance of insurgents up to twelve miles away. Against an enemy that sometimes still used primitive AK-47s, he also had the ability to call in Predator drones equipped with lethal Hellfire missiles, and F-16 fighters carrying five-hundred-pound bombs that could shake an entire village. In the *Infantry* article, Fivecoat described Operation Iron Blade II, a three-company attack in late November. Using surveillance from both a Predator and a blimp, Fivecoat flushed two insurgents into the open and killed them with five-hundred-pound bombs dropped by a pair of F-16s. A third insurgent on a motorcycle was forced out into open terrain and killed with a Hellfire missile.

His efforts had been relentless, and he was one of the top-rated battalion commanders in the theater. But in spite of all the effort, Ghazni remained a tough area where the Taliban were deeply entrenched. Fivecoat's mission had really been to protect the people so that legitimate governance could develop in their districts, resolve local disputes, care for the sick and run schools for their children. That was too much to ask in Ghazni outside its capital at that point. There weren't enough soldiers to support population-centric counterinsurgency operations. So Fivecoat's mission had become to develop the situation. He was told to establish operational bases and check-points, connect with the local people as much as possible and map the enemy situation so that his successor could continue the mission. If the unit coming in to replace the Iron Rakkasans, the 2nd Battalion, 2nd Infantry, was as good, it would take them another year to stabilize Andar and Deh Yak—if the Taliban chose not to reinforce. Only then could the coalition expect real and enduring progress in governance and development efforts. The truth was, the return of the Taliban to Ghazni was not likely to be reversed. With a drawdown of forces coming and the resource constraints faced in the east, there would never be enough American or NATO troops in the area to win over the locals with good governance, decent roads and quality schools. In his heart, Fivecoat felt that his unit had, indeed, put pressure on the insurgents in the area, and he hoped that his successor unit could continue to expand the security bubble across Ghazni and along Highway 1. But, he later reflected, "COIN required a long-term process and six months is too short to convince the population that the government represents the best chance for the long-term future of Andar and Deh Yak."

Fivecoat believed in counterinsurgency, and he believed even more strongly in David Petraeus, a man he had seen overcome the toughest of challenges on the battlefield. But Petraeus could not be everywhere, and America could not afford to put enough troops on the ground in all the places in Afghanistan where, with enough mass and enough time, they might have done some good. Fivecoat was extremely proud of the Rakkasans for taking the fight to the Taliban. But he found the battalion's losses—three dead, 125 wounded—to be a heavy burden. He thought he was mentally prepared to carry that weight, but this was turning out to be harder than he imagined—as most of his peers found, too. He was also frustrated that the surge of 2011 in Afghanistan had not been able to achieve what he saw accomplished in Iraq during the surge in 2007 and 2008. Having been part of a successful counterinsurgency campaign there, he found it tough leaving Afghanistan with so much work still to be done. In retrospect, breaking the back of the insurgency in Ghazni was going to require more combat operations, to kill enough insurgents and persuade others to seek reintegration, with the cumulative effect sufficient to tip the balance of power, perhaps also accompanied by some form of political deal. As Petraeus had frequently observed, Afghanistan was not going to be "flipped" the way Iraq was during the surge there; the circumstances were different, and persistence was going to be required.

As he prepared to fly back to his family in Fort Campbell, Fivecoat sent Petraeus a parting note with a few thoughts about his command of Petraeus's old battalion and about his Afghan experience. Petraeus congratulated him and then cautioned against leaving it too far behind. "Expect to be back here in a few years as a brigade commander," Petraeus wrote.

Fivecoat read the general's e-mail on his laptop and just stared at the screen.

CHAPTER 7

LINES OF OPERATION

One cool morning in mid-January, Brigadier General Mark Martins stretched out in the plush polished-hardwood interior of the Gulf-stream V jet supporting the theater and began to pitch the work of his Rule of Law Field Force to Major General Sayed Abdul Ghafar Sayed Zadah, head of the Afghan Interior Ministry's counterterrorism division. He and Sayed Zadah were flying from Kabul to Kandahar to see the Chel Zeena Criminal Investigative Center, adjacent to Sarposa prison, the first of five planned regional "green zones" for law and justice in Afghanistan. Martins mentioned to Sayed Zadah that there had been 110 assassinations in Kanda-har over the past year. The city's chief prosecutor, Jalat Khan, was doing his best to keep up with the caseload, Martins said, but was simply overwhelmed. Khan needed help. Sayed Zadah listened intently.

Petraeus and Martins had reunited in Afghanistan shortly after Petrae-us's arrival in Kabul. The war's new commander had created a job for his favorite lawyer running what became the U.S.-led Rule of Law Field Force–Afghanistan. Petraeus told Martins to come up with a strategy for getting all forty-nine coalition countries behind creation of a functioning, mod-ern justice system. Petraeus remembered how critical the creation of rule-of-law "green zones" had been in Iraq (an effort also guided by Martins), and he considered them no less crucial in Afghanistan. Significantly, the Afghan implementation differed in certain respects from Multi-National Force–

Iraq's rule-of-law efforts. Martins continued to use the idea of the green zone, but efforts in Afghanistan were also built around the idea that the Afghan government could never compete in providing dispute-resolution services and justice to the people so long as it lacked a minimally capable network to do so. Martins reinforced a traditional Afghan division of functions between national, provincial and district levels of governance. The result was a "hub and spoke" model that emphasized assistance to Afghans as they reinforced key legal institutions at provincial centers and then projected dispute-resolution and governance capacity into surrounding districts.

Petraeus hadn't flinched when it came to handing Martins, a military lawyer, command of hundreds of U.S. combat troops and legal experts to support his rule-of-law initiative. If Martins was going to create a functioning courthouse in the Arghandab River Valley, now that Flynn had cleared it of Taliban, he needed troops to defend it and those manning it, there and around the country. This was Petraeus's Anaconda strategy in action: Flynn and the Top Guns fought the Taliban on the battlefield, and Martins and his Afghan provincial judges and prosecutors fought the insurgents in the courts. Martins was sensitive to concerns that he was "militarizing" criminal justice, but both he and Petraeus thought there was a lack of sufficient civilian capacity to begin this portion of the clear-hold-and-build effort. Senator Graham, a military lawyer in the Air Force Reserve, applauded Martins's command of combat troops, which he thought was "unprecedented in the history of military law."

Back in November, Martins had made a similar plea to Noorullah Sadat, the Karzai government's chief national security prosecutor in Kabul, asking him to appoint three competent and honest subordinates to satellite courthouses he was establishing in Spin Boldak and two other recently cleared districts around Kandahar: Zhari and the Arghandab River Valley. Martins had support from U.S. commanders like Flynn in those areas, and money to boost salaries from the State Department's Bureau of International Narcotics and Law Enforcement Affairs. But what he really needed was specially trained lawyers to assign as trainers and advisers to their Afghan peers before the courthouses were established—amid additional Afghan partners.

After Martins and Sayed Zadah touched down in Kandahar, Martins gave the Afghan official a tour of the Chel Zeena compound. Chel Zeena, built mostly with U.S. funds, was designed as a secure facility where investigators, prosecutors and clerks could do the legal and forensic work necessary for evidence-based criminal proceedings. Despite investment in new equipment, the facility still looked dilapidated. Prisoners, many of them barefoot, sat in open courtyards. One open-air area housed criminals accused of petty crimes. In a separate, smaller holding area, a handful of female prisoners sat chatting while their children played around them. A final holding area housed hard-core prisoners, most of them insurgents.

Martins and Sayed Zadah walked on the roof of Sarposa prison, part of the Chel Zeena compound, a prison infamous for the breakout by more than four hundred Taliban fighters in 2008. After Martins explained the layout of the compound, they proceeded to a conference room to meet with advisers from the FBI and the State Department, military police officers and Afghan police and prosecutorial officials, including chief Jalat Khan.

Khan was a medium-size, salt-and-pepper-bearded, vigorous man with a toothy smile. He was grateful for the international assistance and willing to discuss the Rafiullah case, one that held considerable interest for Martins. "Rafiullah turned himself in after he realized we were on his trail, but was deceptive about his identity," Martins explained through an interpreter. "We questioned him carefully and did follow-up research to find his real name. He was accused of murder and extortion." Other records, however, indicated that he had been involved in supporting insurgents, and it was his connection to organized armed groups seeking to bring down the government that enabled investigation of him as a national security threat and trial under a separate chapter of Afghanistan's criminal code.

"Have you run a full scan of his biometrics with the Cross Match Jump Kit?" Martins inquired, learning from one of the Afghans that, yes, recently trained enrollers had done so. "You should check the coalition database to see if we have any latent prints." The Afghan Ministry of the Interior had over the past year begun distributing the Jump Kits, which digitally scanned fingerprints, recorded iris shape and photographed facial appearance on a laptop computer. Martins had pushed to get the equipment and necessary training to Kandahar and other areas recently cleared of Taliban. The Jump Kits were very similar to the U.S. military's laptop-based Biometrics Automated Toolset and Handheld Interagency Identity Detection Equipment systems. Biometric enrollments of criminal suspects, applicants for the security forces and government jobs, prison inmates and other high-risk populations was a critical enabler for the rule-of-law effort. As tens of thousands of latent fingerprints had been lifted from the surfaces of exploded IED fragments and from weapons found at Taliban hideouts, more and more matches were being made between newly enrolled Afghans and the database of latent prints.

These systems were an important step toward creating identities for friend and foe, denying insurgents the anonymity on which they depended. All Afghan police and military officials were scanned along with prisoners; even enemy KIA were often scanned to compare against target lists. To that point, about one million Afghans had been enrolled in the system, but with a military-age male population of about seven million, the Afghan government was pursuing a biometrically enabled national identification card to increase these numbers. Greater enrollments were needed so that Afghanistan could control its borders more effectively, corner insurgents and criminals and reduce corruption in everything from elections to applications for jobs. Here, even if a database check revealed no matches against fingerprints found on bomb parts, Jalat Khan could definitely benefit by having Rafiullah's exact biometric data on file. There were four "Rafiullahs" in Kandahar police custody, and they all were using aliases.

Sitting at the rectangular table in the conference room, part of the first structure completed at the criminal investigative center, Martins urged one of the FBI agents only recently posted to Kandahar to offer technical assistance. "How can you corroborate Rafiullah's partial confessions for conviction, Jalat?" the agent asked. Evidence gathering was a major challenge for Afghan investigators, who rarely made it to the scene of a crime. Jalat responded, "We need a much fuller background check. Some of these brave investigators here should visit the places where witnesses say Rafiullah did his crimes. We need to reinterview these and other witnesses. And then we need to reinterview Rafiullah." This kind of attention to a case was only just now becoming possible, due to the improved security situation and the training and facilities being devoted to investigation.

Major General Sayed Zadah interjected in Pashto, "Prosecutor Khan, this is your case, but I would consider conducting a fresh investigation, because the investigators who compiled the file you already have may have been corrupt or incompetent: the care taken to select and train the investigators here was not present with that team. I recommend you do all of these things with the newly vetted team that you have here, and I pledge my support. If Rafiullah truly is linked to Quetta [the home in Pakistan of the Taliban headquarters], this is an important case."

"You all are the experts," Martins offered, per the military's habit of steering clear of direct technical advice on legal matters, "but from what I've seen, even a promising case can fall apart before an Afghan judge if the accused recants his confession, so please let us know how the coalition can assist you in building a strong case."

"For instance," Martins asked, "are the Case Management System advisers able to spend enough time with you and the investigators, Prosecutor Khan?" International donors had provided a large grant to the Afghan government to create a uniform process for managing criminal cases. The seven Afghan government elements involved with law enforcement and national security had signed a memorandum of understanding, committing their organizations to the new management system and to using specific formats for recording and more transparently managing case-file data. Implementation was in its infancy, however, and one of the problems in still-violent places like Kandahar was simply getting the contractor employees hired by international donors out and in position to help Afghans stand up this new system. Martins and Jalat Khan knew that better file management could greatly help Afghan officials determine whether other members of Rafiullah's network were already in custody. The greater transparency and uniformity of the system could also reduce opportunities for bribes and illegal influence as Rafiullah's case wound its way toward trial. The new system could reduce delays in case processing stemming from Afghanistan's archaic and inefficient record-keeping system. Under Afghan law, Jalat Khan pointed out, Rafiullah should be tried no more than a month after arrest.

"Meanwhile, Prosecutor Khan," Martins continued, "the secure housing for you and the criminal investigators should be done for you here at Chel Zeena by next month. You will need the protection." Sayed Zadah piped up: "And I spoke with the police zone commander for Kandahar by phone this morning, and he is prepared to issue the investigators the trucks they need to visit crime scenes safely." The afternoon dialogue continued.

It was clear there was still a lot of work to be done in the Rule of Law Field Force. Martins was a driven officer, often on e-mail until three in the morning and out the door for a six-mile run or a battlefield circulation shortly after 6:00 A.M. Like Petraeus, whom he considered a mentor, he drove the mission at times through sheer personality. What he lacked was a large enough team of rule-of-law advisers and support personnel to really gain the traction needed to enable Afghans to take the lead in their own justice system.

WITH MARTINS FOCUSED on how to prosecute and adjudicate criminals in Afghanistan, Brigadier General H. R. McMaster worked on how to identify them—and stop them from looting the country. One evening in January, he walked into Petraeus's office with a folder full of PowerPoint slides he was developing to brief President Karzai on his anticorruption work. McMaster radiated intensity as he briefed Petraeus, who was in the middle of eating dinner at his desk. Petraeus had enormous respect for McMaster, who, like Petraeus with the 101st Airborne, had employed counterinsurgency tactics successfully in northern Iraq well before they were codified in the new *Counterinsurgency Field Manual*. McMaster had, in his anticorruption work with Task Force Shafafiyat, raised eyebrows among some in the State Department and across the international mission by running the task force with the same aggressiveness he had used to drive the 3rd Armored Cavalry Regiment in Iraq. Quietly, the civilians made the same complaint about Petraeus—why were his military guys taking the lead on the anticorruption effort? Petraeus worked in the civilian world as well as any general, but when he really wanted to get something done and there was inadequate capacity elsewhere, his default was to do it with those he had highest confidence in—military officers close to him.

"I wanted to get a quick steer from you, sir, in case you want to give feedback before we meet with Karzai," McMaster said. "As you know, it has been really difficult to get this anticorruption work going in places like airports. We're in a race to do that now. This is the 'purpose' slide—to update him what we're doing on our side and how we propose to deal with corruption at border crossings and airports. He's indicated he is interested in this. We can use it to emphasize our common interest."

Airports, in particular the Kandahar airport, had become hot spots for smuggling—drugs, market goods, cash and other matériel. Government officials and well-connected businessmen were able to board flights with suitcases of cash, no questions asked. The U.S. Department of Homeland Security had installed the technology for screening some of this, but the Afghan customs agents' recalcitrance in implementing screening procedures illustrated the challenges of working with certain elements of the Afghan government. McMaster had also learned that some smuggling was being enabled by a criminal patronage network inside the Afghan Air Force. In fact, he was coming to realize that the hardest part of his job was stopping the criminals inside the government, individuals with whom he was supposedly working.

Petraeus, inhaling his food, shook his head as McMaster explained that his audience with Karzai would be with a group of Afghans and Americans. Then Petraeus cut him off.

"You won't get access to Karzai through that group," he said. "You'll get it through me."

Petraeus was the Karzai gatekeeper, at least for his subordinates; other avenues seldom worked. But he saw McMaster's work as a critical line of effort and would remain closely involved.

"Yes, sir, okay," McMaster said. "We thought this working group would be powerful. It would be a symbol." Petraeus agreed but pointed out that he would be the one who would get McMaster access to Karzai, given that the working group had not yet even had a meeting with the president.

McMaster rolled through the slides, explaining at one point how Karzai seemed supportive but that his government was slow in executing reforms. There had been something of a chill, he said, since the Salehi case came to light.

Salehi, a member of the National Security Council and an aide to Karzai, had been accused and arrested in July for soliciting a bribe in exchange for the dismissal of a corruption investigation. In November, officials dropped corruption allegations, sparking an outrage among Afghan police and officials. No one, it seemed, advised the American advisers to the Afghan team on the political implications of arresting a high-level Karzai aide in a pre-dawn raid by heavily armed special Afghan police, which put a damper on Afghan-U.S. cooperation. It also taught McMaster that he had to understand the political context of every move he made.

General Petraeus took some time to critique his presentation. "Reduce the number of bullets, and don't use sentences," he told McMaster, referring to the bullet-point items in his briefing. "Ensure that President Karzai has to listen to you because you don't put everything in the bullets. Right now, he'll just read the slides himself."

McMaster laughed at himself and shot back: "At least all the bullets start with verbs."

"Okay," Petraeus conceded with a grin, "you get credit for parallelism."

After McMaster flipped to the next slide, which explained the prosecution of doctors for stealing millions in prescription medicines from the National Military Hospital, Petraeus stopped him. "Be clear on who is doing what. Is this ISAF or U.S.? Which Afghan officials? He'll ask you for some examples."

"Yes, sir," McMaster said. "One theme we want them to take in is the concept of joint investigations. And we are going to hit 'Afghan first,'" explained McMaster.

"Good," nodded Petraeus, now wearing his reading glasses, explaining that he had already briefed Karzai on this case. "But it would be good to double-tap him on this."

McMaster had another case study to review for Karzai. "The major crimes task force uncovered a major corruption ring at one of the key border crossings. No surprise. They were able to prosecute that network. After that happened, revenue at that border crossing went up considerably," he said. "But since then, some of the individuals were released from prison, and the head of the ring is back in a customs job in a different area without having served his sentence."

He moved to the next slide, depicting airport corruption.

"It's all about leadership at the end of the day," Petraeus said. "If they have a decent leader [at a border checkpoint or airport], they will get it done. I look forward to laying this out for the president."

LATER, ALONE IN his office, Petraeus seemed weary, even though he'd recently gone for a week to see Holly and other family members in Germany; it was his first leave in several years. He and Holly had repeatedly made plans for leave, but unexpected missions kept interfering. He'd skied with his kids for the first time since they were small children and gone running in the Bavarian hills, but there was still work to be done each day, and that had kept him occupied during much of the break. He was, after all, still the commander of the effort in Afghanistan, even if officially on leave. Some of his aides thought the break hadn't been enough, and they worried that he was losing his edge. One thing or another seemed to keep him up most nights—issues in working relationships with Washington, the relationship with Karzai or, on this night, coalition casualties. "Well, every now and then you gotta get a decent night's sleep," he said. "This wears on you over time, and it wears on you over years. No one else feels the same weight of responsibility that the commander does. . . . Yesterday was a bad day. That takes a toll on a person. The whole command feels the emotional swing, from a period when we had a couple of really decent days."

He was referring to the five U.S. soldiers who'd died on January 12. Staff Sergeant Omar Aceves, 30, of El Paso, Specialist Jarrid L. King, 20, of Erie, Pennsylvania, and Private First Class Benjamin G. Moore, 23, of Robbinsville, New Jersey, members of an engineer battalion attached to the 10th Mountain Division, were killed by an IED in Ghazni Province. Sergeant Zainah C. Creamer, 28, of Texarkana, Texas, serving in the 212th Military Police Detachment, was also killed by an IED, in Kandahar. And Major Evan J. Mooldyk, 47, of Rancho Murieta, California, part of the 19th Sustainment Command, died of a heart attack in Khost. Five soldiers from four states, ages 20 to 47. Petraeus wrote personal letters to the families of every soldier killed on his watch and attended as many memorial ceremonies in Afghanistan as he could. "We try to get out to them, but you have to really commit to that work, because it's not easy to get to some of the bases," he said, referring to the ramp ceremonies where troopers' flag-draped caskets are loaded onto aircraft for return to the United States for subsequent unit memorial ceremonies. Petraeus and his command sergeant major, Marvin Hill, made a significant effort to attend ceremonies in the provinces. "They're out in small outposts, little bases, not exactly C-130 accessible in all cases," he said. Dealing with death on a daily basis, Petraeus had nonetheless dispensed with wearing body armor and a helmet as he moved around the country; in fact, his security chief didn't recall Petraeus ever wearing it on that tour. "If [an attack] happens, it happens, and it doesn't matter what you're wearing," he said fatalistically, adding that he and his wife had been far more worried about their son, Lieutenant Stephen Petraeus. "He was actually getting shot at," he said a few months after his son rotated out of Afghanistan.

Stephen's unit, 3rd Platoon, Alpha Company, 1st Battalion, 503rd Infantry of the 173rd Airborne Brigade Combat Team, serving in Chak District, Wardak Province, had been engaged in numerous gunfights with insurgents. At one point, a deserted compound Stephen's platoon had occupied was assaulted and Stephen had ordered his men to take cover below while he remained on a rooftop calling in support over the radio. Petraeus was very proud of his son. Neither Petraeus nor his wife had pushed their son to enter the military, and during high school and his first year in college at MIT, it didn't appear it was his calling. Stephen was a soft-spoken computer techie, and MIT was quite a contrast with Petraeus's college experience at West Point. But at the start of his second year at MIT, Stephen surprised his parents by joining ROTC on his own. He subsequently was commissioned as an infantry officer upon graduation from MIT, completed the Infantry Officer Basic Course and earned the coveted Ranger tab. He had reported to the 173rd Airborne Brigade Combat Team in Vicenza, Italy, the previous spring and deployed to Afghanistan immediately after arrival.

In Afghanistan, Petraeus knew his son was fighting in one of the tougher areas, an insurgent-infested district that had been an economy-of-force effort until the summer of 2010. By the fall of 2010, there had been hundreds of coalition troops killed or wounded in that area. Stephen's safety was often on Petraeus's mind. But the risk of allowing insurgents or even the Afghans to know that his son was there was so real for him that he would not visit his son until the final week of his tour—to pin a Combat Infantryman Badge on his son's chest and to present Purple Heart medals to some of Stephen's platoon members wounded during their tour.

In mid-January 2011, shortly before Obama delivered his State of the Union address, Petraeus issued a letter to all troops, civilians and NATO officials in Afghanistan with the subject line "COMISAF Assessment." He had been working on it since late December, constantly tweaking it, conscious that it would be read not just by ISAF members but also by the American people, NATO allies, the White House and the Afghan people. It was his measured, carefully calibrated State of the War message, which credited ISAF and Afghan forces with "hard-won progress" in Helmand and Kandahar provinces, as well as advances "in a number of other areas in the east, west, and north, aided by the growth of Afghan and ISAF forces, the commencement of the Afghan Local Police initiative, the beginning of Afghan-led reintegration of reconcilable insurgents, and the relentless pace of targeted operations by ISAF and Afghan special operations forces. . . . Indeed, while there clearly is a need for additional work in numerous areas, it is equally clear that ISAF and Afghan forces inflicted enormous losses on mid-level Taliban and Haqqani Network leaders throughout the country and took away some of their most important safe havens. Now, in fact, the insurgents increasingly are responding to our operations rather than vice-versa, and there are numerous reports of unprecedented discord among the members of the Quetta Shura, the Taliban senior leadership body." But, he cautioned,

Despite the achievements of 2010, there is much work to be done in 2011. And, as always in Afghanistan, the way ahead will be difficult. As President Karzai has made clear, the Kabul security bubble needs to be expanded into neighboring provinces. The gains in the south and southwest have to be solidified, joined, and expanded. Areas of improved security in the east and west need to be connected and extended. And insurgent advances in recent years in the north and mountainous northeast must be halted and reversed.

Obama's State of the Union address contained just two paragraphs about the war in Afghanistan.

We've also taken the fight to al-Qaeda and their allies abroad. In Afghanistan, our troops have taken Taliban strongholds and trained Afghan security forces. Our purpose is clear: By preventing the Taliban from reestablishing a stranglehold over the Afghan people, we will deny al-Qaeda the safe haven that served as a launching pad for 9/11.

Thanks to our heroic troops and civilians, fewer Afghans are under the control of the insurgency. There will be tough fighting ahead, and the Afghan government will need to deliver better governance. But we are strengthening the capacity of the Afghan people and building an enduring partnership with them. This year, we will work with nearly fifty countries to begin a transition to an Afghan lead. And this July, we will begin to bring our troops home.

Obama had committed thirty thousand additional troops and placed Petraeus in command of the war. Even conservatives who found fault with nearly everything Obama did had to acknowledge that he had prosecuted this war with a sense of determination and purpose. They just didn't detect much enthusiasm and were concerned that he might scale down the U.S. effort too soon. Obama deeply respected the effort being put forth by the American military. But he was obviously looking to the drawdown in July and appeared to believe the time was approaching to begin to reduce the U.S. commitment in Afghanistan.

PETRAEUS'S CAMPAIGN PLAN was built upon what he called six "lines of operation." Combat forces covered the first two: "Protect the population" and "disrupt insurgent networks." Martins's Rule of Law Field Force contributed to two more: "Support legitimate governance" and "foster sustainable socioeconomic development." McMaster worked the fifth: "Neutralize criminal patronage networks." The final line was "support the development of the Afghan armed forces," a task headed by Lieutenant General William B. Caldwell, a close associate of Petraeus since Caldwell replaced him as General Shelton's executive assistant.

More than almost any other effort, the development of Afghan forces was the key to Obama's drawdown plan. Since the fall of 2009, Afghan forces had grown in size and capability, financed by billions from U.S. taxpayers. In 2010, the Afghan National Army (ANA), the Afghan National Police (ANP) and the Afghan Air Force (AAF) grew by some 70,000. By the fall, the ANA stood at just under 145,000 and the ANP just above 113,000; the AAF was just over 4,000. The commitment of funds to this enterprise by the United States and its NATO allies was $11.6 billion in 2011, bringing the total for 2010 and 2011 to about $20 billion. Fourteen percent of Afghan recruits were literate, and thousands had gone AWOL, but Caldwell's command was able to keep recruiting enough to ensure 305,000 men in uniform by the fall of 2011. Wages had been substantially increased, paychecks were being delivered to soldiers electronically to cut down on theft, and advanced weaponry was being issued. All recruits were receiving mandatory literacy training so that they could read and write their names, recognize simple numbers and comprehend basic words of text.

Major Fernando Lujan believed fervently in the potential of Afghan forces. To take the CAAT concept inside the Afghan military, Lujan had embedded deep inside the 205th Afghan National Army Corps. He wore an Afghan uniform, grew a beard and fought for two weeks at a time with Afghan units. He spoke to soldiers in Dari, and upon his return to headquarters he briefed the corps's commanding general in Dari. He discovered that Afghan culture was most welcoming to foreigners who took the time to learn Dari or Pashto. At one point he was so impressed with the bravery of Afghan soldiers—their calm in battle and their acceptance of death, which he attributed to their Islamic faith—that he considered converting to Islam. He loved his work: "I'll do [this] in the Army for as long as they'll let me, . . . then I'll get out and do it as a civilian or some other type of governmental actor until I'm too old to walk patrols," he said. "Counterinsurgency is that kind of fight—too fluid and dynamic to draw old lessons from. To develop real insight, you have to stay connected to conflict in a very real, very direct way."

Petraeus had heartily embraced the Counterinsurgency Advisory and Assistance Team initiative a little over a month earlier. The CAAT was Petraeus's kind of organization, driven by big ideas from the battlefield, and Colonel Joe Felter, himself a Stanford Ph.D., had been Petraeus's student in West Point's Department of Social Sciences. Petraeus savored the opportunity to laud a subordinate. "The truth is, you have actually exceeded what I thought were lofty ambitions for the CAAT," Petraeus said to begin a brief ceremony marking Felter's departure.

But Felter's replacement, a spit-and-polish Marine colonel named Rob Tanzola, had a different vision for the CAAT. While Felter was known by those who worked for him as somebody who allowed subordinates considerable latitude, Tanzola seemed to want to exert enormous control over the CAAT's members, and he seemed to loathe what he saw as the team's cowboy ways. One of his first orders to the Afghan Hands in the CAAT was to shave their beards—something the Hands thought was an important signal to gain rapport with their Afghan counterparts. Whatever the CAAT's members thought of him—and there were those who defended his crackdown as long overdue—the disruption that accompanied his arrival exemplified the downside to the U.S. military's penchant for one-year or shorter rotations.

Doug Ollivant, the former lieutenant colonel who had helped plan the surge in Baghdad, was one of the first to go. Tanzola tried to fire Ollivant after he sent an expletive-laced e-mail to a few CAAT hands in Kabul who had ventured into his territory in eastern Afghanistan and, in Ollivant's mind, gotten into areas that were his purview. Ollivant felt blindsided by Tanzola's attitude and mobilized his network of supporters to e-mail Major General Campbell, the commander of the eastern sector, and Lieutenant General David Rodriguez, the deputy ISAF commander, on his behalf. Petraeus offered to help Ollivant find a job, but by then relations had become too strained for Ollivant to stay.

Tanzola began shifting the CAAT's focus from tactical conditions on the ground to the strategic situation in the region, based on a mistaken impression that this was what Petraeus wanted. After Tanzola spent a month following this course, Petraeus finally met with him and other CAAT members, telling them to stay focused on tactics. "'I've got plenty of strategic thinkers running around ISAF,'" one of those present quoted the general as saying. Tanzola shifted back to a tactical focus but continued his hierarchical approach, and his insistence on higher standards for report writing and information collection remained in full force. He had developed a priority list, topped by an initiative to help conventional forces assume responsibility for Village Stability Operations (VSO) and the development of Afghan Local Police detachments, both of which started as Special Forces missions. Lujan's plans for taking the CAAT process inside the Afghan military weren't on Tanzola's list. Tanzola didn't believe Afghans were ever going to be part of the CAAT team, so why bother? In an effort to enforce the chain of command, Tanzola prohibited Lujan from coming to CAAT headquarters in Kabul and directed him to stop interacting with incoming members of the Afghan Hands program, who weren't being assigned to CAAT, as Lujan had hoped.

Lujan worried about what he called "HUGE" gaps on the Afghan side that would badly undermine the campaign when ISAF placed more weight

on the ANSF during transition. "Some of these gaps we don't even fully understand yet," Lujan relayed to colleagues. "The Afghan-CAAT effort is
uniquely poised to gain clarity on these issues and develop innovative solutions." Lujan later voiced his concerns to Tanzola in e-mails that verged on
irreverence. Tanzola stopped responding to Lujan's e-mails. Soon after, Tanzola split up the team and dispersed the members across different regional
commands.

AS LUJAN STRUGGLED to find his way with Tanzola, the first story on
Petraeus's future appeared in the press, in the *Times* of London. The paper
reported what was widely assumed when Petraeus took command in July—
that he would leave Afghanistan by the end of 2011. Speculation about his
next assignment would soon become something of a distraction for him,
which was the last thing he needed.

In late February, at a Sunday afternoon Afghan National Security Council meeting, Afghan officials inquired about reports that as many as fifty civilians, many of them women and children, had been killed in ISAF air strikes
in the remote mountains of Kunar Province, on the Pakistan border. Petraeus later noted that U.S. officials reported that some of the civilians who
had allegedly been injured were children with burned hands and feet, not
shrapnel injuries, as would be associated with air strikes. There had been
reports from that region that children had at times been disciplined by having their hands or feet dipped in boiling water, but Petraeus did not make any
explicit link between these reports and the incident in question. Two days
later, the *Washington Post* reported that Petraeus had shocked Karzai and
his aides by suggesting that "Afghans caught up in a coalition attack in northeastern Afghanistan might have burned their own children to exaggerate
claims of civilian casualties, according to two participants at the meeting."
The *Post* said that neither Petraeus's exact language nor his precise message was known. Petraeus meant nothing of the sort, but leaking inaccurate
statements for political gain was common. "So be it," he said several months
later in an interview. "Welcome to the neighborhood. It's not my first rodeo.

When we have made mistakes, the policy has been to acknowledge them, to explain the facts, to apologize when that is warranted, and obviously not only to take corrective action, but in some cases judicial or non-judicial action."

Petraeus's point man in the Palace Information Coordination Center, Navy captain Ed Zellem, offered to show the videos of the strikes to Afghan NSC staff and even to bring in a trained pilot to explain the video feed and answer questions to convincingly demonstrate that the officials had been duped by locals trying to cause problems for the government and ISAF. But the Afghan officials demurred.

The war was growing increasingly savage and violent for ordinary Afghans. The annual report on civilian casualties in Afghanistan in 2010, released a few days later by the United Nations and the Afghanistan Independent Human Rights Commission, found that 2,777 civilians had been killed, a 15 percent increase over 2009. Seventy-five percent of those deaths were attributed to the Taliban and other "anti-government elements." Homemade bombs, improvised explosive devices and suicide attacks were responsible for most deaths, though the most alarming trend was the insurgents' increased use of assassination as a weapon against Afghan government officials and others who cooperated with the Americans. Half of those assassinations had taken place in southern Afghanistan, where the surge of U.S. and NATO forces left the Taliban with few other options for prevailing at the village and provincial levels. "The social and psychological effects and violations of human rights associated with assassinations are more devastating than a body count would suggest," the report found. "An individual deciding to join a district shura, to campaign for a particular candidate, to take a job with a development organization, or to speak freely about a new Taliban commander in the area, often knows that their decision may have life or death consequences."

The report also noted that deaths and injuries attributed to Afghan and international forces declined. The emphasis by both McChrystal and Petraeus on reducing civilian casualties from air strikes clearly had an impact. The number of women and children killed in air strikes by international forces declined 62 percent and 72 percent, respectively, compared with 2009. Even with Petraeus's reliance on night raids by Special Operations Forces as an important tactic for targeting mid- and upper-level Taliban commanders, civilian casualties associated with the raids fell, the report found. The report also said that clearance operations from July through November in the districts surrounding Kandahar, including the Arghandab River Valley, where Flynn's Top Guns operated, had not produced a "spike" in civilian casualties, "although they resulted in large-scale property damage."

"GUIDONS, GUIDONS. This is Eagle 6. The 101st Airborne Division's next Rendezvous with Destiny is North to Baghdad. Op-Ord Desert Eagle 2 is now in effect. Godspeed. Air Assault. Out," then–Major General David Petraeus, the 101st's commanding general, told his troopers over a field radio the night before they went to war. It was late March 2003. The Screaming Eagles were poised to push across the Kuwaiti border and drive to the Iraqi capital—and beyond.

Six days into the great assault, with U.S. forces stopped dead in their tracks by a blinding dust storm, Petraeus posed his prescient, tell-me-how-this-ends question and answered it with another: "Eight years and eight divisions?" It was a reference to an answer given by the Army chief of staff in the early 1950s when asked by President Eisenhower what it would take to reinforce flagging French forces encircled at Dien Bien Phu, in Vietnam. In Iraq and Afghanistan, it would take nearly as much, and last longer.

In the first combat command of his career, Petraeus led the Screaming Eagles in the fight to Baghdad, supporting the 3rd Infantry Division's bold thrust into Baghdad with deep attacks by the 101st's Apache attack helicopters and conducting major operations on the way to liberate Najaf, then Karbala and, finally, Hillah. Captain Fivecoat would never forget the Battle of Najaf. There were Petraeus, Lieutenant General Scott Wallace, the corps commander, and one of the division's colonels standing on the hoods of Humvees with binoculars, watching "the combined arms attack into Najaf—it looked like something straight out of WWII." Petraeus believed that a commander should seek to be at the "point of decision," where he could best understand what his unit was engaged in, which was often where the fighting was heaviest. In his journal, Fivecoat wrote that Petraeus "habitually wanted to walk forward to watch the action unfold."

While some of his subordinates found him initially overly cautious for not immediately ordering a ground attack into Najaf, Petraeus maneuvered his forces deliberately and skillfully, seeking to understand what he was facing and carefully orchestrating how best to respond. He wasn't casualty averse, he explained, just averse to stupid casualties. Launching light infantry into a city of more than half a million shouldn't commence, he ordered, until all the "enablers"—tanks, artillery, attack helicopters, close air support, air medevac and so on—were positioned to support those on the ground when, inevitably, they ran into dug-in enemies. His approach seemed to work: The 101st accomplished its missions. The fight to Baghdad and subsequent operations to clear Mosul had resulted in relatively light casualties, considering the fighting; by the end of May, three soldiers had been killed and eighty-four wounded in action, including many amputees. The losses awakened Petraeus to the most significant burden of command.

Petraeus mentioned to a friend in an e-mail that it was like a blow to the sternum to receive reports of casualties. He was more guarded with his family. But his face could not fully mask the emotion from his aide Major David Fivecoat, who made a note in his journal that spring: "MG Petraeus was shaken after visiting the injured." Petraeus candidly revealed himself a bit in a letter to West Point classmates that June: "I used to wonder why old men got choked up talking about their comrades; I now know why." But like many of his peers, he knew that the commander's role was to be resolute and offer strength to others. He was learning how to keep the mask of command firmly in place.

Just as the 101st was getting a grip on southern Baghdad, Petraeus received orders to leapfrog, by air assault, five hundred kilometers north to Iraq's second-largest city, Mosul, near the borders with Syria and Turkey. It was here that Petraeus received his greatest acclaim, demonstrating his flair for counterinsurgency, including every task from pursuing—and killing—

Saddam's two sons to performing various components of nation building, and even conducting what some saw as his own foreign policy as he cut a deal with Syria to ensure adequate fuel imports into the city and another deal with a Turkish company for electricity. He cited his experience in Bosnia as having enabled him to quickly gain his bearings. By early May, two weeks after his arrival, Nineveh Province, of which Mosul was the capital, had a provincial council and governor after Petraeus organized elections, which were actually "caucus selections" that he orchestrated to establish a provincial council with representatives of all segments of Nineveh Province so that the 101st had Iraqi partners.

As Petraeus's units, having largely pacified the area, moved into nation building, the Pentagon authorized members of the 101st to sew the division's eagle insignia on the right shoulders of their uniforms, indicating that they had fought with the unit in combat. They already wore the insignia on their left shoulder, representing their unit of duty. "I must say I am extraordinarily proud now to wear the Screaming Eagle patch on both shoulders," Petraeus wrote to his family. "It almost brings tears to my eyes."

Soon he was acting as the viceroy of northern Iraq, cajoling tribal sheikhs ("none has ever had a short conversation in his life, and all want a piece of me right now," he told a colleague), opening schools, negotiating business deals, pleading with his bureaucratic overlords in Baghdad and Washington for help. On May 6, he signed a resolution opening the border crossing with Syria in northwestern Iraq. It began: "Whereas, the Commander of Coalition Forces for Northwest Iraq recognizes an emergency need for the resumption of 'legal trade' in Northwestern Iraq with Syria and Turkey. . . ."

Petraeus's frustration with the Bush administration's Coalition Provisional Authority in Baghdad was a common refrain with all the division commanders. He found the decision by the CPA and senior Pentagon officials to disband the Iraqi armed forces and purge Saddam Hussein's Baath party to the level it did as particularly misguided, since many mid-level bureaucrats and Western-educated academics at the university in Mosul had been party members. Without them, getting the city back up on its feet became endlessly more complicated. The effect of the overall de-Baathification program,

As a West Point cadet,
Petraeus was noted for his drive
and graduated in the top of his class,
a star man in the class of 1974.

Despite the antiwar sentiment of
the time, Petraeus (right) remained
dedicated to following his military
heroes and set his sights on an
infantry post after graduation.

Cadet Petraeus
(fourth from left,
front row) was assigned
to Company C-1
(1970-1974).

Cadet Petraeus with his father, Sixtus, a former officer on a Dutch ship, who came to the United States during World War II and later joined the U.S. Merchant Marines.

Wedding day, July 6, 1974.

Petraeus with his parents and future father-in-law on his commissioning day.

Lieutenant General William Knowlton, superintendent of USMA, was an important early mentor in counterinsurgency and father to Petraeus's wife, Hollister ("Holly").

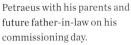

Major General John Galvin, an intellectual force in the post-Vietnam Army, became Petraeus's most influential mentor. Galvin gave Petraeus the "Stampede" as a farewell token in 1982.

Lieutenant Petraeus deployed to Turkey while he was stationed in Vicenza, Italy.

Colonel Keith Nightingale (second from left) mentored Petraeus from their days in Vicenza, Italy. Shown here in France, where Petraeus was serving, on the fiftieth anniversary of D-Day.

The archetypal soldier-scholar completed his dissertation on the influence of Vietnam on military decision-making regarding the use of force at the Woodrow Wilson School at Princeton University.

Following his civilian counterparts, Ambassadors Karl Eikenberry and Mark Sedwill, General Petraeus arrives to take command of ISAF forces in Kabul.

Brigadier General Mark Martins celebrates the launch of the NATO Rule of Law Field Support Mission—part of Petraeus's Anaconda strategy.

Lieutenant Colonel David G. Fivecoat, a Petraeus protégé, commanded the 3rd Battalion of the 187th Regiment, 101st Airborne Division, in Paktika and Ghazni Provinces, with Major General John Campbell, commander of Regional Command East in Afghanistan, and Doug Ollivant, senior civilian adviser for the CAAT, who worked with Petraeus during the Iraq surge.

Lieutenant Colonel David Flynn, who commanded 1st Battalion, 320th Field Artillery Regiment of the 101st Airborne Division in the Arghandab River Valley.

Father and son, Second Lieutenant Stephen Petraeus, who served as a platoon leader in Wardak Province.

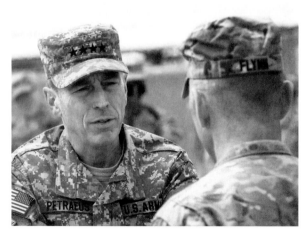

Petraeus with Lieutenant Colonel Flynn, who oversaw an artillery unit conducting classic counterinsurgency operations.

Doug Ollivant (right) visited Ghazni Province and met with local Afghans as part of his CAAT advisory mission.

Upon their return home, Lieutenant Colonel David Flynn's troopers were reunited with their wounded comrades. IEDs remain the greatest cause of injuries for ISAF soldiers.

Major Fernando Lujan (second from left), ISAF CAAT member, with troopers in the Afghan National Security Force. Lujan's initiative met with resistance from some but with praise from Petraeus.

Campbell and Fivecoat touring a battlefield circulation in Ghazni Province.

Lieutenant Colonel J. B. Vowell (far right) with Major General Campbell and members of the No Slack battalion, near the entrance to the Korengal and lower Pech valleys.

Petraeus with Chairman of the Joint Chiefs of Staff Admiral Mike Mullen, in Petraeus's Kabul office. Mullen was a key supporter for Petraeus in Iraq and Afghanistan.

Petraeus with Senators McCain, Lieberman, and Graham.

President Obama announcing the decision to send Petraeus to Afghanistan to command ISAF in June 2010.

The president announces Petraeus's nomination to become the new director of the Central Intelligence Agency.

Petraeus relayed, "was that tens of thousands of former party members were unemployed, without any salary, without any retirement, without any benefits, and therefore, to a large degree, without any incentive to support the new Iraq."

"Had some [American] leaders from Baghdad up here yesterday," Petraeus wrote to a friend on June 5. "Told them we sometimes wonder whether the most important objective to the folks above us/in Washington is winning the peace or getting the paperwork right. The bureaucracy is killing us. We were trusted to fire million dollar munitions out the kazoo (during the fight to Baghdad), but now have to account for even small purchases/contracts, with documents scanned in to be sent digitally to higher headquarters. We could win this thing if they'd just give us money (or get the folks here who are supposed to help—very slow in arriving). And I told them that in no uncertain terms."

Before Paul Bremer, the head of the CPA, visited Mosul in late June, Petraeus wondered whether he would be willing to listen or whether he would be in a "directive mode." Petraeus found the hubris emanating from Baghdad very frustrating and thought it must have been similar to that present in Vietnam when Robert McNamara was Defense secretary. But his conversation with Bremer was a good one. It would later spur Bremer to get authority to provide captured Iraqi funds to division commanders for the conduct of emergency reconstruction initiatives. And a subsequent conversation would gain Petraeus the authority to support Iraq-run reconciliation initiatives.

Nevertheless, Petraeus's frustration surfaced in a later e-mail to an associate:

You had to give people hope and, again, you have to have incentives for people to support the new Iraq, not to oppose it. And, if you don't provide those incentives, then don't be surprised if you have an insurgency in the morning. . . . Did [the military] need to be dissolved without any announcement about what its future was? We went five long weeks without that announcement and it wasn't addressed until some of us talked to some individuals in Baghdad and said, "You know, your policy is killing our troopers." That was a pretty stark statement. . . . Week after week the demonstrations were turning into near riots.

Two weeks prior to the Coalition Provision Authority's announcement that there would be stipends for former military members, Petraeus attempted to quell a fifteen-thousand-man demonstration, some of them holding weapons, outside the Nineveh Provincial Governorate Building, where the governor's office was located and where the provincial council met. It was, he later observed, "the worst nightmare of any commander—a [large, angry] crowd."

Standing on a wall, Petraeus started to speak through a bullhorn to the agitated crowd: "We understand your concerns and have been conveying them to Baghdad." The crowd quieted down, and the angry faces turned toward him. Petraeus assured them that he would take their leaders inside to the provincial governor's office to discuss the concerns further so that the governor—a retired general and Iraqi army hero in the Iran-Iraq War who had been put under house arrest by Saddam in the 1990s—could accurately convey the concerns to the Iraqi Governing Council in Baghdad. The crowd was pacified, but not for long. The violence came a week later. The same day, violence in Baghdad and Basra resulted in deaths due to riots that got out of control.

By late October, after a visit by an aide to deputy Defense secretary Paul Wolfowitz, Petraeus wrote that his visitor from Washington "said they should have put us in charge of the whole thing. I told him just send money and there's no limit to what we can do." Petraeus famously saw money as "ammunition" and prided himself on how much emergency response funds he and his brigade commanders spent fixing roads and schools and putting Iraqis to work—more than any other division. He constantly asked his troops, "What have you done for Iraqis today?" and, practicing the counterinsurgency tactics he would come to codify three years later, he told his soldiers that if they ever damaged an Iraqi's property, they needed to offer immediate compensation, or show up the next day and fix what they had broken. His performance in Mosul became the subject of a case study in public policy and management at Harvard's Kennedy School of Government, "The Accidental Statesman: General Petraeus and the City of Mosul, Iraq." The study concludes: "Petraeus is given little guidance, is in an unfamiliar venue, sets ambitious goals and develops a strategy that finds considerable success." In a detailed self-evaluation done as part of an Army War College study in 2004, Petraeus rated himself most highly as an "entrepreneur" for his nation-building efforts in Mosul, among categories that included vision, diplomacy and personal energy.

Petraeus returned from Iraq in early May, only to be told six weeks later to return to Iraq immediately to assess the state of Iraqi security forces. He quickly assembled a team from the 101st and spent several weeks in April and May flying around Iraq to conduct the assessment. After returning to the States and reporting out to Secretary Rumsfeld and the Central Command commander, he was told to change out of command early, move his family and get back to Iraq in early June to establish and command the effort to organize, train, equip and build the infrastructure for the new Iraqi security forces of the ministries of Interior and Defense. He would be promoted to lieutenant general in May 2004 and return to Iraq in June to take charge of creating the Iraqi military and police and their ministries and all institutions, virtually from scratch, a job he once described as "building the world's largest aircraft, while in flight, while it's being designed, and while it's being shot at."

None of the handful of Iraqi army battalions he inherited upon taking his new mission was operational. Several had mutinied to avoid fighting in Fallujah in the spring of 2004, after four security contractors working for an American firm called Blackwater had been killed in March, their bodies mutilated and hung from a bridge. In one of his first acts, he had to go to Defense secretary Donald Rumsfeld and tell him that the number of Iraqi security forces that the embassy team responsible for the police mission had been reporting had to be lowered, because seventy thousand of the troops that had been counted were actually untrained ministry security guards, not trained police. At the time he arrived, neither the Iraqi Ministry of Defense nor his own command, the Multi-National Security Transition Command–Iraq, even had a headquarters building. It was a true start-up, as the mission in Haiti had been, but everything about it was harder. Petraeus's problems with bureaucracy only intensified. He would submit program requests and wait weeks for action. He was never entirely clear on what exactly was going on. President Bush had said Iraqi forces represented America's ticket out of the country, and General John Abizaid, head of Central Command, promised Petraeus whatever support he needed. Yet the bureaucracy above him never produced all the staff or resources that Petraeus and his team identified as being vitally necessary.

It was staggering what he was being asked to do with less than 30 percent of the staff he needed at the outset. Petraeus reacted the only way he knew how—by putting his shoulder to the wheel and pushing forward as hard as he could, all day, every day. In his mind was his father's admonition: "Results, boy!" The only time he went home during the entire fifteen-and-a-half-month tour was in the late spring of 2005, to attend Stephen's graduation from high school—that after never going home during his first year in Iraq.

Petraeus's experiences along the way occasionally bordered on the surreal: At one point, he encountered an Iraqi commander who was particularly adept at recruiting talented commanders. Petraeus asked him how he knew these men, and the Iraqi replied that they'd all been in prison together. It made sense to Petraeus: Saddam had imprisoned all the most capable people, because they represented the greatest threats to his regime. One of Petraeus's worst moments came after he had flown to a desert base to address a newly formed Iraqi unit, only to find out later in the day that fifty of the new recruits had been ambushed after leaving the base to head home on leave, pulled out of their vehicles and shot in the backs of their heads.

December 2004 was a particularly bad month. Petraeus found himself working with his Iraqi counterparts to deal with high rates of desertion among Iraqi units and, with Fallujah and Anbar Province mostly lost to insurgents, the inadequate combat performance of the Iraqi forces. A number of key Iraqi senior leader partners were assassinated. The situation became so bad that Petraeus found solace in T. E. Lawrence's *Seven Pillars of Wis-*

dom, his book about fighting alongside the Arabs during their uprising in World War I. Petraeus recalled how one scene in the book hit very close to home: One morning, Lawrence came out of his tent to find that everyone with whom he had been fighting was gone. They had vanished in the night. "He was an insurgent without a force," Petraeus said, "without allies, and there were a couple of days where I felt like that as well." But by the time Petraeus left in September 2005, his command and its Iraqi partners had fielded a large, well-equipped and increasingly capable force and created a considerable semblance of order from the early chaos. There were 211,000 soldiers in fifteen Iraqi army and police brigades, up 100,000 over the previous nine months. The ministries of Defense and Interior were functioning, as were basic and advanced training centers, police and military academies and even growing high-end Special Operations Forces. It hadn't been pretty, but the progress had been real and substantial.

When Petraeus returned to the United States from Iraq for the second time, in September 2005, after a brief tour through Afghanistan to assess the same ongoing mission there, Army Chief of Staff General Peter Schoomaker named him commander of the Army's Combined Arms Center at Fort Leavenworth. Many thought Petraeus was being sidelined by Rumsfeld for his brash and headstrong behavior in Mosul and Baghdad, where he had clashed on occasion with General George Casey and others. But that was belied by his marching orders from Schoomaker: "Shake up the Army, Dave." Petraeus used the vast responsibilities that he had to do just that: help to usher in the new counterinsurgency era. They'd put an insurgent in charge of the Army's engine of change.

Undeterred by his clash with Tanzola, Lujan had arranged for one of his CAAT teammates to preside in early March over a two-day *shura* on counterinsurgency for junior officers of the 205th Afghan National Army Corps, which was conducted in Dari and Pashto. Lujan had come up with this idea after Petraeus, back in December, had challenged him to help "change the culture of the Afghan military." By the second day, the Afghan officers had started to open up. The CAAT team was amazed what a difference it made to sit with them in a *shura* circle, without more senior officers around, and speak with them in Dari. "We agree, we need to be the ones engaging with the locals," stated one Afghan officer in the *shura*. "But the coalition never lets us. They always want to be the ones leading, talking with locals. They have us pull security. How do we get them to let us do it?"

The CAAT team came away energized. "These were committed, engaged Afghans who were sharing really great lessons. And they wanted to do more, and thought the coalition was limiting them—not giving them enough information, not trusting them, not allowing them to engage with locals, not respecting their culture." To Lujan, it all flew in the face of the standard narrative that Afghan soldiers were lazy and incompetent. "After a while you have to accept that we share some of the responsibility," he said. One of the most interesting observations to emerge from the *shura* came when several officers observed how the Americans would drag them around on patrol until an IED was encountered, and then the Americans would say, "Put the Afghans in front—it's their country." To the Afghans, who already believed Americans were overly fearful and hid behind their technology, Lujan said, this was seen as blatant cowardice.

As the *shura* was wrapping up in Kandahar, Petraeus was in Kabul, formally apologizing to Karzai's government for an errant air strike in RC East, in Kunar Province's Pech Valley. Nine boys gathering firewood were killed when they were mistaken by the crews of attack helicopters for insurgents shooting from the same area. It was the third incident in three weeks in which Karzai's government accused Petraeus's forces of recklessly killing civilians. Petraeus considered the prevention of civilian casualties an enormous challenge in a war in which the enemy often sought refuge among the people or, worse, hid inside compounds that housed innocent people. The most important standard he insisted upon was positive identification before a strike, which had obviously not been adhered to in the attack that killed the boys. The tactical mistake had grave strategic implications. Karzai rejected his apology.

Defense secretary Robert Gates also offered his own apology when he arrived in Kabul on March 7. He had come in advance of a U.S. negotiating team that was to begin hammering out the shape of a U.S. military presence in Afghanistan after its current combat role was fully handed over to Afghan forces by the end of 2014. Karzai, who ultimately accepted Gates's apology, favored a post-2014 "strategic partnership." Gates said he thought the United States was "well positioned" to begin drawing down its troops in July, although he indicated that the reductions would be limited.

The next day, Gates flew to Kandahar for a visit to a village called Tabin, in the Arghandab River Valley. It would have been hard to imagine the scene six months earlier: the American secretary of Defense walking down a one-lane dirt road in lush terrain that the Taliban had controlled and ultimately laced with deadly homemade bombs. The children in the area would not go outside if insurgents were nearby. Lieutenant Colonel David Flynn and his converted artillerymen, the Top Guns, led the way through the region they had fought so hard to clear. "A year ago, even as recently as six months ago, I wouldn't have driven a vehicle down that road, let alone walked down it," said Major Tom Burrell, Flynn's operations officer. With the spring fighting season approaching, villagers remained skeptical that this new reality was permanent. "You're talking about people who have seen far worse for decades," Burrell said, "and now we're talking about a change that's only months long."

In Tabin, a village of about a thousand residents, Flynn explained that there were now ten "vetted and confirmed" members of the Afghan Local Police providing village security. They had been trained by Flynn's troops using techniques first developed by Special Forces involved in the Village Stability Operations, the effort that laid the foundation for the ALP. Nine more villagers, all recommended by village elders and screened by U.S. forces, were being trained and vetted in order to join the detachment. The Tabin Local Police had received uniforms and weapons, and they were being paid slightly less than members of the National Police. Once the village force was in operation, it would be transferred to the Afghan Ministry of the Interior for ongoing oversight and administration, Flynn said. Gate's team sent a follow-up e-mail: "One of the best visits . . . in 4 years."

Back in Kabul, Petraeus sat down for an interview with the *New York Times* on the eve of his departure for testimony on Capitol Hill in Washington. He was beginning to see the six lines of operation come together for real effect, even though each new week seemed to bring new insurgent attacks and bombings, while ISAF's advances were maddeningly incremental. The *Times* described the interview with Petraeus as "a preview of what is likely to be his argument next week when he testifies before Congress for the first time since he took over command of coalition forces in Afghanistan eight months ago."

The Taliban's momentum, Petraeus said, had been halted in much of Afghanistan and reversed in Helmand and Kandahar. Afghan forces were continuing to grow in number and capability. Special Operations had taken a number of key insurgent leaders off the battlefield. He acknowledged that efforts to persuade Taliban fighters to lay down their arms and become part of a reintegration program had been only modestly successful. He insisted that relations with Karzai were good, despite periodic evidence to the contrary. He said that ISAF forces would focus in the months ahead on a strategy called "defense in depth" to make it difficult for Taliban fighters to leave their redoubts in Pakistan and infiltrate back across the border into Afghanistan and make their way to Kabul. Only time would tell how that strategy would fare on the ground in Afghanistan—and the hearing rooms in Washington.

CHAPTER 8

WASHINGTON AND BACK

Petraeus flew into Washington under the media radar on Friday, March 11, and spent a quiet weekend reunited with his wife, Holly, and their daughter, Anne. Holly had moved from Tampa to a house on the base at Fort Myer, in Arlington, Virginia, overlooking the Potomac. Anne was home on spring break from graduate school. She was studying to become a dietitian and chided her father about his new slow-carb diet, but he would not be deterred. She wrote a popular blog about food and fitness that Petraeus had been following with great pride, pleased that she had gained nearly ten thousand followers.

Undetected by the press but shadowed by Petraeus's security detail, father and daughter ran seven miles along the Potomac on Saturday morning. Petraeus had been slightly irked by various news reports that he was "worn out." He was still running or riding a stationary bike nearly every day. After he'd run at Kabul's 5,800-foot elevation, the run at sea level was nothing. The opportunity to run on a level path, along a clean river, was uplifting. He had been away from his family for more than seventy months since 9/11. He gave his team a day off, their first in more than eight months. Several of his close aides were able to see their families for the first time since their unexpected departures the previous June. His personal security guard, Mark Howell, returned home to Arkansas for just thirty-six hours. That afternoon, the Petraeus clan went to see Matthew McConaughey in *The Lincoln Lawyer* at a theater in downtown Washington. He and Holly loved to watch movies together. He could let go of the immense weight of the war he carried, for a moment.

On Monday morning, Petraeus attended his "murder board," a practice session for his testimony before the Senate and House Armed Services committees. The term was a play on one used to describe the promotion board for noncommissioned officers. Candidates must memorize tactical and operational detail to pass. Petraeus used a Washington-based lobbying-and-communications firm headed by a retired Marine Corps major general who had been the staff director for the Senate Armed Services Committee to conduct the exercise. Petraeus performed well in congressional testimony in part because he conducted these practice sessions. They were at least two painful hours, without a break, to simulate the testimony, but they were beneficial. Lieutenant Colonel Tony DeMartino, Major Keith Benedict and Alston Ramsay, members of his Commander's Initiatives Group, participated with the corporate simulators, asking questions "for elephants—" the big game four-star generals.

The intense session prepared Petraeus for any question, as well as a hostile audience, although neither he nor his inquisitors anticipated one this time. He expected there to be questions about the cost of the war and whether the nation could continue to make that kind of massive financial commitment, with Congress focused on the deficit and proposing huge budget cuts. Petraeus knew that he had to make a persuasive argument that members of Congress could convey to their constituents, many of whom were unaffected by the war and focused more on pocketbook issues than national security. He also expected questions about Afghan corruption, reintegration and reconciliation and the Afghan Local Police initiative, as well as various concerns that revolved around Pakistan. Petraeus would decide what information was essential to highlight while making sure he did not disclose anything that was classified. It was a complex calculus. After the practice session, members of the Commander's Initiatives Group were quickly assigned to research areas in which Petraeus felt he needed more information.

Later that afternoon, Petraeus and Gates met with Obama at the White House to discuss progress in Afghanistan and Petraeus's upcoming testimony. The meeting needed to appear on the president's public schedule to show solidarity, but it was also a good opportunity to provide the president with an up-to-date assessment. Petraeus explained the progress coalition forces had made in recent months. There were no surprises about the war, since the three had spoken together in recent months on several occasions in secure video teleconferences. Petraeus also provided weekly updates on the war via teleconference for Gates, Mullen and Marine General James Mattis, head of Central Command, that were retransmitted to the White House and the secretary of State.

The White House issued a two-sentence summary of the meeting that night, emphasizing the issues most important to the president:

The President, Secretary of Defense Robert Gates, and General David Petraeus met today to discuss our ongoing efforts in Afghanistan, including the effectiveness of the military surge, the growth of the Afghan National Security Forces, and President Karzai's expected March 21 announcement on beginning transition to Afghan security lead. They also discussed the plan to begin the reduction of U.S. forces this July, and the path to completing the transition to full Afghan responsibility for security by the end of 2014.

While Washington was filled with rumors about Petraeus's next assignment, no mention was made of it in this statement from the White House. Nor was there any discussion of it at the meeting between Petraeus and Obama. Petraeus knew he was not in the running to be named chairman of the Joint Chiefs of Staff following his command in Afghanistan, as Gates had made clear to him in December when they discussed the matter in Kabul and Petraeus first floated the idea that he become CIA director. Gates had reported that Obama had been intrigued by the idea, and Petraeus looked forward to discussing it directly with the president. He was encouraged by Obama's interest, and he realized that this trip to Washington was his chance to validate the tough decisions Obama had made in late 2009, since the surge had succeeded in clearing key Taliban strongholds in Kandahar and Helmand provinces.

Some reporters and military officers who had seen Petraeus in action over the past eight months continued to speculate that he was worn out, and that perhaps the president would surmise that a break was in order. This irritated Petraeus to no end. The summer and fall campaign had without a doubt taken a toll. There had been a steep learning curve his first few months in theater, and he would often yawn his way through meetings, chew on Atomic Fireballs and drink coffee nonstop, even into the evenings, but by winter the campaign was showing signs of progress, and the pace of insurgent fighting slowed in its cyclical winter pattern. Petraeus felt energized by spring.

The following morning, the clicking of camera shutters sounded when Petraeus took his seat before the Senate Armed Services Committee in the Dirksen Senate Office Building. Undersecretary of Defense for Policy Michèle Flournoy sat next to him at the witness table, facing the horseshoe-shaped dais of senators. Members of Petraeus's military team wore their Class A uniforms, neatly pressed. They had awoken that morning to a headline on the front page of the *Washington Post* that read, "Afghan War Isn't Worth Fighting, Most in U.S. Say." A poll by the *Post* and ABC News had found that nearly two-thirds of Americans thought the war was no longer worth fighting, "the highest proportion yet opposed to the conflict." The newspaper said Petraeus was expected to face "tough questioning" on the war. Yet, aside from two protestors who had made it into the room, there was a relaxed feeling. Petraeus was well prepared, and the senators were relatively deferential to a commander who had appeared before them numerous times in the previous six years. Taking his seat at the witness table always took Petraeus back to Iraq and all the passions the war had unleashed as violence exploded in 2004 and grew steadily straight into the surge at the beginning of 2007.

A MONTH AFTER he arrived at the Army's Combined Arms Center at Fort Leavenworth in the fall of 2005, Petraeus set out to create a new field manual on counterinsurgency. He would launch this ambitious effort by hosting an inclusive workshop at Fort Leavenworth, the Army's schoolhouse, in February 2006. He considered creation of a new doctrinal manual for commanders and troops fighting in Iraq and Afghanistan to be a critical need.

The situation in Iraq, the U.S. military's main effort, had spiraled downward, with the country beset by extreme sectarian violence that many thought would lead to civil war between Shiites and Sunnis. Petraeus thought he had a chance at Fort Leavenworth to help the military provide doctrinal concepts to address the problem. There had already been speculation that he might be the next overall commander in Iraq, and the chief of staff had told him that he was just being given an opportunity to "take a knee" for a while before deploying again. That made it all the more imperative to identify and codify best practices in counterinsurgency.

The manual, developed jointly with the Marine Corps, would be published on an unprecedented timeline. Petraeus commissioned Dr. Conrad Crane, his West Point classmate and director of the U.S. Army Military History Institute, to lead the effort, helped by Lieutenant Colonel John Nagl, Rhodes Scholar, West Point Department of Social Sciences alum and author of a notable book on counterinsurgency. Within a month of taking command, Petraeus e-mailed the manual as it existed at the time to several intellectuals, including Eliot Cohen, whom he'd known since Petraeus's days teaching at West Point, and members of the "LICimites," the low-intensity-conflict acolytes of the 1980s, some of whom he'd met in Central America in 1987. He sought feedback on its content—another example of his crowd-source approach to decision making.

The day before Christmas, Petraeus brought his boss, General William Wallace, up to speed on his plans for the conference that would kick off the effort, noting that he planned to invite "a broad mix of approximately sixty influential practitioners, academicians, journalists and others," including the full spectrum of typically liberal skeptics, to participate in a quest for "infotopia." He was also planning to invite fifteen foreign liaison officers at Leavenworth to participate, along with additional representatives from the United Kingdom and Australia. Tentatively, the Carr Center at Harvard University was going to cosponsor the workshop, contingent upon approval by the Army's General Counsel.

The manual spelled out the focus for all U.S. counterinsurgency operations: Protect the people from violence, harassment or intimidation by insurgents. Killing the enemy and disrupting insurgent networks remained critical areas of emphasis. But the most important area—the center of gravity—was protecting the people. This led to better intelligence from them. It enhanced prospects for effective local governance. And it made it difficult for insurgents to operate. It was published in late 2006, the fastest doctrinal endeavor in anyone's memory.

The manual was lauded inside and outside the military, but it also energized military skeptics, who said bad strategy in Afghanistan and Iraq could not be fixed with sound tactics. Petraeus welcomed the constructive criticism, and a spirited debate ensued among defense intellectuals. The skeptics' concerns were perhaps best symbolized by Ralph Peters, a retired Army lieutenant colonel and novelist whom Petraeus had long respected but who had become a font of criticism of the wars. "It's appallingly bad—a prescription for defeat," he wrote. "We're not at war with ideologies, but with religious convictions and ethnic identities. Those are profoundly different matters. We're not in Malaya in 1959. We don't have to like it, but our core enemies are waging religious warfare, and they're not susceptible to friendly persuasion."

Petraeus realized the political sensitivity of the manual, personally editing the opening chapter thirty to forty times. "Let me assure you that there is no reluctance to kill religious extremists (or Saddamists or any others) who want to kill us," Petraeus responded to Peters in an e-mail.

"The 101st Airborne, e.g., remains proud to have killed [Saddam Hussein's sons] Uday and Qusay—and to have done it in a way that took them out without blowing up the rest of the neighborhood. Nor did we shrink from taking out Ansar al-Sunnah's number three, or from killing or capturing a host of other extremists, insurgents, or Saddamists. Our objective, though, was always to try to take more bad guys off the streets than we created by the way we conducted our operations. That's not politically correct; it's the way to win—when complemented by a host of other activities, of course, many of them nonmilitary in nature. . . . One can, to be sure, defeat an insurrection or insurgency by killing lots of people. The Romans did it long ago, and people like Saddam and Assad have done it more recently; however, that's obviously not an approach that is available to us."

The 419-page manual was not only published by the Army but also made into a trade version that was favorably reviewed. That version included an introduction by Sarah Sewall, director of the Carr Center for Human Rights at Harvard, that began, "This counterinsurgency field manual challenges much of what is holy about the American way of war. It demands significant change and sacrifice to fight today's enemies honorably. It is therefore both important and controversial. Those who fail to see the manual as radical probably don't understand it, or at least understand what it's up against."

Beyond the manual, Petraeus focused his efforts during his fifteen-month tour at Fort Leavenworth on advancing the concepts of full-spectrum operations and preparedness of leaders and units for deployment. A significant part of the latter was overhauling the military's "road to deployment"—a systematic road map that charted the training activities that a brigade combat team, a division headquarters and corps headquarters went through during the approximately twelve months of preparation for deployment. Up until 2006, Petraeus had discovered, deploying units were still going through an outdated "Military Operations in Urban Terrain" (MOUT) seminar as their first step down that road. The MOUT training did not reflect the combat and stabilization operations in which troops had been engaged in recent years. The deploying units needed guidance, training and rehearsals for counterinsurgency operations, he believed. The training needed to include an understanding of the cultural nuances of the area to which the unit was to deploy, the concept that protecting the people was the overarching objective and a recognition that soft-power governance and development efforts had to complement military clearing operations. Few, if any, had demonstrated this better than Petraeus in Mosul in 2003.

Petraeus remembered visiting Fort Sill, Oklahoma, home base of Army artillery, and going for a run with a group of captains, all of whom were required to write five operations orders during their six-month Captain's Career Course. "All of those orders were the same as they would have been prior to our operations in Iraq," he recalled later. "In other words, they were still large artillery operations, standard missions, massing of batteries and battalions—essentially the old Cold War missions. I asked, 'Well, what did you do in Iraq or Afghanistan? You are all veterans of one or, in many cases, two tours downrange already. How much of your battalion actually shot [artillery] in Iraq?'"

Most of the captains responded that one battery, at most, was prepared to fire at the enemy. The rest of the battalion would be broken down performing convoy or base security, or security for a geographic area. In some cases entire artillery units were devoted to detainee operations. And yet, Petraeus noted, "not a single one of the operations orders addressed any of those tasks at all." After Petraeus shared this with the field artillery center commander, the commander shut down the Career Course, using the seasoned captains to help overhaul the curriculum and restarting the course within two weeks. Petraeus also came to believe that mission rehearsal exercises at the Army's training centers required further refinement. There had been some change to the war games that troops participated in before deploying. Iraqi- or Afghan-American civilians role-played Iraqi or Afghan citizens and local officials during the mock battles, and U.S. soldiers simulated IED cells, host-nation troops, and suicide car bombers and local leaders with whom the exercise unit had to engage. But Petraeus wanted to see far more unpredictable scenarios driving the mock engagements. It was the same principle of surprise and emphasis on realistic training that Petraeus had sought as an operations officer in the 24th and 3rd infantry divisions, and as a battalion and brigade commander. The Army was still adjusting preparation for deployment activities to follow one of its most basic tenets: to train the way we will fight.

Petraeus sought as well to inculcate a culture of constant learning in the leaders who attended the courses in the centers and schools he oversaw. Speaking to a group of staff college students at Fort Leavenworth, Petraeus explained his philosophy.

> Each of you is one part student and one part teacher, and in your year at Leavenworth, each of us . . . will be . . . part of what we call the "engine of change," the combination of elements overseen by the Combined Arms Center are helping the U.S. Army respond to the challenges that face the United States. . . . Change, in fact, is critical. . . . A military is a living organism. Like all living organisms, the military obeys the fundamental law of nature—the law of survival of the fittest. Today, our militaries are confronted with the problem of how best to adapt to changes in the operational environment. At stake here is not simply the survival of our militaries but the security of our nations, which is, of course, what our militaries exist to protect. The requirement, therefore, is to adapt along with the threat to our nation. . . . So we must change the way we train our units and our leaders—you. Change is, indeed, hard, but it is also a must.

The Army, in short, had to be a learning organization. Petraeus's 2006 *Counterinsurgency Field Manual* expressed it clearly: "The side that adapts the fastest tends to prevail."

THAT CERTAINLY remained the case in Afghanistan late in the winter of 2010–2011, as Senator Levin knew well. He pounded his gavel promptly at 9:31 A.M. on March 16. He harked back to Obama's speech at West Point in December 2009 and noted that Obama had set July 2011 as the date "when U.S. troops would begin to come home." And just last week, he said, Secretary Gates, on a trip to Afghanistan and NATO headquarters, had said that the

United States would be "well positioned" in July to begin transferring authority to Afghan forces and drawing down American troops. But as Levin also noted, Gates had also told NATO defense ministers that "there is too much talk about leaving and not enough talk about getting the job done right."

"Both messages and the thread that unifies them are part and parcel, I believe, of General Petraeus's counterinsurgency strategy, which is so instrumental in turning the tide in Afghanistan," Levin said. "The success of the mission depends on Afghan security forces holding the ground, which they are helping to clear of Taliban." Levin was mindful of the cost, in blood and treasure, and wanted to start to bring U.S. forces home as soon as was feasible. He also took it upon himself to defend his president from anticipated Republican attempts to paint him as weak or unpatriotic for insisting that the drawdown of forces begin in July, especially in light of the surge and everything else Obama had been willing to invest in the war, including Petraeus's talents.

Throughout the hearing, Levin and the Democrats defended Obama's decision to announce that he would begin drawing down forces in July 2011 as necessary to force the Afghans to take their responsibilities seriously, and Republicans criticized it for undercutting U.S. efforts and emboldening the Taliban. Levin clearly supported the planned drawdown but hardly could be seen as opposed to the war effort, given the push for building up Afghan forces he had strenuously backed. To defend the planned drawdown, he quoted General Mattis, who'd replaced Petraeus as head of Central Command and who said that the transfer of authority to Afghan forces "'undercuts the enemy's narrative when they say that we're there to occupy Afghanistan.'"

Senator McCain, the ranking Republican, underscored the political tension, saying that "we need to be exceedingly cautious about withdrawal of the U.S. forces this July. The wisest course of action in July may be to reinvest troops from more secured to less secured parts of Afghanistan, where additional forces could have a decisive impact. In short, we should not rush to failure. . . ."

After Levin and McCain staked out their positions, Undersecretary Flournoy read her prepared statement. It neatly summarized what the Obama administration had inherited in Afghanistan upon taking office in January 2009:

> While our attention was turned away, al-Qaeda, the Taliban and associated extremist groups reconstituted their safe havens along the borderlands between Afghanistan and Pakistan. As a result of this inattention, we risked the return of a Taliban-led Afghanistan that would likely once again provide a safe haven for terrorists who could plan and execute attacks against the United States. When President Obama took office, he immediately undertook a thorough review of our strategy in Afghanistan and Pakistan and reaffirmed our core goal: to disrupt, dismantle and eventually defeat al-Qaeda and to prevent its return to Afghanistan. In the course of that review, we found that the situation in Afghanistan was even worse than we'd thought and that the Taliban had seized the momentum on the ground.

Petraeus, a black plastic 101st Airborne Division coffee mug on the table in front of him, then read his opening statement; it was largely an update of the speech he had delivered in November at the Lisbon conference.

> As a bottom line up front, it is ISAF's assessment that the momentum achieved by the Taliban in Afghanistan since 2005 has been arrested in much of the country and reversed in a number of important areas. However, while the security progress achieved over the past year is significant, it is also fragile and reversible. Moreover, it is clear that much difficult work lies ahead with our Afghan partners to solidify and expand our gains in the face of the expected Taliban spring offensive. Nonetheless, the hard-fought achievements in 2010 and early 2011 have enabled the joint Afghan-NATO transition board to recommend initiation this spring of transition to Afghan lead in several provinces. The achievements of the past year are also very important

as I prepare to provide options and a recommendation to President Obama for commencement of the drawdown of the U.S. surge forces in July.

Petraeus described how ISAF forces, fighting alongside Afghan troops, had cleared the Taliban out of its birthplace around Kandahar, and how the Afghan forces were not only greater in size but better in quality. He lauded Lieutenant General Caldwell for leading the effort to train and equip Afghan forces, which he described as "a huge undertaking, and there is nothing easy about it." He described the growth of the Afghan Local Police "a community watch with AK-47s," an important addition to the overall campaign that he hoped would spread to seventy districts, each averaging three hundred ALP members. Twenty-seven of those districts, he noted, had been "validated for full operations.

"This program is so important that I have put a conventional U.S. infantry battalion under the operational control of our Special Operations Task Force in Afghanistan to augment our Special Forces and increase our ability to support the program's expansion," he said, tacitly acknowledging that Flynn had been correct in his belief that conventional forces such as the Top Guns could indeed train Afghans to protect their own villages. The augmentation of the Special Operations Task Force with conventional forces—initially criticized by some—was proving to be an important addition to the Afghan Local Police initiative, enabling the Special Forces to create Afghan Local Police detachments much more rapidly and in many more provinces, a key to defending against Taliban infiltration at the village level. He would later augment the effort with a second conventional infantry battalion, this one from the 82nd Airborne Division.

In reviewing each component of his campaign plan, Petraeus might well have projected his Anaconda strategy slide on the hearing room wall. There were his six lines of operation—protecting the population, disrupting insurgent networks, building the Afghan armed forces, supporting legitimate governance, fostering sustainable development and neutralizing criminal patronage networks. Petraeus told the senators that reintegration of reconcilable insurgents at local levels also remained an important element of his plan, because "we recognize that we and our Afghan partners cannot just kill or capture our way out of an insurgency in Afghanistan." In recent months, he said, seven hundred Taliban had officially reintegrated with the Afghan government, and another two thousand were in the process of reintegrating.

On the issue of civilian casualties, he pointed out that the recent UN study had concluded that civilian casualties caused by ISAF operations had decreased 20 percent in 2010. But he revealed that he had ordered "a review of our Tactical Directive on the use of force by all levels of our chain of command and with the aircrews of our attack helicopters," due to the incidents in February that had left him apologizing to Karzai. However challenging his relationship with the Afghan president had been, he gave no hint of it during the hearing. At one point, he paraphrased a remark that Gates had made recently—that sometimes American leaders didn't listen well enough to Karzai. "What he says is understandable about civilian causalities," Petraeus said. "We cannot harm the people that we are there to help protect. And we have to protect them from *all* civilian casualties, not just those at our hands or those of our Afghan partners, but those of the insurgents as well."

The following week, Petraeus said, Karzai would announce which provinces would be turned over this year to Afghan forces as the transition process, scheduled to run through 2014, officially began. "The shifting of responsibility from ISAF to Afghan forces will be conducted at a pace determined by conditions on the ground," Petraeus explained, "with assessments provided from the bottom up so that those at operational-command level in Afghanistan can plan the resulting battlefield geometry adjustments with our Afghan partners." After Petraeus finished reading his opening statement, Levin began by asking whether he supported the beginning of troop reductions in July. Petraeus acknowledged that he was accepting of the plan.

"And why do you support the beginning of reductions this July?" Levin asked.

"If I could come back perhaps to your opening statement, Mr. Chairman,

I think it is logical to talk both about getting the job done, as Secretary Gates did with his NATO counterparts, and beginning transition and 'responsible'— to use President Obama's term—reductions in forces at a pace determined by conditions on the ground," Petraeus said. "As my good friend and shipmate General Jim Mattis noted, it undercuts the narrative of the Taliban that we will be there forever, that we're determined to maintain a presence forever. And it does indeed, as I have told this committee before, send that message of urgency that President Obama sought to transmit on the first of December at West Point in 2009, when he also transmitted a message of enormous additional commitment in the form of thirty thousand additional U.S. forces, more funding for Afghan forces and additional civilians."

McCain focused on the front-page story in that morning's *Washington Post,* saying that most Americans believed the Afghan war wasn't worth fighting. "Could you respond to that poll and maybe have a few words for the American people about this conflict?" McCain asked. "And you might mention the consequences of failure."

"Up front, I can understand the frustration," Petraeus responded, knowing this was an important moment to sustain support for the war among the American people, who ultimately paid the bills and contributed the soldiers.

We have been at this for ten years. We have spent an enormous amount of money. We have sustained very tough losses and difficult, life-changing wounds. I was at Walter Reed [Army Medical Center] yesterday seeing some of our troopers whose lives have been changed forever by their service in our country's uniform in a tough fight. But I think it is important to remember why we are there at such a time. It's important to remember that that is where 9/11 began. That's where the plan was made. That's where the initial training of the attackers took place before they went on to Germany and then to U.S. flight schools. That is where al-Qaeda had its most important sanctuary in the world, and it had it under the Taliban. At that time, of course, the Taliban controlled Kabul and the vast majority of the country. And, indeed, we do see al-Qaeda looking for sanctuaries all the time, frankly.

Petraeus never wavered in his belief in the cause. He saw the conflict, and the broader global war on terror, as an ongoing effort to contain and confront the enemy, much like the Cold War. There was no end date. His refusal to quit inspired his admirers. It drove the war's skeptics, including the vice president and more than a few national security officials in the West Wing, crazy. In their minds, Petraeus only wanted more troops. In their minds, Petraeus would keep fighting forever.

Senator Graham began his questioning on a personal note. "General Petraeus, how long have you been deployed since 9/11?" he asked. "Do you even know?"

"Well, it's more than six years, because there was a year in Bosnia, nearly four years in Iraq and then, you know, eight and a half months here, and then it depends on your accounting rules for CENTCOM, I guess, where we spent, I think, 300 days of the first 365 on the road."

"What keeps you going?" Graham asked.

"Obviously it is the greatest of privileges to serve with our young men and women in uniform. When the president turns to you in the Oval Office and asks you to do something that's important to our country, there can only be one answer, frankly," Petraeus said. "I strongly believe that our young men and women in uniform in places like Afghanistan and Iraq and elsewhere around the world have more than earned the title 'new greatest generation.'"

After questioning from nine more senators, alternating back and forth between Republicans and Democrats, Levin gaveled the hearing to a close, noting that the cost of an Afghan security force in excess of 300,000 troops was still a "tiny fraction of what the cost is of having our forces in Afghanistan"—$8 to $10 billion per year, versus $80 billion. (Later, Petraeus and Caldwell would undertake an effort to bring the projected annual number down to the $3-to-$4-billion-per-year range.) Finally, Levin noted that Petraeus had provided a helpful set of charts to accompany his testimony but had left his name off of them as one of the "inputs." McChrystal's name remained. Perhaps it was undue modesty, Levin told the general, but your name belongs on them. Then, addressing Petraeus, he said: "We thank you. You've got great staying power."

The invitation for a Friday meeting with Obama at the White House arrived that afternoon as the press filed generally upbeat news stories about progress in Afghanistan based on Petraeus's testimony. There was no indication to his team what the meeting would be about, but they hoped the president would discuss choices for Petraeus's next assignment. He could be told, "Thanks for your service, well done," or maybe there would be a surprise. Only one member of Petraeus's inner circle—Colonel Hickman—and Petraeus's wife, Holly, knew that becoming the director of the CIA was a serious option and that it was what Petraeus wanted to do.

The following morning, a line of more than a hundred people stretched down the hallway outside the hearing room in the Rayburn House Office Building, with only sixteen seats inside for Petraeus's testimony before the House Armed Services Committee. Petraeus covered much the same ground as he had the day before in his testimony before the Senate committee, where the political objectives dividing Republicans from Democrats were even more pronounced.

Representative Walter Jones, a North Carolina Republican whose district includes Camp Lejeune, the Marines' home on the East Coast, read from a serviceman's letter: "'It makes no difference if we're there four or 40 years. The result will be the same. The war is costing the United States billions of dollars a month to wage. We'll still continue to get more young Americans killed. The Afghans have no end state for us—this has no end state for us. I urge you to make a contact with all the current and newly elected members of Congress and ask them to end this war and bring our young men and women home.'

"For God's sakes, how much more can we take?" Jones asked. "How much more can we give treasure and blood?"

"If I ever felt that we couldn't achieve our objectives, I would be very forthright with my chain of command, with the president of the United States and with all of you," Petraeus responded evenly. Jones's pointed question, fraught with emotion, challenged Petraeus in a way no one else had. Petraeus answered with his most heartfelt response in two days of nonstop testimony. He revealed that his own son, 1st Lieutenant Stephen Petraeus, had led a combat platoon through intense fighting in 2010. "We're very proud of what he did," Petraeus said. "He thinks he was doing something very important." Without belaboring the point, Petraeus had made clear what he was willing to contribute and sacrifice. Stephen Petraeus had served on the front line and heard the crack of incoming rounds as an infantry platoon leader on nearly every patrol.

Then came Representative Loretta Sanchez, a liberal Democrat from Southern California who opposed the war, mistrusted the military and wasn't afraid to make that abundantly clear. She had challenged Petraeus many times over the years, and Petraeus was ready. She gave voice to the frustrations of many in America who questioned the strategic importance of endless fighting in Afghanistan and did not believe Petraeus's "optimistic assertion" that we had wrested momentum from the Taliban. "I have a couple of questions for you, General," she said. "We've been in Afghanistan about ten years, and we've lost over fourteen hundred U.S. lives, and we've spent more than $300 billion on this military operation alone.... What does success look like in Afghanistan?"

"Well, thanks very much, Congresswoman," Petraeus responded. "Success in Afghanistan is a country that can secure and govern itself and, in so doing, prevent the reestablishment of sanctuaries by al-Qaeda and like-minded groups," Petraeus said.

Sanchez noted that he and Gates were now talking about having troops in Afghanistan past 2014. "Somehow mission creep's gotten into this thing," she said. After she and the general sparred over the subject of training Afghan forces and the commitment of America's NATO allies, Sanchez turned to corruption in Afghanistan. "Corruption, by and large, is the Afghan state," she said.

Petraeus, who admired Sanchez's feistiness and enjoyed the challenge she presented, mentioned McMaster's work and said he welcomed the opportunity to "lay that out for you in detail." Sanchez raised a number of legitimate issues, and Petraeus thought it was important to make sure she got good answers. He didn't think it would change her mind, but he considered it his duty to describe the good work his people—some of whom were her constituents—were doing in Afghanistan.

In the weeks prior to Petraeus's testimony, reports had surfaced in the media that Obama planned on naming him CIA director. While Petraeus knew that the president was contemplating that possibility, he had yet to speak to Obama about his next assignment and did not know precisely what to make of the leaks. Senator Graham confirmed during a meeting the day after Petraeus's House testimony that Petraeus was, at the very least, a strong contender for the CIA job. Graham said that he and other senators from both parties had heard that he was out of the running for chairman of the Joint Chiefs but that he would be offered the CIA director's job and would probably retire from the military before assuming the post. But if he were allowed to take the post and remain in uniform, as General Michael V. Hayden had been allowed to do, Graham said, an "unholy alliance" of Republican and Democratic senators would push to get him a fifth star for all he had accomplished in Iraq and Afghanistan. A fifth star was a very political move, but Graham was determined to make it happen if he got the chance. Petraeus told Graham that he appreciated the thought but politely offered that such ideas verged on nonsense.

The testimony, as smoothly as it went, didn't receive much attention, with the press focused on a tsunami in Japan, the stalled economy and budget fights. It wasn't clear that anyone in Congress had changed his or her stance on the war. With the hearing behind him, Petraeus filled up the rest of the week with additional engagements. In between, he conducted closed-door meetings with Senate and House leaders. After he'd run the gauntlet of testimony on the Hill, the pressure was off. "How's the general's morale?" one journalist asked Petraeus's personal security bodyguard, Mark Howell. "Exceptionally high, I should think," Howell said. "Usually when we come back for testimony, everybody suffers a little from what we [the staff] call 'PTSD'—*Petraeus* Traumatic Stress Disorder. But," Howell continued, "I sense a feeling of calmness from the boss that says, 'I'm where I want to be. Let the cards fall where they may.'" Petraeus drove his staff hard and expected those around him to work as hard as he did. The demands on his nonstop schedule during his trips back to Washington were intense for everyone. Although Petraeus worked people hard, he treated them well and let them know how much he depended upon and appreciated their great work. They also knew that his gratitude had no "half-life": once a Petraeus guy, always a Petraeus guy when it came to letters of recommendation, advice, references or other forms of assistance.

Petraeus's schedulers had been waiting for word all week as to when he would meet with the president that Friday. But as of 10:15 A.M. on Friday, the White House still did not have Petraeus listed on the schedule. By noon he had been told that he was supposed to meet with Joint Chiefs chairman Admiral Mullen after Mullen first met with Obama. When he did meet with Mullen at 4:00 P.M., the chairman told him that he was the leading candidate for the CIA job but that if he accepted the position, he would have to retire from the military. His aides and members of his security detail were in a light mood as they drove across the river, even though they were unsure of what to expect. The boss's meeting with Obama gave them some hope that their futures might be resolved. They'd heard the rumors by now and were considering the implications. If he retired and went to the CIA, they'd have to find new jobs. If he took the CIA job in uniform, would they go with him? And if there was some miracle in the making and the president opted to select him as chairman of the Joint Chiefs, then they were most likely moving to Washington for their follow-on tours.

Petraeus maintained a poker face to all. Behind the mask, there was a lingering sense of frustration about the perception of his loyalty. He'd been told that some members of the White House still thought they had a "Petraeus problem." But Petraeus felt he had passed every test of loyalty he'd been given. He had assumed command at the president's behest, even, unbeknownst to most, taking a pay cut by stepping down from the CENTCOM position to take the command in Afghanistan. He'd succeeded in guiding a campaign to take away the Taliban's momentum in Kandahar and Helmand provinces. And he'd supported the policy on the Hill, at NATO and with the press.

Senator Lindsey Graham discussed with Petraeus that as head of the CIA, he could actually have more impact on the war against terrorism. He would direct the work of covert action around the world. The chairman position obviously was of enormous significance as the senior military adviser to the president and secretary of Defense; however, Graham pointed out, the position is not a command, and it is heavily dependent on the relationship between the chairman and the secretary of Defense when it came to ongoing operational matters, as the secretary actually issues orders in the Pentagon. Petraeus demurred. But his closest colleagues and mentors worried that the CIA job was just a way for the administration to keep him at bay. He might not be allowed to attend regular NSC meetings, and he might more or less be leashed in seeking out the public spotlight to market the agency, as he'd done for years with the military. They thought he didn't know the CIA or its rules and regulations, which would make it harder for him to find solutions to problems and use his force of will to manage the bureaucracy. To assume the role, he would have to be a civilian and forgo wearing the medals and awards on his uniform that had served partly as a shield.

At the White House, Obama welcomed Petraeus with a firm handshake. They once again sat down one-on-one next to each other in the same two armchairs in which they'd sat in late June 2010, when the president asked Petraeus to go to Afghanistan. Obama observed that the hearings on Afghanistan that week had seemed to go well. According to aides briefed after the meeting, he then raised the issue most on Petraeus's mind. He noted that he had, for some time, been "intrigued" by the notion of making Petraeus the director of the CIA. He told Petraeus he thought he would be a great director. There was no better place than the CIA, Obama said, for Petraeus to continue to contribute to the missions in which he'd been engaged throughout much of the past decade. Petraeus's field experience, including that with the intelligence community in Bosnia, Iraq, Afghanistan and the greater Central Command theater, and his intellectual acumen seemed to make him a natural fit.

Obama added, however, that he thought that Petraeus should run the agency as a civilian. The CIA wasn't the military, and Obama was sensitive about the already blurry lines between the two. Having Petraeus in uniform would only further confuse the matter, especially when he traveled to the CENTCOM area and met with national leaders. Petraeus said he understood completely and had already discussed the issue with Secretary Gates and decided that he would retire from the military if offered the job. He told Obama that he thought taking the uniform off would send a powerful message to the CIA workforce. Obama agreed. They then discussed how Obama felt the CIA director should operate. He thought the director should represent the agency's analysts' positions on issues, but Obama would welcome Petraeus's personal views on occasions when they might differ somewhat from those of the analysts. Petraeus agreed, and Obama closed the conversation by saying he needed to discuss Petraeus's selection with others and he would finalize the decision in the weeks ahead.

Petraeus was in a light mood as he left the White House and jumped into his black Yukon. He opened his laptop and read an e-mail that had the letter "U" as the subject line.

"Good luck. Think U won," wrote his mentor Keith Nightingale.

Petraeus was elusive in his responses.

"Thx, Keith, pretty good week, in fact. Just leaving one-on-one with CINC," Petraeus replied.

"Congrats. Good guys win. When is it official?" Nightingale replied.

"Don't jump to the wrong conclusion, Ranger! Good, though . . . ," Petraeus replied, elusively.

"If you are happy we will be also. Press on!" wrote Nightingale.

"RLTW," Petraeus responded—short for "Rangers Lead the Way."

"Get some sleep. U earned it. The world can wait. Yes. RLTW!" Nightingale responded.

"Indeed, it can, Keith. Great week . . . And exciting prospects . . . ," Petraeus said.

"What counts is your view of the task and your assessment as to what you can do with it to further meaningful service. All else is superfluous. Carpe diem," Nightingale said.

"Spot on, Keith. Or, as a tanker would say, 'Target!' RLTW—Dave."

Petraeus drove to the Capitol building for an awards ceremony for a team of Floridians who had gone above and beyond in supporting Central Command troopers—a ceremony originally scheduled for last July that had been delayed eight months—and he then hosted a small dinner, with Holly, at a local restaurant. He was gregarious, but his mind was preoccupied with all that had transpired that week, especially the job prospect. As far as the team around him knew, even his closest aides, they would be heading back to Afghanistan with their future uncertain. The meeting, they thought, had not brought any resolution for them, but it had not closed any doors, either.

Overall, Petraeus and his team were pleased with how the week had gone. Petraeus's team usually conducted after-action reviews after congressional testimony to brainstorm how he might have answered questions better, what went well, and what "questions for the record" his Commander's Initiatives Group would have to draft answers for over the next few weeks. This round of testimony was probably the "most uneventful" he'd ever delivered, his aides believed. "They only threw softballs," said one inner-circle member who had been with Petraeus for every congressional appearance since he assumed command of the surge in Iraq in 2007.

The team flew back to Kabul via London. Petraeus briefed Prime Minister David Cameron, the ministers of Defence and Foreign Affairs, and the chief of Defence Staff on the state of the war in Afghanistan and the dynamics in Washington. The team stayed two nights in London and followed their normal routine. They stayed at the Grosvenor House Marriott, across from Hyde Park, with rooms for entourage members, "designated thinkers" on the CIG and all of their classified communication equipment. The Grosvenor House staff knew Petraeus, and he enjoyed the stark contrast to his Conex container housing in Kabul. The team couldn't wait for a run in Hyde Park— a 4.2-mile loop at sea level in the relatively clean London air. It contrasted starkly with their runs around the eight-hundred-meter loop at ISAF headquarters, where the air was heavy with the acrid smell of burning garbage. The first evening in London, Petraeus attended a dinner hosted by the chief of Defence Staff, General Sir David Richards, ISAF commander in 2006 to 2007, along with Sir Max Hastings, a British journalist and Oxford-educated historian. They quietly discussed the war's progress and challenges as they sat in a booth at Wiltons restaurant.

The next day was full of meetings with VIPs. In the morning, Petraeus met Queen Elizabeth II and gave her one of his COMISAF brushed-steel coins, given to recognize noteworthy achievement and a prize coveted by soldiers in his command. It was engraved with his signature and had a red four-star flag embossed over a black silhouette of Afghanistan. FOR EXCELLENCE was printed across the top, along with COMMANDER, NATO INTERNATIONAL SECURITY ASSISTANCE FORCE on one side. On the other, an embossed picture of the ISAF NATO-OTAN patch in black and tan. "And here is another one for your grandson, Harry," he said as he gave her a second coin. Prince Harry, in his early twenties, had been quietly serving in Helmand Province, Afghanistan, as a forward air controller the previous year, guiding jets toward suspected Taliban targets, until he was "outed" by the press a month or so before the end of his tour. Petraeus could relate to the concerns about one's offspring serving in a war zone. He also expressed his gratitude for the U.K.'s continuing support. "She is one well-informed lady," he mentioned to his staff on the way out of Buckingham Palace. That afternoon, Petraeus headed to 10 Downing Street to meet with Prime Minister Cameron, who had been well briefed on progress in Afghanistan. The team then went out the back door to meet with the secretary of State for Foreign and Commonwealth Affairs, William Hague, to discuss the forthcoming announcement by Karzai of the first phase of the ISAF transition of provinces to Afghan control. They also discussed campaign progress and the challenges of the political process. Petraeus felt these stopovers with a key ally were beneficial for bilateral relations, and they also helped ease the jet lag between continents.

On March 22, shortly after Petraeus's return to Kabul, Karzai made his long-awaited statement on transition as part of his graduation address at the National Military Academy. In July, as the United States began drawing down its forces, he explained, Afghan troops would assume sole responsibility for securing three relatively secure provinces: Panjsher, in northeast Afghanistan, Bamiyan, in central Afghanistan, and Kabul, the capital province. The Afghan troops would also assume responsibility for four province capitals and municipalities: Mazar-i-Sharif, in the north, Herat, in the west, Lashkar Gah, capital of Helmand Province, in the south, and Mehtar Lam, capital of Laghman Province, in eastern Afghanistan. Without mentioning the United States by name, Karzai also used the opportunity to criticize his NATO partners for recent civilian deaths and urged them to stop night raids.

A spokesman for the Taliban called Karzai's transition plan "a symbolic act to deceive the people" that would not "help resolve the main problem, which is the occupation of Afghanistan by foreign forces." Karzai appeared torn in his feelings about the Taliban. On one hand, he saw them as fellow Pashtuns and Afghans. On the other, he considered them extremists who kill government officials and tried to undermine the Afghan constitution.

The same day that Karzai spoke, *Foreign Policy* published an article arguing that the Afghans' ability to assume security control of even limited sectors in Afghanistan was, most likely, a fantasy. Beyond a "staggering attrition rate and a serious gap in quality recruits," the authors wrote, were the obstacles of illiteracy, drug use and medical problems.

Fernando Lujan disagreed. Lujan was just returning from an unprecedented mission in which he and two other members of the Counterinsurgency Advisory and Assistance Team had embedded for a week with an Afghan unit in Zabul Province, the first place in Regional Command South that Afghan forces would begin to operate independently. Lujan was still working toward his goal of taking the CAAT concept inside the Afghan military. Kosh Sadat, an impressive Afghan special forces major who was Petraeus's Afghan military aide, had joined his advisory team. Together, the team's five members—three Americans and two Afghans—ate, slept, showered and patrolled with the Afghan people. The team grew beards, wore Afghan uniforms and conducted all their briefings in Dari or Pashto. Sadat flew down to Kandahar a few days early so that he could participate in planning and team-building exercises. When they briefed an Afghan corps commander before the embed began, Lujan could tell that the general was moved that an Afghan was working as part of the CAAT team. "Kosh told the soldiers and officers everywhere we went that it is possible to rise up through the ranks and make a career for themselves, even if they didn't have money to 'buy' a position," Lujan said once he'd returned from the embed. "He basically said that if they worked hard and set their mind to it, they could become leaders of the army. I know it sounds simple, and we as Americans take it for granted, but I'm telling you, there was something special about what we were doing." At one point, the CAAT team accompanied Afghan troops on an IED-clearing mission. Lujan watched as Afghans, thinking they'd spotted something suspicious in the road, got down on all fours and probed for bombs by hand. "These guys are just fearless sometimes," he said. "It's a whole different perspective riding in the trucks with them."

No sooner had Lujan's team written the report and filed it on a classified computer portal accessible to the Afghans than Tanzola initiated a security investigation of Lujan and his team members. Their team's collective offense: including a minor sentence that contained terminology classified U.S. Secret (NOFORN), as opposed to ISAF Secret, which was releasable to Afghans and NATO partners. As committed as the U.S. military was to its NATO partners, the Pentagon did not share its most sensitive classified information with all of them. Instead, it insisted that U.S. personnel follow highly detailed classification rules that spelled out what could be shared with ISAF partners. "At the very most, this is a minor 'oops'-type incident, but looks like it's going to cloud the whole Zabul report," a senior CAAT officer said. Soon investigators were interviewing the team. "Always a great experience," a few members of the team grumbled. "Now we see why people don't take initiative."

Petraeus, meanwhile, was briefed on Lujan's Zabul embed and said that he was looking for the "right" CAAT leader to replace Tanzola when the time came. He was cheered by the news that his aide Kosh Sadat had been such an inspiring presence among the Afghans. "Kosh is a national asset to Afghanistan," he told his staff. "Good to see how he was able to contribute."

Settling back into the rhythms of command after his visit to Washington,

Petraeus thought of the coming spring and the warming weather as "teeth in the enemy's jugular time" in the south, around Kandahar and Helmand, and in the eastern mountains of Kunar, Paktika and Nuristan provinces. He knew the Taliban would mount a spring offensive. He and his staff had spent the winter formulating plans to disrupt their operations and their thrusts into Afghanistan from across the border in Pakistan. He felt ISAF had the momentum, partly because the Afghan forces that Lujan championed were growing and fighting better. He did not want the Taliban to take the momentum back.

CHAPTER 9

HIGH STAKES

Lieutenant Colonel J. B. Vowell knew he had achieved surprise when armed Taliban fighters scrambled away as the rotor blades announced the approach of the Americans in the dead of early morning. Vowell enjoyed the high ground, in a UH-60 Black Hawk command-and-control helicopter equipped with a suite of specialized communications gear. He ordered the pilots of Apache Longbow helicopter gunships, flying with him to ensure that the landing zones were clear, to target the fleeing Taliban with infrared sensors and kill whatever enemy they identified. A dozen insurgents were killed by the attack helicopters before the ground assault had even begun. Vowell could only hope that the element of surprise would keep the Taliban from ever recovering.

Vowell's 2nd Battalion of the 327th Infantry Regiment, was part of the storied Bastogne Brigade of the 101st Airborne Division. The attack Vowell was leading, code-named Strong Eagle III—the regiment's third major operation in the rugged Kunar Province, in eastern Afghanistan—began at 2:00 A.M. on March 29. Helicopters carrying Vowell's soldiers were approaching two villages, Barawala Kalay and Sarowbay, each in the forbidding mountains of Kunar Province, half a mile from the Pakistan border. The villages were only three miles apart, but separated by nine-thousand-foot mountain ridgelines. Vowell knew these two villages were strongholds of insurgent forces in Kunar, providing security, supplies, natural resources and a pliable population. They were "pivots of maneuver," or staging bases, from which Taliban operations could be planned and executed. No foreign soldiers—not the Americans, the Pakistanis or the Soviets—had ever gone this deep into the mountains. Vowell's spring counteroffensive was designed to deny the Taliban, al-Qaeda and other insurgent groups freedom of movement and maneuver along a corridor, or "ratline," they had used for years connecting the Kunar River Valley and the Pech Valley from which a sister battalion, the 1st of the 327th, had recently withdrawn after handing off their base to an Afghan army battalion.

Vowell had the benefit of earlier air assaults, and his staff had been able to identify landing zones above the villages. His troops could cordon the villages and control all routes to and from them before clearing operations began. The key was holding the high ground, which would draw insurgent fighters to their positions. This kept the Taliban from massing in a defense of the villages and forced them to attack up the mountain, where the Americans were dug in with machine guns.

After the Apaches gunned down the fleeing Taliban outside the village of Sarowbay, three platoons from C Company, the "Cougars," commanded by Captain Tye Reedy, began touching down around 2:00 A.M. As the lead fire team began to approach the village, a third of a mile away, insurgents opened up on them from close range. The Apache pilots had missed some of the enemy, and the Taliban had positioned in trees, from which they were now firing down at the advancing Americans. In the brutal, up-close firefight, Private First Class Jeremy P. Faulkner, 23, of Griffin, Georgia, was killed, and Specialist Dustin J. Feldhaus, 20, of Glendale, Arizona, and Staff Sergeant Bryan A. Burgess, 29, of Cleburne, Texas, were grievously wounded. A platoon leader, Lieutenant Jason Pomeroy, and his soldiers exhibited what Vowell considered "extreme heroism" as they took fire through a wood line to recover the wounded. It would take another forty-five minutes before Vowell could get medevac aircraft to rescue Feldhaus and Burgess, due to intense enemy fire. Both soldiers later died at a trauma center at Bagram Air Base. The operation was off to a tough start.

Soldiers from C Company began moving into Sarowbay to clear a series of compounds. No military-aged males were to be seen, only older women and men. Once the soldiers had worked their way through about a third of the village, a house behind them exploded. It was wired with a house-borne IED, most likely remote-controlled, a common Taliban tactic. Why it wasn't detonated with half a dozen Americans inside would remain a mystery.

As C Company assaulted Sarowbay, Vowell's Headquarters Company, the "Wolverines," joined by an Afghan unit, touched down at a landing zone high above Barawala Kalay. The two companies were supposed to move simultaneously on the villages, though the Cougars landed much closer to their target.

Finally, A Company, the "Gators," commanded by Captain Tom Billig and 1st Sergeant Kenneth Bolin, air-assaulted farther north of Barawala Kalay to isolate the village. If Vowell's hunch was correct, Billig's forces, which included a company of Afghan National Army soldiers, would be in for a stiff fight just preventing the enemy from coming onto the main battlefield. Billig's forces would, in fact, kill forty-five insurgents over the next six days during which the enemy attacked from both close range and with distant fire, but Billig had the assistance of a talented joint tactical air controller and a .50-caliber machine gun with plenty of ammunition. Their defense kept the enemy from getting anywhere near Headquarters Company as it cleared Barawala Kalay.

Vowell landed and linked up with Captain Ed Bankston, commander of Headquarters Company, joining his assault on Barawala Kalay. They had to traverse a very steep, rocky piece of terrain, waiting for daylight just to see their steps in front of them. Each soldier wore body armor and a Kevlar helmet, and carried an assault pack with enough batteries, ammunition, explosives, medicine and water to last for three days. The No Slack battalion would resupply each position once a day by helicopter, but the battle plan depended on the force being able to fight for more than three days in order to prevail. The Taliban believed that the Americans couldn't sustain their high-tech force for more than three days. Vowell was determined to prove them wrong.

After Headquarters Company made its way through the first series of houses, soldiers started finding huge caches of ammunition and weapons—82-mm recoilless rifle rounds, AK-47s, thousands of rounds of 7.62-mm ammunition. There were, however, no men to be seen. Families reported that their husbands and fathers "had gone for work in Jalalabad." Soon, the Americans started to find caches in the tree branches, signs of a hasty retreat by insurgent forces. Vowell's signals intercepts quickly picked up Taliban walkie-talkie chatter that helped corroborate this. His interpreters repeated the words of Taliban commanders: "'We weren't able to get our things out before the Americans arrived.'"

Vowell then joined Captain Reedy and C Company to assess how they were coping with the enemy engagement. The Cougars had not only lost three soldiers shortly after their insertion; several others had been wounded right off the landing zone. Convinced that Reedy's men were in full control, they lifted off and flew to the location of Vowell's operations officer and tactical air controller, who were with the battalion's tactical command post on a mountain ridge half a mile west of his scout platoon, which had assumed a position on a ridgeline separating the two villages. Vowell wanted to link up with his operations and intelligence officers. Where was the enemy? Why hadn't the Taliban attacked since the first firefight that greeted C Company?

No sooner had Vowell landed on the ridge than dense clouds engulfed them in haze and took away their ability to see the other elements, as well as their air support from lithe OH-58 Kiowas and lethal AH-64 Apaches, as well as full-motion video from unmanned aerial vehicles. It was then that Vowell and No Slack discovered where the enemy had gone. They were all around the Americans.

Vowell's position started taking sporadic fire, then well-aimed fire. The scout platoon to his east came under heavy fire. Then Reedy called—they were under intense, concentrated enemy fire. Vowell could hear attacks on all of his positions even as he was pinned down. With a radio on his chest rack, Vowell quickly tried to figure out what to do. With no helicopter air support, only mortars and artillery, Vowell divided up his weapons systems to defend units that were all being severely pressed.

Sergeant First Class Ofren Arrechaga and Staff Sergeant Frank Adamski of Headquarters Company were hit several times in the middle ground between two compounds at Barawala Kalay. Bounding from one compound to the next, they had moved into an intense barrage of accurate fire. Both were severely wounded, shot multiple times and losing blood. Specialist Jameson Lindskog, the newly assigned platoon medic, moved to help Arrechaga, who was trapped in the kill zone. Moments after he started triage, Lindskog was shot in the chest. In excruciating pain, Lindskog kept on treating Arrechaga. Soon other soldiers reached them, just as Lindskog was starting to lose strength and could no longer help Arrechaga. They dragged Arrechaga and Lindskog out of immediate danger. Lindskog continued to explain how to treat Arrechaga. He slowly drifted out of consciousness, saying that he was "sorry" that he didn't have the strength to help. He died moments later.

Once the weather cleared, Vowell's helicopter lifted off from the ridgeline between the villages, but Vowell stayed behind because the position allowed him to talk to all three engaged companies assaulting the villages. Vowell had lost a total of six soldiers by then. Part of him wanted to go back and join Headquarters Company at Barawala Kalay, as they would have a tough time clearing the village. If he moved, though, he would lose the ability to communicate with C Company, given the mountain range separating them and their objectives.

As the battle raged throughout the day, Vowell asked his brigade commander, Colonel Andrew Poppas, to commit an Afghan commando unit from Forward Operating Base Fenty that night. The Afghans, 120 strong, had been trained by U.S. Special Forces and were highly effective for twenty-four to forty-eight hours of intense combat operations. They were lifted in during darkness, and their arrival and reinforcement of the Cougars proved decisive, enabling C Company to consolidate and continue the clearance of Sarowbay.

The assault of the two villages ultimately involved eight hundred coalition and Afghan soldiers. The added combat power was needed to overcome an intense enemy defense in which insurgents occupied the middle ground between the village and the top ridgelines above the village. The insurgents attacked from this middle ground for the next four days, until they were exhausted. When night fell, Vowell turned a number of sophisticated sensors on the enemy positions, using electro-optical, radar and infrared intelligence, surveillance and reconnaissance capabilities to direct Apaches to the Taliban hiding places. Once Vowell found them with weapons, it was easy for the pilots to engage, killing more and more of the insurgents. With each day, the enemy attacks grew weaker. In short order, the Taliban could no longer precisely target Vowell's forces. Every time they tried, they would expose themselves to a myriad of withering fires from both the air and the ground. Vowell called in a total of ninety-six precision-guided bombs on enemy positions.

Headquarters Company wound up clearing Barawala Kalay by itself, with just A Company to the north providing protection. C Company, along with the Afghan commandos, cleared all of Sarowbay, finding arms cache after arms cache, including one with more than two hundred hand grenades. The scout platoon found the long-sought Radio Shariat transmission center, which the insurgents had used to broadcast Taliban propaganda to Kunar Province and into Pakistan as well. Captain Billig and his platoons found weapons, six dead fighters, communications equipment, wads of Pakistani rupees and numerous cell phones on a ridgeline south of Sarowbay. They also found six machine guns, including one that was hidden in the wall of a home, and collected biometric data that would help determine which leaders were among the dead. When the smoke cleared, Vowell's forces had confirmed killing 132 enemy fighters between the northern Marawara Valley and Ganjgal Valley. No Slack lost six soldiers, and the Afghans fighting alongside them lost three, all in direct firefights.

This was what the war in the eastern mountains was like as U.S. commanders tracked insurgent movements with drone reconnaissance and human intelligence and then responded, either with large-scale air-assault operations, smaller Special Operations Forces raids or drones firing Hellfire missiles at specific high-value targets. These tactics would enable them to keep the insurgents off-balance. But the days when the United States would think of establishing dozens of combat outposts in the mountains and valleys of eastern Afghanistan were over. With U.S. forces drawing down, there would never be enough soldiers deployed to man such efforts; nor, as American and Afghan leaders had come to recognize, were such outposts the answer in some of the more remote areas.

AS THE BATTLE raged in the mountains of Kunar Province, 220 miles to the southwest, in the lush vineyards of the Arghandab River Valley, Lieutenant Colonel David Flynn, the commander of the 1st Battalion of the 320th Artillery Regiment, the "Top Guns," sat amid the dignitaries at the opening of a new mosque at Tarok Kolache, the empty, IED-infested village he had flattened with saturation bombing in October. The villagers who had been driven out by the Taliban were back, now that Tarok Kolache was free of all the homemade bombs that had made it uninhabitable. There'd been no gunfire there for five months. The day began with Flynn meeting reporters at the helipad and walking with them to the village, describing battles from the previous fall as he proceeded.

The new mosque was part of a major reconstruction project that included rebuilding every home and replanting every field of pomegranate trees destroyed in the bombing. The project also included the building of a combat outpost in the village to keep the Taliban from intimidating the villagers for working with Flynn's soldiers and civilian engineers and builders. The public affairs office at Regional Command South at first did not want any Americans present, but Flynn would have none of that. The locals had worked very closely with Flynn and his men for several months, and they expected him and some of his key leaders to be there.

Flynn thought the threat of an attack on the mosque opening was low, and he didn't want security officers to flood the zone as they had for Secretary Gates's recent visit. This time, Flynn kept them behind the tree line so they were not visible from the road. When he picked up the reporters, he went "slick," leaving his Kevlar body armor and helmet behind. Though out of sight, security was still substantial.

With the fighting season again upon Afghanistan, the Taliban had shown themselves to be a tough and adaptable enemy. The Top Guns in the Arghandab River Valley and the No Slack battalion in the mountains of Kunar made it clear that massing force against the Americans was a losing proposition. So the Taliban had turned to infiltration attacks on ISAF and Afghan forces, in addition to resuming its campaign of suicide attacks and assassinations.

On his way to see the governor of Kandahar Province several days later, Petraeus flew over Tarok Kolache so he could get a peek at the new mosque and progress on the houses. He had tracked developments there closely and had been heartened by the progress. However, the Taliban had pulled off a brazen attack that day in Kandahar, sending insurgents wearing suicide vests to attack a police and military training center, followed by an ambulance that the Afghans assumed was there to pick up casualties from the first attack. The ambulance was actually loaded with explosives that detonated inside the compound. The twin attack killed six Afghans and wounded twelve others. It was Kandahar's third eruption of violence in a week.

In his appearance with the governor in Kandahar, Petraeus addressed the recent burning of a Koran by a minister at a church in Florida, calling it an "inhumane action." It had, in fact, been a catalyst for violence in Kandahar and several other cities in Afghanistan and left many Afghans badly shaken. Later, he stopped at Forward Operating Base Wilson to see Flynn and his boss, Colonel Arthur Kandarian, commander of the 101st's Strike Brigade, which had done much of the heavy fighting around Kandahar. Petraeus acknowledged that Kandarian's brigade had weathered a tough fight over the past year. Flynn arrived after Petraeus and joined him as Petraeus chatted with Kandarian and several other officers.

The Strike Brigade was in the final weeks of its deployment and understandably felt a sense of considerable accomplishment, albeit tempered by recollection of the human price paid along the way. Petraeus was there to pay tribute to the Strike Brigade's troopers and to speak to their leaders. They should, he told them, be very proud of what their troopers had accomplished. Several days later, Lieutenant General David M. Rodriguez, head of ISAF's Joint Command, informed Flynn that he would be awarded the Silver

Star for courage and valor under fire in rallying his forces during the Battle of Bakersfield. Flynn and his unit had been down a tough road since their first operation with the paratroopers of the 82nd, establishing themselves as among the finest counterinsurgents Petraeus had ever seen. He told Flynn as much in private.

LESS THAN a week later, Petraeus lifted off from the soccer field at ISAF headquarters in his Black Hawk to visit Vowell's No Slack battalion in the Kunar River Valley, several days after Vowell's troops had cleared Barawala Kalay and Sarowbay in Operation Strong Eagle III. He had last met with Vowell and his soldiers in August, following their opening victories in the mountains, Operations Strong Eagle I and II. Accompanied by Major General John Campbell and Colonel Andrew Poppas, commander of the 101st's Bastogne Brigade, Petraeus had come to pin on medals, present awards, receive an intelligence briefing and review lessons learned from the battlefield, all tasks he never tired of doing.

Following the removal of all U.S. forces from the northern part of the Pech Valley in February, Operation Strong Eagle III had been conceived to create "time and space" for the realignment of those forces elsewhere in the region. At the time of the withdrawal, Petraeus had said that "the math didn't add up," meaning there simply weren't enough troops there to sustain U.S.-led population-centric counterinsurgency operations, as had been envisioned for the area years prior. Nor were they necessarily the answer in that area. In fact, he had come to agree with Lieutenant General David Rodriguez that the small outposts were not achieving what had been intended when they'd been emplaced years earlier. Consequently, they made the decision to consolidate forces elsewhere. Building forty bases over five years in an effort to extend the reach of the Kabul government in the rugged mountains of the east had cost more than dozens of Americans their lives. But the people who lived in this forbidding region had no interest in aligning with the Karzai regime, or with the Taliban, for that matter. "The failure in the Pech does not mean that counterinsurgency is a failed concept," Petraeus disciple Ollivant said in Washington. "But it shows that it certainly will fail—or be exponentially more difficult—when it is attempted against isolated peoples who have consciously opted out of the state system. Yes, these non-state spaces do leave room for terrorists to find sanctuary. But it's awfully hard to attack Manhattan from the Pech Valley."

Petraeus sat between Campbell and Poppas for the intelligence briefing, conducted by the No Slack battalion's intelligence officer. The Taliban, he said, called Kunar the "Gateway to Afghanistan." It was largely an unrestricted transit area from Pakistan, a rugged route for fighters and munitions. It also contained remote training areas for insurgents, some of whom had relocated their families there. The enemy typically moved at night. They sometimes even wore women's clothing for cover. This was the same area where Linda Norgrove, a British woman working for a USAID contractor to build roads and bridges and improve agriculture in the area, had been kidnapped in September by insurgents wearing Afghan army uniforms. She had been killed in early October by a grenade thrown by a member of a Navy SEAL team attempting to rescue her. Generally speaking, Afghans in this area were not particularly forthcoming. The intelligence officer noted that "significant activities"—typically attacks—had increased in the area from 77 in 2009 to 234 in 2011. The increase, he told Petraeus, was due, in part, to the past two mild winters. There had been no snow in the area until February, so insurgents had freedom of movement throughout much of the normally bitter winters. Beyond that, the insurgents had sought to expand their footholds in this forbidding area with few coalition and Afghan forces.

There were different groups of insurgents in the area, Petraeus noted, and competition among them that needed to be understood. He knew the Pakistan side of the border from his days at Central Command, and his focus since July had been on the southern and southwestern regions of Afghanistan. In recent months he had been focusing more on achieving "granular knowledge" of the east, and he pressed the commander about the way forward. "You know the enemy will return in months if you don't ultimately find a way to hold," Petraeus said, offering that Afghan security solutions had to be the answer.

The discussion then turned to the recent operation. Vowell and his operations officer explained that they had established three communications centers to maintain adequate command and control of the battle. With temperatures dipping into the twenties at night, they had conducted fourteen complex air assaults with only four helicopters available: two UH-60 Black Hawks and two large CH-47 Chinooks. In the treacherous mountain terrain, there were few cleared areas where helicopters could safely land. All of the attack and maneuver operations had to be planned around available points of insertion. "We used historic sites, but we also had to clear several new areas," he explained. "Sir, it was the most demanding operation we've ever done."

Petraeus, who had commanded numerous huge air-assault operations in Iraq as commander of the 101st Airborne, asked Vowell question after question about the insertions, and how they had worked the synchronization of air support and communications. Then he shifted the focus from tactical to strategic. "Your task right now is to 'disrupt,'" he told Vowell. "Once you've cleared this area, your task will have to become to 'deny' the enemy his safe havens. They will use Kunar if it is wide-open. You must figure out how to hold by employing various local security solutions. That's the only way to deny the Taliban additional safe havens." He also stressed the importance of their partnership with Afghans. "Ultimately, as you know, you'll have to shift your mission to work more with the Afghan National Police and the Afghan National Army. Use every tool you can use so that we can eventually hand off to ANSF. . . . The main effort in the larger campaign will eventually shift here to the east, but, perhaps sooner than that, we will have to begin the drawdown. We won't get more U.S. forces."

The Afghans had already shown that they were capable of working with the Pakistanis on some parts of the border at the tactical and operational levels. Given the porous state of the border, the location of which was unclear in many areas, Pakistanis and Afghans in tribes straddling the border had grown up knowing one another. Campbell explained how he and other ISAF officials had worked directly with the "PakMil" on a plan for this area, an initiative Petraeus applauded, as a comprehensive border plan was one of the greatest challenges for ISAF commanders and their Afghan partners.

Beyond attempting to disrupt the ability of both the Taliban and al-Qaeda to reestablish themselves in the mountain passes and the border, Vowell's battalion was also involved with the creation of Afghan Local Police detachments, as well as a small "allegiance" program for individuals who wanted to lay down arms and reintegrate.

"The formula doesn't matter," said Petraeus, explaining that the exact size and nature of the programs employed for convincing the insurgents to stop fighting was less important than the outcome, as long as the programs met certain redlines. "If the concept includes locals running acceptable governance mechanisms, and they are not engaged in violence or causing problems, that equals success," assured Petraeus. "We have to see how Pech plays out; it is a test case." Petraeus thought the challenge in Kunar was in determining the right mix of U.S. and Afghan forces, given the inevitable limitations on forces.

As he had noted in his conversation with Vowell, the goal was not only to *disrupt* the enemy, as Vowell's forces had done, but to *deny* them safe havens. He believed the ultimate solution would rest with Afghan Local Police detachments, partnered with small U.S. Special Forces elements and integrated with the growing Afghan army and police forces. The surge in Afghanistan would begin to recede in the months ahead, and Petraeus hoped the momentum Vowell and Flynn had helped create could be sustained by Afghan forces. He had seen it work before.

IN EARLY 2007, President Bush had made Petraeus not just the commander but also the face of the war in Iraq. The new four-star was to command a last-ditch effort to salvage the administration's faltering effort in Iraq. A force of five additional combat brigades would "surge" into Baghdad and other parts of Iraq to quell the raging sectarian violence, protect the Iraqi people and arrest Iraq's slide into civil war—the exact counterinsurgency concept Petraeus had spent the previous fifteen months defining at Fort Leavenworth.

In advocating what came to be known as the surge, a coterie of colonels, generals, defense intellectuals and retired officers parted company with many in the Army and pinned their hopes on the counterinsurgency tactics that had fascinated Petraeus since he was a young officer. There were few other officials who believed that a surge could effect change, but Bush did. Approving the brigades, he tasked the chairman of the Joint Chiefs, General Peter Pace, to identify the forces and deploy them as rapidly as possible.

"Figure it out," Pace, in turn, told the Pentagon operations team on December 24, 2006. Petraeus and the operational-level commander, Lieutenant General Raymond Odierno, and the respective division commanders would determine the employment of the forces in Iraq. Petraeus was adamant about the commitment of all five brigades from the outset. He couldn't be forced to ask for each brigade, month after month, as the serving commander in Iraq had proposed.

"The situation in Iraq is dire," Petraeus told the Senate Armed Services Committee during his confirmation hearing on January 23, 2007. "The stakes are high. There are no easy choices. The way ahead will be very hard. Progress will require determination and difficult U.S. and Iraqi actions—especially the latter, as, ultimately, the outcome will be determined by the Iraqis. But hard is not hopeless."

After the confirmation hearing, Petraeus went to see Bush in the Oval Office. Betting his presidency on the success of the surge, Bush described the commitment of additional forces as a "double down" strategy. Petraeus said it was more than that, according to a source briefed after the meeting. "This isn't double down, Mr. President. It's all in," Petraeus stated. "And we need the whole U.S. government to go all in, not just the military."

On February 11, 2007, the day after Petraeus took command in Baghdad, he went out on his first battlefield circulation. At the Dora Market, in the Rasheed District of south Baghdad, where death squads had dumped many bodies, Petraeus's escort said it was too dangerous to stop. No bodies were visible, but the walls of buildings bore blast marks and bullet holes, and the police station Petraeus's organization had built in his previous tour had been blown up by a car bomb. No one was on the streets, and the fear in the neighborhoods was palpable. Petraeus was stunned to see the damage to the area, one that he recalled from a previous tour as a vibrant upper-middle-class neighborhood. He found the same in Ghazaliyah, in northwestern Baghdad.

"Gonna be nothing easy about this," Petraeus noted that afternoon in an e-mail to Michael O'Hanlon, of the Brookings Institution. Petraeus immediately energized the senior staff and commanders. But his will was sorely tested. "You have to be able to take bad news," Petraeus would say later. "A day in Iraq during the surge was multiple items of bad news throughout the day. Some of these were just like a massive emotional blow."

As U.S. forces poured into Baghdad, the insurgents counterattacked, using more and more ruthless tactics and bigger, deadlier bombs. Attacks on U.S. forces throughout Iraq ultimately reached 220 per day. "In truth, the sectarian genie may be tough to put back in the bottle," Petraeus wrote to O'Hanlon on March 1. "I was taken back by the situation in Baghdad; however, we must do all we can, as the alternative would be grim, as you clearly recognize." U.S. combat deaths increased from 70 in February and 71 in March to 96 in April, ultimately topping out at 120 in May.

It was "just one blow after another," Petraeus later observed.

If it wasn't a bomb in the cafeteria of the Iraqi Parliament, it was the remaining minaret of the Samarra Mosque complex being blown up or a major market leveled in Baghdad or an explosion on Mutanabbi Street, the intellectual heart of Baghdad. In my second month of command, there were three car bombs per day on average in Baghdad alone, just staggering. We would fly to the green zone from Camp Victory, and . . . if you didn't see a plume of smoke from a car bomb or an oil pipeline that was blown up or some other attack, it was a great day. But there weren't many great days.

Joe Biden, then a Democratic senator from Delaware, pronounced the surge doomed in April. In June, what little political backing existed for the surge all but disappeared. Even Senator Dick Lugar, a Republican, said it was time to end the surge. Petraeus later recalled:

We were getting hammered. And Iraqi civilians were getting hammered, we were taking really tough casualties and it was not uncommon to lose five, six troopers in a single attack in a single location, with other attacks similar to that in a day. One hundred and twenty troopers were killed in the month of May 2007 alone. And so we'd have these really tough days. You wanted to go out and just fly around and look out the window and see that there were kids playing soccer and road construction ongoing and a bridge being completed. There were all these canaries in the mine shaft out there that we would revisit to remind myself that this was doable, because it was excruciatingly difficult.

He had faith in the new strategy—conventional U.S. and Iraqi forces clearing areas of insurgents and then holding them by moving into the neighborhoods; reconciliation with elements of the Sunni insurgents and Shia militia who were willing to lay down their weapons; targeted special operations raids to capture or kill key insurgent and militia leaders; support for governance and economic development to build on security gains; support for the development of Iraqi forces and institutions; and so on. It all would eventually work, he believed, but he couldn't pinpoint when the results would become tangible.

A few long months into the surge, Petraeus wondered when the violence would start to ebb. He was keenly aware that it was a race against time, with U.S. public support eroding and congressional hearings scheduled for September. There were 156,000 U.S. forces on the ground and more on the way, yet enemy attacks were increasing and casualties were escalating. Even surge believers began to wonder when, and if, things would improve. "When do we think this baby's gonna turn?" Petraeus remembered asking the operational commander, Lieutenant General Odierno, after one morning stand-up.

Attacks on U.S. forces increased at least in part because the soldiers moved off their big, fortified bases and established small outposts in neighborhoods, seventy-seven of them in Baghdad alone. Living among the people exposed the troops to attacks by suicide bombers, militiamen and insurgents. But this action was one of the strategy's most important components, and Petraeus and Odierno pushed to accelerate it. U.S. and Iraqi troops started walking the streets, befriending store owners, fixing clogged sewers, repairing pockmarked schools. Soon they started receiving tips about insurgent hideouts. The intelligence they would gain became a key factor in the success of their operations as well as in the night raids overseen by Special Operations Forces, commanded at the time by Lieutenant General McChrystal.

"They displayed incredible resilience and courage," Petraeus said of the conventional surge forces. "They demonstrated enormous initiative. I think [those qualities] are a strength of our country in general—innovativeness, determination, sheer courage at various times as well as in really difficult positions and conditions. And steadfastness in the face of just really horrific losses and casualties."

Petraeus put a huge premium on initiative at the small-unit level:

That's exactly the kind of attitude that you're seeking to foster, the kind of culture that you're seeking to establish in an organization that's conducting a counterinsurgency campaign as difficult as what we were doing in Iraq. I gave captains my e-mail address and said if there's ever something that's so vexing that you just want to throw your hands in the air, don't do that. Send me an e-mail. If you really care that much, then you gotta have the guts to do it, because you're talking about life-and-death issues and you have an awesome responsibility to your troopers. So don't ever hesitate to do that if it's reached that point.

Finally, attacks and U.S. combat losses started to drop precipitously in July. Surge skeptics and revisionists argued that the improvement came not from anything the surge troops were doing but because ethnic cleansing had run its course, but Petraeus and Odierno differed. The key for them was living with the people. Meanwhile, Petraeus was busy beginning the process of putting 103,000 Sunnis and Shiites, former insurgents or militia, on the U.S. payroll. Petraeus's decision to reconcile with former Sunni insurgents and later with Shiites was one of the riskier parts of his strategy. He did not initially tell the Iraqi government of Prime Minister Nouri al-Maliki, a Shiite, that he planned to put many opponents of his regime on the American payroll, though he forged cooperation as early as he could, and ultimately there was partnership on the approach. Nor did he clear the move with Bush. He just did it, informing Washington but not asking permission.

Petraeus agrees that signing neighborhood truces with Sunni and Shia militants helped reduce violence. But ultimately violence came down, he said, for a variety of different reasons: broad reconciliation with the Sunni and Shia group leaders, targeted night raids on al-Qaeda and Shia militia leaders, major clearance operations in insurgent strongholds, and Maliki directing action against the fighters of anti-American Shia cleric Muqtada al-Sadr. "I think August is going pretty well," Petraeus wrote to O'Hanlon on August 12. "We've continued to make substantial progress against al Qaeda in Iraq and do have them on the run. Looks like sectarian deaths, IEDs, and attacks are all trending down—and the latter two may be approaching statistical significance."

By the time Petraeus went back to Capitol Hill to brief Congress on the surge in September 2007, he had ample metrics to show that the surge was, in fact, succeeding. As he would do later in describing the gains in Afghanistan, he called the gains in Iraq fragile and reversible. For this reason, the full-page "General Betray Us" ad placed by MoveOn.org in the *New York Times* on the day of his Senate testimony seemed particularly unfair in its assertion that Petraeus wasn't being honest with the facts. Petraeus never minimized the difficulties in Iraq, even after conditions improved. "There are endless, innumerable problems that just cause one to want to explode in frustration," he wrote to O'Hanlon on October 28. "And attacks do continue—including a possible kidnapping, yesterday, of sheiks who came to see the prime minister about reconciliation." On November 28, he wrote to O'Hanlon: "You won't hear us talk about turning corners, [reaching] culminating points, [achieving] success, or any of that. In fact, I have repeatedly said that we won't know that we turned a corner until 6 months after we did so; moreover, I have said repeatedly as well that there will be plenty of tough days and tough weeks in the months ahead."

In March 2008 came a climactic series of battles when Prime Minister Maliki made a courageous, if somewhat impulsive, decision to confront the Shia militia in Basra, in southern Iraq, and then in the Baghdad suburb of Sadr City, among other locations. The subsequent fighting was some of the most intense of the war, but U.S. and U.K. forces backed up the Iraqis in the south, while Americans in Baghdad massed assets to take on the militia groups in pitched fighting in the city.

The U.S. forces and Iraqi offensives were relentless, taking control of one area after another, steadily building Iraqi forces in quantity and quality, and supporting the slow but continuing development of local, provincial and national governance and economic development, including important initiatives overseen by then–Colonel Mark Martins in the rule-of-law arena and numerous efforts to enable the development of political consensus and legislation on which further progress hinged. The comprehensive civil-military COIN campaign proved itself.

By the time he left Iraq in mid-September 2008, after more than nineteen months in command, Petraeus and his surge forces and Iraqi partners had clearly regained the initiative across the country. Given the conditions they had inherited in early 2007, that was a historic accomplishment. The surge had been violent and bloody. U.S. combat losses totaled 1,124 soldiers killed, with 7,710 wounded. But the surge proved to be Petraeus's finest hour as a field general. As he said in his final letter to his troops, on September 15, 2008, "your great work, sacrifice, courage, and skill have helped reverse a downward spiral toward civil war and wrest the initiative from the enemies of the new Iraq."

IN MID-APRIL 2011, the enemies of the new Afghanistan seemed to be everywhere. As Major General John Campbell prepared to lift off from the RC East command headquarters at Bagram Air Base, east of Kabul, for a day's battlefield circulation. He thought of these battlefield circulations as critical parts of his job, not social events. Commanding Afghanistan's eastern sector on yearly rotations was a challenge for anyone, given the vast and difficult terrain, the diversity of tribes and the depth of knowledge necessary to tell good guys from bad guys in dozens of villages. But by this point, approaching the end of his tour, Campbell had started demonstrating real mastery. Petraeus noticed how skillful Campbell had become and valued his counsel. Then urgent word arrived: There had been a suicide attack by a man wearing an Afghan army uniform at Forward Operating Base Gamberi, in Laghman Province, to the east. Several members of the 101st Sustainment Brigade—the "Lifeliners"—had been killed in the attack, along with Afghan soldiers and possibly others. Unfortunately, such attacks had become commonplace, but it didn't make them any easier for a commander at any level in the chain of command, including a division commander, to stomach. Campbell was in immediate contact with the commander on the ground; he'd allow that commander the opportunity to conduct consequence management; then, he decided, he'd go to the scene to view it for himself.

While he continued to monitor the developments via radio at the scene of the suicide attack at Gamberi, Campbell continued his battlefield circulation on the cloudy and dreary day. He next touched down at the headquarters of the 2nd Battalion of the 506th Infantry Regiment, home to Task Force White Currahee. Lieutenant Colonel Don Hill greeted him, walked him to a briefing room and described the unit's largest air assault during the deployment, Operation Overlord, which was still under way in the nearby Naka District. Naka was the last insurgent stronghold in the region, the place where enemy soldiers slept, planned, recovered and staged their attacks. They had been expecting an attack by the Americans. But when it came, the rapid insertion of 350 U.S. soldiers and their Afghan partners left the insurgents nowhere to go and little to do but attack the Americans' blocking positions, to little effect. As Hill briefed Campbell, U.S. soldiers occupied the final insurgent stronghold in the region.

The climactic air assault was the logical culmination of operations emanating from Combat Outpost Zerok, about twelve miles from the Pakistan border. As recently as that summer, it had been under near-constant attack by the insurgents with small arms and mortars. The base had nearly fallen to the insurgents in 2009 and was considered one of the most dangerous places in Afghanistan. When Lara Logan and a team from *60 Minutes* embedded at Zerok the previous August, a month after Petraeus assumed command, they had found themselves in a fierce rocket attack in their first hour at the base. Two soldiers were wounded.

At first, the Currahees' chances for success in the region seemed remote. As in the Korengal and Pech valleys, to the north in Kunar Province, where the ultimate decision would be to withdraw forces from the most remote areas, the area was difficult to clear of insurgents with force levels that were relatively light compared with those in the south, around Kandahar. But Echo Company had made strong gains since its arrival in August 2010. Zerok hadn't been shelled since the previous summer, in part, according to Major Mark Houston, the battalion operations officer, because of a shift in tactics that included relentless foot patrols in the mountains. By patrolling at night, the Currahees had taken away the insurgents' vantage points and disrupted their freedom of movement to the extent that engagements had virtually ceased. As U.S. forces were gradually drawn down, this coverage would be assumed by Afghan forces, border police or, in some areas, the Afghan Local Police.

By April, villagers in this part of Paktika Province enjoyed greater freedom of movement. A new hotel had opened in the local bazaar, in part to accommodate the increased flow of travelers coming into the larger villages to buy and sell goods and larger numbers of elders returning to represent their villages in district *shuras*. Two hundred fifty elders had attended a *shura* the month prior, Hill noted, helping to mediate land and timber disputes. In an area where the Taliban's shadow government had resolved disputes in the past, now elders—and by extension the Afghan government—had begun to reassert their authority.

Campbell was scheduled to visit the Sarobi District Center at 1:00 P.M. to attend a "validation" ceremony there for the six new ALP detachments that the Special Forces in the area had helped create, building on their earlier

Village Stability Operations. On the brief flight to Sarobi, Campbell told an aide to find out the latest from FOB Gamberi, which was reeling from the suicide attack that morning that appeared to have been carried out by an Afghan insider. Six, maybe nine, were dead. Many were wounded, but there was still confusion at the base. Had an Afghan soldier conducted the attack, or had an insurgent infiltrated and stolen a uniform in order to penetrate security? It sounded as if the suicide bomber was recognized by other Afghans in the room. How many more of these could the command expect? Campbell had ordered all units to be on guard for this type of infiltration attack, but completely preventing such attacks was hugely difficult. Intelligence warnings from earlier in the year indicated that the insurgency's focus this fighting season would be on infiltrating the Afghan military and police.

Once the helicopter landed at Sarobi, it quickly lifted off to avoid small-arms fire. The security situation, while improved, was not good enough to allow for the "birds" to stay on the ground long. Campbell and his aides walked briskly toward a white concrete walled structure while his security team set up a hasty perimeter. It was the district center for local governance, and nearly all three hundred new members of the Afghan Local Police were present for the ceremony. If Petraeus was to have any hope of keeping the Taliban from reasserting control over this area, these newly minted village constabulary units constituted an important part of the blocking force. Campbell exchanged handshakes and placed his hand over his heart in the traditional Afghan gesture of respect and thanks. A few elders greeted him, but there were long, awkward silences.

The ceremony had been moved inside a large community room in the district's central building because of the rain, and all of the Afghan elders crowded inside. Campbell and the other Americans and ISAF officials waited outside the main room. This was an Afghan ceremony, run by Afghans for Afghans. The expanding security inkblot, as Petraeus liked to call it, was slowly spreading in this area, thanks to the new local police units. "We are in the beginning stages of this, but I believe this will be a game changer here in Afghanistan," said Campbell.

Campbell then flew to FOB Gamberi, one part of which was in ruins after that morning's attack. He spoke quietly to all the survivors who had been in the room when the attack happened and pinned Purple Hearts on those in the base aid station who had been wounded. It had been another long day in America's longest war.

In spite of the additional forces deployed and the tactical victories his soldiers had achieved in the forbidding mountains of eastern Afghanistan along the Pakistan border and in the rolling hills closer to Kabul, Campbell's sector remained an "economy of force" area. The "surge" of an additional 30,000 soldiers to Afghanistan had raised the total U.S. forces to 100,000. But Afghanistan was vast and had been swallowing up foreign troops for centuries. Taliban could still easily travel through Paktika and other eastern provinces bordering Pakistan along footpaths, unchecked roads and ungoverned valleys with relative ease. There was still only a nascent border plan for this part of Afghanistan. It was hard to claim that 5,000 additional ISAF troops, mainly Americans, sent to Paktika over the past year accomplished much more than displacing insurgents. An Afghan Paktika protection-force concept was under way; until those Afghans could conduct sustained security operations at a higher level, or until additional ISAF forces were stationed in the area—which was not likely—no one was certain the gains would hold.

THAT NIGHT, back at ISAF headquarters in Kabul, Petraeus spoke by secure phone to the commander of the Sustainment Brigade whose soldiers had been killed in the infiltration attack at Forward Operating Base Gamberi. Such a loss inevitably brought him to a moment of assessment. "It was a tragic, very tough event out there for the Lifeliners," Petraeus reflected, his voice cracking slightly. "Very tough." He thought for a long moment when asked how he handled soldiers dying. "You just keep it all in," he said. "You bite your lip." There would certainly be more to come in the months ahead as the Taliban returned to the battlefield and fighting resumed, given what Petraeus was anticipating—"key-leader attacks, suicide attacks, tough fighting." As he summarized conditions on the ground, he focused on expanding the security bubble around Kabul. In addition to the gains made in Kandahar and Helmand provinces, conditions were still touch-and-go in Logar and Wardak provinces, to the south and southwest of Kabul, and more effort was being focused there. The same combination of conventional and Special Operations Forces, along with Afghan special forces, was achieving results in Laghman Province, east of Kabul. This layered defense forced the Taliban into valleys where they could be tracked, if not directly through ISAF checkpoints.

Petraeus was now fluent down to the district level, from Herat Province in the west, on Iran's border, to governance challenges around Kandahar, where the Taliban had been effectively cleared. In his own assessment, there was fragile progress to report. He was pleased with the "hold"-phase actions of conventional Afghan and ISAF forces in the south and with the still-burgeoning effort to build Afghan Local Police units in villages across the country, as well as with Brigadier General H. R. McMaster's work fighting corruption. Karzai was accepting McMaster's ideas—he'd even fired his surgeon general, Ahmad Zia Yaftali, for selling medical supplies donated by the international community and relieved the leadership of the Afghan Military Hospital. But working with the international community, Petraeus observed, introduced a whole new level of complexity and occasional frustration. The coalition was now forty-nine nations (plus Afghanistan), and persuading all to "make way together" took considerable energy, engagement and determination—all of which Petraeus had in spades and committed to this aspect of his responsibilities.

What seemed to worry him most, though, was not conditions on the ground but the adjustments that would be necessary with the drawdown of forces in July and the inevitable transition in the war effort. "Transition is, in some respects, a philosophical issue," he said. "But it's hugely important. Big ideas matter. The mission is not transition. The mission is to achieve conditions in security and governance and development that enable irreversible transition. If the mission becomes transition, we can do that—we can hand off—but we may not achieve the goals of the U.S. or NATO forces. I'm very sensitive to this," he explained, recalling the situation in Iraq in 2004 and in 2006, when the mission seemed to become precisely that.

"Commanders thought they'd be judged based on how well they did with transition readiness," he said. "Some people kept telling the commander they were going to be able to transition, when the situation was going south." By late 2006, with violence escalating in Iraq, the mission paradoxically seemed even more focused on transition. "We stopped that when I took command—we stopped transition," he noted.

In Afghanistan, he observed that, "even with commencement of the drawdown, enough troops and civilians will remain in Afghanistan to pursue all the campaign plan's lines of operation—protecting the people, dismantling insurgent networks, building Afghan forces, aiding local government, fostering development, attacking corruption. Progress still needs to be made in all of those areas before transition is possible in additional areas." Clearly, as troops "thin out," Petraeus explained, more and more emphasis will need to be placed on helping the Afghan government build its capacity to deliver services and provide security. "If transition is the mission, well, we can hand the ball to these guys and step off the field now," he said. But, he clearly implied, the mission was to accomplish more than that: The intention was to hand the Afghans a situation they could sustain.

PETRAEUS HAD BEEN TOLD by a Fox News reporter, interviewing him in his office, that Obama would give him the CIA job as a way to muzzle him, although Petraeus did not believe that to be true. The reach and capability possessed by the agency in the global war on terror clearly intrigued him. "They should use me," he said to a close friend about those in the Obama White House. "I've been their most loyal guy for quite a while; sure, I haven't hesitated to provide forthright advice . . . but that's what a commander in chief should want."

The Fox News interview eventually touched on Petraeus's family. Holly was in Oklahoma, speaking in her new role as assistant director of the government's new Consumer Financial Protection Bureau, heading the Office of Servicemember Affairs. "The Dude," as Petraeus referred to his now–1st lieutenant son Stephen, was getting ready for his Expert Infantryman Badge test before going to Jumpmaster School and possibly off to the Rangers. His daughter, Anne, continued in graduate school, her blog attracting more and more readers—with her dad commenting on it nearly every day.

At the end of the interview with the reporter, there was a long pause in the conversation. Finally, Petraeus said, "You know . . . in Iraq, there were days when you asked yourself, 'Is this going to work in the time we need it to work?' You know, tough days," he shared as he explained the fallout from the suicide attack that Major General Campbell's unit had experienced that day. The higher up you got, the heavier the weight fell, the more responsibility rested on your shoulders. "And at the end of the day," Petraeus reflected, "there is only one guy in charge in a theater."

THE TOUGH NEWS would continue. Two days later, an insurgent in an Afghan National Army uniform got inside Afghanistan's Defense Ministry, in Kabul, and killed two soldiers before he himself was shot and killed. A Taliban spokesman said the attack had been aimed at Afghan defense minister Abdul Rahim Wardak and Gérard Longuet, the visiting French defense minister. French dignitaries were in Kabul to visit Afghan leaders and to present Petraeus with the Commandeur de la Légion d'Honneur. In accepting the award, Petraeus thought how proud Holly's father, General Knowlton, would have been. Knowlton had also been a recipient of the Légion d'Honneur.

Petraeus's days were a kaleidoscope of events and emotions. He and Command Sergeant Major Marvin Hill, along with a congressional delegation headed by House Speaker John A. Boehner, attended a memorial ceremony for the six soldiers killed at FOB Gamberi by the Afghan soldier. Petraeus put his commemorative coins by the boots in front of the upside-down rifles and Kevlar helmets of the fallen troopers. Boehner added his coins, too. It was a tough moment but also a moving one for Petraeus, who felt the strength of U.S. soldiers was once again on full display.

As Petraeus was receiving his honor that day from the French, Flynn was awarded the Silver Star by Lieutenant General David M. Rodriguez at Forward Operating Base Wilson, in Kandahar, the Strike Brigade's headquarters, for "exceptionally valorous conduct in the face of a determined enemy." The recommendation for the award, submitted and signed by six of Flynn's men, began by citing Flynn's actions during the Top Guns' battles in the Arghandab. While Flynn was on leave in January, his operations officer, Major Brendan Raymond, had asked the brigade commander for his endorsement on the award, and he agreed. Raymond had submitted other troopers in the unit for valorous award nominations, but while writing them up he reflected back on the significant impact that he felt Flynn had had on the unit, their civilian and Afghan partners, the Afghan people and the Taliban.

"The award was intended to recognize the unparalleled courage that [Flynn] demonstrated during the arduous fight last summer," Raymond shared in an e-mail. "We had many heroes in our ranks, and I think that we did a good job recognizing their efforts with valorous awards. But, as in all fights—leaders are often overlooked. I felt it was my responsibility for seniors, peers and subordinates to acknowledge LTC Flynn's acts of valor. He, more than any soldier in our TF, deserved this award. Soldiers identified with him throughout the train-up and recognized his courage in combat; and because of this, they followed him without question. He shared every hardship and inspired his men and women to greatness."

Flynn was eloquent five days later at Forward Operating Base Terra Nova as he handed authority over to Lieutenant Colonel Mike Kirkpatrick, commander of the unit replacing the Top Guns. "Our task force . . . defeated the Taliban in the Arghandab District, rebuilt mosques and homes in villages used as enemy sanctuaries . . . and, most importantly, provided hope for a peaceful and prosperous future for the Afghan people that is closer in sight now than at any time in the past six years. The price was paid in blood spilled by our soldiers." The final toll suffered by the Top Guns and the Afghan battalion with which they fought shoulder to shoulder: eight killed in action and 104 wounded, including more than twenty amputees. "Notwithstanding our success, this war is not over, and there is much to be done still in the Arghandab," he said. "Our collective optimism is cautious, and the gains are certainly fragile as we see the Taliban begin to reseed the district."

Flynn felt a weight in his stomach flying out of Terra Nova a short while later. He found himself wondering how he would ever get through all of the memorials back home when the families of the fallen troopers arrived.

THE DAY AFTER Flynn left, the Taliban engineered a massive jailbreak from Sarposa prison, in Kandahar, with an estimated 476 prisoners escaping through a tunnel dug beneath the Kabul-Kandahar Highway. Just two days earlier, Gates had called 2011 a "critical year" in Afghanistan and said that by the end of the year it was possible that the United States and its allies may have "turned a corner" in the country. On many days, that seemed like an ambitious statement.

Despite all that Brigadier General Martins and his team had done to help build a functioning judicial system, the Afghan Ministry of Justice officials who were running the prison sometimes seemed incapable of hanging on to their prisoners. While it was hard to see the escape of 476 Taliban insurgents, on one level, as anything other than a major setback, Martins could also point to the fact that all of the escapees had had their biometric data—eye scans, fingerprints and facial images—entered into a giant database. Petraeus had supported the ambitious biometric data program in Iraq, both for Iraqi detainees and Iraqi employees, during the surge in 2007. The program had proven so successful that he encouraged Martins and his boss to do the same in Afghanistan, where biometric data from 1.5 million Afghans existed in a database at the time of the Sarposa jailbreak. But that info would be useful only if the escapees were killed or detained again in the future.

THE NIGHT of the Sarposa escapes, Gates called Petraeus and told him to be ready to return to Washington on short notice for a likely announcement of his selection to be the next director of the CIA. Late the next night, Obama called Petraeus and formally offered him the job. With the news spreading all over Washington, Team Petraeus geared up for another trip. They departed from Kabul on April 27 for an eight-hour flight to Ramstein Air Base, in Germany. Petraeus went for a run while the plane refueled, then flew for another eight hours to Andrews Air Force Base, outside Washington. The mood was light. Petraeus and his spokesman, Erik O. Gunhus, monitored speculation about Petraeus's nomination, whether he was qualified to run the CIA, and whether he would further militarize the agency.

Petraeus landed at Andrews at 6:25 P.M. and spent the night at his Fort Myer home. The next morning, he went running and then spent some time working from classified computers in his little office at the Fort Myer quarters. That afternoon, he appeared alongside the president, Gates, Panetta and his replacement as commander in Afghanistan, Lieutenant General John Allen, in the East Room of the White House. After naming Panetta to succeed Gates, Obama said:

I'm also very pleased that Leon's work at the CIA will be carried on by one of our leading strategic thinkers and one of the finest military officers of our time, General David Petraeus. This is the second time in a year that I've asked General Petraeus to take on a demanding assignment. And I know this one carries a special sacrifice for him and his wife, Holly. After nearly forty years in uniform, including leading American and coalition forces in some of the most challenging military missions since 9/11, David Petraeus will retire from the Army that he loves to become the next CIA director, effective early September, pending Senate confirmation. As a lifelong consumer of intelligence, he knows that intelligence must be timely, accurate and acted upon quickly. He understands that staying a step ahead of nimble adversaries requires sharing and coordinating information, including with my director of national intelligence, Jim Clapper. And even as he and the CIA confront a full range of threats, David's extraordinary knowledge of the Middle East and Afghanistan uniquely positions him to lead the agency in its effort to defeat al-Qaeda. In short, just as General Petraeus changed the way that our military fights and wins wars in the 21st century, I have no doubt that Director Petraeus will guide our intelligence professionals as they continue to adapt and innovate in an ever-changing world.

Petraeus took Holly and his mother-in-law, Peggy Knowlton, out to dinner that night. And he ran again on Friday morning before taking off at nine o'clock. from Andrews to return to Kabul. By the end of the trip, he had spent more time in the air than on the ground.

As Petraeus flew back to the war, Flynn's Top Guns were touching down at Fort Campbell. The most emotional moment for Flynn came on the tarmac as he led his soldiers to Hangar 3 for the homecoming and he saw the line of wounded warriors waiting to greet them: Lugo, Macari, Bixler, Gatson, Kent, Malin, Bryant, Brown, Kuehl, Stinnett, Siler and the others, in wheelchairs or standing on prosthetics with canes, their family members by their sides. They were exceedingly proud to be there with the rest of the battalion to celebrate its homecoming. Flynn had to struggle to fight back tears. As they were all falling into formation outside the hangar, the wounded soldiers were made to stand off to the side. Flynn asked the homecoming organizers if they could walk in with the rest. When he was told that they would have to fall into the back of the formation, Flynn exploded. "Bullshit," he said. "They are going to walk in right up front with me!" The wounded men lined up next to Flynn at the front of the formation and led the Top Guns back into the hangar.

That night, Flynn set up a dinner with all of the wounded at a local restaurant in town. An older woman with her husband told Flynn, with tears in her eyes, that the first round of drinks was on her. They were quite a spectacle: a long table filled with legless young men in wheelchairs. Flynn finished the night with a short speech in their honor. He told all of them that he was committed to them for life.

CHAPTER 10

TRANSITION

Petraeus sat in the small common room off his bedroom reading e-mails later than usual on Sunday, May 1, the night after his return from Washington. He had stayed up in anticipation of what he knew was about to happen—and had told no one about. He left his quarters in ISAF headquarters' "Florence Village" compound in workout shorts and a T-shirt fifteen minutes before midnight and walked in the darkness to the Joint Special Operations Command's Situational Awareness Room that supported ISAF headquarters. He was the only person on the compound who knew the full details of the impending operation: Navy SEALs were about to raid a compound in Abbottabad, Pakistan, where the Central Intelligence Agency was reasonably confident they would find Osama bin Laden.

Though Petraeus had gotten wind of the developments of the hunt for bin Laden when he'd been in Washington in March, he hadn't taken it overly seriously. That changed when he was in Washington on April 28, after meetings at the White House to discuss his next job. The Central Command commander, Marine general James Mattis, had called Petraeus with an alert, and shortly after, the vice chairman of the Joint Chiefs of Staff called Petraeus to provide additional details. Vice Admiral William H. McRaven, commander of the JSOC, briefed him in Kabul two days later, upon his return, with the concept, timeline and planning for various contingencies, some of which could have significant consequences for ISAF and U.S. forces in Afghanistan.

The stakes were enormous. Petraeus, however, didn't get excited about many operations; he strove to keep a steady demeanor. He had geared up for big military operations in the past, only to have them canceled due to weather delays or some other last-minute glitch. To be sure, some operations—like the killing of Saddam's sons, Uday and Qusay, by the 101st Airborne and Special Operations Forces, in the summer of 2003—had been executed roughly as scheduled. But the Abbottabad raid had already been postponed twenty-four hours due to weather. Petraeus flashed back to his airborne days, sitting in the aircraft, hesitating to get too psyched up before conditions for a drop were confirmed at the drop zone. He'd learned to keep his emotions at bay.

As he walked through the night, he thought of the importance of the operation, and he calculated the second- and third-order effects of the raid. He had flown over Abbottabad the week prior with the Pakistani army's chief of staff, General Ashfaq Kayani, and a year earlier he had spoken at the military academy a mile or so from the compound. He could picture the city. He also thought of the 1979 Iran Hostage Rescue Mission that had been aborted in the Iranian desert before ever getting to Tehran, much less to the U.S. Embassy there. Petraeus understood, in great detail, why the nation's nascent special operations community had failed in 1979, particularly in the intelligence and aviation arenas, just as he now knew how the JSOC had flourished in the most lethal sense to become a key force in Afghanistan—and in the broader war on global extremism. But would the Special Operations Forces be good enough on this night? If they failed, as they had in Iran more than thirty years ago, what would it mean for U.S.-Pakistani relations? And if they succeeded in capturing or killing the al-Qaeda leader, the casus belli that had brought Petraeus and hundreds of thousands of U.S. soldiers to Afghanistan, what would that mean for the war?

Petraeus knocked on the unmarked secure, vaulted door to JSOC's Situational Awareness Room and surprised the night shift. He'd dropped by many times before, but never unexpectedly so late at night. He asked everyone to leave but the senior officer in the room, a colonel who was the liaison officer between Joint Special Operations Command and Petraeus. After the room had been cleared, Petraeus asked the colonel, "Do you know what's going on?" The colonel told him he was monitoring nine operations ongoing in Afghanistan that night and that there were a few others "on deck." Petraeus sat down at a computer terminal, logged in to a Special Ops "chat room," and waited for midnight Kabul time, when the helicopters were to arrive at the bin Laden compound. It was only when the helicopters carrying Navy SEALs were on the ground at the objective in Pakistan that Petraeus told the colonel that an operation was under way to target bin Laden.

The Situational Awareness Room was filled with large computer screens for streaming video of ongoing operations and flashing SIGACTS—significant actions—alerts. But they were focused on the normal operations inside Afghanistan. To maintain situational awareness on the bin Laden raid, Petraeus used a special online "chat room" that connected him to individuals in the operations center in eastern Afghanistan that was overseeing the mission. There was no radio or video feed available for him, but Petraeus, making occasional phone calls and using the secure online chat, was able to track the mission, since he'd be the one to commit some of ISAF's U.S. assets if any of various contingencies arose. Some of the Special Operations Forces under his control were on alert, even though the mission was not "operationally controlled" by the military.

The Title 50 authority for this operation, which allows the U.S. government to conduct covert action or "deniable" missions, dictated that the operational chain of command went from the president to the CIA director to the commander of the Joint Special Operations Command to the Special Operations Forces element conducting the raid, meaning that Petraeus and the Pentagon were effectively out of the chain of command. For the raid, members of Navy SEAL Team 6 and other JSOC elements had been placed under the agency. Still, Petraeus was read into the raid, because various contingencies—none of them good—could have required soldiers under his operational control to serve as a rapid-reaction force. It was amazing for him to closely follow the operation as commandos stormed the highly secure compound in Abbottabad and opened fire on four occupants until they found

"Geronimo," bin Laden's code name, on the third floor of the building in which bin Laden had apparently spent years. After forty minutes inside, the message finally came: "Geronimo EKIA." Bin Laden had been killed by a shot each to his chest and to his head above the left eye.

Petraeus clenched his fist and reflected on all that had transpired since the hunt for bin Laden had begun. There were no high fives; rather than celebrate, Petraeus and the colonel focused on what came next—the extraction of the body and the exfiltration of the SEAL team—and the possible implications of various contingencies for the forces in Afghanistan. The operation was not unlike those the colonel monitored from his post each night. There were, in fact, now thirteen Special Operations raids under way that night in Afghanistan, executed by the same highly trained troops, based on precise intelligence and employing stealth tactics. Several that night were judged to be "more demanding" in various respects than the operation in Pakistan, but none had even remotely the same strategic significance—though the operations that night resulted in the capture of five important Taliban leaders. With all that activity, the colonel quickly tuned back to monitoring the operations in country, while Petraeus continued to monitor the events in Abbottabad and allowed the other JSOC personnel back into the room.

The raid team had reported killing "Geronimo," but JSOC commander Admiral McRaven wanted to confirm bin Laden's identity further, in part through DNA tests. While bin Laden's body was flown out of Pakistan to an aircraft carrier, hair and other samples were expedited for verification. After the fastest DNA test run in the history of Bagram Air Base, McRaven and all the other observers in Afghanistan and Washington breathed a sigh of relief. There was a very high probability, McRaven said later that morning, that they'd killed "number one."

Petraeus remained in the windowless room in Kabul for a few hours more, monitoring the continuing operation and tuning in to open-source news in Pakistan to try to gauge what the reactions would be as night turned to day. Given the eight-and-a-half-hour time difference between Washington and Kabul, it was nearing time for the president to deliver the extraordinary news to the American public, planned for approximately ten o'clock on a Sunday night. The president's announcement, however, was delayed an hour. Petraeus and his team gathered to hear it, delaying—for only the second time in his command—his regularly scheduled morning stand-up briefing and directing all stations within the ISAF Command to turn on their televisions to observe the president's announcement from Washington.

"Today, at my direction, the United States launched a targeted operation against [a] compound in Abbottabad, Pakistan," Mr. Obama said. "A small team of Americans carried out the operation with extraordinary courage and capability. No Americans were harmed. They took care to avoid civilian casualties. After a firefight, they killed Osama bin Laden and took custody of his body."

Following a moment of excitement for those at ISAF headquarters, Petraeus quickly returned to the business at hand. Bin Laden's death would not immediately change the dynamic on the ground, he suspected. But the global implications could be enormous, affecting U.S.-Pakistani relations, the future of al-Qaeda and, ultimately, the coalition's will to fight in Afghanistan, now that the iconic terrorist leader who had plotted the 9/11 attacks in camps along the Afghan-Pakistan border was dead. Still, Petraeus remained cautious. He wasn't sure it was the end of an era, just an important inflection point in America's longest war; and it wasn't clear that the effects in Afghanistan would be that significant, in the near term, at least.

TWO DAYS BEFORE the bin Laden raid, the Defense Department released a document it had produced for Congress, "Report on Progress Toward Security and Stability in Afghanistan and United States Plan for Sustaining the Afghanistan National Security Forces." It confirmed Petraeus's most recent testimony on Capitol Hill. The U.S. troop surge had arrested the Taliban's momentum and wrested safe havens in Kandahar and Helmand from its control. Governance and economic development, however, were lagging behind these tenuous security gains. "Overall, the progress across Afghanistan remains fragile and reversible, but the momentum generated over the last six months has established the necessary conditions for the commencement of the transition of security responsibilities to Afghan forces in seven areas this summer." The Afghan Local Police had expanded from eight districts in September to thirty-four in March and were helping put "unprecedented pressure on the insurgency." The Afghan military was growing in capability as well. According to a Defense Department report, by the spring of 2011, 95 percent of all ISAF military operations were being conducted in partnership with Afghan forces. Afghans, in fact, had provided 60 percent of overall force strength during Operation Hamkari, in Kandahar Province in September 2011. By contrast, the Afghans' force contribution to Operation Moshtarak, in Helmand Province in March 2010, had been only 30 percent.

An Afghan public opinion poll showed the Taliban were less popular than ever, with 75 percent of Afghans surveyed saying that it would be bad for the country if the Taliban returned to power. The report also referenced "indicators" that ISAF attacks were "steadily eroding insurgent morale." And yet the insurgents continued to fight at undiminished levels and continued killing Americans at a steady rate. More Americans had been killed (122) and wounded (1,178) during the first four months of 2011 than during the same period a year earlier. While the report noted that community council elections had actually been held in March in Marjah, in Helmand Province, the scene of heavy fighting by the Marines in March 2010, security incidents had increased in both Helmand and Kandahar. "The Taliban's momentum has been halted and much of their tactical infrastructure and popular support removed," the report concluded, "although hard fighting is expected through the spring, summer and fall of 2011." Progress was tough to judge.

The Taliban announced the start of their spring campaign the very next day. In a prepared statement, the Taliban said they would target NATO troops as well as contractors, Afghan and foreign, who were assisting them and the Afghan government. The Taliban said they would take special pains to avoid harming Afghan civilians, warning them to stay away from troop convoys and military installations.

Forecasting that the nexus of the war would eventually shift from the orchards around Kandahar, now cleared, to the forbidding mountains in eastern Afghanistan, which were still teeming with insurgents, Petraeus went to visit Major Jim Gant, "Lawrence of Afghanistan," in eastern Kunar Province, on the Pakistan border. Petraeus considered Kunar perhaps the most difficult province for which to develop a strategy for moving forward, given the low density of NATO and Afghan forces, the difficult terrain, the porous border with Pakistan's tribal areas, a myriad of local government challenges and a number of tribes—Malik Noorafzhal's was the exception—who rejected outsiders. For two years Petraeus had been looking forward to meeting Gant again, ever since he'd recommended Gant's monograph, *One Tribe at a Time*, as required reading throughout the U.S. military and helped change Gant's orders from Iraq to Afghanistan. Gant first met Petraeus in Iraq after he had been awarded the Silver Star. Gant had spent the year since running Village Stability Operations in Mangwal.

After Petraeus's helicopter touched down, Gant briefed him on conditions in Mangwal and walked him to Malik Noorafzhal's home, where the two had lunch and spent several hours deep in conversation. Though some in the Special Forces community thought Gant took too much credit for initiatives and a philosophy that had already been embraced by many key leaders in the community, Petraeus thought Gant's monograph had laid the basic groundwork for the whole Village Stability Operations program—and, by extension, the Afghan Local Police. Petraeus knew that while Gant might not have been the first to develop the concept, he had been the first and most effective in describing the concept and writing about it. The ALP were establishing the patches of security that would make up the patchwork quilt of a pacified Afghanistan, assuming they could be stitched together as part of a campaign involving both conventional troops and special forces—which would increasingly be Afghan.

Petraeus was impressed by how Gant had blended soldiers from the Iron Rangers, the 1st Battalion of the 16th Infantry Regiment, 1st Infantry Division—an infantry unit Petraeus had (over the objections of some other senior officers) assigned to the Special Operations Task Force to augment the nationwide Village Stability Operations effort—into his Special Forces A-Team. This unusual partnership had helped "thicken" the Green Berets, the nickname for Special Forces troopers, so that Special Forces ODA teams like Gant's could multiply, covering more terrain. It remained to be seen whether the conventional military units could adapt to the Special Forces culture, or merely provide security and support. They wore the "modified" uniforms Gant favored and sported beards, some quite wispy on young men barely old enough to shave.

Malik Noorafzhal, whom Gant had given the nickname "Sitting Bull," told Petraeus that he needed jobs for young men in his tribe. He wanted Mangwal to be connected to the electrical grid, and he requested both an expanded local force and an assurance that local forces would be robust enough to keep the Taliban away. Petraeus left impressed by Gant and the malik.

The Taliban's first big attack in their spring offensive came in the south, that same day, May 7, as if to remind the general that the gains his troops had made in Kandahar were indeed fragile. Teams of insurgents, including suicide bombers, fanned out across Kandahar and opened fire on a series of government buildings. The fighting shut down the Taliban's onetime home city. The insurgents never came close to regaining control of the city, though their ability to drive bomb-laden vehicles through the streets suggested that they had had some inside assistance. The Taliban's new reliance on assassinations—and their infiltration of Afghan police and military units—illustrated the enemy's resilience. As Petraeus and his forces planned for transition, so did the Taliban.

Vowell and the No Slack battalion returned to Fort Campbell in May. Vowell was convinced they had left their replacements in a much better position than they had been in a year earlier, thanks to all of the Taliban they had killed and cleared and their work with the district governments in Kunar. With Operation Strong Eagle III, he believed they had preempted the Taliban's spring offensive.

Vowell was firmly of the opinion that the war would be won at the district level. It was the same point his friend Doug Ollivant had made to Petraeus a year earlier. The United States had spent enormous amounts of money on the central government, Vowell believed, and had little to show for it beyond Kabul. No one had ever truly governed effectively at the district level. The notion of Afghanistan as a modern state was more of a concept than a reality, Vowell had come to realize.

He had lost eighteen soldiers and had nearly two hundred injured. The price, he thought, was almost too high. The three key districts they'd fought to secure, Noor Gul, Khas Kunar and Sarkani, continued to be examples of effective and independent local governments. As Vowell had counseled Campbell and Ollivant back in the summer of 2010, they never had to be reinforced to progress on their own. Two Afghan battalions had been added to No Slack's area of operation over the winter, and by the time the battalion left, the Afghans were taking the lead for daily security in many areas of the valley.

Upon his return to the United States, Vowell learned that the hardest part of the deployment was knowing how to talk to the wives of the six soldiers killed in Operation Strong Eagle III. They wanted to know why it had been necessary for Vowell to take on this mission a month before rotating home. Why hadn't he just sat tight? He had no immediate answer, except explanations of military necessity that he knew didn't translate to young women who had lost their husbands. He remembered something Petraeus had said when he visited the battalion in the aftermath of those six deaths: Do everything humanly possible to reduce the risk of casualties on the battlefield. "I now understand what General Petraeus was getting at: Casualties are inevitable, but the cost is expensive," Vowell said. "Whereas we move on in the military and our own lives, our families pay that burden forever."

Vowell vowed to take time to remember, on Memorial Day and Veterans Day, his men who lost their lives. "With their names inscribed on bracelets I now wear, I will remember and reflect. Then it'll be time to put them away and focus forward until the next holiday, where I'll bring their names out and remember yet again. It is how I will cope."

Vowell now serves as operations officer on the 101st Airborne Division staff, a post once held by David Petraeus. Vowell's picture hangs on the wall a few places down from Petraeus's at division headquarters. "Not a day has gone by," Vowell said, "that I don't try to live up to his legacy and what would most certainly be his expectations."

ALONE AND IN LIMBO, Major Fernando Lujan walked a hot and dusty road with Afghan forces from the 215th Corps in Nad-e Ali, Helmand Province, near Marjah. Like the handful of other integrated advisers on the ground, Lujan had developed a nuanced feel for the capabilities of the first Afghan forces patrolling independently in the transition sectors Karzai had identified in March. The security investigation Colonel Tanzola had initiated against Lujan and his colleagues on the Counterinsurgency Advisory and Assistance Team (CAAT) had been quietly buried, but so had the offending twenty-page report on his Zabul embed. Nonetheless, relations with the Marine colonel had improved. Tanzola had agreed to start processing Afghan-CAAT memos and including Afghan advisers like Major Kosh Sadat, Petraeus's Afghan special forces aide, in CAAT communications. But Lujan had not yet succeeded in getting a Special Forces officer to replace himself in his work with the Afghans. He had little confidence that anything he had built over the past year would remain when he returned after rotating back to Washington.

A year earlier, as the Marines fought to solidify their hold on Marjah, Nad-e Ali had been a particularly bad place. U.S. and other NATO troops would almost surely draw fire once they'd moved a couple of hundred yards off any base, but now Lujan moved freely across the countryside, embedded in Afghan units, without incident. The poppy harvest was just ending, which meant the fighting season was about to resume. Lujan kept waiting for some spectacular attack, but it hadn't happened—yet. He traveled from base to base with Afghans in a single Ford Ranger. This was totally counter to ISAF rules, which required him to move only in armored vehicles or MRAPs. Tanzola was under the impression that this was what Lujan was doing, but Lujan knew that waiting for armor to arrive would completely erode his credibility with the Afghans. He was taking more risk than he really wanted to, in terms of both his safety and his career, but he was doing what he needed to do to accomplish the mission. Besides, no one had said no.

He also knew that he had only one chance to make an impression on the Afghan commanders of the 215th Corps, who had seen plenty of U.S. advisers before him. After one embed with Afghan forces, Lujan was beside a stream when a group of Afghan soldiers surrounded him. They were curious about this American in an Afghan uniform who spoke their language and treated them respectfully. The hair on Lujan's neck stood up. They pummeled him with probing questions.

"Are you a spy? What do you think of America? Are you trying to control our country? You're an infidel."

Lujan stayed calm. He responded in Dari. "No, I am not here to tell you what to do," he said. "And we're not leaving soon. I'll be here for years," he continued, trying to explain the Afghan Hands initiative. "I work for the corps commander, and I want to learn from you." The situation was defused, but he remained cautious. Nobody knew exactly where he was right now, and he had very limited communication capability. But these were risks he was willing to take to build rapport and illustrate to the Afghan troops that he trusted them and genuinely wanted to help.

He'd been received by the 215th Corps commander in Helmand only because the commander of the 205th Corps, in Kandahar, with whom Lujan had bonded, had sent word to Helmand that "Jagaran (Major) Farid"—the nickname he'd been given—could be trusted. Lujan's initial briefing in Dari did the trick. He was in with the commander. For the embed, Lujan asked for two officers to work with him—one from operations and one from intelligence. The ops officer, an older man, wore a belt buckle with a Soviet hammer and sickle—he had helped ambush the Soviet unit as a mujahideen fighter back in the 1980s. The intelligence officer had been in the military since he was fourteen and was skilled at mining intelligence from everyone he met on the streets and in villages. He spoke Pashto, Dari and Uzbek. If only the U.S. government had a cache of officers who could do the same, Lujan thought.

In his travels, Lujan had spent time observing the relationship between

British troops and the Afghans. The Brits were trying what Lujan thought of as "tough love" with the Afghans, attempting to foster independence and avoid a dependency culture. But Lujan thought the disparities in living conditions were hard to justify. The British operated from bases with tents, air-conditioning, Porta-Johns and satellite television. Next door, the Afghans lived with open latrines and trash burning in open pits, the smoke blowing into the soldiers' sleeping areas. The Brits told Lujan that the disparity didn't affect their relationship. The Afghans asked him, "Why won't they help us?" Lujan thought the Brits would be better off doing what Flynn had done in the Arghandab River Valley, treating the Afghans as equals and partners. He also thought the Americans and other international partners could do more to improve logistical support for Afghan troops. The theory at work was that denying the Afghans the matériel support ISAF received would keep them from becoming dependent on the foreigners. But Lujan thought the inequities were troubling in their own right.

Some aspects of the Afghans' performance were troubling as well. He didn't think the Afghan soldiers spent enough time communicating with Afghan villagers to understand their needs. Several Afghan officers told him that they would never sit and have tea with the locals, because it would invariably be a trap, or they would be poisoned. Lujan also came away from the embed feeling that these Afghan forces were overconfident. They would walk the same routes day after day, a poor operational practice they had adopted merely because they hadn't been hit recently. They had a good intuitive feel for the countryside, but whenever Lujan would ask them precisely where they were on a map, they were always a mile or two off, which would have made calling in a quick-reaction force or artillery in the event of an attack a nightmare.

But Lujan believed ISAF and its Afghan partners were clearly winning. In his mind, there was no denying that they had taken terrain, and the initiative, from the Taliban. He heard this from Afghans everywhere he went: "'Things are better. Last year we couldn't even move two hundred meters down the road without being fired upon or hitting an IED. Now we can move all over our area. The Taliban are much weaker here. Local villagers are starting to be brave enough to send them away." The change was real and palpable. Lujan also noticed a big difference between older Afghan officers and the new generation of younger ones. The younger officers were incredibly brave, throwing themselves into battle and sleeping on tiny bases with little but wire barriers protecting them. They were truly committed, and they gave him hope.

AS ISAF BEGAN to focus on the disruption campaign in the rugged mountains along the Pakistan border southeast of Kabul, the Currahee Brigade of the 101st Airborne joined forces with the Duke Brigade of the 1st Infantry Division in Paktika Province to clear terrain and shut down two infiltration routes from Pakistan. This area would not be ready for transition to Afghan control anytime soon, but the disruption mission remained critical until ISAF could reinforce the economy-of-force effort there. It was critical that the insurgents be forced to fight their way into Afghanistan and suffer losses as they did so.

A large-scale air assault launched the last major engagement fought by the Screaming Eagles in 2011. Captain Ed Churchill's D Company of the Currahee Brigade's 2nd Battalion, 506th Infantry Regiment, were flown into forbidding terrain on May 14 aboard twin-rotor Chinook helicopters. Insurgent fighters watched, gathered their weapons and prepared to ambush their visitors. At 1:15 P.M. on May 16, insurgents opened fire on the company's 3rd Platoon with machine guns, rocket-propelled grenades and small-arms fire from four positions along a steep ridgeline. The barrage was so intense that Sergeant First Class Adam D. Petrone could see bullets striking rocks and shrubs around him as he dashed from position to position, desperately attempting to gain some semblance of fire superiority.

Churchill's Dog Company had been assigned the task of securing two engagement areas and shutting down one of the infiltration routes, called "Route Civic." Churchill was almost a mile away, on a hilltop overlooking the battlefield, when the insurgents opened up on 3rd Platoon. Just three hundred yards from the Pakistan border, Sergeant First Class Petrone left his fortified position and bounded across twenty-five yards of open ground to where Private First Class Christopher W. Mioduszewski was manning the only machine gun between the insurgents and his platoon's exposed flank. Petrone showed him the insurgents' positions, and Mioduszewski opened up with his MK-48, firing on multiple targets with his weapon set on cyclic, then rapid. Under fire himself from twenty-five insurgents, he covered a sector of nearly sixty-five degrees for three minutes, enabling 3rd Platoon to regain the initiative, move to covered and concealed positions and return fire. After Mioduszewski's barrage, Petrone dashed back to his original position and radioed Captain Churchill with a battle update.

Insurgents continued firing a machine gun from the ridge, pinning down his men in three positions. When Petrone finally figured out where the fire was coming from, he marked the location with tracer fire for Private First Class James R. Morrison, the platoon's best shot with a recoilless rifle. Morrison ran twenty yards through enemy fire to a spot from which he could set up his weapon, crouched and then fired two quick shots at the insurgents, who were as close as fifty yards away. The initial ambush was broken. Sporadic fire continued throughout the day as Churchill and Petrone called in air strikes and 105-mm artillery. But the insurgents, dug into caves and other rock formations on the side of the mountain, were shielded from 30-mm cannon fire and 2.75-inch rockets. At 7:00 P.M., Churchill called in an attack by a fighter bomber, which dropped a five-hundred-pound GPS-guided bomb on the insurgents' position. When the bomb malfunctioned, the plane dropped another, silencing the enemy for the next several hours.

At 1:00 A.M. on May 17, Dog Company's 1st Platoon and Headquarters Platoon moved to reinforce Petrone's 3rd Platoon. In the darkness, Mioduszewski spotted the enemy with his night-vision goggles and fired on them as the platoon leader called in air strikes. When the enemy approached to within fifty yards of the company's perimeter, Morrison left his primary position and maneuvered with his 90-mm recoilless rifle, firing at the insurgents at point-blank range.

As the company consolidated its position, Apache helicopters fired on an insurgent spotted near the area where the bombs had been dropped. The pilots soon realized that they were taking fire not from insurgents but from a Pakistani military base just over the border—the same base from which the insurgents had launched their attacks. After one helicopter was hit by small-arms fire, the other opened up on the Pakistani base. Insurgent fire then ceased for the rest of the day, allowing all of Churchill's units to clear their objectives and establish a unified company position.

As dusk approached on May 18, the insurgents attacked again. They had reestablished three positions on the mountain above the force and were firing with machine guns and small arms. Churchill ran to the company's easternmost gun position, directed automatic weapons and the 60-mm mortars to fire at all three insurgent positions, then ran back to his command post and called in air strikes and artillery. There was a lull, and Churchill reported to battalion headquarters. Minutes later, the insurgents attacked again, raining effective machine-gun and small-arms fire down on the eastern end of the company's perimeter. Churchill ran back to the east, assessed the situation, organized fires and returned to the command post. First Lieutenant Chase M. Derbin played a similar role, moving from cluster to cluster to direct machine-gun fire at the insurgents from the company's southernmost position. After the second attack was defeated, a sergeant in the Afghan Border Police fighting alongside the Americans saw insurgents running to the Pakistani military base on the Pakistan side of the border, dragging injured and dead comrades.

When Apaches arrived overhead, they saw two Mi-17 helicopters on the Pakistan side of the border, but the Pakistani aircraft turned south and headed down the border. The battle was over. Churchill's company had blocked Route Civic and disrupted insurgent operations in the gap between the Gayan and Spera districts. There were no further insurgent attacks during the company's final five weeks in Afghanistan.

As a result of the operation, the insurgents had lost their ability to affect the population, as well as the ability to move men, weapons and equipment across the border. The population had seen the enemy attack the Americans and their Afghan partners twice, and twice be defeated. Twenty-one insurgent fighters had been killed, with six wounded. Now Churchill worked with his partners in the Afghan military to move immediately into the villages and initiate security operations. Their message was simple, and powerful: We are here to protect you.

AMID THE NOISE and hubbub of Café Milano, the best place at ISAF headquarters, in Kabul, for cappuccino and free WiFi, Brigadier General H. R. McMaster spoke with confidence. With Petraeus's strong support and help, he had assembled a small army of military and civilian go-getters, including top investigators from the FBI, the DEA, State and Treasury. But before they could begin fighting corruption, they had to understand the nature of the organizations they were up against. They soon realized that they were looking at organized crime—criminal networks fueled by international aid that often made even more money trafficking in Afghanistan's number-one export, opium. And those working with the insurgents could then purchase Afghanistan's top imports: weapons and fertilizer, for use in making roadside bombs. McMaster's team had to understand how these networks worked with one another internally, and how they worked externally with criminal syndicates in Pakistan and places like Dubai.

As ever, the Afghans understood their country far better than the Americans ever would, so working closely with trusted Afghans was the key. With Afghanistan invariably ranked as one of the world's most corrupt nations, McMaster and his cohorts also had to find a way to talk about and describe the problem without insulting their hosts. They finally constructed a narrative that everyone could buy into: Corruption in the country was the byproduct of thirty years of conflict. Vast amounts of international assistance had flowed in without adequate oversight, and the government lacked strong institutions that might have been able to ensure transparency and accountability. Part of the problem stemmed from how the wars had been funded in the past—by dumping huge amounts of money on proxy forces, followed by various political settlements that empowered the warlords, whose corruption then solidified their strength and power. The Afghans—at least those working with McMaster—could see how corruption robbed the state of revenues, perpetuated dependence upon international aid, weakened institutions, undermined the legitimacy of the government and eroded international support.

The first key to Shafafiyat's progress had come through the counterinsurgency contracting guidance that McMaster had drafted and Petraeus had edited and then signed on September 8. Before that, the Americans were ostensibly letting contractors operate the way they did back home—hiring a prime contractor and letting him police all the subcontractors. It was too much work to do otherwise. But in Afghanistan, McMaster learned, you had to know who the subcontractors were, because some of them were skimming money and underwriting the Taliban. Petraeus said in the counterinsurgency manual that "money is ammunition," and McMaster was finding that U.S. aid had—unintentionally, through inadequate contracting practices—been giving ammunition to the enemy. Now, in accordance with the contracting guidance, to win a contract, a contractor had to name all of his subs; and McMaster now had sufficient intelligence to figure out who the subs were—and to track them on the job. As Petraeus noted in the contracting guidance, "If money is ammunition, then we need to get it into the right hands." Now, if strange things started happening to the money, there were real consequences: suspension and debarment, which meant no more lucrative contracts for three to four years. "If you want to make money with contracts, you better start policing your own end of the business, right?" McMaster said. "Because if you get debarred, you're not gonna have that business opportunity."

When McMaster had started his work nearly a year earlier, more than a few eyebrows had been raised by those in Kabul's vast international mission: Why were Petraeus and the military focusing on corruption? Didn't Petraeus have enough to worry about on the battlefield? Petraeus and McMaster, however, had quickly recognized that if the so-called criminal patronage networks were not taken on, they would destroy the very Afghan governmental institutions to which ISAF and the international community were soon to begin transferring important tasks. The mission was not, therefore, optional; it was critical to the overall effort. So McMaster had launched his assessment, and made progress, recognizing over time that Petraeus's ability to achieve "unity of effort" among all the players—military and civilian, Afghan, American and international—allowed for the progress through his task force.

PETRAEUS AND RETIRED general Jack Keane had sat chatting in Petraeus's office in Baghdad in the fall of 2008 when Petraeus's direct phone line rang. It was the senior military assistant to the secretary of Defense, Lieutenant General Pete Chiarelli. "The secretary wants to talk to you in thirty minutes; will you be available?" Petraeus said he would. "You know what that's going to be about, don't you, Dave?" Keane asked. Petraeus did; he suspected he was going to be offered command of U.S. Central Command, the Florida-based combatant command covering an area of responsibility of twenty countries across the broader Middle East, upon completion of his tour in Iraq.

He had had a few reservations as, after spending four of the previous five and a half years in Iraq, he thought a new landscape might be more intellectually stimulating. But he responded that command of Central Command would be an honor, and after a few months in the new position, he found it to be the best assignment he could have in the military. No one operated at the strategic political-military level better than Petraeus, and heading CENTCOM was the ultimate pol-mil job. His combat tours in Iraq had brought him in contact with officials from Turkey, Jordan and virtually all the Gulf states. Now he had a chance to utilize those relations and security networks.

As head of Central Command, he oversaw two wars that were under the command of subordinate four-star generals in Iraq and Afghanistan. Three-star generals representing each of the four services reported to him as component commanders. The Joint Special Operations Command, also under him for operations in the Central Command theater, was a key player across the region in the war on terror. The full scope of the responsibility, beyond overseeing and resourcing the two ground wars and regional counterterrorist operations, was enormous. He was involved in formulating the drawdown of forces from Iraq and the buildup in Afghanistan. He oversaw counterterrorist operations in Yemen and other locations. He was responsible for regional security, working to turn bilateral relations into multilateral ones that would collectively promote air and ballistic missile defense and shared early-warning systems. He worked on maritime freedom of navigation and counter-piracy operations. He gathered Arab perspectives on the Middle East peace process. And he paid special attention to what some experts on his team thought could be a fundamental strategic reordering of the region, given the confluence of Iran's apparent efforts to develop nuclear weapons, the potential of the Saudis and the Gulf allies to follow suit, and various ethnic, sectarian and tribal tensions, any of which could manifest as conflicts in short order.

The day after he took command, Petraeus was on his plane for Pakistan and Afghanistan. Shortly after that, he and his team headed to the Central Asian states. Among his first priorities, after assessing ongoing operations in Afghanistan, Pakistan and Iraq, was development of the so-called Northern Distribution Network, the logistical arrangements to transport supplies and matériel into Afghanistan from the north instead of through Pakistan. The existing dependence on Pakistan as the primary supply route into land-locked Afghanistan was a strategic vulnerability. A considerable threat to the major supply routes existed in Pakistan, and at the time—shortly after the Russian intervention in Georgia—there seemed to be few alternatives. Cutting off supplies to the war theater would put the mission in jeopardy. When Petraeus and his team landed in Uzbekistan for high-level meetings, Petraeus's team's efforts and those of his U.S. Transportation Command counterparts and their staffs made great strides. Soon, new air, land and rail networks had been established to support logistical flow to Afghanistan, reducing the dependence on Pakistan and reducing the strategic vulnerability, just in time for the surge of forces to arrive in Afghanistan.

In January 2009, after meetings with key leaders in Central Asia, sessions with Pakistan's president and the army chief in Pakistan and a dinner with President Karzai in Afghanistan, Petraeus was beckoned back to Washington for a meeting on the day after the inauguration at the White House to launch a review of the policy for Iraq. "Don't head back to Tampa yet," one National

Security Council official told Petraeus after the meeting on Iraq. "We are going to begin the review on Afghanistan tomorrow." Petraeus, having flown in that morning from Afghanistan, and the Obama team, having just celebrated the inauguration, were exhausted. But there was no time to waste as Bruce Riedel, a former CIA official now at the Brookings Institution, was selected to commence the sixty-day review.

Petraeus, according to Riedel, "was the unacknowledged third co-chair," along with Ambassador Richard Holbrooke, who had been selected to be the special representative to the president and the secretary of State for Afghanistan and Pakistan. "Petraeus knew more than all other members of the team," Riedel said in an interview, but he and Holbrooke also knew enough not to make Petraeus, whom Holbrooke called his "wingman," the face of the policy, given the perception at the time that Petraeus was a "Bush guy."

The Riedel review followed on the heels of a review that Petraeus had chartered using a CENTCOM assessment team of interagency players that looked at the key issues across Afghanistan and seven subregional problem sets. The effort was codirected by Brigadier General H. R. McMaster and three other senior officials—from Treasury, State and the CIA. Conceptualization of the five-month review began at Petraeus's behest even before he took command. It included one of the "most robust interagency teams in anyone's memory," according to State Department codirector Dawn Liberi, with fifty core players and more than 150 subject-matter experts, working out of office spaces at the National Defense University, in Washington. The findings presented Petraeus with "a bird's-eye view through multiple lenses," recalled Liberi, "in part because it brought in a political, policy and intel perspective, but also the views of NGOs, think tanks and academic personnel."

Liberi was struck by Petraeus's guidance to look at the issues from an interagency perspective. He also recognized "the importance of bringing in voices that the military wouldn't ordinarily have . . . and bringing in an academic perspective that had intellectual rigor to it." Liberi, a senior development expert who had served with Petraeus in Iraq and would subsequently serve in Afghanistan from 2009 to 2011, explained the significance of the assessment team and one of its key conclusions: that a comprehensive civil-military counterinsurgency approach was needed in many areas of the region, requiring varying numbers of U.S. troops on the ground, depending on the capabilities of the host nations.

Interagency elements would also play key roles in counterterrorism efforts. Drawing on models he had employed in Bosnia and Iraq, Petraeus built an interagency counterterrorism working group to address problems that required international, interagency cooperation, including creation of a cell to track terrorist financing, a regional initiative to choke the flow of foreign fighters, and efforts to interdict the flow of weapons and materials sought by regional countries for illicit reasons. A major concern for the entire intelligence community was the growing problem presented by al-Qaeda in the Arabian Peninsula, in particular the facilitation and training locations in Yemen. The response would not be large numbers of boots on the ground, but a counterterrorism strike program powered by quality intelligence, Predator drones armed with lethal Hellfire missiles, and lightning-fast Special Operations raids like the one that would kill Osama bin Laden. It was an example of what seemed to be becoming the U.S. grand counterterrorism strategy: "whack a mole."

The key to whacking moles, in whatever country, Petraeus felt, was engaging with the country leader and seeking agreement on cooperative efforts, ideally with the host nation conducting the operations, and with the United States providing security assistance, training, intelligence and other help. The other key was, as he put it, "whacking all the moles in the region simultaneously" so that operations didn't just displace the terrorists from one sanctuary to another. Less than two months into his command, Petraeus and his team made a trip to Yemen to meet with President Ali Abdullah Saleh, but little was accomplished other than posturing. The next fall, Petraeus returned again after Admiral William McRaven, the head of the JSOC at the time, and John Brennan, assistant to the president for homeland security and counterterrorism, had also visited. The threat was now more apparent, Saleh had seen Central Command deliver on past promises, and the tone was much different. Soon the U.S. security force assistance effort had grown from $60 million in the first year to $150 million the next year. The robustness of the assistance package was supported by the mutually defined priorities of all the component commanders serving under Central Command. Conventional, Special Forces and Special Mission units all played important parts, together with intelligence and diplomatic elements.

The meeting opened the gates for improved interagency cooperation and operations against al-Qaeda leaders who found sanctuary there. Al-Qaeda in the Arabian Peninsula, the intelligence community believed, had grown beyond a national or regional threat and now posed a serious extremist threat to Europe and the United States. The increasing importance of American-born Anwar al-Awlaki, who'd emerged as a very charismatic extremist figure in cyberspace, confirmed that the assessment of the threat in Yemen was well founded. Al-Awlaki would be killed in a CIA drone strike in late September 2011, shortly after Petraeus took over as CIA director.

At Central Command, Petraeus would constantly tell members of his team, "Your job is to identify significant trends and good ideas and bring them to my attention." Petraeus's political adviser, Ambassador Mike Gfoeller, an Arabist with decades of experience, remembers Petraeus telling him that he had "complete freedom to think about and investigate anything that you might think is important, as long as you keep me informed periodically. . . . You report to me and shouldn't worry about anyone else; don't tolerate any attempts to circumscribe what you are doing for me." Petraeus moved to empower his associates to think more openly about problem solving.

One of the greatest challenges Petraeus would face at CENTCOM was Pakistan. The reviews in 2009 all concluded that Pakistan had to remain a priority. Petraeus would labor with other U.S. officials, including Ambassador Holbrooke, to support Pakistan's military with security force assistance initiatives. Gaining approval for these assessments meant closed-door congressional sessions together with Holbrooke to support the Kerry-Lugar-Berman bill, among other initiatives. Petraeus felt these efforts had, relatively speaking, helped to improve relations with Pakistan, especially military cooperation programs, by the spring of 2009.

Pakistan's General Kayani, Petraeus believed, had skillfully guided the military, national and political leadership, as well as the Pakistani religious community, to recognize the imperative of operations in the Swat Valley. This was where Tehrik-i-Taliban Pakistan—the Pakistani version of the Taliban—had taken over in the spring of 2009. When Pakistani forces launched operations, the decision was made in Washington to assist. "They'd run low on artillery ammunition, we'd find some, and we'd fly it into the country," Petraeus recalled. "We substantially augmented our Special Forces on the ground from probably a couple of dozen to well over a hundred."

U.S. Special Forces were there to provide foreign internal defense assistance, especially helping rebuild the Pakistani special operations forces, which had sustained significant losses while employed as light infantry in heavy fighting in prior years. U.S. forces helped to arm and train Pakistani forces and to build training facilities and other infrastructure for them. Improved cooperation, however, was not guaranteed. That was why Petraeus, from the moment he moved from Central Command to commander in Afghanistan, focused on Taliban sanctuaries in Pakistan.

IN WASHINGTON, Doug Ollivant tried to explain why RC East had just pulled out of the nearby Pech Valley, in Kunar Province, near the Pakistan border. He was beginning a new career as a writer and think-tank analyst and, he hoped, a government contractor specializing in data applications. In an op-ed for the *Washington Post,* Ollivant argued that there were actually three wars in Afghanistan. The first was against al-Qaeda and related terrorist groups. The second, fought on behalf of the Karzai government, was against the Taliban. And the third pitted the country's "urban modernizers" against its "rural, tribal, anti-modern peoples" who live in the forbidding mountain villages.

When the U.S. military had seized on population-centric counterinsurgency operations as the appropriate strategy in 2006, it built forty bases in the Pech, Korengal and Waygal valleys of Kunar Province, only to realize three or four years later that this move was not well founded. The people in these villages, by and large, didn't want to be part of modern Afghanistan, and attempts by American soldiers to win their hearts and minds had the perverse effect, in many instances, of driving them closer to the terrorists, who also frequented these border environs. "The Pech will not be ignored," Ollivant wrote in justification of the withdrawal of American forces from the Pech. "The U.S. military will continue to hunt down terrorists there and in a host of other valleys. What it will not do is attempt to remain in these remote regions, attempt to alter the way of life of their people or attempt to extend the reach of Kabul into places where it is decidedly unwelcome. That is an exercise in futility, a lesson the troops withdrawing from the Pech have paid in blood to learn."

Petraeus found the piece sensible and thought it accurately described what he and RC East commander Major General Campbell had sought to do in redirecting troops to key districts, although Petraeus still thought it was essential, over the long haul, to deny even rugged areas like those in Kunar to the enemy as sanctuaries. But occupying them, as commanders had tried to do from 2006 to 2010, wasn't the right approach. Rather, Afghan troops, working with Afghan Local Police at the village level, should work with the tribes on denying the enemy sanctuary, with help from drones and Special Operations Forces and occasional large-scale air-assault operations like those conducted by Vowell and Churchill.

The downside of this light footprint in the eastern provinces was apparent on May 25, when the Taliban took control of a government center in the hotly contested Do Ab District of Nuristan Province, which borders Kunar to the north. Taliban fighters overran the facility after attacking a lightly armed Afghan police contingent with mortars and rocket-propelled grenades. They held it for hours before ISAF responded with a hundred helicopter-borne U.S. and Afghan troops to dislodge the insurgents.

Petraeus was agitated about ISAF's slow response when he met privately two days later with Lieutenant General Rodriguez, head of ISAF's Joint Command and deputy commander of U.S. forces. If there was anyone who knew the nuances of the Afghan battlefields, it was Rodriguez, the principal architect of the operational portion of the war plan Petraeus had inherited from McChrystal. The two couldn't have been more dissimilar. Rodriguez had been selected for promotion to four-star general but had not been selected as Petraeus's replacement. This was not because he didn't understand the war but rather because he had not gained Secretary Gates's confidence in his ability to operate at the highest of strategic levels in Washington and other coalition capitals. A truly exceptional soldier, Rodriguez was also given to a certain awkwardness at times, and that reportedly gave Gates and others pause. But Rodriguez had achieved Petraeus's respect and a depth of devotion from those he commanded. No one had served in Afghanistan longer in recent years—a total of forty months over the past four and a half years. Nonetheless, while Gates, Petraeus and others thought highly of Rodriguez, they agreed that Lieutenant General John Allen, Petraeus's former deputy at Central Command, was the better choice for Petraeus's successor, feeling he had a certain strategic touch, gravitas and experience at high levels that Rodriguez lacked.

Petraeus brought up the attack on the Do Ab district center in Nuristan with a touch of irritation. Why had it taken so long to get a quick-reaction force on the scene? Rodriguez had initially wanted to give Afghan forces a chance to execute the mission. But Petraeus made clear his view that ISAF simply couldn't afford the delay that had allowed the Taliban to hold a district government center. He repeated the point during his stand-up briefing the following morning, and he was still aggressively preaching the gospel of rapid response at that afternoon's weekly security *shura* with ISAF and Afghan officials. He sugarcoated his disappointment with profuse praise for Afghanistan's deputy interior minister, who had flown to Do Ab during the battle to get a firsthand read of the situation, but he was clear that responses needed to be swifter.

The next morning, Petraeus again repeated the point during his stand-up briefing, when the results from an investigation by Rodriguez's ISAF Joint Command were reported: We needed to commit earlier. Today, another issue bothered him—an allegation that morning by officials in the Afghan Ministry of the Interior that civilians had been killed by ISAF forces in Do Ab. "What's the status with that?" he asked out loud, in a concerned tone, but to no one in particular. Petraeus's Afghan-American interpreter and adviser, Abdullah, piped up, "Sir, I called the MOI last night," referring to the Ministry of the Interior. "There was no news of any civilian casualties." Petraeus turned around in his chair to face Abdullah and asked him to relay a message to the deputy interior minister. "The deputy MOI needs to understand how exercised I am when he publicly claims there were civilian casualties before there has been an investigation. This is a big concern to me. And such behavior makes a commander want to withdraw his pledge to not let a district center fall. Tell them we are partners all the way through this, or not. The choice is theirs."

But the Do Ab attack, for all its complexity and ambiguity, immediately became a footnote in the war, eclipsed in an hour or two by news of another dramatic attack in the north, this one in Taloqan, capital of Takhar Province, in far northern Afghanistan, on the border with Tajikistan, where a suicide bomber dressed as an Afghan policeman had attended a security *shura* and detonated a bomb that killed Lieutenant General Mohammed Daud Daud, the police commander for all of northern Afghanistan, and wounded Major General Markus Kneip, a German general heading NATO's northern command. Daud was much beloved in northern Afghanistan for his exploits fighting the Taliban. The attack that left him dead was the latest of a number in which the attacker had dressed in an Afghan uniform. Taloqan had been in turmoil for more than a week following a demonstration by thousands of Afghans on May 18. They attacked a police station and a NATO base to protest a night raid by U.S. and Afghan forces that had killed four people, including two women who had pointed weapons at the forces when asked to surrender.

Compared with the number of civilians killed by Taliban suicide bombings and buried IEDs, the ISAF nights raids were, for the most part, surgical strikes that harmed few civilians. But many Afghans hated the operations. Petraeus remained a staunch proponent of night raids as a key element of his counterinsurgency strategy, despite their unpopularity, because he knew how devastating they had been at eliminating mid- and upper-level Taliban commanders. Afghanistan's security leaders agreed with him.

During Petraeus's tenure, the effectiveness of night raids run by the Joint Special Operations Command increased in terms of Taliban leaders captured, while shots fired and civilian casualties decreased. Increasingly, steadily improving Afghan special forces were in the lead. There were some twelve thousand Afghan special operations forces trained and equipped by Lieutenant General John Caldwell's and Brigadier General Scott Miller's trainers, and they were growing in capacity and capability with each passing week, though no one could predict when the Afghans would have enough helicopters and intelligence capabilities to mount their own night raids. "We all agree that we cannot achieve our mutual objectives without night raids," Petraeus said at one stand-up, echoing an assessment he had provided to President Karzai. "However, we also all agree that we cannot achieve our mutual objectives if we don't change how we conduct night raids—we have to Afghanize them further."

During his morning five-mile run the next day at ISAF headquarters, he said to some newcomers running with him, "Welcome to the roller-coaster ride of combat command," referring to the latest civilian casualty accusations and the tragic attack that had killed General Daud and wounded the RC North commander, General Kneip. "You never get truly hardened to the losses and bad news," he observed. "You just have to be extremely resilient, all the time. Stay even." He ran for several minutes in silence, then added, "Buckle your seat belt and get ready for the ride."

There were more sudden dips to come. NATO confirmed that an air strike in the Now Zad District of Helmand Province, fifty miles north of Lashkar Gah, the provincial capital, had killed nine innocent civilians on May 28. Afghan officials put the toll at fourteen, saying seven boys, five girls and two women had been killed in their sleep. The air strike, according to NATO, had taken place after a band of five insurgents attacked a coalition foot patrol, seriously wounding a U.S. Marine before seeking refuge in a compound occupied by the sleeping women and children. Pinned down by the insurgents and unable to call in a medevac helicopter for their wounded comrade, the Marines called for the air strike.

No matter how hard Petraeus tried, civilian casualties bedeviled his command. Just two weeks earlier, he had issued new guidance "concerning civilian casualties." The one-page document said that "no issue highlights more [than civilian casualties] the need to balance tactical aggressiveness with tactical patience—both of which are critical to achieving our objectives." Petraeus said that "we are now at a pivotal moment in our work here" and urged all leaders to review not only this latest guidance but also his counterinsurgency guidance, the Tactical Driving Directive that prohibited reckless vehicle use, and a document called "Standard Operating Procedure 373: The Guidance for Escalation of Force," that emphasized the need to balance risks with prudence while keeping in mind the criticality of reducing civilian casualties. "Through hard work and many sacrifices, we and our Afghan partners have achieved considerable momentum across Afghanistan," Petraeus wrote. "Building on that momentum will demand exceptional skill, bravery, and above all, judgment from every trooper involved in the campaign as we seek to protect the Afghan people." Teaching what General McChrystal had termed "courageous restraint" remained a challenging proposition in counterinsurgency.

As the summer approached, there was growing apprehension across the country that naturally raised questions about the transition from ISAF to Afghan forces that was about to take place in Mazar-i-Sharif, where General Daud had been based. Although the Marines defended their position—insurgents had used a civilian compound as cover—Karzai was furious. Petraeus was frustrated, too, at the morning stand-up. He insisted that if there was too much fog and friction, troops should pull back, not press on. Few tactical objectives were worth the civilian casualties. Karzai insisted on May 31 that the U.S.-led international coalition cease all air strikes aimed at Afghan homes.

Like night raids, air strikes had surged on Petraeus's watch. Air strikes had peaked at 1,043 in October. While they had declined to several hundred a month during the first four months of 2011, they remained 80 percent higher than the previous year, when McChrystal had clamped down hard on airpower, precisely to limit civilian casualties. Karzai had no legal power to restrict international forces in his country, which were there under a NATO mandate. But that did not stop him from essentially calling the foreign troops an occupying force. "History," he said, was a witness to "how Afghanistan deals with occupiers."

His rhetoric roiled Washington at a time when President Obama was deciding how rapidly to draw down U.S. forces and U.S. officials were negotiating a strategic partnership after the full transition of security responsibility to Afghan forces in 2014. His eruptions were making Petraeus's job harder and harder, creating operational obstacles on the ground in Afghanistan and even more nettlesome political ones back in Washington, particularly with those on Capitol Hill.

LUJAN, WRAPPING UP his embeds with Afghan troops in Helmand Province, prepared for an off-site meeting of the Counterinsurgency Advisory and Assistance Team that was scheduled to begin in Kabul in early June. He would soon be heading back to Washington for a year's fellowship at the Center for a New American Security and language training in Pashto. Then, he figured, it would be back to Afghanistan for another year working for the CAAT. But after that, he wasn't sure where his career was heading—the National Security Council staff or early retirement because of his history of irreverence. Despite his difficulties with Tanzola and what he took as a personal failure to institutionalize the Afghan-CAAT, he told Petraeus in an e-mail that the past year had been his most rewarding in the Army. "Come see me when you're back in Kabul," Petraeus replied.

When the CAAT convened at ISAF headquarters the next day, Petraeus addressed the group and talked about its unique contribution. "Your work is about quality, not quantity," he said. "In you, we have found people capable of independent action. You are willing and empowered to take prudent risks and are real subject-matter experts who benefit from repeat tours here.

We've incorporated, in the campaign plan, a strategic line of effort called 'Understanding the Environment,' and you've worked hard to support our progress in it, from the squad to brigade level, with coalition forces and Afghans. Let your guys grow a beard. Let them accept risk." He singled out Roger Carstens, the CAAT's senior counterinsurgency adviser, and Lujan, for praise. "Make this an intellectual stone soup organization—keep adding good people one at a time and stir.

"Now I want you to think about preparing for the period beyond 2014, about Afghan-COIN Advisory and Assistance initiatives," he added. This had, for the most part, been Lujan's brainchild. Lujan had thought that, after his row with Tanzola, it was dead. Petraeus indicated that it was not, before going around the room and asking for lessons learned from key CAAT leaders, including the French and Italian representatives.

"Partnership in everything is critical," said one colonel.

Petraeus agreed and said that it was particularly important to partner with the Afghan security forces, especially when it came to organizing the Afghan Local Police. Lujan added that getting Afghans to partner with one another was also important. The Afghan armed forces, he said, considered the Afghan National Police "hopelessly corrupt."

"Write something on it for me, please," Petraeus responded. Then, addressing everyone in the room, including Army historians there to gather lessons learned for the military's training colleges, he challenged them. "Think back to when you were a lieutenant. What is relevant at that level? Everyone wants to write a *Foreign Affairs* article or op-eds for the *Washington Post*, but the incoming leaders want to read about what they will and should do at their levels. My son, a lieutenant, didn't care about his old man's great published works. He wants small-unit vignettes."

Lujan later told Petraeus that he had done everything possible to get Major Stephen Hopkins, an Army Green Beret with six previous Afghan tours, to replace him at CAAT, to no avail. Lujan and Hopkins had been in communication over the past nine months, and Hopkins had spent a year learning Dari. But rather than continue Lujan's work embedding with Afghan forces, Hopkins was now slated to be a liaison officer to the interagency intelligence community. Petraeus later told his executive officer, Colonel Bill Hickman, to make sure Hopkins was assigned to replace Lujan. "I'm firm on this," Petraeus said. He also told Lujan to give the December memo to Tanzola's replacement "on the QT" and say that Petraeus had directed him to do so.

The next few weeks would be dominated by preparation for the trip back to Washington for his confirmation hearing and President Obama's discussions of and decision on the numbers and pace of the U.S. drawdown. Only Petraeus and two others at ISAF headquarters, as well as Rodriguez and two trusted planners at the IJC headquarters, knew what Petraeus intended to recommend to Obama when he returned to Washington in just over a week. He even decided against telling Hickman, his executive officer, or members of the Commander's Initiatives Group staff, much less other staffers, anything about troop numbers or timetables, to avoid leaks. He remembered how the White House had felt boxed in during its Afghan policy review in the fall of 2009 by Mullen's testimony before the Senate Armed Services Committee and McChrystal's speech in London. He was adamant about preventing leaks that might create such a situation once again. Outside ISAF, Petraeus would tell only General Mattis at CENTCOM, Admiral Mullen, chairman of the Joint Chiefs, and Defense secretary Gates what he intended to provide to President Obama.

Petraeus was reminded of how little time he had left in Afghanistan when Gates arrived for what became an emotional final visit—his twelfth—to Afghanistan as Defense secretary. Gates met with Petraeus and Ambassador Eikenberry in Kabul and suggested that the war might be at a turning point following bin Laden's death if U.S. officials could make progress in their fledgling talks with the Taliban. With some in the White House speaking publicly in favor of a bigger drawdown of forces than the Pentagon favored, Gates expressed concern about pulling troops out of the country too quickly. He also appeared at a news conference with Karzai, who remained highly agitated over the Helmand air strike and the continued reliance on night raids by ISAF forces. "We cannot take this anymore." Petraeus apologized again to Karzai for the recent deaths of civilians in Helmand and explained how the air strike had gone awry, noting that a young Marine had died as his comrades fought to bring in a medevac helicopter during a firefight.

After appearing with Karzai in Kabul, Gates boarded a helicopter for a series of visits with troops. His first stop was Forward Operating Base Walton, outside Kandahar. On June 6, the anniversary of the D-Day invasion of 1944, Gates flew to Forward Operating Base Sharana, in Paktika Province, to say farewell to the 101st Airborne's Currahee Brigade, the last of the Screaming Eagles in Afghanistan. The Currahee mission on D-Day had been to jump into Normandy on the high ground near Utah Beach to secure the causeways, link up with the beach infantry and then move south to take Carentan. The Currahees jumped in prior to the landing of the invasion force on the beaches of Normandy, and 184 paratroopers were killed in the subsequent fighting. All of their names were read during a memorial ceremony, along with those of seventeen Currahees who had been killed over the past nine months in Afghanistan. Gates, dressed in a starched blue button-down oxford dress shirt and standing in the bright sun, took questions from soldiers. One asked what effect he felt bin Laden's death would have on the war. Gates replied:

> I think that it's too early to tell what the impact of bin Laden's death is on the situation here in Afghanistan. I think we'll have a better idea of that by the end of the year. . . . If I were Taliban, I would often be asking what did al-Qaeda ever do for me except get me kicked out of Afghanistan? So my hope is that, if we can keep the military pressure on through the remainder of this year, keep what we've captured from these guys in the south, keep disrupting them as you are up here and they see that they are not going to win, that that then creates the opportunity for a political reconciliation in the future, because one of the redlines for both the Afghan government and the coalition is that the Taliban have to renounce any connection or support for al-Qaeda. . . . We are still on track and, frankly, making a lot of progress in breaking the momentum of the Taliban, denying them control of

populated areas, degrading their capabilities, enhancing the capabilities of the Afghan National Security Forces and going after al-Qaeda. I think we've made tremendous strides in all of those areas in the last fifteen to eighteen months, but my view is we've got to keep the pressure on. We're not quite there yet.

Gates struggled to maintain his composure as he said his good-byes. "I really did want to come out here and thank you one last time for your service and your sacrifice," he told the soldiers, his voice catching with emotion.

Probably more than anybody except the president himself, I'm responsible for you being here. I'm the guy who signed the deployment orders that sent you here. That has weighed on me every day that I've had this job for four and a half years. So I've taken it as my personal responsibility to make sure that you had what you need to accomplish your mission, to come home safe, and if you get hurt, be medevacked as quickly as possible and get the best possible care. I think about all of you every moment of every day. I feel your hardship and your sacrifice and your burden more than you can possibly imagine, and that of your families as well. I think you're the best America has to offer. My admiration and affection for you is without limit, and each and every one of you will be in my prayers every day for the rest of my life. Thank you.

He left Kabul the following day after remarks before officers at ISAF headquarters. Gates thanked Rodriguez, his former military assistant, for building the ISAF Joint Command and said he believed the coalition force was close to delivering a "decisive blow" to the Taliban. Then he headed for Brussels for a meeting of NATO defense ministers. Petraeus would soon join him there, but in the meantime, in Kabul, the stream of guests from Washington continued.

No sooner had Gates departed than a congressional delegation—U.S. rep-

resentatives Doug Lamborn of Colorado, Richard Nugent of Florida, Austin
Scott of Georgia and Rob Woodall of Georgia, all Republicans, and William
Keating, a Massachusetts Democrat—arrived in Kabul. Petraeus gave them
an executive briefing that began with a description of what he called "Getting
the Inputs Right"—a description of the effort since early 2009 to get the
strategy right, deploy the forces and civilians needed, build the organizations required and get the right people into key positions. He walked them
through a cast of characters that included Eikenberry, Rodriguez, Caldwell
and even Afghan Hands, a nod to the likes of Fernando Lujan. He talked
about the new initiatives he'd pushed since he arrived, including McMaster's
Task Force Shafafiyat, enhanced intelligence fusion efforts, reintegration,
the Afghan Local Police and Martins's Rule of Law Field Force. The briefing also included a diagram of his Anaconda strategy, with its clouds and
arrows and circles—all connoting pressure points squeezing the Taliban, the
Haqqani network and other insurgent groups. Petraeus explained to the congressmen the progress achieved by clear-and-hold operations in the south,
and how there were now forty-one Afghan Local Police detachments operating in villages, with another thirty-six coming online. He showed them a
ninety-day summary of raids by Special Forces—1,843 operations, 509 insurgent leaders killed or captured, 2,573 insurgents captured. And he explained a reintegration process through which 1,737 Taliban members had
renounced their arms and decided to support the government.

The biggest problem, he told the congressmen, was the sanctuaries in
Pakistan. Petraeus thought America's relationship with Pakistan was at a
crossroads. On the one hand, ISAF depended on Pakistan for the vital lines
of communication and supply. On the other hand, Pakistan was seen as complicit in its inability to control the Federally Administered Tribal Areas, a
breeding and training ground for the endless flow of fighters moving into
Afghanistan. But he was also quick to defend Pakistan. "Pakistan has gone
after some groups, and they have sustained many losses. We have to walk a
few miles in their shoes periodically."

Petraeus was back onstage reciting a similar script the following day at
NATO headquarters, in Brussels, having flown there the previous night to

join Gates for closed-door meetings with NATO defense ministers. With Petraeus at work on the recommendations for drawing down forces that he would present to Obama, Gates told reporters after meeting with the NATO ministers that the drawdown would not be "rush to the exits on our part, and we expect the same from our allies."

From Brussels, Gates returned to Washington as Petraeus made an eighteen-hour stopover in Rome, where he enjoyed the ride into town in an armored Maserati with a Carabinieri escort. At a dinner later that night, Petraeus was awarded the Croce d'Oro—the Carabinieri Golden Cross—by Italian defense minister Ignazio La Russa. He was out of his hotel near the Via Veneto at six the next morning on a clear and cool day for a six-mile run that he thought was one of his most scenic ever, down the Via Veneto, through and around the Colosseum, past the Trevi Fountain and up the Spanish Steps before a fast finish back down the Via Veneto.

EVEN AS PETRAEUS'S FOCUS necessarily shifted a bit to his next job, running the CIA, the war in Afghanistan demanded his full attention. Petraeus thought there had been an interesting dynamic during his briefing among newer members of Congress who may not have fully appreciated all that was going on inside Afghanistan. He also read a four-page weekly update from Lieutenant General Caldwell on recruiting and training the Afghan military. Over the next six months, the American government would provide those forces with 14,000 vehicles, 33,000 weapons and 40,000 radios. Petraeus wished he could be there when the shipments arrived. He was pleased to learn that the U.S. military would soon begin providing food and other relief supplies to 28,000 Afghans in northern Sar-i-Pul Province who were in danger of starving to death in drought conditions, another initiative he'd been tracking.

Preparing for his final embed with Afghan forces in Helmand Province before returning to Washington himself, Lujan sent Petraeus a note to let him know that the Army staff had approved his request for a fellowship at the Center for a New American Security, in Washington, which—with its former leaders now at State (Assistant Secretary Kurt Campbell) and the Pentagon (Undersecretary Flournoy)—was run by retired Army lieutenant colonel John Nagl, an ardent Petraeus mentee who had helped write the new counterinsurgency manual. "Definitely could not have done it without your assistance," said Lujan. Petraeus replied, "You get what you earn in life, Fernando, and you more than earned the fellowship. It was a privilege to help."

CHAPTER 11

DRAWDOWN

Petraeus landed early on June 11, 2011, at Andrews Air Force Base. He was planning to stay in Washington for nearly two weeks. The first would be dominated by a series of White House meetings on the drawdown of forces from Afghanistan. The second would revolve around his confirmation hearing as CIA director before the Senate Select Committee on Intelligence.

As Petraeus began work on his opening statement for his CIA confirmation than the UN mission in Afghanistan released a statement that said May had been the deadliest month for Afghan civilians since records were first kept in 2007. The tally was chilling: 368 dead, 593 wounded. The Taliban and other insurgent forces were responsible for 82 percent of the deaths, international forces were responsible for 12 percent, and 6 percent died in crossfire between the two sides. A fresh wave of attacks made headlines in Afghanistan. A roadside bomb killed fifteen civilians, including eight children, in the Arghandab River Valley, and a suicide bomber attacked a police headquarters in Khost, killing its Afghan commander. Furthermore, the *Washington Post* ran a piece about Democratic leaders in Congress, led by Senator John F. Kerry, chairman of the Senate Foreign Relations Committee, urging Obama to draw down troops faster than the Pentagon wanted. Times were tough.

The workweek began with a media report on "Obama's Secret Afghan Exit Formula"—which was to pull out thirty thousand troops but do so slowly, over twelve to eighteen months, under military guidance. Petraeus, however, had no idea how valid the piece was or where the White House was headed—he had yet to present his recommendations. He had worked with only a handful of select individuals in Kabul, all sworn to secrecy. Outside Kabul, his discussion circle had gone no further than Mattis, Mullen and Gates, who had excluded their personal staffs. He was adamant about avoiding the perception that the military was trying to box in the president by leaking its recommendations to the press.

Petraeus began his day on Tuesday with an early-morning five-mile run through the neighborhoods around Fort Myer before meeting on Capitol Hill with three members of the Senate Intelligence Committee. Then it was on to the White House's West Wing for a meeting with John Brennan, the administration's counterterrorism chief, followed by meetings back across the river with Gates at the Pentagon. From there, he met with the director of national intelligence, Jim Clapper. He finished his day over dinner at the Matisse, in Georgetown, with Walter Pincus, a veteran intelligence correspondent at the *Washington Post*.

On Wednesday Petraeus presented his recommendations for drawing down troops in Afghanistan to President Obama and other senior national security officials in the White House Situation Room. According to accounts from aides close to other participants, Petraeus described a range of options for the president, options that the Obama team had been seeking. The one Petraeus reportedly preferred: Remove 3,000 to 5,000 troops by the end of 2011 and leave the rest of the 33,000 surge troops in Afghanistan through the 2012 fighting season, which would end around November. Petraeus tried to remain sanguine about the White House's likelihood of supporting his recommendation. He would be happy if most of the surge forces could stay through a second fighting season in 2012, even as he personally wanted to stay and oversee the fight through the 2011 fighting season. At the end of the meeting, Obama asked him to come up with an alternative assessment for a second meeting. "Tell me," the president said, "what I can and cannot do if you have to recover 15,000 by end of this year, and another 15,000 by July 2012. And how would that change the strategy?"

After the White House meeting, Petraeus contacted Major General Mick Nicholson, his ISAF deputy chief of staff for operations, and asked him to assess the risks associated with the alternative the president had requested. In Kabul, Nicholson's portfolio covered everything from Pakistan to transition to the drawdown planning. The drawdown decision would have implications for every line of effort. Nicholson was asleep in Kabul when his aide woke him at 2:00 A.M. It had to be urgent, Nicholson realized. Petraeus relayed the president's tasking. By the next morning, Nicholson and a subordinate had put together the briefing that Petraeus needed to answer Obama's questions and sent it to him over the classified Internet network.

Petraeus wasted not a moment as he made the Washington rounds, maintaining simultaneous e-mail conversations from his laptops in the backseat of his black GMC Yukon. He maintained his poker face, even on e-mail with trusted confidants. Not only did he not want to share any information on the ongoing deliberations on the drawdown, he also didn't want to deal with his own transition just yet. Thursday began with more rounds of meetings with senators on the Senate Intelligence Committee on Capitol Hill. The relationship with Pakistan dominated the conversation. Petraeus hadn't seen General Kayani, the head of the Pakistani army, since his last visit a week prior to the bin Laden raid, but he looked forward to seeing him again shortly after Petraeus's return to Kabul, when he would host the next trilateral meeting with senior officials from Afghanistan and Pakistan.

Friday morning included the second meeting on Afghanistan in the White House Situation Room. According to staffs of some of the principals, Petraeus presented an edited version of Major General Nicholson's matrix and the associated risks to accomplishment of various missions that would be involved with the president's alternative course of action. Petraeus and Mullen cautioned about the risks to the military effort of drawing down more rapidly than recommended, as was to be anticipated, while some other participants explained why they felt additional risks could be taken, in accordance with the alternative the president had proposed.

Gates reportedly had several meetings with the president in anticipation of the third meeting, when it was believed that the president would announce his decision. Gates knew where Petraeus stood on his recommendations, and he supported him. But he also understood the president's challenges, and he sought to craft some kind of compromise.

That afternoon, Friday, Petraeus and his wife flew from Andrews Air Force Base to Maine for a casual meeting and dinner at the Bush compound in Kennebunkport with former president George H. W. Bush and his wife, Barbara. The feast of lobsters, swordfish and vintage red wine was an opportunity for Petraeus to speak with another former CIA director, the one for whom the CIA campus was named. The former president turned it into a reunion of sorts when he called Bill Clinton and his son, George W. Bush, so they could also pass on their regards to Petraeus and offer brief insights on the president's use of the CIA. Petraeus came away from the evening humbled and amazed at how far life had taken the first-generation son of a crusty Dutch sea captain from a modest home in Cornwall-on-Hudson.

As the White House and Pentagon teams deliberated, Karzai stated publicly that American officials were secretly negotiating with the Taliban. These talks had been reported but never confirmed by the U.S. government. Karzai's own government had also been negotiating with the Taliban, but he used the speech to question the tactics and motivation of U.S. and other foreign troops fighting in Afghanistan. "The nations of the world which are here in our country are here for their own national interests," he said. "They are using our country."

An official from the U.S. Embassy communications team immediately contacted the palace spokesperson, Wahid Omar, who calmly advised the official to "ignore" Karzai's statements concerning the talks with the Taliban, because these were "not planned." Karzai's speech was full of other negative statements, which seemed to have become his hallmark of late. "Ignore those, too," Omar said. Officials in Washington struggled to see them as anything less than betrayal by an ally. In Afghanistan, Ambassador Eikenberry reacted strongly, denouncing Karzai's remarks as "hurtful and inappropriate."

Eikenberry's relationship with Karzai was tense, to put it mildly. In a secret cable to Secretary of State Clinton in 2009, subsequently leaked in Washington and then made public by WikiLeaks, Eikenberry had bluntly stated his objections both to Karzai as a strategic partner and to McChrystal and Petraeus's recommended addition of 40,000 troops to support expanded counterinsurgency operations in Afghanistan. "President Karzai is not an adequate strategic partner," he wrote. "The proposed counterinsurgency strategy assumes an Afghan political leadership that is both able to take responsibility and to exert sovereignty in the furtherance of our goal—secure, peaceful, minimally self-sufficient Afghanistan hardened against transnational terrorist groups. Yet Karzai continues to shun responsibility for any sovereign burden, whether defense, governance or development. He and much of his circle do not want the U.S. to leave and are only too happy to see us invest further. They assume we covet their territory for a never-ending 'war on terror' and for military bases to use against surrounding powers." In the cable, Eikenberry also said that "we underestimate how long it will take to restore or establish civilian government" in Afghanistan and predicted that "more troops won't end the insurgency as long as Pakistan sanctuaries remain."

Eikenberry had offered a far more charitable view of Karzai during an interview in Kabul just ten days before this latest controversy. He explained that while Karzai viewed Pakistan as Afghanistan's existential threat, he thought his countrymen were paying a far higher price for Pakistan's bad behavior than Pakistan itself. "You're going to someday get a son or daughter of Sigmund Freud to do a great story of Karzai," Eikenberry said. "He is an extraordinarily complicated man. He's under unimaginable amounts of pressure every day. I don't know how anyone could do that job well. You just get worn down and then it becomes a matter of surviving day to day. He's an emotional man, truly he's an emotional man, with a heart that causes that emotion to come out. So he looks at a picture of Afghan children dead, maimed horribly, unfortunately with the staff around him, the few that try to spin him up at just the wrong moment, right before a press conference, and he reacts to that." Karzai faced mounting problems, Eikenberry said, that were related to corruption, his own leadership failings and his faltering

relationship with the parliament, not to mention the never-ending Kabul
Bank scandal, in which the nation's largest private bank had made hundreds
of millions in questionable loans to its own shareholders, including a number who were Karzai's relatives or backers.

E-mailing from D.C. Petraeus asked his staff for a more complete analysis
of Karzai's remarks. Petraeus agreed with a NATO official's assessment that
the ongoing Kabul Bank scandal was the pressure point looming over Karzai's intemperate remarks, and he sought to reassure officials in Washington,
while avoiding comment to the press himself.

"IT'S 'OPEN THE ENVELOPE time,'" Petraeus told his security team as his
SUV approached the White House for the final meeting with Obama on the
drawdown of forces. On the way, retired Army general Jack Keane, one of
his mentors, e-mailed him with rumors of what he was hearing: The White
House was going to recommend 10,000 depart by the end of 2011, with the
rest out by the summer of 2012. Petraeus acknowledged Keane's e-mail but
was noncommittal.

Keane was protective of his prodigy. "Given we are already 10K short
from initial request by you and Stan and that this decision not only protracts
the war but risks the mission, should you consider resigning?" he e-mailed
to Petraeus. "I don't think quitting would serve our country," Petraeus responded. "More likely to create a crisis. And, I told POTUS I'd support his
ultimate decision. Besides, the troops can't quit. . . ."

Petraeus refused to discuss his interactions with the president, but accounts from officials briefed on the White House meeting indicate that
Obama, Petraeus, Mullen, Biden, Gates, Clinton and other senior national
security officials engaged in a lengthy discussion, tense but respectful, over
the pace of the drawdown. Obama expressed his gratitude that there had
been no leaks and said the frank exchanges during their two prior meetings
had been a great help to him. The president believed that Petraeus and ISAF
forces had made gains that justified his commitment of extra forces but that
now it was important to signal to the American, Afghan and international

communities that the coming year would be one of transition. There was general agreement with Obama's desire to draw down 10,000 troops by the end of 2011, though that was a larger figure than Petraeus and the military had recommended. But there was sharp disagreement over when the remaining 23,000 surge troops should leave Afghanistan.

Obama began the discussion by explaining that he wanted the 23,000 forces out of Afghanistan by July 2012—five months sooner than the after-the-end-of-the-fighting-season drawdown Petraeus had recommended. Mullen thought a drawdown by July would sacrifice virtually the entire fighting season. Both Gates and Clinton also expressed reservations. When Obama looked to Gates in an attempt to achieve consensus, Gates said there was a big difference between July and an "end of summer" drawdown. After further discussion, Obama voiced a willingness to consider splitting the difference and leaving the troops in Afghanistan through the end of the summer, but he was against waiting until the end of 2012. Gates, Clinton and Mullen all then said they could support an "end of summer" timetable. When Obama turned to Petraeus, the general was reportedly respectful, but he was not budging. He expressed concern that removing the troops before the end of the fighting season would increase risk considerably and could invalidate the campaign plan. Biden expressed the counterpoint, favoring the original July deadline—or one even sooner. Susan Rice, U.S. ambassador to the United Nations, suggested being flexible about the exact drawdown timetable for the 23,000 by saying they would leave in "mid- to late summer" of 2012. As momentum seemed to shift toward a late-summer drawdown, Petraeus again made it clear that he remained in favor of keeping the troops in Afghanistan until the end of the year in order to achieve the six objectives the president had laid out at West Point. The mission in Afghanistan, he said, was not transition; it was achieving conditions that allowed for *successful* transition. Obama asked whether those three extra months would make that much difference; Petraeus said he thought they would.

Petraeus again assured the president that he would faithfully support and execute his decision, but he noted that he would have to say, if asked at his confirmation hearing in two days, that the timeline was more aggressive

298 | **ALL IN**

than he had recommended. The president understood the obligation of military witnesses at congressional hearings to provide their personal views on issues when asked. Nonetheless, it was a tense moment. Finally, the president made his decision: 10,000 forces would leave Afghanistan by the end of the year, and the remaining 23,000 surge troops would be out by the end of summer 2012.

When Petraeus left the White House, he reportedly felt he had been heard. His recommendation had not been adopted, but he believed in and supported the process, and he recognized that only the president could truly weigh all the factors—many of which went beyond the military's purview. He'd acknowledged as much at the first meeting. He accepted the president's decision—and was ready to execute. He wanted to get in touch with his headquarters in Afghanistan to reassure them that all was well; he knew many would feel disappointed. It was time, as he liked to say, "to look forward and take the rearview mirrors off the bus." He wrote a statement and asked Lieutenant General James Bucknall, his deputy at ISAF headquarters, to read it at the morning's stand-up. He added one important instruction: Do not forward it to anyone via e-mail. The president had not yet made his public announcement, but Petraeus wanted his team to be prepared to deal with, if not shape, the troops' and coalition members' reaction. His statement read:

> Today, I participated in the final session with President Obama on deliberations over the drawdown of the US surge forces (i.e. the final 33k). President Obama will announce his decision on Wednesday evening, US time. I provided the President various options and assessments of risk to the military campaign plan for each option, and we had excellent discussions during the course of three meetings; indeed, he gave a very full hearing to all participants and I had ample opportunity to describe our campaign plan and the way ahead. US Forces will, needless to say, execute the president's decision; that is, of course, our constitutional duty and we embrace it. The mission will not change; it will remain hard, but doable. We will not lose focus on the initiation of the execution of the drawdown; in fact, we will redouble

our efforts to help our Afghan partners develop the capabilities to secure and govern themselves, thereby ensuring that this country does
not once again become a sanctuary for Al Qaeda and its affiliates. We
will likely have to work harder in some cases, as we begin to reduce
forces over the course of this year and continue in 2012; that is understandable but doable. Consequently, I will expect more, not less, of
each of you. So will General Allen. And we will, of course, continue to
take the fight to the enemy, along with our Afghan partners, with our
Afghan counterparts increasingly in the lead. We will continue to
help our civilian counterparts, international and Afghan, build on
the gains ANSF and ISAF forces have achieved as they seek to help
establish local governance, stimulate economic development, support provision of basic services, promote establishment of the rule of
law, pursue reintegration, and so on. I will work with the staff when I
return late this week to tweak our campaign plan to reflect the adjusted force levels and timelines, to ensure that we continue to drive
the campaign forward, and to build on the achievements of ANSF and
ISAF forces in the past year, in particular, as well as to set General
Allen up for success. I look forward to getting back to Kabul and the
mission of the largest coalition in history! Best from Washington—
COMISAF.

"BIDEN WINS, PETRAEUS LOSES" was the headline the following morning
as news of the president's decision began to leak. "That's not the issue," Petraeus told one of his confidants. "This is not about one person's rep; it's
about achieving our national objectives." Obama saw Afghanistan as a "war
of necessity" but was reducing forces more rapidly than advised. To explain
the president's position, the White House held a background briefing for
reporters that afternoon, several hours before the president's nationally
televised address. Officials described what the president would announce:
10,000 troops would leave Afghanistan by the end of the year, and all 33,000
surge troops would be out by the end of the summer of 2012—in fifteen

months, faster than Petraeus had recommended. He and Obama were only three months apart—but those three months would have left those troops in country through the end of the 2012 fighting season, which Petraeus considered critical in consolidating the gains he had achieved over the previous year.

A reporter asked the White House spokesperson point-blank whether Petraeus had endorsed Obama's plan. The fuzzy answer he got back bespoke the extreme sensitivity of the issue. "In terms of General Petraeus, I think that, consistent with our approach to this, General Petraeus presented the president with a range of options for pursuing this drawdown," one official said. "There were certainly options that went beyond what the president settled on in terms of the length of time that it would take to recover the surge and the pace that troops would come out—so there were options that would have kept troops in Afghanistan longer at a higher number. That said, the president's decision was fully within the range of options that were presented to him and has the full support of his national security team."

The New York Times soon quoted two administration officials as saying that Petraeus had not endorsed Obama's decision, while Gates and Clinton reluctantly had. Keane denounced the decision and told Petraeus in an e-mail that it "appears to undermine the entire COIN campaign at a time when we finally have gained momentum. My god, Dave, they just pushed your recommendations aside and changed the war fundamentally. What a mess." Petraeus did not respond.

President Obama addressed the nation at 8:00 P.M. from the White House. Petraeus watched it with his wife, Holly, from their home at Fort Myer. Obama called the decision he had announced at West Point in December 2009 to order 30,000 additional American troops into Afghanistan one of the most difficult decisions he had made as president. But the objectives were clear: Refocus on al-Qaeda and reverse the Taliban's momentum and build an Afghan military capable of defending the country. A drawdown of those forces would begin in July.

"Tonight I can tell you that we are fulfilling that commitment," Obama said. "Thanks to our extraordinary men and women in uniform, our civilian personnel and our many coalition partners, we are meeting our goals." The president did not credit Petraeus by name for assuming command and overseeing the effort to gain momentum on the battlefield. Obama continued:

> As a result, starting next month, we will be able to remove 10,000 of our troops from Afghanistan by the end of this year, and we will bring home a total of 33,000 troops by next summer, fully recovering the surge I announced at West Point. After this initial reduction, our troops will continue coming home at a steady pace as Afghan security forces move into the lead. Our mission will change from combat to support. By 2014, this process of transition will be complete, and the Afghan people will be responsible for their own security. . . .
>
> Of course, huge challenges remain. This is the beginning but not the end of our effort to wind down this war. We'll have to do the hard work of keeping the gains that we've made, while we draw down our forces and transition responsibility for security to the Afghan government. . . . We do know that peace cannot come to a land that has known so much war without a political settlement. So as we strengthen the Afghan government and security forces, America will join initiatives that reconcile the Afghan people, including the Taliban. Our position on these talks is clear: They must be led by the Afghan government; and those who want to be a part of a peaceful Afghanistan must break from al-Qaeda, abandon violence and abide by the Afghan constitution. But, in part because of our military effort, we have reason to believe that progress can be made. . . . We've ended our combat mission in Iraq, with 100,000 American troops already out of that country. And even as there will be dark days ahead in Afghanistan, the light of a secure peace can be seen in the distance. These long wars will come to a responsible end.

Conservative writer Max Boot, whom Petraeus respected, was outraged by the speech. He told Petraeus that if he wanted to quit and run for president, he would work on his campaign. Petraeus told him that his position would undoubtedly be known during tomorrow's confirmation hearing but that quitting was not the answer. He certainly didn't intend to run for president, either. As a student and practitioner of civil-military relations, Petraeus had thought at length about the subject of resignation in protest, turning it over in his mind many times. He was well steeped in the theory and practice and pitfalls of civil-military relations. Military decision making and the use of force as they related to civil-military relations had been foundations of his doctoral research.

Petraeus strongly believed that "military leaders should provide advice that is *informed* by important nonmilitary and military factors beyond their strict purview, but is *driven* by the situation on the ground and military considerations." In other words, a military leader's advice was premised first and foremost on his or her areas of expertise—military affairs, not political ones. Petraeus fully subscribed to the oath of office, including obeying "the orders of the President of the United States and the officers appointed over me." Obama's decision to draw down forces faster than he had recommended did not, in his mind, begin to approach the threshold for such an extraordinary action as resignation. He thought it would have been a selfish, grandstanding move with huge political ramifications. He had had ample opportunity to provide input and give his best advice, and now it was time to salute and carry on.

Some politicians thought otherwise.

Senator Joseph Lieberman issued an immediate statement saying that Obama's speedier drawdown would "put at risk the substantial gains we have made in Afghanistan."

Soon after, Gates's press secretary sent Petraeus's team a statement from Gates supporting the president. "Over the past 18 months our troops have made tremendous progress degrading the capability of the Taliban while enhancing the Afghan security forces," Gates said. "It is critical that we continue to aggressively prosecute that strategy. I support the President's decision because it provides our commanders with enough resources, time and, perhaps most importantly, flexibility to bring the surge to a successful conclusion."

A short while later, Petraeus's executive officer sent him the prepared statement that Joint Chiefs chairman Mullen would use to open a hearing in the House Armed Services Committee on Thursday morning:

Let me start by saying that I support the President's decisions, as do Generals Mattis and Petraeus. We were given voice in this process. We offered our views—freely and without hesitation—and they were heard. As has been the case throughout the development and execution of the Afghanistan strategy, the Commander-in-Chief presided over an inclusive and comprehensive discussion about what to do next. I am grateful for that.

AT UNION STATION over drinks and dinner that evening, Senator Graham took a cell phone call from his colleague and fellow Afghan war booster Senator McCain. The two strongly disagreed with Obama's decision. "This is now his policy; he needs to own it," Graham told McCain. "He did not take the advice of his military advisers, and it has put the mission in jeopardy. This assumes too much risk. His decision was political, and we need to pin it on him." Graham was livid. "You know, as a ranking GOP member, I have supported the war and the president's position, but he is about to lose that support and the rest of those in the party who have backed this war," he said as he closed his cell phone.

Petraeus was determined to avoid getting sucked into the politics of either side. He knew some senators would question the drawdown decision during his confirmation hearing the following day. He needed to keep the troops in Afghanistan focused, to give them energy and reassurance that the president's decision did not call for such doomsday political rankling. Initially, he intended for his deputy commander to read the statement he had provided at the stand-up in Kabul on Thursday morning, the morning after the president's announcement. But Petraeus quickly decided that wasn't enough; the best point of influence as the battlefield commander was for him to be with the troops, to the extent that he could from D.C. He had his communications team arrange for him to deliver a revised statement personally via a secure video teleconference from his Fort Myer home that evening at 11:00 P.M.

Whatever he may have felt about the decision that day, there was no trace of disappointment on his face or in his message, a modified version of what he'd sent his deputy earlier:

As was noted earlier, President Obama announced this evening in Washington his decision on the drawdown of the US surge forces. As he explained, the drawdown will entail a reduction of 10K US forces by the end of this year and the remaining 23K by the end of next summer. This culminated a decision-making process that was rapid and thorough, in which three meetings were held in the past week alone, during which I was provided ample opportunity to contribute and in which I offered forthright, professional military advice that included options for implementing the policy, assessments of risk for each option, and recommendations. As President Obama noted, this decision will fulfill the drawdown commitment he made in his speech at West Point on 1 December 2009. And, as he observed, it is a decision made possible in large part by the hard-fought progress made over the past 18–24 months by ISAF and ANSF troops. Needless to say, with the decision being announced, all of us will support the decision and strive to execute it effectively. That is our responsibility as military leaders. As we contemplate the way ahead, we should recall that during the course of the drawdown of the 33K US troopers over the next 15 months, ANSF numbers will increase likely by some 70K, if we count, in addition to the additional ANA and ANP to be fielded, the additional APPF, ALP, and specialty forces, such as the Khost Protection Force and various NDS Counter-Terrorist Pursuit Team elements.

We should recall that when the president initially ordered additional US forces into Afghanistan, the Taliban controlled much of Helmand Province, were on the verge of taking Kandahar, were threatening Kabul, and were posing an increasingly existential threat to the Afghan state. Because of the hard-fought and skillful operations that ISAF and the ANSF have conducted over the past 18–24 months, none of those conditions still holds. We have driven the enemy out of many of his safe-havens in Helmand and Kandahar, we have increased security in and around Kabul, and, above all, the Taliban no longer poses an existential threat to the Afghan state. To be sure, the fighting remains tough and levels of violence have gone up in certain areas; that was what we predicted, and our troopers and Afghan partners have met the challenges and are in the process of dealing with them. A key reason for the progress in the past year, in particular, has been the dramatic expansion in the size and capabilities of the Afghan security forces themselves. While the United States added the final 30,000 surge troops to the effort, the Afghans have added more than 70,000. The quality of those Afghan forces has also improved because of your partnering, mentoring, and enabling, and because of our Afghan partners' growing ability to shoulder security tasks in their country. Indeed, no figure better demonstrates this than the fact that 3 Afghan troopers have been killed in action for each coalition member killed in action in recent months.

Having spent time in European capitals and here in Washington over the past few weeks, I know that the international commitment to succeeding in Afghanistan remains firm and support for ISAF remains very high. Our capitals believe that we can achieve the vital mission they have given us. The reduction in US forces is, in many respects, based on that confidence, not on any erosion in the will to succeed. Even after this surge of forces ends, our nations are committed to supporting Afghanistan with significant military efforts through 2014, and that commitment has not changed. In short, this is not a time to start thinking about going home. Rather, we need to stay focused on protecting the Afghan people from all threats and on helping our ANSF partners develop the ability to defend their people. We need to continue to take the fight to the enemy. We need to remain on the offensive, to ensure that we do not allow the enemy any breathing space or respite. I am confident that you will be more than equal to the continuing challenges we will face and that our path forward provides the best opportunity for achieving our objective in this critical mission. As always, thanks for your great work!

"How'd it go, GEN P?" an aide asked him later via e-mail. "It went fine," Petraeus responded at 12:15 A.M. "Tried to be realistic, reassuring, circumspect, and determined."

BY THE DAY of his confirmation hearing, Petraeus had prepared as though he were expecting a grilling from members of both parties. He'd participated in a two-and-a-half-hour murder board the previous morning at CIA headquarters. And, in between the NSC backgrounder and the president's address the previous night, he'd spent half an hour on the phone with George Tenet, another former director of the CIA. By the time Senator Dianne Feinstein gaveled the hearing to order Thursday afternoon in the Hart Senate Office Building, Petraeus had met privately or spoken with every member of the committee and met or spoken to all former living CIA directors except one whose health precluded a conversation.

Senator Lieberman introduced Petraeus to the committee. The conservative and hawkish Connecticut Democrat-turned-Independent felt a special connection to Petraeus. The feeling was mutual. The two had met during Petraeus's first year in Iraq, and Lieberman remained a staunch ally in Washington during the surge, virtually the only Democrat/Independent who supported it—and Petraeus never forgot that. Lieberman had written a number of strong op-ed pieces that influenced public opinion in favor of the war. Petraeus respected him immensely and was grateful for his conviction.

"At a moment when too many of our fellow citizens fear that America's best days are behind us," Lieberman said, "Dave Petraeus's life and leadership have been a reminder that America is still a land of heroes and that individually and as a nation we are still capable of greatness."

Petraeus began his prepared remarks, which he had been working on for the past two weeks, by recognizing Holly, his partner for "thirty-seven years and twenty-three moves." He then addressed, up front, some of the skepticism about his move to the CIA and what it meant. Responding to some who had wondered in print whether he would be able to "grade my own work," he said he was "keenly aware" that as CIA director he would be an intelligence officer, not a policy maker. He noted that he had twice offered war assessments that were more positive than those of the intelligence community—in Iraq in September 2007 and in Afghanistan in 2010—and twice he had been less positive: in Iraq in 2008 and 2009. "In short, I have sought to provide the most accurate view possible," he said. "My goal has been to speak truth to power, and I will strive to do that as director of the CIA if confirmed."

To others who had voiced concerns about the "militarization" of the CIA—the extension, since 9/11, of America's lethal military force through the agency's paramilitary branch and the increased use of drone missile strikes—Petraeus noted his intention to retire from the Army before becoming director to "allay those concerns." He also said he had no plans to bring members of his military brain trust to Langley and would instead surround himself with the many "impressive individuals" at the CIA. Panetta was taking a few of his inner circle with him, but Petraeus felt he could fill those gaps with internal hires. "If confirmed, I will, in short, get out of my vehicle alone on the day I report to Langley," he said.

When the questioning began, Senator Saxby Chambliss, the Georgia Republican and committee vice chairman, said he was "somewhat disappointed with the scale of the drawdown" announced by Obama and asked Petraeus whether that plan jeopardized his gains in Afghanistan. If Chambliss was hoping to use the general to score partisan points, he got nowhere. Petraeus explained that the president's plan called for removing the 33,000 surge troops over a fifteen-month period beginning in July. He supported the president's decision and recognized that Obama had to take factors into consideration that went well beyond those of a battlefield commander. He noted that 70,000 additional Afghan troops would be added in that period.

Echoing what Joint Chiefs chairman Mullen had told the House Armed Services Committee that morning, where Mullen stated that "the president's decisions are more aggressive and incur more risk than [Mullen] was originally prepared to accept," Petraeus stated it was "more aggressive" too, noting specifically that he, Mullen and General James Mattis, the head of Central Command, had recommended to keep those forces in place through the end of the 2012 fighting season. But Petraeus termed it a "small difference." As if to cut off Chambliss's further lines of attack, Petraeus pointed out that a transition to Afghan forces would soon begin in seven districts in three provinces, including Kabul—all told, areas encompassing 25 percent of the nation's population.

The next questioner, Senator Jay Rockefeller, the West Virginia Democrat, elicited the most newsworthy response of the hearing when he asked Petraeus to share some of his thoughts about running the CIA. "As I told you behind closed doors, I'll say here: I wanted this job," Petraeus said. "This is something that was not . . . a month or two or three in the making. Secretary Gates and I discussed this all the way back last year."

Senator Levin was clearly irked by Karzai's most recent speech, in which he said U.S. forces were essentially an occupation force "using our country." "I was absolutely dismayed," Levin said, "because I thought the comment of his talking about us as occupiers plays right into the hands of a common enemy, the Taliban. And I would hope that in your determination to speak truth to power, which is your commitment here as the new CIA director, that you also will speak truth to President Karzai."

"I can assure you, Mr. Chairman, that I have always sought, albeit in private and on many occasions one-on-one, to have very candid and forthright conversations with President Karzai," Petraeus said.

"Were you dismayed by that comment?" Levin asked.

"It did cause concern, without question," Petraeus said.

Feinstein expressed similar dismay, calling Karzai's remarks "insulting" and "misleading." "You have the automatic reaction 'Why the heck are we here then?' " she commented.

"Well, look, I am entirely sympathetic to that, needless to say, and so I will certainly ensure that that sentiment is shared with our Afghan partners." Petraeus wanted to preserve the relationship he had with Karzai and wasn't about to criticize him in public, but he couldn't help but express that he, too, had been disturbed by such statements.

By far the most dramatic moment, and a lesson for students of civil-military relations, came when Levin asked Petraeus whether he supported the president's drawdown plan and what would have to happen before he would ever consider resigning his command. "I obviously support the ultimate decision of the commander in chief," Petraeus said. "That is, we take an oath to obey the orders of the president of the United States and indeed do that."

"And if you couldn't do that—if you couldn't do that consistent with that oath—you would resign?" asked Levin.

"Well, I'm not a quitter, chairman," Petraeus said. "I've actually had people e-mail me and say that I should quit, and actually this is something I've thought a bit about."

"I'm sure you have," Levin said.

"And I don't think it is the place for a commander to actually consider that step unless you are in a very, very dire situation," said Petraeus. He went on:

This is an important decision. [The president's decision] is, again, a more aggressive approach than the chairman, General Mattis and I . . . put forward, but this is not something I think where one hangs up the uniform in protest or something like that. . . . I actually feel quite strongly about this. Our troopers don't get to quit, and I don't think commanders should contemplate that, again, as any kind of idle action. That would be an extraordinary action, in my view. And at the end of the day, this is not about me, it's not about an individual commander, it's not about a reputation. This is about our country. And the best step for our country, with the commander in chief having made a decision, is to execute that decision to the very best of our ability.

CHAPTER 12

MASK OF COMMAND

D uring his final three weeks in command of the war in Afghanistan, Petraeus masked his emotions. He believed in projecting strength, and while he did not consider his emotions a weakness, he also didn't feel they were something he necessarily needed to show to others. As the end of his military service approached and the outcome of the war remained uncertain, he kept the mask of command firmly in place. Even more than giving up command, he dreaded taking off the uniform. Retired general Fred Franks warned him not to underestimate the emotional impact of the next few weeks. He urged Petraeus to give himself some space and time to reflect. "Sometimes," Franks told him, "emotions ambush us." Petraeus was grateful for the counsel, but he thought the best strategy was to control his emotions, not give in to them. He'd rarely if ever gotten choked up during a ceremony, and he didn't plan to start now. Avoiding self-reflection, as much as possible, seemed to be the way to go. Another close friend urged him to just let it out in private so he didn't have a weak moment in public, or, better yet, to just let the public see his human side. But Petraeus had seen others struggle to regain control, and he was having none of it. He knew what to do. Stay busy. Don't think. Compartmentalize.

Petraeus would be serving his seventh Independence Day in the nine years since 9/11 in a combat zone: commanding the 101st Airborne in Mosul in 2003, training Iraqi forces in Baghdad in 2004 and 2005, commanding the war in Iraq in 2007 and 2008 and commanding the war in Afghanistan in 2010 and 2011. Always the competitor, Petraeus noted in an interview with David Ignatius of the *Washington Post* that the answer would have been eight in eleven years, had the question been how many Fourths he had spent deployed overseas since 2001—as he was serving in Bosnia on July 4, 2001.

Though Petraeus knew he was sacrificing time with his family during those absences, he loved to be where the fight was. To that end, he thought he should have fought harder to remain in command through the end of the fighting season in October. But he wasn't sure what else he could have done. He understood why the White House wanted him in place at the CIA before the September 11 anniversary. He also recognized that it was undoubtedly a good idea to have General Allen and Ambassador Crocker getting off to a fresh start together as they assumed the reins for the war.

PETRAEUS'S ASSESSMENTS of how the war was going were quite measured. He always predicted hard fighting ahead. He always said the gains were fragile and reversible. After the first week in command, he never talked about winning; rather, he talked about progress—or, in some cases, lack of progress. But he never sounded defeated. What Petraeus's critics saw as his "spinning" of events was really a by-product of two of his greatest strengths: his unrelenting optimism and his insatiable appetite for facts and information, wherever he could find them. There would be no victory lap, however, in his final weeks of command, only relentless attention to detail to the very end. His immediate focus was getting his staff to work on planning to implement the president's drawdown decision—first, the reduction of 10,000 troops by the end of 2011, and then the rest of the 23,000 by September of the following year. He wanted the planning effort well under way by the time Allen took over.

Petraeus's workweek back in Kabul had begun that Monday morning, June 27, with a security briefing to a large gathering of more than seventy senior civilian representatives of the countries helping in Afghanistan. The meeting was hosted by the Afghan Foreign Ministry and was the first time such a session had been held in Kabul. Jet lag hit Petraeus hard; it was a "fireball" session. (An officer close to him said he had eaten four Atomic Fireballs in one hour.) Petraeus stayed only for the meeting's first hour before heading off to convene a tripartite meeting of Afghan, Pakistani and NATO military commanders, including General Ashfaq Kayani, head of the Pakistani military, and General Sher Mohammad Karimi, his Afghan counterpart. Petraeus later noted to his staff that Afghan intelligence chief Major General Abdul Khaliq had been impressive in his briefing on the current threat situation and the Afghan security posture along the Afghanistan-Pakistan border. But tensions persisted. Pakistan remained concerned about insurgent infiltration into its tribal areas from Afghanistan; the Afghans countered with their objections to numerous cross-border mortar and rocket attacks from Pakistan.

A report released that day by the International Crisis Group came into his e-mail inbox as he returned to his office. The ICG is an influential nonprofit that seeks to find peaceful solutions to global conflicts. The report concluded that the Taliban had moved into the country's center, around Kabul, far beyond its home in Kandahar and Helmand provinces, and that combat gains in those two provinces had not arrested the Taliban's momentum elsewhere. Violence had peaked in the country despite the troop surge, the report contended, and Karzai's government was hopelessly corrupt, ineffectual and close to collapse. "On the surface, security conditions in the capital city appear relatively stable," the ICG report said. "The nexus between criminal enterprises, insurgent networks and corrupt political elites, however, is undermining Kabul's security and that of the central-eastern corridor. . . . Tasked with quelling the violence, NATO's International Security Assistance Force (ISAF) is perceived as unable or unwilling to distinguish between civilians and insurgents and to reduce dependence on corrupt government officials in its counter-insurgency strategy." The group's conclusion: "Failure in Afghanistan is not inevitable, but without a recalibration of the current counter-insurgency strategy, success is far from guaranteed."

Petraeus countered the group's pessimism the following day in his own guidance to the troops on Obama's decision to draw down forces. "The prog-ress of the past year, in particular, has been significant," he wrote. "Together, ISAF and Afghan forces have driven insurgents out of a number of impor-tant safe havens in Helmand and Kandahar. Security in Kabul, home to one-fifth of Afghanistan's population, has been improved. Broadly speaking, we have broken the Taliban's momentum and reversed it in many areas."

He also managed to keep an eye on his successor's upcoming confirma-tion hearing before the Senate Armed Services Committee. He had immense respect and affection for John Allen, whom he had fought to have assigned—and be given a third star—as his deputy at Central Command after the two had worked together in Iraq. Allen, like Petraeus, had a reputation as a stra-tegic thinker and a deft communicator. He was highly respected by the NSC staff and principals. Petraeus's admiration for Allen was born during Petraeus's command in Iraq, when Allen, as deputy commander in restive Anbar Province, was credited with helping to convince Sunni tribes there to reject the insurgency and take part in the Sunni Awakening. Petraeus felt he was a great leader who developed a vision and was then calm but determined in carrying it out. He also thought Allen was very good in the interagency and international arena and understood how to navigate the U.S. military hier-archy, skills not all attributed as fully to Rodriguez, the man Allen had edged out to replace Petraeus as commander in Afghanistan.

As the confirmation process approached for Allen, Petraeus was con-cerned that Senators John McCain and Lindsey Graham would try to pin Allen down on the difference between Obama's drawdown and Petraeus's recommendation. Mindful that this was Allen's first Senate confirmation, Petraeus coached him on how to provide context before directly taking on a hard question such as "What does this mean in terms of risk for the troops?" Petraeus knew the Republicans would try to drive a wedge between Allen and Obama. At the hearing, Graham asked Allen whether Obama's draw-down plan was one of the options Petraeus had presented.

"It was not," Allen said.

"So I just want the country to understand that this is not the Petraeus strategy any longer," Graham said. "The commander in chief has the perfect right to do what he did. I just hope that it hasn't undercut what I think could be a very successful outcome."

Levin took the opposite tack.

"I think it's important that even though this apparently was more aggressive than General Petraeus recommended, that military leaders of our country support this decision and feel it was an appropriate decision for the president to make. Is that correct?"

"Chairman, we're in execution now," Allen replied.

"But you also felt it was a proper decision for the president to make?"

"It is the prerogative of the president to make—to take the recommendations of his commanders and to make the decision—and he made the decision and we are executing," Allen said.

"All right," said Levin. "And it's something you agree with."

"I agree," Allen said.

Petraeus thought his protégé had done well and told him so immediately following the Senate hearing.

The same day as Allen's confirmation hearing, a small group of insurgents blew up a vehicle at the gate of the historic Hotel Intercontinental in Kabul and stormed the building just as Afghan officials were preparing to hold a meeting elsewhere in Kabul of provincial governors to discuss the upcoming transfer of security responsibilities to Afghan forces. Reports indicated that at least some of the attackers had worn Afghan police uniforms. Eleven civilians were killed and eight were wounded in the assault, which shattered the sense of security in Kabul. While Afghan police and commandos ultimately cleared the hotel of insurgents, the siege didn't end until well after midnight, when an ISAF sniper aboard a NATO helicopter finally killed the last three insurgents, who had sought cover on the hotel's roof. The attack made the ICG report citing weaknesses in Kabul's security seem all the more prescient.

Petraeus thought the attack demonstrated real capability on the part of the insurgents. The silver lining, in his mind, though, was that the Afghan National Police's Crisis Response Unit and the Afghan National Army Commandos had responded capably and courageously, with an official from the Ministry of the Interior and the Kabul police chief on the scene commanding the response. Several Afghan troopers had sacrificed their lives going after the attackers. In the end, all nine insurgents were killed, and a fire they set was extinguished. While attending a security *shura* later in the week, Petraeus noted that the attack had been carried out by the same number of insurgents as had raided hotels in Mumbai, India, in the deadly 2008 attacks, but with a far different result—the Afghans having resolved the situation during a single night, in far less time and with far less loss of life than in Mumbai, where 166 were killed.

FRESH FROM Lieutenant General Allen's confirmation hearing, Senators McCain, Graham and Lieberman arrived in Kabul for the Fourth of July weekend, far more focused on what they considered the "unnecessary risk" inherent in Obama's drawdown plan than was Petraeus, who had clearly moved on. McCain repeated the words "unnecessary risk" in an interview, and Graham, appearing on *Fox News Sunday* from Afghanistan, continued doing his best to saddle Obama with the consequences of his drawdown plan. "No military leader recommended the decision the president chose," he said. "So it is now the Obama-Biden strategy."

The senators and Petraeus had dinner that evening with Karzai. At one point, the Afghan leader mentioned that he loved a song that he thought was called "Down on the Bayou." After dinner, Petraeus put his communications team on it. His aides quickly found the tune—"Born on the Bayou," by Creedence Clearwater Revival. For Petraeus, it brought back memories of Cadet Hops at West Point in 1972. His team burned a CD of Creedence's greatest hits, and Petraeus gave it to Karzai two days later. The president beamed.

When the morning of the Fourth arrived, Petraeus felt a bit of a dull ache but hoped his jam-packed day would keep him from thinking too much about his final Fourth in uniform. He flew to Kandahar and presided over a reenlistment ceremony for 235 soldiers, commemorating the 235th anniversary of the United States. Before the ceremony, he promoted his son Stephen's best friend from the 173rd Airborne, who had volunteered to return to Afghanistan to serve under Brigadier General Martins. He also used the occasion to formally establish the NATO Rule of Law Field Support Mission, making Martins's work to build a functioning justice system an international effort.

McCain, Lieberman and Graham carried the message of urgency to President Karzai during dinner with him that evening at the palace. They also warned him about his repeated eruptions in the media. The three senators impressed on Karzai that the U.S. Congress was running out of patience. Graham was frank with Karzai, whom he sometimes referred to as "the Lion." "The Lion will never be your friend," he confided later. But you still wanted the Lion on your side.

"The best chance for your country's survival, and for *your* survival," Graham advised Karzai at the dinner, "is a meaningful relationship with the United States." Graham was referring to a long-term commitment to permanent basing and partnership, an initiative he had first raised exactly a year earlier with Karzai in the same room. Karzai was less than sanguine.

The deal was a hard sell, Graham said, "when most people have written Afghanistan off as a hopeless endeavor, too corrupt to be saved. I don't believe that. But to convince them, you're going to have to step up your game.

"My biggest fear is that people will use lack of progress on governance and corruption as a reason to accelerate withdrawal. . . . There's a growing frustration on the right," but "we're not going to walk off a cliff for Obama's deal," he continued, noting that "a lot of Republicans feel like it's now his war." But he reassured Karzai: "I don't; I feel like it is our war."

To Graham's pleasant surprise, Karzai seemed to be more willing to embrace reform than at any of their past meetings. "You have to show the American people that you are dealing with corruption," Graham told him, explaining how worrisome the status of the Kabul Bank failure was to decision makers. "In no uncertain terms, if you sweep this under the rug and it becomes a legal matter, it's going to be very hard to sell. . . . We're hanging by a thread. This unholy alliance I've been worried about for a couple of years is becoming real," Graham said, referring to the union of some of his colleagues on the far right and the far left. "But I think we're okay in the short term; we just need to show progress." If there was not continued demonstrable progress, the senators told Karzai, then Karzai and Afghanistan would be the losers.

The senators emphasized the importance of a strategic partnership that would keep air bases with trainers, Special Forces elements and various support assets in the country past 2014. If not, they said, all the momentum from the surge would eventually be lost. They all saw progress from Petraeus's utilization of the surge troops. But this latest announcement about reducing surge forces had reignited the old debate about America's enduring commitment. Graham hoped the Afghans' stubbornness at the bargaining table reflected a desire to get the best deal possible, and not a lack of commitment to an enduring partnership.

By late summer, progress in negotiating the strategic partnership declaration had foundered on Afghan demands that the document include binding deadlines for their assumption of authority for detaining insurgents and controlling night military raids—deadlines the American negotiators did not think should be part of the declaration. The Afghans also wanted the United States to provide their armed forces with F-16 fighter jets and Abrams tanks, which the Pentagon had no intention of doing.

Petraeus told reporters in an interview late on the Fourth of July that the focus of the war would shift east later in the year—not by putting many more boots on the ground but by sending more Special Forces, more intelligence capability, more helicopters, more reconnaissance, more drones, more airpower. He was pleased to have "the three amigos" (McCain, Lieberman and Graham) with him and the troopers for their third Fourth of July together in a war zone. But he also said it was "probably time to stop second-guessing the decision that only the president can make." Petraeus said of the president, "Only he has the full range of considerations that he has to deal with. That decision has been made. . . . It is our job to get on with it and do the absolute best we can."

Three days later, Petraeus made his final battlefield circulation, visiting the Currahee Brigade, the 506th Infantry Regiment of the 101st Airborne Division, at Forward Operating Base Sharana, in Paktika Province, more than a hundred miles south of Kabul on the Pakistan border. Petraeus had been commander of the 101st in 2004, when plans to reactivate the storied Currahee Brigade were first discussed. The unit was the final brigade deployed as part of Obama's surge, and it would be leaving Afghanistan in early August. "I want you, above all, to have pride, quiet pride, in what it is that you have achieved," Petraeus told several hundred soldiers gathered before him in battle fatigues. "You all have done a magnificent job over the course of the last year [in] very difficult terrain against a very difficult enemy—right up against the [Pakistan] border. You have truly distinguished yourself in that fight; you've made inroads, especially as you've come to the end of your tour."

Still, the fighting and dying were not over. When the Pentagon announced ten fatalities for the week ending July 12, the total number of Americans killed in Afghanistan since October 2001 had reached 1,552. A staggering 12,593 had been wounded. The ten men killed that week had been attacked in six different provinces across Afghanistan. During their year in the Hindu Kush, the Currahees would lose eighteen soldiers.

Back in Kabul that evening, Colonel Jim Seaton of Petraeus's Commander's Initiatives Group forwarded a guest post from the *Best Defense* blog of Thomas E. Ricks, former Pentagon correspondent for the *Washington Post,* who had written two seminal books on the Iraq war: *Fiasco* and *The Gamble.* The blog post was written by an anonymous Army major who had spent four months in intensive Pashto language training as part of the Afghan Hands program—the baby of Joint Chiefs chairman Admiral Mullen, McChrystal and Petraeus while he was at CENTCOM and theater commander. Due to personnel shortages in the Army Corps of Engineers, the anonymous major had been transferred to a desk job. Three other Afghan Hands in the corps had reportedly received similar transfers. According to the major, Army bureaucrats apparently cared little about developing real language and cultural expertise in a counterinsurgency campaign. The officer wrote, "I just want someone to help me get the word out that maybe the CJCS is not aware of how his top priority is being run in the war zone." The blog post ended with a note that "'A.P. Hand' is based in Kandahar, Afghanistan, at least until his boss reads this."

"Let's try to find him, Jim," Petraeus told Seaton. "Our kind of guy, actually. Let me talk to him. And let Tom [Ricks] know I want to find him, talk to him and get him to the right billet. And get to the head of the Afghan Hands program. No recriminations. Let's just fix it." Petraeus had eleven days left in country. He was going to do as much as he could in each one.

EVEN THOUGH his year of service in Afghanistan was over, Major Fernando Lujan agreed to go back out on one more embed with Afghan forces, at the request of Marine lieutenant colonel Wade Priddy, another Afghan Hand on the Counterinsurgency Advisory and Assistance Team. Newly arrived on the CAAT, Priddy wanted to see how Lujan embedded with the Afghans, and Lujan wanted to go back to Zabul Province and spend time with two Afghan battalions, or *kandaks*. One of them was the unit Lujan had embedded with back in May, and he was curious to see whether any of the issues he had raised about its performance had been resolved. The other was the first Afghan battalion authorized to operate with complete independence from the Americans and NATO. Once they got out into Zabul's parched, desolate, dangerous countryside, on the border with Pakistan between Paktika, to the northeast, and Kandahar, to the southwest, Lujan was disappointed to see that most of the same old problems still existed in the first *kandak*. The Afghans walked the same routes day after day. They were careless, unimpressive.

But after a day with the newly independent battalion, Lujan was glad he had agreed to extend his tour and lead this mission. These Afghans were exceptional—a validation of all he had worked for and believed in. An Afghan captain invited the American platoon to go along on a night ambush. Lujan remembered thinking, *I can't believe these guys are doing this*. In the field, the Afghans moved stealthily, the Americans loudly, with their radios initially turned up too high. "The Afghans were more aware of their surroundings and more capable of connecting with the locals," Lujan said. The Taliban never showed, and there was no one to ambush. But these Afghan soldiers were well trained and willing to fight.

Petraeus had made it clear that independent Afghan units should continue to receive the full array of combat support assistance from the Americans, including intelligence, surveillance and reconnaissance help from drones and other technical means. Lujan tried to explain this to the commanders of this superb battalion, in hopes that they could communicate Petraeus's intent to more Afghan units. Lujan's fear was that the Afghan units would essentially be cut loose—and left completely to their own devices. Still, to watch this multiethnic battalion operate with skill and esprit de corps was, for him, exhilarating.

Lujan finally left Afghanistan in early July and returned to the United States just after the Fourth. It was a jarring transition, but it felt good to be home. Then, three days later, his fiancée, a Harvard graduate who worked in international development, announced she was leaving him— she couldn't handle the deployments. She realized, at some point, that Lujan had a mistress he was never going to give up: the war in Afghanistan. She handed him a list of all the bills he needed to pay. Welcome home. Then he found out that Major Stephen Hopkins, the Special Forces officer and Afghan Hand who—at Petraeus's request—had replaced him on the CAAT, had abruptly quit. He accused Lujan of selling him a false bill of goods after arriving in Helmand and concluding that no one there really cared about Lujan's quixotic mission to take the CAAT evaluation process into Afghan units. So Lujan headed home to Texas and hit rock bottom for a month. "I'll know I'm fully adjusted when I don't have the urge to jump back on a plane and go to Afghanistan," he said.

But he was back in Washington by mid-August, ready to begin his fellowship at the Center for a New American Security (CNAS). During his interview at the upstart think tank, known as COIN Central by the defense intelligentsia, Lujan told John Nagl and Nate Fick, the president and CEO of CNAS, that he thought COIN "would be a dirty word in a year." Lujan just couldn't help himself. That kind of honesty had rendered him "PNG'd"—

persona non grata—back when he was teaching at West Point, and it had certainly destroyed his relationship with Tanzola. But Nagl and Fick didn't judge; they welcomed Lujan to the fold. He may have thought COIN was passing from vogue, but he still believed in it. He knew that it had opened up a lot of "white space" in the toughest areas of Kandahar and Helmand provinces, where Afghans could now go about their daily lives without fear of the Taliban. And he believed in Afghan troops—at least the Afghan National Army. He'd had an inside look at more Afghan battalions than any other American officer over the past year—probably twenty battalions in all. "The Afghan army is just much better than it was," Lujan said. "I was humbled by them—young lieutenants and NCOs who were full of fire, aggressive and wanting to do the right thing. This really gave me a lot of heart."

WITH A WEEK in his new job, Defense secretary Leon E. Panetta was making news before he even arrived in Kabul, telling reporters that the United States had al-Qaeda "on the run" and was within striking distance of strategically defeating the terrorist organization. As Petraeus's predecessor at the CIA, Panetta's rhetorical flourish stood in contrast to Petraeus's under-promise/overdeliver mantra. Once on the ground in Kabul on July 8, Panetta continued with the press in a similar vein, predicting that victory against al-Qaeda was "within reach."

Petraeus had a close relationship with Panetta, whom he liked personally and considered a strong leader. Panetta had hosted Petraeus at the CIA for dinner a few weeks earlier and instructed the agency staff to help the general prepare for his confirmation hearing in every possible way. As head of Central Command, Petraeus had similarly sought to support Panetta in early 2009 as Panetta approached confirmation as CIA director. After that, the two would talk to each other on at least a monthly basis about various operations in the global war on terror in the Central Command region. They also cohosted every four to five months what they referred to as the "counterterrorist board of directors," with the commander of the Special Operations Command, the commander of the Joint Special Operations

Command, the Treasury undersecretary for counterterrorism, the heads of the CIA's Counterterrorism Center and the DNI National Counterterrorism Center, the State Department's assistant secretary for counterterrorism and representatives from other military commands as well as the National Security Council staff. It had been during one of the last such gatherings cohosted by Petraeus that General McChrystal called Petraeus to alert him to the *Rolling Stone* article that led to McChrystal's resignation.

After arriving in Kabul, Panetta, together with Petraeus and Ambassador Eikenberry, had dinner with Karzai, with whom he'd had a good relationship as CIA director. He thought a new team in Kabul consisting of himself, incoming ambassador Ryan Crocker and Lieutenant General John Allen, Petraeus's replacement, stood to improve relations with Karzai, who had never gotten along with Eikenberry. Petraeus did not take offense at Panetta's remark, even though he prided himself on how hard he had worked to maintain a close working relationship with the Afghan president.

Petraeus remained a bit more circumspect than Panetta in characterizing progress against al-Qaeda and in Afghanistan. But he couldn't help disclosing that for the first time since 2006, the number of insurgent attacks in Afghanistan had declined in June when compared with June a year earlier, even though there were eight thousand more coalition forces in the country than in 2010, which analysts had predicted would result in a 20 to 30 percent increase. He cautioned that it was too early to say the insurgency had been significantly weakened.

Petraeus cited the trend in declining insurgent attacks during his interview the following day with the *New York Times,* explaining that attacks were down from the previous year in May and June and heading the same way in July. This, he said, was the first real indicator since 2006 that the insurgents had been degraded, although he noted that their ability to assassinate Afghan leaders, plant roadside bombs, infiltrate Afghan units and cause mayhem across the country was still substantial. He outlined the campaign plan for the coming year: Consolidate gains in and around Kandahar and in central Helmand, push into Taliban redoubts in northern Helmand, then transfer some intelligence capabilities and combat support elements to the eastern provinces in the winter of 2012 to shut down infiltration routes, with an emphasis on restive Kunar and Nuristan provinces, along the border with Pakistan in the far northeast. U.S. forces could help disrupt insurgent activities, but the ultimate solution in many areas would be a local one. Undergirding it all would be an expansion of the Afghan Local Police across Afghanistan and the minting of an additional sixty thousand Afghan forces. "It is very hard, but it is doable," he said.

Asked during an interview with NATO TV about increasing violence levels in the context of a counterinsurgency campaign intended to protect the Afghan people, Petraeus said that most of the night raids involved the capture of insurgent leaders with no shooting at all—and when the raids did involve shooting, he said, "they are quite precise in their effects."

His assessment of the quality of Afghan forces was measured. "You have to acknowledge, I think, an unevenness among some of the forces," he said, noting that the more than twelve thousand Afghan special operations forces were "really quite capable" and leading nearly a quarter of all night raids. They performed creditably and courageously, he said, in response to the recent attack on the Hotel Intercontinental. They now led all night raids in the Kabul area. Beyond that, he felt that many regular Army units were also developing impressively. The quality of the police ranged from very good to inadequate in some areas. But the conditions for transition had been set.

PETRAEUS WAS EFFUSIVE at Lieutenant General Rodriguez's change-of-command ceremony on July 11. "General Rod is, in many respects," Petraeus explained in his remarks, "the operational architect of the campaign plan that has guided the progress of the past year. But what he has done pales by comparison to the way in which he has done it. . . . He is always out there, meeting with ISAF troopers and Afghan counterparts, explaining our concepts, overseeing their execution, and keeping his finger on the pulse of every situation."

Rodriguez chatted briefly with reporters before he left later in the day from Kabul's military airport. "The violence has gone down where we've focused our efforts," he said on the tarmac, his tour at an end. "You have to watch it very carefully, because the violence is now outside instead of inside the populated areas. It takes a lot to really understand the nuances of what's happening. But, look, these things go up and down, and we're going to have to sustain that with our partners. Afghan forces are stepping up more and more. I'm confident the withdrawal will be all right now."

WELL PAST MIDNIGHT on the night following Rodriguez's departure, Petraeus wrote to Bob Gates, the now-retired secretary of Defense, thanking him for a formal letter Gates had written to him a few days earlier on official Pentagon stationery and for a more personal handwritten note several days later.

Dated June 27, 2011, Gates's official letter read:

> *Dear General Petraeus,*
>
> *Please accept my congratulations and my deepest appreciation as you retire after nearly four decades of military service. To call that service remarkable is an understatement.*
>
> *The strength of the United States military throughout our history has been its resilience and adaptability in the face of new threats and challenges. You have stepped forward as the indispensible soldier/scholar of this era, transforming the U.S. Army, and the entire military approach to warfighting, from training to capabilities.*
>
> *In the field, you have changed the course of two wars, an unprecedented accomplishment. I especially commend you for answering the call to serve as Commander, International Security Assistance Force in Afghanistan after sacrificing, and achieving, so much over the long fight in Iraq. But I believe your greatest legacy will be as the leader, mentor, and role-model of one of the most battle-tested, adaptive, and innovative generations of military leaders the United States has ever*

*known—a generation ready and able to defend the United
States against whatever threats the future may hold.*

*You have risen to every challenge and fulfilled every charge
your country has asked of you and more. As you lay down one
heavy mantle of service and responsibility, only to pick up
another as you assume my one-time post as Director, Central
Intelligence Agency, it has been a privilege and a pleasure to
work with you these past 4 1/2 years.*

I wish you and your family the very best for the future.

Sincerely,
Robert M. Gates

The handwritten note, dated June 29, on a secretary of Defense note-
pad, read:

Dear Dave,

*As I leave this position, I want to tell you how much I have
enjoyed working with you over the last 4 1/2 years. We have had
a unique partnership spanning two wars. I would be hard
pressed to identify a secretary and a field commander who
worked more closely—and beneficially—together. I suspect we
will write about these times, and I, for one, would be gratified to
have Dr. Petraeus review my draft.*

*I wish you all the best at CIA and thank you from the bottom
of my heart for your brilliant and courageous service.*

All the best,
Bob Gates

Petraeus responded in a note that "Dr. Petraeus" would be honored to
help, adding, "Allow me, also, to thank you again for your determined, prin-
cipled, and visionary leadership over the past 4 1/2 years—and, again, for

'having my back' and 'having our troopers' backs' throughout that time!" He
followed up with a formal letter of his own, on July 12:

> *Dear Mr. Secretary:*
>
> *Thank you for your letter of June 27, 2011.*
>
> *I cannot tell you how much I appreciate your kind words.
> I remain deeply grateful for your support, counsel and
> mentorship over the past 4 ½ years. As I noted when you were
> here in June, you "had my back" throughout that time. More
> importantly, you had our troopers'—and our families'—backs
> throughout that time, too. You were masterful in ensuring they
> received the support and resources they needed, even when
> there was institutional resistance. As you well know, we never
> would have gotten MRAPs, more UAVs, M-ATVs, much of the
> Counter-IED systems, and a host of other vital enablers, were it
> not for your determined leadership. Please accept my sincere
> appreciation for that leadership and for your steadfast
> commitment during your time as our Secretary.*
>
> *Best wishes to you and the Gates tribe as you begin the next
> chapter of your life. And thanks again for all that you have
> done for our Soldiers, Sailors, Airmen, Marines and Coast
> Guardsmen and their families.*
>
> *Very respectfully,*
>
> *David H. Petraeus
> General, United States Army Commander*

LATER THAT MORNING, Ahmed Wali Karzai, the president's half brother
and the most powerful man in Kandahar, was killed at his home by one of
his security force commanders, his trusted aide, Sardar Muhammad. Muhammad was immediately shot and killed by Karzai's bodyguards. Ahmed

Wali Karzai and Muhammad were so close that the killing was at first seen as a personal vendetta. But in the days following the assassination, Afghan officials and members of the Karzai family began to express their suspicions that the Taliban had somehow turned Muhammad. It was ultimately determined, however, that Muhammad had become a heavy narcotics user and that he had learned that Ahmed Wali Karzai was going to fire him. Muhammad confronted Karzai, and the argument escalated into Muhammad shooting and killing Karzai. Even so, the mere suspicion of Taliban involvement sowed fear and made those Afghans closest to the United States realize that if someone as powerful and well guarded as the president's half brother could be assassinated, no one was really safe. Indeed, two days later, a suicide bomber with an explosive hidden in a turban attacked a memorial service for the slain Karzai at a mosque in Kandahar, killing himself and three others.

The attack came on the same day that the United Nations Assistance Mission in Afghanistan released its midyear report, *Protection of Civilians in Armed Conflict*. Its stark conclusion: "In the first six months of 2011, the armed conflict in Afghanistan brought increasingly grim impacts and a bleak outlook for Afghan civilians." Civilian deaths totaled 1,462, a 15 percent increase over the same period a year earlier. The UN attributed 80 percent to the Taliban and other insurgents, and it noted that the overall number killed by the Taliban had increased by 28 percent. Fourteen percent of the deaths were attributed to ISAF and Afghan forces, and the number killed had decreased by 9 percent from the previous year. The deaths occurred during an overall escalation of violence.

"The mounting toll of civilian casualties in the first six months of 2011 represents a deepening entrenchment of violence in the everyday lives of Afghans," the UN concluded. Behind the grim statistics, there were a number of alarming developments. The UN documented the first two confirmed cases of attacks on hospitals. The recruitment and use of children as suicide bombers was also noted. The UN found that the increasing use of "night raids" by U.S. and Afghan special forces—three hundred a month, on average—had resulted in fewer civilian deaths: thirty fewer than were seen in the first six months of 2010. Still, the UN said that night raids "remain one of the most despised tactics in the eyes of the Afghan population." While night raids produced fewer civilian casualties, ISAF air strikes produced more, despite all of Petraeus's efforts. Air strikes were the leading cause of civilian deaths, claiming seventy-nine lives in the first half of 2011, a 14 percent increase.

Petraeus noted that there had been more than 1,600 strikes involving improvised explosive devices in June, the highest number recorded for any month during ten years of war. U.S. military officials knew that the Taliban's deadly reliance on IEDs was the direct result of Pakistan's inability or unwillingness to stop large quantities of ammonium nitrate fertilizer from being smuggled into Afghanistan. Petraeus had become increasingly concerned about the insurgent sanctuaries in Pakistan and other Pakistani support for the Taliban from the moment he'd arrived in Afghanistan a year earlier; in fact, he had been seized with it as the Central Command commander as well. He had less influence while in command in Afghanistan, but it didn't stop him from engaging when he could.

Even as U.S.-Pakistani relations had deteriorated in the wake of the bin Laden raid in Islamabad and the Obama administration had suspended $800 million in military aid, Petraeus tried to remain relatively optimistic—publicly, at least—about his ability to work with the Pakistanis. As the UN released its midyear report, Petraeus and Allen flew to Pakistan to meet with General Ashfaq Kayani, the head of the Pakistani military. As bad as the relationship was, the situation could only get worse in Afghanistan if that relationship fell apart completely. As Petraeus noted in a video teleconference he gave that week to Princeton alumni, "We've seen that movie before." He was referring to the American withdrawal of support for Pakistan and lack of interest in Afghanistan after the end of the so-called Charlie Wilson's War—the support through Pakistan of the mujahideen fighters who forced the Soviets to withdraw from Afghanistan in 1989, after nearly ten years of war.

THAT SATURDAY, July 16, Petraeus attended his final senior security *shura* at the Ministry of Defense, attended by Defense minister Wardak and the deputy minister from the Ministry of the Interior, among others. Listening to the discussion topics that day, Petraeus knew the future in Afghanistan was tenuous but far from hopeless. There had been setbacks, chief among them the recent infiltrations of the Afghan armed forces by insurgents and the worrisome Taliban assassination campaign. When Petraeus had the chance to speak at the end of the two-hour session in the crowded room, he wanted to assuage concerns, which had spread like wildfire, about the U.S. drawdown. He reminded the senior Afghan leaders in the room that the Afghan armed forces would be increasing by 70,000 by the time the last of the surge forces left the country next fall. "The U.S. drawdown is made possible by our combined progress," he said. "We'll draw down 10,000 by the end of 2011, and 20,000 more by September 2012. This will allow us to fulfill our original surge timeline and allow Afghans to assume increasing responsibility for security." He also wanted to assure them that there was no run to the exits. "The U.S. drawdown is not a reflection of a changing strategy or overall campaign plan. It does not undermine the 2014 commitment and post-2014 commitment," he said. "We will not abandon our partners before you are capable, nor will we withdraw precipitously."

PETRAEUS WAITED UNTIL the last possible day, his second-to-last in command, to preside over his first-ever battlefield promotion. He had a special place in his heart for Sergeant Landon Nordby, a member of his personal security detail in Iraq and then in Afghanistan, a highly professional NCO and one of the greatest all-around athletes Petraeus had encountered in the Army. Petraeus had fought to bring back battlefield promotions in 2008, during the latter part of the surge in Iraq. The practice had been discontinued after the Vietnam War, with the advent of the Army's centralized promotion system. But Petraeus pushed the idea when he was commanding the effort in Iraq, based on his belief that promoting soldiers at war purely on the basis of "extraordinary performance of duties while serving in combat or under combat conditions"—with no promotion boards or time-in-grade requirements necessary—would be hugely motivational. "Today," he said, "I am enormously proud, as is Command Sergeant Major Hill," who had helped him gain approval of the battlefield promotions in Iraq, "to promote Sergeant Landon Nordby to staff sergeant, in recognition of his performance and proven ability to carry a few more rocks in his rucksack of responsibility." It was a special moment for Petraeus and his inner circle, many of whom had uprooted their lives to follow Petraeus to Afghanistan—a number after having followed him to Central Command from Iraq.

PETRAEUS ALSO released his farewell message to the troops that day:

As I prepare to depart Afghanistan, I want you to know what an honor it has been to be your commander for the past year. During that time, you and our Afghan counterparts have achieved important progress in a hugely complex, enormously important mission. In the face of resilient enemies and innumerable other challenges, you and our partners have halted the momentum of the insurgents in much of the country and reversed it in a number of key areas. While much hard work clearly lies ahead, the achievements of the past year have enabled gains in security, governance, and development and have helped bring new hope to the Afghan people in a number of villages, districts, and provinces.

He ended with a reference to his impending retirement, the event he dreaded as much as relinquishing command.

When I take off the uniform for the last time on 31 August 2011, I will recall with deep respect and enormous gratitude the extraordinary troopers with whom I have been privileged to serve in my 37 years in uniform. That is particularly true for those with whom I have served on deployments in the past decade in tough, important coalition missions. Among those in the front rank of such troopers will be each of you with whom I have had the honor of soldiering during the surge here in the Shadow of the Hindu Kush.

But the Taliban were determined to keep Kabul on edge as Petraeus prepared to depart. On the eve of his change of command, two gunmen broke into the Kabul home of Jan Mohammed Khan and killed the former governor of Uruzgan Province. Khan was a close adviser and political ally of President Karzai. The gunmen also killed Mohammed Hasham Watanwal, a member of Parliament from Uruzgan. A Taliban spokesman called Khan a "stooge of American invaders." As Petraeus occasionally observed, it is the rare day in command that does not have bad news. His final day in command was no exception.

THE NIGHT BEFORE his change of command, Petraeus was scheduled to attend a ramp ceremony on the military tarmac of the Kabul International Airport to honor soldiers who had been killed in action. Petraeus continued to work in his office until he was summoned to the memorial. This ramp ceremony was for seven fallen French soldiers killed in three separate incidents that week in Kapisa Province. Five of them had died in a suicide attack earlier in the week that also killed an Afghan civilian. It was the worst loss of life for French forces since August 2008, when ten soldiers were killed in a Taliban ambush east of Kabul. Seventy French soldiers had died in Afghanistan since the war began in 2001. Around four thousand French troops were serving in Afghanistan, most in Kapisa, and Petraeus was impressed with their counterinsurgency efforts and grateful for their contributions. He had met French president Nicolas Sarkozy earlier in the week and expressed his gratitude, especially given the ambivalence of French citizens over the war. He had strived to keep the coalition together, and paying his last respects to these French soldiers was, in his mind, a commander's responsibility in support of coalition cohesion.

Finally, as midnight approached, Hickman signaled that it was time to head to the ceremony. Petraeus walked with his team and Lieutenant General Allen to the ISAF compound soccer field to catch his helicopter to the airport. They lifted off to the *whup-whup-whup* of the rotors into the Kabul night. Petraeus sat looking out the window in silence as they flew.

There were more than two hundred French troopers in blue berets lined up to form a single-file man-made tunnel from the open-ended French cargo plane that would carry the fallen soldiers home. The night was dark, but rampside stadium lights and headlights from parked military vehicles shone on the entourage. Somber music began to play. Senior French officers then slowly marched from the aircraft down the long line of steely-faced troops, saluting slowly on every fifth step. French troops hoisted the French blue-white-and-red-draped coffins to their shoulders. They walked slowly, in a quiet cadence, with the bodies of their comrades on their shoulders, down the two-hundred-yard tunnel of soldiers and dignitaries and up the yawning rear ramp into the belly of the plane. A moderator gave remarks in French as the troops paid their respects. Many of the soldiers standing at attention on that dark, quiet night didn't know who the fallen troopers were or how they had died. Neither did Petraeus. Ramp ceremonies in Afghanistan were held anytime a soldier gave the ultimate sacrifice. An attempt was made to send the remains of the fallen home within twenty-four hours of their deaths. It was optional for troops to attend, but there was always a substantial turnout, even after midnight.

Petraeus, Allen, UN special representative Staffan de Mistura and the other leaders stood at attention as still as statues, close to the French cargo jet. Petraeus had attended too many of these in his years in the military; these young men were the same age as his son, Stephen, he thought to himself. The melancholy songs reminded him of his first real exposure to significant casualties after seventeen of his men from the 101st Airborne died in a tragic helicopter crash in Iraq. The emotion triggered had been so strong at times over the years that he would occasionally put his head down on his desk, but only when he thought his staff was not watching. Petraeus never let anyone see this side of him. He had learned to hide the heavy burdens of command during his first tour in Iraq in 2003. But on the night before his final day in command, at a 1:00 A.M. ceremony for more of the war's dead, the mask felt heavy.

"At the end of the day, there is only one commander, and he is the one who feels the ultimate responsibility for committing these troops who made the ultimate sacrifice. We are all changed by this," he later relayed to a friend. "You carry a sense of responsibility for those who never go home or whose lives are changed forever from catastrophic injuries. And there is an added feeling of guilt from departing the theater earlier than planned as well, of leaving your guys, your team while they are still in combat. A commander feels, understandably, this extraordinary weight of responsibility. It is impossible to understand it without having lived it. You cannot explain it to others. It doesn't get easier and you don't get hardened to it."

THE DAY OF HIS change of command, Petraeus awoke at 5:00 A.M. He hadn't returned to his room after the ramp ceremony until 1:30 A.M., and he hadn't slept well. Petraeus had his personal security detachment meet him at 6:00 A.M. for a final morning run. Three soldiers arrived to accompany the general on what would be his final laps around the ISAF and U.S. Embassy compound. Normally inquisitive and humorous when he ran, he was now serious and contemplative; despite the early hour, he wore sunglasses. He barely spoke. His focus, he later confessed, was basic: Get to the other end of the day.

After the run, Petraeus donned his camouflage battle fatigues and was driven to the palace, where he would receive an award from President Karzai. It was the highest Afghan award, the Medal of Ghazi Wazir Mohammad Akbar Khan. Karzai made the presentation in front of Afghanistan's National Security Team. Petraeus thanked Karzai, expressed his gratitude and said he had always thought of himself serving President Obama, the secretary general of NATO *and* Karzai, the head of the Afghan state. "I've always regarded myself as your soldier and your commander," he said, pledging continued support once he became director of the Central Intelligence Agency. He departed as swiftly as he had come, heading back to ISAF headquarters. He attended the ceremony for the promotion of his successor, Lieutenant General Allen, to the rank of general and paused for a moment at a short reception in Destille Gardens, across from the headquarters, as the crowd of guests arrived. Then it was time for the change of command.

As the ceremony began, the sun poured down on the peach-colored building that had been first a military installation and then a military sports club but now served as the ISAF headquarters. With the building as the backdrop, Petraeus stood ramrod straight and saluted as the 1st Cavalry Division Band and the Afghan Army National Band played the national anthems of both Afghanistan and the United States. Spectators sat under blue tents. Ambassador Eikenberry began the ceremony, recalling Petraeus's comments to him from the previous year's Fourth of July celebration at the embassy: "Civil-military cooperation is not optional." Then he presented the State Department's Secretary's Distinguished Service Award to Petraeus on behalf of Secretary of State Hillary Clinton. The ambassador was followed on the podium by Admiral Mullen, the chairman of the Joint Chiefs of Staff, General Wolf Langheld, Petraeus's NATO boss, and the Afghan minister of Defense, all of whom praised Petraeus for his effort and his sacrifice. Petraeus then formally handed the colors of command of ISAF and U.S. Forces–Afghanistan to his close friend and colleague General Allen, a fourth star now on Allen's collars. Petraeus delivered his address at a wooden podium, his battle fatigues decorated with two additional medals he had just been awarded, the Defense Distinguished Service Medal and the NATO Meritorious Service Medal.

After encapsulating the year, he closed simply:

> For the better part of the last decade, I have been deployed in Bosnia, Iraq, the greater Central Command region and, now, Afghanistan. Culminating that time by serving with you this past year here has

been an extraordinary honor. At countless dusty outposts and operating bases across Afghanistan, on innumerable patrols through marketplaces and bazaars, I have had the opportunity to see you in action. Each of you has demonstrated extraordinary professionalism. In crushing heat and in numbing cold—from the deserts of southern Afghanistan to the peaks of the Hindu Kush—you have shown initiative, determination, innovativeness and courage. You have been diplomats as well as warriors, statesmen as well as soldiers. Your performance has been, in a word, awesome.

In a poem published a few years ago, a British trooper who was deployed here in Afghanistan captured eloquently the emotions of those who serve and those who sacrifice. He wrote:

> *And what is asked for the service we give?*
> *No high praise or riches if we should live,*
> *Just silence from friends, our name on a wall,*
> *If this time around, it is I that fall.*

To the families, friends and countrymen of those who fell *this time around*—and to *all* those who have served and sacrificed here—you have my deepest respect and my eternal gratitude. The coalition and Afghanistan can never thank you enough for all that you have given as we have carried on with this enormously difficult, hugely important endeavor.

Petraeus clearly was moved, but he kept the mask in place.

Less than an hour later, after shaking hundreds of hands in a long receiving line, he walked briskly to the soccer field and jumped into his seat in the back of his helicopter. Accompanied by Colonel Hickman and a cadre of his closest aides, Petraeus watched the ISAF compound shrink in size as the Black Hawk lifted off to fly him over to Kabul International Airport, where he would begin the next phase of his journey home.

Once inside the Gulfstream V, he kept himself occupied, distracted and engaged. He had wanted to hand General Allen a neatly wrapped package, a war that had taken a decisive turn for America and for the people of Afghanistan, but he knew that, despite the hard-fought progress, that wasn't yet the case. He had done all he could for the war effort, Petraeus believed, trying to put various thoughts behind him and compartmentalize his feelings. He felt Allen was prepared to carry that baton. He answered numerous e-mails, read through letters given to him at the ceremony and conversed for much of the four-hour flight to Turkey.

Petraeus had grown accustomed to the intensity of combat command, to the adrenaline of always needing to be "on," to the fatigue he fought off after fast-paced eighteen-hour days, one after another. "The feeling of leaving combat command is like being in a car and slamming on the power brakes, pulling the emergency brake and deploying a drogue chute all at once," he later explained, trying to provide an appropriate metaphor for the feeling a wartime commander has when it all comes to an end. "It's hard on the system—be it vehicle or man—to slow down." And Petraeus really didn't want to slow down, at least not yet.

CHAPTER 13

STILL ALL IN

After he relinquished the final command of his career to General Allen at ISAF headquarters, Petraeus flew from Kabul to Europe for a tour through several ISAF-contributing national capitals: Ankara, Berlin, Paris and London. He did not think of it as any kind of victory lap. In private, he was still processing his command and setting aside his regrets about departing before the end of this fighting season. Thankfully, the schedule was tightly packed, and there was barely time to think about it as his team jetted through four coalition countries en route back to Washington. He had helped to prevent a rush to the exits over the past year, and he wanted to express his gratitude to some of the key members of the alliance.

The stay in London was longer than the others. This would be his final opportunity in uniform to say thanks to the partner who had contributed the most in Iraq, Afghanistan and the greater CENTCOM area. In addition to the usual calls at Number 10 Downing Street with the prime minister and at the Defence and Foreign ministries, he had time for dinner with colleagues with whom he'd been through some tough times. On the second night, Ambassador Mark Sedwill, the talented British diplomat who had departed Kabul in April after serving with Petraeus as the NATO senior civilian representative in Kabul, hosted a private dinner and roundtable discussion for him with diplomatic and military officials in London. Sedwill and Petraeus had teamed up to corral the coalition into a cohesive team the prior year. Moving the endgame to 2014 was perhaps the most significant accomplishment of the past year, and Sedwill had played a key role in that effort. With Sedwill now serving as the U.K.'s special representative for Afghanistan and Pakistan, Petraeus would no doubt be seeing him again in his new position at the CIA. Officials from the British foreign ministry and intelligence services joined the dinner as well; their focus was on the future. They all knew the significance of Petraeus's next post, and they were eager to begin thinking about how they could all work together with him in that role.

On his last night, Petraeus attended an intimate dinner with a half-dozen old friends, the British "Band of Brothers" with whom he'd served in Iraq, most of whom had also served in Afghanistan or at a minimum were presently dealing with the war from the Ministry of Defence. His former deputy from Afghanistan was there among them—a great officer whose son had lost his legs to an IED in Helmand Province. The dinner was hosted in the quarters of the senior U.K. military officer, General Sir David Richards, who lived within the grounds of Kensington Palace. The evening was a time for reminiscing about some of their shared memories, but it left Petraeus wistful about relinquishing command and leaving this brotherhood behind.

Petraeus had volunteered to remain in Kabul through the end of the fighting season in the fall, although he later acknowledged that the president had been wise to ask him to be in place as CIA director in time for the tenth anniversary of the 9/11 attacks, particularly when an explicit threat emerged in the days prior to the anniversary. He had convinced himself that he was more of a surge guy than a drawdown guy anyway, and he'd set up Allen to take the reins for the rest of the fighting season. Beyond that, Petraeus had never wavered in his desire to "stay in the fight" by moving to the CIA. He had been approached with lucrative book deals and equally remunerative consulting positions, but they held no appeal, especially when compared with running the CIA. He wanted to continue to serve his country and felt very privileged to have been provided such an opportunity.

The trip through Europe had been productive with members of the alliance and for Petraeus personally. He'd shown the flag and expressed appreciation. He had had a few brief moments to reflect and walk down memory lane with old battlefield friends who reassured him that his military career had made a difference. And he'd made a point to take a little time for himself, which included his favorite way to reflect—running through Hyde Park, getting up to twelve miles with some of his team the final morning he was there.

As he left his final command behind and began the transition to a new chapter in life, Petraeus lamented his unfamiliarity with Afghanistan when he'd first arrived in Kabul. He noted that he had lacked the fingertip feel he'd developed for Iraq after two and a half years on the ground there prior to taking command of the surge in 2007. "[Afghanistan] was a heck of a fast ride, and in truth, there was a lack of preparation," he said. "Don't get me wrong: I'd made numerous visits, led the civ-mil conferences, participated in the policy reviews, and conducted innumerable video teleconferences and intelligence 'deep dives.' But that's very different from being the commander of the theater of Afghanistan, learning about it village by village, valley by valley, developing the kind of granular understanding that is needed even at the strategic level."

Looking back, he reckoned that while he'd gained a handle on the south pretty quickly, it had taken him "a good six months or more," in particular, to develop a coherent vision for eastern Afghanistan's twelve provinces, each with its own government and cast of tribal leaders, warlords and enemy commanders. His ultimate plan involved a greater focus on confronting the insurgents while seeking to build local and national Afghan forces and governance. Too many combat units, he had found at the outset, were focused solely on partnering with Afghan forces and helping the local Afghan government—and insufficiently focused on countering the Taliban.

Overall, Petraeus felt that the military campaign, while facing innumerable challenges, was moving in the right direction. He had enormous confidence in the new civil-military team of General Allen, U.S. ambassador Ryan Crocker, and NATO senior civilian representative Ambassador Simon Gass, another British diplomat who had impressed Petraeus. Across Afghanistan, enemy-initiated attacks from January to August were down 3 percent compared with 2010, although ISAF had *expected* a 17 to 30 percent increase, given the increase in troop strength—25,000 ISAF forces and 60,000 ANSF troop and police forces. In fact, enemy-initiated attacks for the period June–August 2011 were 17 percent lower than in the same period in 2010, and in seventeen of the previous twenty-two weeks (through September 2011) they were lower than in the same week in 2010. The command had not seen this sustained year-on-year level of decrease since the insurgency had begun to intensify in 2007. The trend ultimately would continue through September and into the fall, though sensational attacks would continue as well.

A concern Petraeus shared with others in the command, given the faster-than-originally-anticipated drawdown, was the inability to hold and build in the important areas that the surge of military forces had successfully cleared. Even while commencing the scheduled drawdown of troops, Petraeus maintained hope and confidence that the Allen-Crocker-Gass team would maintain the momentum of the previous year. Overall, the progress that the troopers had achieved in key areas had set the conditions for further progress across the Afghan theater, especially as Afghan forces continued to grow.

The west and north were relatively pacified and on the way to transition, although they would experience periodic attacks and require continued attention. The gamut of Anaconda strategy activities was under way in those areas, albeit with relatively low levels of ISAF and Afghan forces. The latter needed to be built up as local police, governance, reintegration and rule-of-law initiatives were also pursued. These efforts continued to be enabled by focused conventional force-clearance operations, targeted special operations, and reintegration, which had made a dent in the insurgent ranks in the northwest, in particular.

The campaign plan for the east that Petraeus had inherited from McChrystal and with considerable modification bequeathed to General Allen was now redesigned to try to cut off the insurgents' infiltration routes through the mountains from Pakistan. The east had not been the main effort for the surge of forces in the past year, and the security situation remained tenuous, as Vowell's and Fivecoat's tours had shown. Attacks continued to increase in the east, up 17 percent for the period June–August 2011, compared with the same period the previous year. The east's importance could not be overstated, given the buffer it provides for Kabul. "Keep in mind that Kabul is vastly more important . . . than Baghdad was in Iraq," Petraeus observed. "In Baghdad, there were three car bombs per day on average in the second month I was the commander there, but the country still survived. If that happened in Kabul, or even if there was one car bomb per day, you'd lose the nongovernmental organizations, the international organizations, embassies and other elements, all of which support Afghanistan to a much greater degree than was the case in Iraq." Petraeus considered Kabul the key security inkblot or oil spot in the counterinsurgency lexicon: "You can't have a high level of violence [in Kabul] and have the country overall survive. So we put a lot of effort into determining how to move forward in the east; it probably took us a good six or more months, in fact, to develop a coherent plan for that."

Part of that plan, across the theater, included ensuring that there was a proper focus on defeating the insurgency. "In some cases, the mission statements when I took over read, 'Our mission is to partner with Afghan forces and connect GIRoA to the people,'" Petraeus recalled. He continued:

Yet in some areas, there was an insurgency raging and there was no mention of either defeating, disrupting or denying the insurgents and the insurgency in that area—whatever was appropriate—although [security] was the prerequisite for progress in any of the other areas. Security was essential to enable progress in governance, local economic revival, provision of basic services, and construction of schools, health clinics, roads and all the other infrastructure. There needed to be a sharpened focus on the insurgency and the vital importance of achieving a sufficient level of security so that you could then focus on connecting GIRoA to the people. If there was a sufficiently "good GIRoA" then it *should* be enabled [by security] to be connected to the people.

In the southwest and south, Petraeus had seen the Marines and British forces solidify gains in Helmand Province and the U.S. soldiers and Canadian forces make noteworthy gains clearing the Taliban from its birthplace around Kandahar. According to the Afghan Mission Network, "attacks during the period June–August 2011 were 40 percent lower than the same period in 2010," and "some districts in the Central Helmand Valley saw reductions in violence of nearly 80 percent." In the same period in RC South (principally Kandahar Province), "enemy-initiated attacks reported during the period June–August 2011 were 10 percent lower than the same period last year." Flynn's area in the Arghandab had been virtually pacified. Pundits argued that the selective lethal application of force used there would turn the local population against the coalition and that the rebuilding strategy, disparaged by some as shortsighted, would not survive transfer to the next U.S. unit. To the contrary, Flynn's replacement later reported, Flynn's security gains enabled the reconstruction of Tarok Kolache and other villages as well as other economic and developmental infrastructure, such as canals and roads. Decreased violence and evidence of popular support—including an increase in local-resident tips about IEDs, a functioning district center, the consistent attendance by village maliks at district *shuras,* and the turnover, by the fall, of six U.S. Army strongpoints to ANSF—seemed to indicate that the surge in that area had been effective. But even there Petraeus had not declared victory. As he turned command over to Allen, violence was, to be sure, increasing across Afghanistan, as it did every summer. Counter to all predictions, however, the increase was at lower rather than higher levels compared with the previous year.

Civilian casualties, numbers of attacks and troop casualties had been critical concerns all year. Petraeus kept track of those many times on a given day. ISAF-caused civilian fatalities were down, although overall civilian casualties were up. Coalition-force casualties, which included battlefield injuries and deaths, were significant, but overall, ISAF trooper deaths in Petraeus's final months were down from the previous year. Such metrics were a challenge to compare, but the increase in forces over that time normally would have meant an increase in deaths, not a decrease.

As long as total numbers of incidents were almost where they had been the previous year and overall civilian fatalities were up—even though an overwhelming majority were caused by insurgents and not ISAF—it was difficult for analysts to conclude that the security environment on the whole was significantly improved. The Taliban had advanced their own special operations strategy, powered not by drones and missiles and night raids but by infiltrators into Afghan army units, control over cell-phone-tower use, continued use of suicide bombers, targeted assassinations and spectacular attacks—all of which drew greater media attention and psychological weight over attacks against troops in the field. Petraeus wished he had been able to quell more of that. But to argue that violence and use of such tactics was a sign that ISAF and Afghan forces had failed was to miss the point that progress and violence can coexist in a war zone. If analysts had made that mistake in March 1945, they would have argued that the Allies were on the verge of losing World War II.

There were other lessons to be learned in this theater, including the challenges and virtues of coalition warfare. The greatest challenge, of course, was the high maintenance required to keep the members marching together and, Petraeus frankly reflected, staying in the formation. The national caveats and the variance in levels of training, capability and readiness required a nuanced understanding of partner capabilities. The innumerable visits by national leaders required an extraordinary amount of time in key-leader engagements. Petraeus had had several visits each week from visiting coalition delegations, sometimes several a day. Even so, he enjoyed the intellectual stimulation and the opportunity to help diplomatic partners expand the coalition. By the end of his tour, forty-nine international partners and Afghanistan were contributing forces to the mission, and other countries contributed substantial financial resources.

"Coalition management is a hugely important function of a coalition commander," Petraeus observed, noting that ISAF had the largest number of countries ever united in a theater of war. Iraq, by contrast, was "essentially a coalition dominated by one, with the 165,000 American troops vastly outnumbering the coalition contribution, though the U.K. and other countries did, indeed, make important contributions. And keep in mind as well," Petraeus noted, "that Afghanistan is vastly more dependent on what these coalition countries and the international organizations and the NGOs and other groups provide to them. Because unlike Iraq, which had a substantial revenue stream—$100 billion a year at the height of the oil prices— Afghanistan generates only about $1.8 billion. [Although they are] very proud of the steady increase in their revenue, Afghanistan is a country that is, nonetheless, dependent to a huge extent on donors."

Petraeus recognized that one requirement for keeping the coalition together was coming up with an overall transition concept and mechanism; developing these concepts, he believed, was one of his most important contributions. Many of these ideas, of course, he had learned in Haiti, Bosnia and Iraq, all of which required varying levels of both coalition warfare and multi-year transition road maps.

It took true civil-military effort to corral the forty-nine contributing nations into staying the course to ensure that transition happened properly. In order to ensure that coalition members remained engaged and subscribed to a proper transition process, ISAF leadership would have to buy more time—an effort that happened in the fall of 2010 at the Lisbon conference. Petraeus noted, "We had an eye on the Lisbon summit which took place in November 2010 from the very beginning of my time. . . . Ambassador Sedwill and I in particular put a lot of effort into informing individual [contributing nations] about all the different [lines of effort] . . . laying out and refining transition concepts and then plans and assessments, and then also . . . encouraging the idea that the focus should be extended from that of July 2011 to that of the end of 2014, the date by which President Karzai publicly had said Afghan forces should be in the lead across the country for security tasks." The national leaders at the Lisbon summit embraced this concept, and by September 2011, three provinces and four districts had successfully been transitioned.

Transition meant a shift from ISAF-led military operations to Afghan National Security Forces–led operations and local security initiatives. The continued growth of the Afghan National Security Forces had, therefore, become a critical component of transition. Lieutenant General Caldwell had done a "very impressive" job, Petraeus thought, leading that endeavor and building a largely U.S.-led effort into what became the NATO Training Mission–Afghanistan. Petraeus had lived through the same industrial-strength effort in Iraq as he worked to stand up the security force training effort there, and he knew how daunting the task was; he sought, therefore, to give Caldwell the total support that many perceived he himself had not had in full while in Iraq. The effort was challenged by issues of Afghan desertion, illiteracy, inadequate infrastructure, insufficient numbers of trainers and cost sustainability—challenges similar to what Petraeus had seen in Iraq, though the challenges associated with some of these shortcomings were higher in Afghanistan. But those issues were being addressed, to varying degrees, and by the end of Petraeus's tour, Afghan troop numbers had risen from approximately 191,000 in the fall of 2009 to 305,000 in the fall of 2011.

At the end of the day, however, the numbers of ANSF were not yet enough to provide security for the entire country; Petraeus hoped the local police could be the putty between the locations ANSF did control. He felt, in fact, that one of the most important initiatives on his watch was gaining President Karzai's approval for the Afghan Local Police program. It had been one of his key agenda items early on, even before he arrived in Kabul. Petraeus acknowledged that he may have had a catalytic effect of convincing the Afghans to embrace the concept, "but the fact is that Karzai honestly drove it."

Some analysts felt Petraeus put too much emphasis on the ALP, given that there were only 6,500 by the time he left; these skeptics also speculated about the risks of untethered, autonomous local defense initiatives that were not linked to the government but whose links to the Ministry of the Interior and U.S. partners were solid. The ALP elements, Petraeus firmly maintained, were vital to linking and expanding the security inkblots in order to ensure that the insurgents, especially those hiding in sanctuaries across the border, would meet with resistance. In remote areas—often border-crossing areas—where ANSF members might not have a presence, the perfect counterinsurgent, Petraeus thought, was a local who could detect and deter insurgent movement from the sanctuaries in Pakistan into Afghanistan. And the partnership with U.S. Special Forces and Afghan uniformed police meant that good links were maintained with ISAF and the Afghan Ministry of the Interior, especially as the latter paid the salaries for ALP members.

Petraeus knew from his first days in Kabul that insurgent sanctuaries in Pakistan, especially those in the FATA and Balochistan, could conceivably doom the war effort. If anything, the U.S. relationship with Pakistan had deteriorated during his year in command, through no fault of his own. How America could be fighting a war against an insurgency that was allegedly supported by, to some unclear degree, Pakistan's intelligence service, the Inter-Services Intelligence agency, incensed many in Washington. The issue would undoubtedly follow Petraeus to his next assignment.

As Petraeus left the war theater, some of his staff reflected on the comprehensive efforts related to the campaign. "What is significant," shared Colonel Mike Meese, Petraeus's ISAF deputy chief of staff, "is not any one of these activities—ALP, security, special operations, economic development, rule of law or the other lines of effort—but that Petraeus continuously pushed all of us to think broadly about how to get *everything* to work in warfare, which is ultimately a human endeavor, not just a video game."

In his year in Afghanistan, Petraeus reaffirmed what he'd first learned as a student of Vietnam and counterinsurgency and, soon after his academic days, in person in Central America: the importance of developing host-nation governance and rule-of-law capacity, at all levels, in order to achieve legitimacy in the eyes of the people and gain their support. The aforementioned challenges with Karzai, however, including the Kabul Bank scandal and reconciliation initiatives, were beyond Petraeus's purview. Although he, and ISAF, remained involved on some levels, these were primarily civilian initiatives. But in spite of the civil-military campaign's best intentions, including Brigadier General McMaster's—and Karzai's own—best efforts to counter corruption, Karzai's government remained beset by corrupt elements. In this vein, Petraeus reaffirmed that the "establishment of rule of law is very difficult in the presence of criminal patronage networks and an illegal narcotics industry." He maintained that the rule of law was essential to earning support of the people (as the Taliban can provide speedy justice if the government doesn't). The ISAF and embassy teams had made strides in the past year, but there was significant work to be done to build capacity.

As the war rages on, it remains difficult to make a conclusive judgment about the outcome. On the one hand, Petraeus succeeded in establishing the momentum Obama needed to begin the drawdown of U.S. forces from a position of reasonable strength. The president's selection of Petraeus for the CIA position seemed to confirm that the administration believed Petraeus was someone who constantly produced "results." On the other hand, the challenges of holding and building in areas where ISAF and ANSF efforts had cleared, especially in light of the drawdown surge, along with the challenges presented by Pakistan's terror sanctuaries and a host-nation government of limited capacity, presented formidable hurdles for Petraeus's comprehensive civil-military counterinsurgency strategy. Nothing would be easy for his successor there.

His critics argued that Petraeus's unwavering optimism had become a weakness, although he had long rejected the term "optimist"; rather, he repeatedly asserted, he was a "realist," and he went to great lengths to acknowledge the challenges of reality on the ground. He understood that Osama bin Laden's demise in late May had added to a growing sentiment that the rationale for the effort in Afghanistan—to keep al-Qaeda from regrouping in the country—suddenly made less sense than it had previously, but he wouldn't concede the argument. Petraeus believed that abandoning Afghanistan again would have disastrous consequences for America and for the region. It was vital that Afghanistan not once again be a sanctuary for al-Qaeda. He would never give up.

PETRAEUS'S LEGACY to date extends across the Army and the entire U.S. military. He is credited with ushering in a new focus on counterinsurgency while in northern Iraq as a division commander, codifying it in the new

COIN field manual and influencing the Army's preparedness by adapting the institutional training programs constituting the "Road to War " for leaders and units preparing to deploy. He became the face of the war in Iraq while he commanded the surge in 2007 and 2008 and oversaw a campaign that dramatically reduced the violence there, at a time when many senior leaders in America had lost credibility and the nation had come to see Iraq as mission impossible. He helped craft the campaign strategy for Afghanistan, and then, unexpectedly, executed it.

Far beyond his influence on the institutions and commands in Iraq and Afghanistan, Petraeus also left an indelible mark on the next generation of military leaders as a role model of a soldier-scholar-statesman. American military strategist Bernard Brodie noted several decades ago that civilian think tanks and academics were doing more strategic thinking than were military officers. Petraeus sought a different path for himself and encouraged the same for many of his protégés. He advocated civilian graduate school for the benefits of getting out of one's intellectual comfort zone. Creative thinking and the ability to wrestle with intellectual challenges are hugely important in counterinsurgency but also in any campaign's design and execution, he felt; and equipping oneself with new analytical tools, civilian and academic experiences, and various networks had been invaluable for him and—he hoped—for those whom he'd mentored and led.

One of those individuals, Colonel Bill Ostlund, a former platoon leader during Petraeus's battalion command days who later served with him in Afghanistan, remembered being out in the woods at Fort Campbell on a battalion field exercise when Petraeus asked, "Bill, what does 'senseless slaughter' mean to you?" "It means nothing to me, sir; I've never heard that before," then–2nd Lieutenant Ostlund, a former enlisted Ranger, replied. Petraeus responded, "It is the Battle of the Somme, where sixty thousand Brits were killed or wounded on the first day of battle. You not knowing that is an example of why you need a higher education to understand the larger concepts and reasons we train the way we do." That led later to discussion, Ostlund shared, about a quality graduate education, which Ostlund ultimately pursued. "I used to explain," Petraeus shared, "that officers should have sufficient knowledge of history that words or phrases like 'the Somme' mean something to them. The Somme was a tragic event in which part of a generation of young British men were ground into the mud because their senior leaders didn't have the right big ideas."

For the rising generation of the military's leaders, Petraeus not only encouraged the pursuit of intellectual development and a willingness to accept risk; he encouraged initiative and the pursuit of independent action. As Major Lujan's endeavor to stand up an Afghan COIN Advisory and Assistance effort and his sojourns to military operational areas illustrated, many of these young leaders operated with great autonomy in high-risk environments. This generation also assumed diverse leadership roles as engineers, mediators, police, and jobs-placement and military mentors.

They sometimes operated in the "gray area" of moral ambiguity, which forced junior leaders to balance the hard realities of complex situations— such as relatively restrictive rules of engagement, and the presence of innocents on the battlefield—with their need to accomplish the mission and protect their troopers. As in the case of Lieutenant Colonel Flynn's decision to call in an air strike on a bomb-laden village, officers are often held accountable for recognizing the *strategic* implications of their *tactical* actions in a complex moral environment. In truth, their choices can have global repercussions. The leaders of what Petraeus termed the "New Greatest Generation" have shouldered tremendous responsibility since 9/11, bridging the tactical and strategic realms. They have demonstrated resilience and commitment and accrued years of wartime experience—in some cases with five years or more of deployments.

Both the Army and the Marines had shown themselves, in some units at least, capable of effective counterinsurgency operations before Petraeus and Mattis teamed up to draft the new *Counterinsurgency Field Manual* in 2006. But counterinsurgency tactics in Iraq and Afghanistan before the surge in Iraq had been wildly uneven. Petraeus made comprehensive counterinsurgency concepts the primary focus of ground forces in both conflicts and insisted that best practices be followed by all units under his command. His critics in the Army thought the heavy focus on counterinsurgency was myopic in a world where combat action and high-tech missile readiness were equally important for the next war. What would happen, they asked, if the Army had to intervene in a war between North Korea and South Korea? Similarly, counterinsurgency tactics would accomplish little in a conflict with China in which firepower and maneuver would be far more essential.

Petraeus never argued that counterinsurgency was the only way America should fight—only that it was the best way to pursue the wars at hand in Iraq and Afghanistan. In fact, while he was commander at Fort Leavenworth, he advocated readiness for "full-spectrum" military operations as the prudent goal, and he oversaw development of a field manual that emphasized that concept. He always noted that counterinsurgency includes plenty of hard-edged combat—including conventional clearing operations, counterterrorist force raids and use of airpower. Petraeus would later reflect that he might have spent too much time early on in Afghanistan talking about the success of the night raids. As a result, both the media and the Karzai government focused on them. His approach more correctly was a comprehensive one that also included "stability operations"—activities to support establishment of local governance and rule-of-law capability, foster economic development, counter corruption and drug trafficking, train host-nation security forces and reintegrate reconcilable members of the insurgency. These efforts aimed to improve basic services for the people so that they would support the legitimate government rather than the insurgent alternative. A comprehensive approach, and comprehensive readiness, were most prudent.

At his retirement ceremony, Petraeus reiterated this point, noting that "it will be imperative to maintain a force that not only capitalizes on the extraordinary experience and expertise resident in our ranks today but also maintains the versatility and flexibility that have been developed over the past decade in particular. I do believe . . . that we have relearned since 9/11 the timeless lesson that we don't always get to fight the wars for which we are most prepared or most inclined. Given that reality, we will need to main-

tain the full-spectrum capability that we have developed over this last decade of conflict in Iraq, in Afghanistan and elsewhere."

MUCH LIKE AFGHANISTAN for him at the outset, the inner workings of
the CIA will be somewhat unfamiliar terrain to Petraeus. With his passion
for mastering new systems and developing teams and people, he is likely
to be a quick learner. Although the mission and personalities at the CIA will
be somewhat new for him, Petraeus's leadership style there is unlikely to
change.

From Central America and Haiti to Kuwait and Bosnia, from Iraq
to Afghanistan and throughout the Central Command area, Petraeus succeeded in convincing fractious elements to work together. But he could have
his work cut out for him in the U.S. intelligence community, where cooperation has never been a natural instinct. Most immediately, he will have to
gauge how his approach is playing to members of the agency's powerful
Clandestine Service, which includes a surging Special Activities Division,
the CIA's paramilitary arm. Within his first month of assuming its director-
ship, in fact, CIA drones had killed two high-value al-Qaeda terrorist targets
in Yemen: Anwar al-Awlaki, a Yemeni-American imam, and a Saudi-born
American militant, Samir Khan, who produced an English-language al-
Qaeda Web magazine. Several "high value" al-Qaeda leaders were killed in
the rugged tribal areas of Pakistan as well.

On the analytic side of the CIA, Petraeus will have to craft a constructive
relationship with analysts in the Directorate of Intelligence who judged
the war in Afghanistan a "stalemate" in an assessment issued as Petraeus
was leaving Kabul (though, as Petraeus wryly noted, that judgment was an
improvement over the CIA's assessment of the situation in the summer of
2010). Obama had already told him that he expected him to represent the
position of his analysts—but that he also welcomed Petraeus's personal
thoughts when they differ from the agency line.

As the eighth of twenty directors who came to the CIA from a military
background and the second serving out of uniform, he is the first CIA direc-

tor to have commanded large-scale combat operations and overseen a theater full of war and conflict. If the personal informs the professional, he will be well schooled in employment of these national assets.

PETRAEUS'S FORT MYER retirement ceremony, on August 31, 2011, marked the end of one career and the beginning of a new one. Petraeus had requested a joint military parade, not an Army-only procession, to symbolically mark his succession of joint commands in combat. A communion of friends and family—from West Point classmates and Screaming Eagle comrades to diplomatic partners and beyond—and generous remarks from his friend and colleague Admiral Mike Mullen brought Petraeus a sense of closure. As Mullen put it:

> What sets Petraeus apart is not just his ability to visualize the way to victory, but the will, the determination and the resilience to see it through. Afghanistan is now a more secure and hopeful place than a year ago, and while Dave would be the first to tell you that a lot of hard, deadly work remains, the progress has never been more real or the prospects more encouraging. David, you've run the race well, swifter and surer than the rest, and you now stand among the giants not just in our time but of all time, joining the likes of Grant and Pershing and Marshall and Eisenhower as one of the great battle captains of American history. You've expanded our view of the possible, inspiring our military on to historic achievements during some of the most trying times America has ever known. And today you depart our ranks with the sincere thanks of a grateful nation.
>
> As you take the helm of the Central Intelligence Agency, your ability to see the next shot and around the corners will never be more important, and we are blessed that you will continue to serve and lead during these dynamic and uncertain times. T. E. Lawrence, a man who knew a thing or two about insurgencies, once said, "All men dream, but not equally. Those who dream by night, in the dusty recesses of

their minds, wake in the day to find that it was vanity. But the dreamers of the day are dangerous men, for they may act their dreams with open eyes to make it possible." David Petraeus has indeed been a dreamer of the day, dangerous to our enemies but no greater friend to those with whom he fought alongside and fought for. He's been a dreamer with a vision and a plan to get there.

Petraeus, in his farewell address, spoke in terms of gratitude and caution. He thanked his family, his mentors and the troops for all that for which he had been lauded. He warned of cutting the military budget precipitously and beckoned decision makers to take care of the people—the cornerstone of the military. He noted the need to maintain full-spectrum operations capability, recalling once again that the military has to be ready for all contingencies, not just those with which they are the most comfortable. Implicit in his words was the question of whether the military would forget the hard-won lessons it had learned, or take the wrong lesson altogether, from the past decade of war.

He could have used the words he'd written in the concluding pages of his 1987 dissertation:

The senior military thus find themselves in a dilemma. The lessons taken from Vietnam would indicate that, in general, involvement in a counterinsurgency should be avoided. But prudent preparation for a likely contingency (and a general inclination against limiting a president's options) lead the military to recognize that significant emphasis should be given to counterinsurgency forces, equipment, and doctrine. Military leaders are thereby in the difficult position of arguing for the creation of more forces suitable for such conflicts, while simultaneously realizing that they may advise against the use of those forces unless very specific circumstances hold.

Petraeus ended his final address in uniform by quoting his favorite passage, from Teddy Roosevelt's 1910 "Man in the Arena" speech.

"It is not the critic who counts, not the man who points out how the strong man stumbles or where the doer of deeds could have done them better. The credit belongs to the man who is actually in the arena, whose face is marred by dust and sweat and blood, who strives valiantly, who errs and comes up short again and again, because there is no effort without error or shortcoming, but who knows the great enthusiasms, the great devotions, who spends himself for a worthy cause; who, at the best, knows, in the end, the triumph of high achievement and who, at the worst, if he fails, at least fails while daring greatly so that his place shall never be with those cold and timid souls who knew neither victory nor defeat."

The White House seemed prepared to embrace the man whom pundits had tried to pit as an adversary. Immediately following Petraeus's ceremony, President Obama called to congratulate him on a historic career of service in the United States Army and commented on his "extraordinary contributions to our national security in Iraq and Afghanistan." The words meant a lot to Petraeus, and so did the president's expression of gratitude for Petraeus's continued commitment to public service.

A week later, the irony at Petraeus's swearing-in as CIA director was unmistakable as Vice President Biden, the White House's leading Petraeus skeptic, administered the oath of office in the Roosevelt Room while Holly Petraeus held a tan-colored Bible Petraeus had received from his West Point roommate, Chris White, thirty-seven years earlier. Biden had opposed Petraeus's troop surge in Afghanistan and had reportedly seen the general, during the 2009 Afghan policy review, as an inflexible commander whose response to every request had been to demand more troops; more recently, Biden himself had pushed for a more aggressive drawdown in 2011, against the military's recommendations.

Yet those tensions seemed behind both of them now. Biden, in fact, revealed that he had been the one who had suggested to Obama in June 2010 that Petraeus assume command in Kabul. Now, as was customary for cabinet appointees, the vice president had been chosen to preside over swearing Petraeus in as director of the CIA. Petraeus, dressed in a tailored gray suit and burgundy-colored tie, placed his right hand on the Bible and repeated the oath of office after Biden.

"Duty, honor and country," Biden said to Petraeus after reading the oath. "You've led and trained the 9/11 generation to become the greatest group of warriors this country has ever seen—I would argue that the world has ever seen. And not only your personal leadership but your strategic leadership has been invaluable. And now you've been called on to lead what I believe to be the leading intelligence agency in the world."

Petraeus had gone through a transformation that summer. After six straight military commands leading up to the end of his career, the prospect of taking off his uniform had initially left him pensive. But he was grateful to have a demanding new job on the horizon, another opportunity to serve the nation. He hadn't lost his will to win by leaving the military. He hadn't forsaken his competitive nature. David Petraeus was still "all in."

ACKNOWLEDGMENTS

This book is an extension of my Ph.D. dissertation research that began as an examination of Petraeus's role in military innovation in the wake of 9/11. For two years, I had traced Petraeus's steps from Cornwall-on-Hudson to Central Command, exploring the arc of the development of his philosophy of war. In June 2010, while Petraeus was standing in the Rose Garden with the president, I thought the time had arrived to turn the dissertation into a book, and I thought I might nest my research on his intellectual development within the bookends of his command in Afghanistan. I asked an associate, Tom Ricks, a reporter at the *Washington Post* and author of *Fiasco* and *The Gamble,* about approaching a publishing house. He graciously referred me to Scott Moyers, a star agent at Wylie Agency. Scott wanted me to "go big" and helped craft a vision for what a first-time author might actually achieve; he remained involved as he moved from Wylie to become the publisher at Penguin Press. Tom and Scott led me to Vernon Loeb, a former war correspondent and now the senior metro editor at the *Washington Post,* who became my writing partner and coach. Vernon has been an exceptional partner, helping to craft a vision for the story line and the design for how to nest my dissertation into the book. His constant enthusiasm for the project gave me energy to keep the pace. My editor at Penguin Press, Ginny Smith, became a tremendous guiding light as we developed the cast of characters and important themes. I value her judgment, enthusiasm and commitment to making this book the best it could be. I am also greatly indebted to Will Palmer, my copy editor, whose exacting attention to detail is truly unmatched. I also thank Andrew Wylie, my new agent; Ann Godoff, president of Penguin Press, for investing in an unknown writer; and the ever-patient Veronica Windholz and the rest of the team at Penguin for their expertise. Writing a story about an ongoing war seemed a daunting project; in the end it has been one of the most enriching, humbling and inspirational experiences of my life, in great part because of their encouragement and support.

Family and friends were instrumental in support of this endeavor. Most of all, I thank my husband and best friend, Dr. Scott Broadwell, who played Mr. Mom for our two little boys while I was in Afghanistan or Washington, D.C., and shielded them from any concerns about their adventure-seeking mother's travels in a third-world country. (He also taught our boys where Afghanistan is on the globe. We imagine they'll have to keep an eye on it in the future.) Scott showed admirable tolerance for my absence and the many late nights and early mornings at the computer; I am grateful to have such an amazing and supportive partner. I am also extremely indebted to my boys' grandparents, especially my mother, Nadene Kranz, for the countless weeks she came to stay with my kids while I was away from home for extended periods. She and my in-laws, Sharron and Russ Broadwell, tried to make the transition nearly seamless for my boys, and that means a tremendous amount to a working mother. I'm grateful to my brother and sister-in-law, Steve and Carolynn Kranz, for generously hosting me in Washington during my frequent visits. Many girlfriends (Alica, Kathy, Suzanne, Anna, Sarah and sister-in-law Heather), working mothers themselves, provided moral (and kid) support and helped fill the mothering gap in my absence. I also would have been lost without the assistance, at the eleventh hour, of Beckie Johnson and her team of transcribers, and Lieutenant Jamie Lynn De Coster, all of whom ran beside me on the final lap.

The book would not have been possible, of course, without the cooperation of General David Petraeus. Petraeus's willingness to indulge my endless questions and allow me to explore all corners of the war theater provided me with a once-in-a-lifetime education, and I am grateful for his candor, trust and support. His personal staff were essential in this pursuit; they all gave generously of their time and insights over the year, and I appreciate their patience with all of my requests and their toleration of my constant presence. I especially thank Colonel Mike Meese, Colonel (Promotable) Bill Hickman, Colonel Erik Gunhus, Lieutenant Commander Kimberly Brubeck, Captain Eric Prazinko, Chief Petty Officer Josh Treadwell—an extraordinary photographer who provided many images for this book, Captain Chip Walter, Chief Warrant Officer Five Charles Clayton, Command Sergeant Major Marvin Hill, Lieutenant Colonel Andy Gebara, Lieutenant Colonel Tony DeMartino, Lieutenant Colonel Aaron O'Connell, Alston Ramsey, Master Sergeant Mike Wallace, Sergeant A. J. Santi and Mary Kohler. I also thank Chief Warrant Officer Four Mark Howell, Staff Sergeant Landon Nordby and Sergeant First Class Kevin Cheeley—Petraeus's security detachment, with whom I'd never felt so safe on a run. Special thanks to Brigadier Generals Mark Martins and H. R. McMaster, Major General Mick Nicholson and Captain Ed Zellem, for allowing me to be a participant observer in their activities in their respective pursuits. I am especially grateful to Brigadier General (Promotable) Scott Miller, who was gracious enough to allow me to hitchhike to VSO-ALP sites and sit in on key meetings in Kabul and various FOBs and COPs around the country, as well as Master Sergeant Joseph Burke, Captain Geno Paluso and Commander (Promotable) Travis Schweizer and his right-hand men. Many others assisted in my effort to understand the complex environment in Afghanistan, and three of the most supportive were battalion commanders Lieutenant Colonels David Fivecoat, David Flynn and J. B. Vowell and their respective teams. I appreciate their willingness, in the midst of a war, to host my visits, arrange for meetings with Afghans when possible and respond in a timely fashion to endless inquiries for the facts. Their stories in these pages illustrate tremendous leadership; I remain humbled and inspired by their collective dedication. I thank their troopers who were willing to afford me a seat in their MRAPs or on a cot, who covered me on patrols and who overlooked their own spartan lives with a passion to serve. Other characters in the book were already friends, and they offered candid perspectives into the war; these include five of my West Point peers who served as aides to Petraeus over the years, and other friends, including Major Fernando Lujan, Major Abi Linnington, Colonel Joe Felter, Roger Carstens, Doug Ollivant, Mark Jacobson, Lieutenant Colonels Chris Riga and Bob Wilson, and especially Michael O'Hanlon, who helped me think about the big picture and was always a voice of reason and balance. Several senior officials were also gracious with their time, including Senator Lindsey Graham, Admiral Mike Mullen, Lieutenant General Bill Caldwell, Lieutenant General David Rodriguez, Major General John Campbell, UN special representative of the secretary general in Afghanistan Staffan de Mistura, Saad Mohseni, Afghan minister of the Interior Bismallah Khan and minister of Defense Abdul Rahim Wardak.

I am grateful as well for the support of my dissertation adviser, Sir Lawrence Freedman, of King's College London, and David Gergen, director of the Harvard Center for Public Leadership, for their patience and willingness to allow me to write a book while completing my dissertation. I thank Professors Sarah Sewall and Toni Chayes, who were guiding lights for me in the early days of trying to reorient my professional azimuth in my attempt to balance motherhood with professional goals; they remain inspirational role models.

I am indebted to Generals (Retired) Keane, Galvin and Vuono and Colonel (Retired) Nightingale for sharing their perspectives at the beginning of my dissertation pursuit, but also as General Petraeus began his final military assignment. Their collective mentoring of Petraeus, from lieutenant to four-star general, has been inspirational to observe. I especially thank Keith Nightingale for his mentorship, insights and trust along my own journey. Other Petraeus mentors, including General (Retired) Fred Franks and Brigadier General (Retired) Jim Shelton, were wonderfully helpful, too. In addition to the mentors, I am indebted to the other individuals in Petraeus's network who provided insights for the biographical digressions. Special thanks go to Holly Petraeus, Alan Seidman, Dan Kaufman, Conrad Crane, Steve Trauth, Chris White, Dave Buto, Rob Reese, Bob Bassler, George Oliver, Rich Clifford and Pat Schado. Petraeus's colleagues at Princeton, including John Duffield, and others from his various assignments have been helpful with historical material, especially Colonel Fred Johnson, Colonel Bill Ostlund, Colonel Charlie Miller, Major Jeanne Hull, Lieutenant Colonel (Retired) Fred Wellman, Colonel Patrick Frank, Lieutenant Colonel

Kevin Petit, Major General Ben Hodges, Colonel (Retired) Rich Hatch, Colonel (Retired) Rich Whitaker, Lieutenant Colonel (Retired) Mike Bailey, Major General (Retired) Joe Kinzer, Colonel (Retired) Bill Hudson, Colonel Paul Olsen, Lieutenant General Frank Helmick, Colonel (Retired) Jim Coffman, Colonel (Retired) Andy Milani, Sadi Othman and the many, many others who were all extremely helpful along the way. I thank Susan Lemke at the National Defense University for her team's support during the oral history interviews.

Triangulating opinions and insights always presents a challenge to a writer, but as such, any errors in this text are solely mine. Although not all will agree with my analysis or the presentation of what I observed, I am extremely grateful for their assistance in trying to accurately capture the story.

APPENDIX A:
COUNTERINSURGENCY GUIDANCE LETTER

HEADQUARTERS
International Security Assistance Force/
United States Forces-Afghanistan
Kabul, Afghanistan
APO AE 09356

COMISAF/CDR USFOR-A   1 August 2010

FOR The Soldiers, Sailors, Airmen, Marines, and Civilians of NATO ISAF and US Forces-Afghanistan

SUBJECT: COMISAF's Counterinsurgency Guidance

Team, here is my guidance for the conduct of counterinsurgency operations in Afghanistan. In keeping with the admonition in this guidance to "learn and adapt," I will update this document periodically in the months ahead. Indeed, this edition is my first update, as I received useful feedback on the initial draft from Afghan partners and also received advice from elders and Special Forces teams in Herat Province's Zericho Valley. I welcome further feedback.

As I noted during my assumption of command remarks, it is a privilege to serve with each of you in this hugely important endeavor. And I appreciate all that you will do in helping to turn this guidance into reality on the ground.

Secure and serve the population. The decisive terrain is the human terrain. The people are the center of gravity. Only by providing them security and earning their trust and confidence can the Afghan government and ISAF prevail.

Live among the people. We can't commute to the fight. Position joint bases and combat outposts as close to those we're seeking to secure as is feasible. Decide on locations with input from our partners and after consultation with local citizens and informed by intelligence and security assessments.

Help confront the culture of impunity. The Taliban are not the only enemy of the people. The people are also threatened by inadequate governance, corruption, and abuse of power – recruiters for the Taliban. President Karzai has forthrightly committed to combat these threats. Work with our Afghan partners to help turn his words into reality and to help our partners protect the people from malign actors as well as from terrorists.

Help Afghans build accountable governance. Afghanistan has a long history of representative self-government at all levels, from the village shura to the government in Kabul. Help the government and the people revive those traditions and help them develop checks and balances to prevent abuses.

Pursue the enemy relentlessly. Together with our Afghan partners, get our teeth into the insurgents and don't let go. When the extremists fight, make them pay. Seek out and eliminate those who threaten the population. Don't let them intimidate the innocent. Target the whole network, not just individuals.

COMISAF
SUBJECT: COMISAF's Counterinsurgency Guidance

Fight hard <u>and</u> fight with discipline. Hunt the enemy aggressively, but use only the firepower needed to win a fight. We can't win without fighting, but we also cannot kill or capture our way to victory. Moreover, if we kill civilians or damage their property in the course of our operations, we will create more enemies than our operations eliminate. That's exactly what the Taliban want. Don't fall into their trap. We must continue our efforts to reduce civilian casualties to an absolute minimum.

Identify corrupt officials. President Karzai has said, "My government is committed to fighting corruption with all means possible." Help the government achieve that aim. Make sure the people we work with work for the people. If they don't, work with partners to enable action, or we will appear to be part of the problem. Bring networks of malign actors to the attention of trusted Afghan partners and your chain of command. Act with your Afghan partners to confront, isolate, pressure, and defund malign actors – and, where appropriate, to refer malign actors for prosecution.

Hold what we secure. Together with our Afghan partners, develop the plan to hold an area (and to build in it) before starting to clear or secure it. The people need to know that we will not abandon them. Prioritize population security over short-duration disruption operations. And when we begin to transition to Afghan lead, thin out rather than handing off and withdrawing, maintaining headquarters even as we reduce combat elements.

Foster lasting solutions. Help our Afghans partners create good governance and enduring security. Avoid compromises with malign actors that achieve short-term gains at the expense of long-term stability. Think hard before pursuing initiatives that may not be sustainable in the long run. When it comes to projects, small is often beautiful.

Money is ammunition; don't put it in the wrong hands. Institute "COIN contracting." Pay close attention to the impact of our spending and understand who benefits from it. And remember, we are who we fund. How we spend is often more important than how much we spend.

Be a good guest. Treat the Afghan people and their property with respect. Think about how we drive, how we patrol, how we relate to people, and how we help the community. View our actions through the eyes of the Afghans and, together with our partners, consult with elders before pursuing new initiatives and operations.

Consult and build relationships, but not just with those who seek us out. Earn the people's trust, talk to them, ask them questions, and learn about their lives. Inquire about social dynamics, frictions, local histories, and grievances. Hear what they say. Be aware of others in the room and how their presence may affect the answers you get. Cross-check information and make sure you have the full story. Avoid knee-jerk responses based on first impressions. Don't be a pawn in someone else's game. Spend time, listen, consult, and drink lots of tea.

Walk. Stop by, don't drive by. Patrol on foot whenever possible and engage the population. Take off your sunglasses. Situational awareness can only be gained by interacting face-to-face, not separated by ballistic glass or Oakleys.

Act as one team. Work closely with our international and Afghan partners, civilian as well as military. Treat them as brothers-in-arms. Unity of effort and cooperation are not optional.

Partner with the ANSF. Live, eat, train, plan, and operate together. Depend on one another. Hold each other accountable at all echelons down to trooper level. Help our ANSF partners achieve excellence. Respect them and listen to them. Be a good role model.

Promote local reintegration. Together with our Afghan partners, identify and separate the "reconcilables" from the "irreconcilables." Identify and report obstacles to reintegration. Help our partners address grievances and strive to make the reconcilables part of the local solution, even as we work with our partners to identify and kill, capture, drive out, or "turn" the irreconcilables.

Be first with the truth. Beat the insurgents and malign actors to the headlines. Preempt rumors. Get accurate information to the chain of command, to Afghan leaders, to the people, and to the press as soon as possible. Integrity is critical to this fight. Avoid spinning, and don't try to "dress up" an ugly situation. Acknowledge setbacks and failures, including civilian casualties, and then state how we'll respond and what we've learned.

Fight the information war aggressively. Challenge disinformation. Turn our enemies' extremist ideologies, oppressive practices, and indiscriminate violence against them. Hang their barbaric actions like millstones around their necks.

Manage expectations. Avoid premature declarations of success. Note what has been accomplished and what still needs to be done. Strive to under-promise and over-deliver.

Live our values. Stay true to the values we hold dear. This is what distinguishes us from our enemies. We are engaged in a tough endeavor. It is often brutal, physically demanding, and frustrating. All of us experience moments of anger, but we must not give in to dark impulses or tolerate unacceptable actions by others.

Maintain continuity through unit transitions. From day one, start building the information you'll provide to your successors. Share information and understanding in the months before transitions. Strive to maintain operational tempo and local relationships throughout transitions to avoid giving insurgents and malign actors a rest.

COMISAF
SUBJECT: COMISAF's Counterinsurgency Guidance

Empower subordinates. Resource to enable decentralized action. Push assets and authorities down to those who most need them and can actually use them. Flatten reporting chains (while maintaining hierarchical decision chains). Remember that it is those at tactical levels – the so-called "strategic sergeants" and "strategic captains" – who turn big ideas in counterinsurgency operations into reality on the ground.

Win the battle of wits. Learn and adapt more quickly than the enemy. Be cunning. Outsmart the insurgents. Share best practices and lessons learned. Create and exploit opportunities.

Exercise initiative. In the absence of guidance or orders, figure out what the orders should have been and execute them aggressively.

David H. Petraeus
General, United States Army
Commander, International Security Assistance Force/
   United States Forces-Afghanistan

APPENDIX B:

COMISAF'S COIN CONTRACTING GUIDANCE

NATO / ISAF UNCLASSIFIED RELEASABLE TO GIRoA

Headquarters
International Security Assistance Force

Kabul, Afghanistan

08 September 2010

COMISAF/CDR USFOR-A

For the Commanders, Contracting Personnel, Military Personnel, and Civilians of NATO ISAF and US Forces-Afghanistan

SUBJECT: COMISAF's Counterinsurgency (COIN) Contracting Guidance

The scale of our contracting efforts in Afghanistan represents both an opportunity and a danger. With proper oversight, contracting can spur economic development and support the Afghan government's and ISAF's campaign objectives. If, however, we spend large quantities of international contracting funds quickly and with insufficient oversight, it is likely that some of those funds will unintentionally fuel corruption, finance insurgent organizations, strengthen criminal patronage networks, and undermine our efforts in Afghanistan.

In view of these points, contracting has to be "Commander's business." Indeed, I expect Commanders to consider the effects of our contract spending and understand who benefits from it. We must use intelligence to inform our contracting and ensure those with whom we contract work for the best interests of the Afghan people. We must be better buyers and buy from better people. Consistent with NATO and national contracting laws and regulations, we must:

Understand the role of contracting in COIN. Purchases we make for construction, goods, and services can bolster economic growth, stability, and Afghan goodwill toward their government and ISAF. Contracts with Afghan firms that procure Afghan goods and services generate employment and assist in the development of a sustainable economy. However, if we contract with powerbrokers who exclude those outside their narrow patronage networks or are perceived as funneling resources to one community at the expense of another, the effect on Afghan perceptions and our mission will be negative. Thus, we must incorporate COIN Contracting topics into training for Commanders.

Hire Afghans first, buy Afghan products, and build Afghan capacity. Use contracting to hire Afghan workers and Afghan-owned companies. If we are unable to contract with an Afghan company, encourage companies to hire Afghans and sub-contract with responsible Afghan firms. Emulate successes such as NTM-A/CSTC-A's Afghan First program that created a boot making industry in Kabul. Find solutions that tap existing, but sometimes limited, Afghan capacity, such as maximizing the opportunities for local small and medium-sized companies to compete for our contracts. Adapt procedures, such as facilitating base access, to remove obstacles to hiring Afghans. Wherever appropriate, use in-country sourcing rather than imports. Look for opportunities to incorporate maintenance and repair training in existing contracts to build Afghan skills and to create long-term employment. Focus efforts on promoting industries with immediate and long-term growth potential, such as agriculture, food processing, beverages, and construction. Adopt a fair wage and fair price approach that minimizes market shock and inflation. Guard against "front businesses" that fraudulently claim to be Afghan-owned.

Know those with whom we are contracting. Where our money goes is as important as the service provided or the product delivered. Establish systems and standard databases for vetting vendors and contractors to ensure that contracting does not empower the wrong people or allow the diversion of funds. Support contracting agencies and officers so they can get out in the field and build relationships with local businesses and community leaders. Gain and maintain visibility of the sub-contractor network. Contract with vendors that have fewer sub-contractors. Excessive sub-contracting tiers provide opportunities for criminal networks and insurgents to divert contract money from its intended purpose. Hold prime contractors responsible for the behavior and performance of their sub-contractors. Ensure that prime contractors provide detailed information on all sub-contractors consistent with coalition requirements and with CENTCOM Contracting Command's new sub-contractor clause.

Exercise responsible contracting practices. While we all desire fast results, haste in contracting invites fraud, waste, and abuse. Plan ahead, establish reasonable timelines, and ensure transparency and oversight so that contracting and procurement reinforce rather than detract from our objectives.

Integrate contracting into intelligence, plans, and operations. Commanders must know what contracting activity is occurring in their battlespace and who benefits from those contracts. Integrate contracting into intelligence, plans, and operations to exert positive influence and to better accomplish our campaign objectives. Commanders should use COIN Contracting Management Boards to coordinate contracting efforts and ensure contracts support campaign goals. Commanders and contracting agencies should share best practices, align policies and procedures, and exchange information on contractor performance—positive or negative (using digitally linked CIDNE/INDURE databases).

Consult and involve local leaders. Use local shuras and Afghan government and private sector leaders to prioritize projects, identify viable companies, vet potential contractors, improve oversight, hold contractors accountable, and provide post-award feedback to inform future projects. Work with and through the Ministry of Rural Reconstruction and Development to leverage existing monitoring, procurement, and implementation capabilities and to build long-term Afghan institutional capacity.

Develop new partnerships. Contracts with a broader range of Afghan companies will help break monopolies and weaken patronage networks that breed resentment. In situations where there is no alternative to powerbrokers with links to criminal networks, it may be preferable to forgo the project. Broadly advertise contract opportunities to local communities beyond bases. When appropriate, use NGOs to identify potential contracting partners and train them to navigate our contracting processes.

Look beyond cost, schedule, and performance. Evaluate the success of a contract by the degree to which it supports the Afghan people and our campaign objectives. Include operational criteria in decisions to award contracts such as the effect of the contract on security, local power dynamics, and the enemy.

Invest in oversight and enforce contract requirements. Ensure post-award oversight of contractors and their performance to get what we pay for and to ensure the contract supports our mission. Because the number of contracts each contracting officer oversees has increased, commands must devote additional personnel to oversight. Designate top-performers to serve as Contract Officer Representatives and ensure that they are trained and understand the operational importance of contracting.

Act. Upon identification of linkages between contractors and criminal networks, we must take appropriate actions, such as: suspension and debarment of the individuals or the company, contract termination, or not renewing a contract option period. Recognize that some of these actions may have broad or significant ramifications and plan accordingly. Establish rapid, flexible, and thorough processes to develop, coordinate, approve, and implement contract actions to end contracts that undermine our mission.

Get the story out. We must improve our contracting practices to ensure they fully support our mission. However, we must also recognize what our contracting has accomplished. Our contracting efforts have sustained widely dispersed and high tempo operations and helped build Afghan national security capacity. Our contracting has also improved the lives of many Afghans, enhanced infrastructure, delivered essential services, supported local businesses, increased employment, and fostered economic development.

David H. Petraeus
General, United States Army
Commander, International Security Assistance
Force/United States Forces-Afghanistan

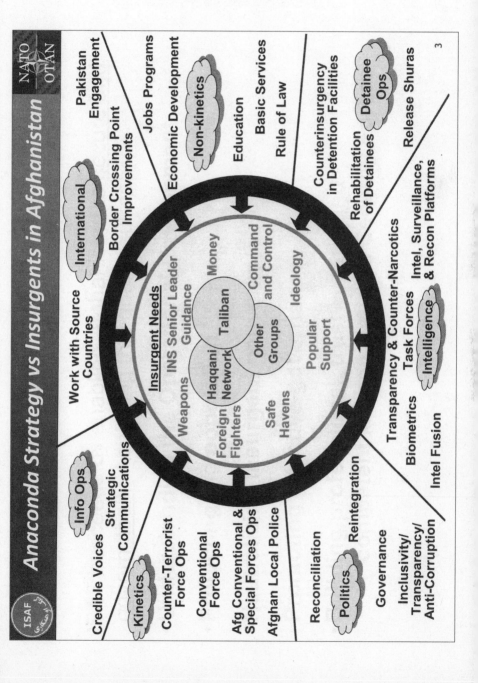

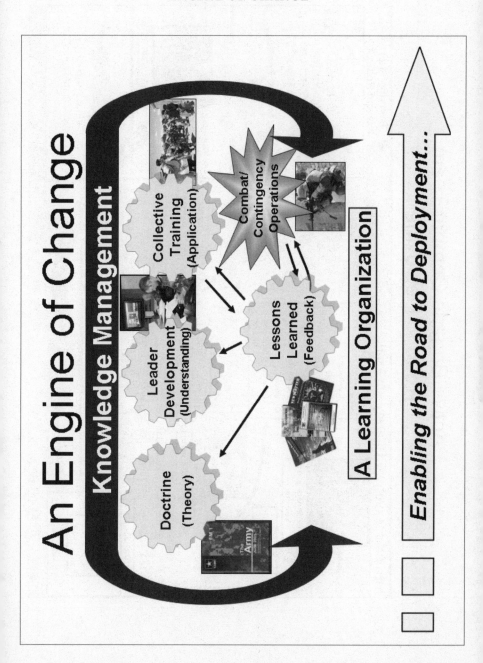

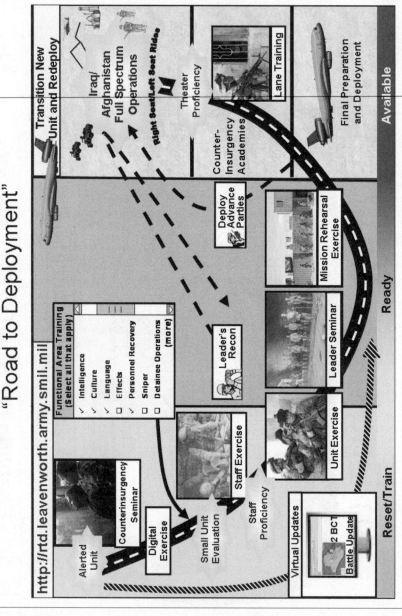

Active Brigade Combat Team "Road to Deployment"

NOTES

The core of this book comes from interviews and interviewees' responses to my inquiries via e-mail, many of which were provided on background, others on the record. The interviews were conducted over the course of 2008–2011, though the majority were conducted in the past fifteen months in Afghanistan. Information was supplied by more than 150 individuals and hundreds of hours of interviews, totaling approximately 700 interviews over three years (including multiple interviews with some sources). Many military officials provided insights, as did senior and well-placed military, civilian and diplomatic officials. I also attended General Petraeus's congressional testimonies and participated in his oral history interviews at the National Defense University prior to his retirement from the U.S. Army. Additional information was derived from personal notes, letters and e-mails exchanged with or among various individuals referenced in the book. I also participated in meetings at ISAF and with Afghan officials at the MOD and MOI, and I embedded with various units in the field; in all these locations I was able to view (limited) unclassified reports, cables, calendars, transcripts and various PowerPoint briefings. On occasion, a source indicated that information was off the record, in which case I could use the information if I found it in an open source. I have vetted, with the oversight of senior DOD officials, the information in this manuscript to ensure there are no violations of operational security.

EPIGRAPH

vii *General Petraeus said this to President George W. Bush in the Oval Office on January 23, 2007, on the eve of the Iraq surge.*

CHAPTER 1: GROUND TRUTH

4 *He'd already been deployed over five and a half years:* General David H. Petraeus, interview by Jennifer Griffin, Fox News, August 25, 2010.

7 *"I've had a certain affinity for leaders":* General David H. Petraeus, e-mail message to author, April 19, 2011.

16 *the largest combat loss in a single day:* Bradley Graham, "Ambush at Takur Ghar," *Washington Post,* May 24–25, 2002. (Graham wrote a powerful two-part series on the Battle of Takur Ghar.)

16 *"Every tiny piece of terrain":* Major Fernando M. Lujan, e-mail message to author, August 4, 2010.

20 *In fact, when McChrystal had arrived in Afghanistan:* General Stanley A. McChrystal, interview by author, November 19, 2010, Arlington, Virginia; Lieutenant General David M. Rodriguez, interview by author, Kabul, Afghanistan, April 15, 2011.

20 *It wasn't until May 2010 that troop strength:* Anthony H. Cordesman, "The Afghan War—Part One: Shaping the Campaign," Center for Strategic and International Studies, September 8, 2010.

21 *Before his demise at the hands of Rolling Stone:* Michael Hastings, "The Runaway General," *Rolling Stone,* June 25, 2010.

22 *"It's not accurate to say Marjah's a failure":* Richard C. Holbrooke, interview by Fareed Zakaria, CNN, July 25, 2010.

22 *The stronghold of the Taliban:* Brett Van Ess, "The Fight for Marjah: Recent Counterinsurgency Operations in Southern Afghanistan," *Small Wars Journal,* September 30, 2010.

23 *"Top 10 insights/recommendations welcome":* General David H. Petraeus, e-mail message to Douglas Ollivant, June 24, 2010.

24 *"We're putting it all on the line":* General Petraeus's e-mail is quoted both in Linda Robinson's book *Tell Me How This Ends* (New York: Public Affairs, 2008), on page 123, and in David Cloud and Greg Jaffe's book *The Fourth Star: Four Generals and the Epic Struggle for the Future of the U.S. Army* (New York: Three Rivers Press, 2009).

CHAPTER 2: RESULTS, BOY

32 *"the best combat leader I have ever known":* Greg Jaffee, "U.S. Is Losing a Savvy Leader in Afghan War Efforts," *Washington Post,* April 19, 2011.

33 *a clicking chorus of . . . laptops:* General David H. Petraeus, interview by author, Kabul, Afghanistan, April 12, 2011.

36 *"But in the long run":* Martha Schiff, "Two Friends from Cornwall Join the Long Grey Line," *The Cornwall Local,* December 19, 1973.

40 *When he arrived in Afghanistan:* General David H. Petraeus, interview by author, Kabul, Afghanistan, October 3, 2011.

42 *It did not go particularly well:* General David H. Petraeus, interview by author, Kabul, Afghanistan, October 3, 2011.

47 *"point of decision" was typically where the fighting was heaviest:* General David H. Petraeus, interview by author, Washington, D.C., April 3, 2009.

50 *Churchill's observation:* General David H. Petraeus, interview by author, Kabul, Afghanistan, September 29, 2010.

51 *a "lick 'em tomorrow" day:* General David H. Petraeus, e-mail message to author, July 20, 2010.

52 *Karzai's government . . . approved creation of the local police:* General David H. Petraeus, e-mail message to author, July 14, 2010.

54 *The number of bombs dropped in Iraq:* Noah Shachtman, "Does Petraeus Mean a Return of Afghanistan Air War?" *Danger Room* blog, Wired.com, June 23, 2010, www.wired.com/dangerroom/2010/06/does-petraeus-mean-a-return-to-all-out-war.

54 *"sometimes the best weapons don't shoot":* Ibid.

CHAPTER 3: TRUE BELIEVERS

58 *Rumsfeld imposed a "force cap":* Thomas E. Ricks, *Fiasco* (New York: Penguin Group, 2009), p. 41.

58 *"a perfect storm of political upheaval":* Seth G. Jones, *In the Graveyard of Empires* (New York: W. W. Norton, 2009), p. xxiii.

60 *These imperatives and others neatly distilled:* Former Army vice chief of staff General Jack Keane makes this point in *The U.S. Army and U.S. Marine Corps Counterinsurgency Field Manual* (Chicago: University of Chicago Press, 2007), p. xiv.

60 *favorably reviewed:* Samantha Power, "Our War on Terror," *The New York Times Book Review,* July 29, 2007.

60 *Nagl . . . wrote in a foreword: The U.S. Army and U.S. Marine Corps Counterinsurgency Field Manual,* p. xv.

61 *Petraeus's counterinsurgency guidance bore some parallels:* Colonel Daniel Roper, director of the Army and Marine Corps Counterinsurgency Center, made this point in a note on the center's Web site, at http://usacac.army.mil/cac2/coin.

62 *"Lawrence of Afghanistan":* Ann Scott Tyson, "Can This Officer Win the War?" *Washington Post,* January 17, 2010.

62 *"a paper written by Special Forces major Jim Gant":* Major Jim Gant, *One Tribe at a Time: A Strategy for Success in Afghanistan* (Los Angeles: Nine Sisters Imports, 2009), available at http://agora.stevenpressfield.com/2009/10/one-tribe-at-a-time-4-the-full-document-at-last.

68 *Petraeus thought Krepinevich's book:* In September 2005, Krepinevich wrote an article that argued for a classic COIN campaign approach in Iraq. Andrew F. Krepinevich, "How to Win in Iraq," *Foreign Affairs,* September/October 2005.

75 *the story broke that Karzai had fired:* Dexter Filkins and Alissa J. Rubin, "Graft-Fighting Prosecutor Dismissed in Afghanistan," *New York Times,* August 29, 2010.

76 *Petraeus thought improvement was possible:* Colonel William B. Hickman (Executive Office to General Petraeus), e-mail message to author, November 17, 2010.

77 *A report released that October found . . . $55.7 billion:* See the October report of the Special Inspector General for Afghanistan Reconstruction (SIGAR) to Congress, October 30, 2010, www.sigar.mil/oct2010Report.asp.

78 *Watan . . . "had been funneling large sums":* "U.S. Blacklists Afghan Security Firm Tied to Karzai," Associated Press, December 9, 2010.

82 *Lawrence's "Twenty-Seven Articles":* A guide T. E. Lawrence wrote for British officers in the *Arab Bulletin,* August, 20, 1917.

CHAPTER 4: SCREAMING EAGLES

84 *Taliban movement was established in . . . Sangsar:* David S. Cloud, "Troops Launch Afghan Assault," *Los Angeles Times,* September 15, 2010.

88 *"There will be time to re-train":* Lieutenant Colonel David S. Flynn, e-mail message to author, November 12, 2010.

89 *"You dudes need to think about my guys":* Brian Mockenhaupt, "The Last Patrol," *The Atlantic,* November 2010.

89 *Flynn's artillery unit "weren't prepared physically":* Dion Nissenbaum, "U.S. Soldiers' Mission Shows Afghan War's Uncertainties," McClatchy Newspapers, August 13, 2010.

89 *"I knew we could prepare our men to be better than the Taliban":* Lieutenant Colonel David S. Flynn, e-mail message to David Mockenhaupt, August 19, 2010.

89–90 *"We all have three, four or five deployments":* Lieutenant Colonel David S. Flynn, comment on "A Reporter to Watch—Brian Mockenhaupt: The Last Patrol," *Blackfive* blog, blackfive.net, comment posted on October 16, 2010.

90 *"Medic!" he heard someone shout:* Captain Andrew Shaffer, e-mail message to author, March 25, 2011.

91 *Pittman was conscious but unresponsive:* U.S. Army, *Official Investigation into the Deaths of Sergeant Stout, Specialist Stansbery, and Mr. Pittman,* September 9, 2010 (statement of Lieutenant Colonel David S. Flynn, Commander, 1st Battalion, 320th Field Artillery Regiment, 101st Airborne Division).

93 *A profile in* **Harper's***:* Matthieu Aikins, "The Master of Spin Boldak: Undercover with Afghanistan's Drug-Trafficking Border Police," *Harper's,* December 2009.

94 *a London tabloid:* Richard Pendlebury and Jamie Wiseman, "Dicing Death in the Devil's Playground," *Daily Mail,* October 26, 2010.

99 *"Until recently, Ghazni . . . was considered reasonably safe":* Nir Rosen, "How We Lost the War We Won," *Rolling Stone,* October 29, 2008.

99 *Their fighting force was thought to number around four hundred:* C. J. Chivers, "In Eastern Afghanistan, at War with the Taliban's Shadowy Rule," *At War* blog, NYTimes.com, February 7, 2011, www.nytimes.com/2011/02/07/world/asia/07taliban.html?pagewanted=all.

100 *"What do you expect after years of our presence here?":* Lieutenant Colonel David G. Fivecoat, interview by author, Kandahar, Afghanistan, October 1, 2010.

101 *six "lines of effort":* Lieutenant Colonel David G. Fivecoat and Captain Aaron T. Schwengler, "Revisiting Modern Warfare Counterinsurgency in the Mada'in Qada," *Military Review,* Nov./Dec. 2008.

101 *"The December assessment will be bad":* Lieutenant Colonel David G. Fivecoat, e-mail message to author, July 28, 2010.

104 *"Petraeus, in his relentlessly positive way":* Lieutenant Colonel David G. Fivecoat, interview by author, Kandahar, Afghanistan, October 1, 2010.

105 *Petraeus had nearly bled to death:* General Jack Keane, interview by author, Kabul, Afghanistan, November 12, 2010.

109 *The division had six dozen Apache gunships:* Rick Atkinson, *In the Company of Soldiers* (New York: Henry Holt and Company, 2004), p. 14.

111 *"The challenges from the sanctuaries":* General David H. Petraeus, e-mail message to author, July 30, 2010.

111 *"We had multiple indicators":* Matiullah Mati, "Dozens of Bodies Found After Clash at Afghan Military Base," CNN.com, October 31, 2010.

112 *Around Margah, there were four:* Department of Defense, Pentagon briefing, Federal News Service, November 2, 2010.

112 *"wonderful American":* General David H. Petraeus, e-mail message to author, December 4, 2010.

CHAPTER 5: ANACONDA

113 *An officer . . . fired off an e-mail:* Major John P. Gallagher, e-mail message to author, September 22, 2010.

115 *White House draft had merely said "disrupt":* Bob Woodward, *Obama's Wars* (New York: Simon & Schuster, 2010), 145.

115 *McChrystal . . . had not planned on asking for more troops:* General Stanley McChrystal, interview by author, Arlington, Virginia, November 19, 2010.

116 *"There was the real work":* General David H. Petraeus, interview by author, Kabul, Afghanistan, October 4, 2010.

116 *"All we were repeating during the subsequent policy review":* Military official, interview by author, Kabul, Afghanistan, October 5, 2010.

117 *restating what Mullen had told the Senate:* Woodward, *Obama's Wars,* 158.

119 *Like McChrystal and Mullen:* General Stanley McChrystal, interview by author, Arlington, Virginia, November 19, 2010; Admiral Mike Mullen, interview by author, Washington, D.C., August 31, 2010.

119 *"This approach is not fully resourced":* Woodward, *Obama's Wars,* 387.

121 *"'They knock you down every chance they get'":* Woodward, *Obama's Wars,* 362.

121 *"fucking with the wrong guy":* Steve Luxenberg, "Obama Battles with Advisers Over Afghan Exit Plan Detailed in Woodward Book," *Washington Post,* September 22, 2010.

121 *He later surmised . . . that it was a field-grade officer:* General David H. Petraeus, e-mail message to author, January 26, 2011.

135 *A headline . . . triggered a counterattack:* Carlotta Gall, "Coalition Routs Taliban in Southern Afghanistan," *New York Times,* October 21, 2010.

136 *A story line emerged that Petraeus was moving away:* In mid-October 2010, three columnists wrote about a shift in the strategic effort in Afghanistan under General Petraeus: Fred Kaplan, "A New Plan for Afghanistan: Less Counterinsurgency, More Killing and Capturing," *Slate,* Slate.com, October 13, 2010; David Ignatius, "Petraeus Rewrites the Playbook in Afghanistan," *Washington Post,* October 19, 2010; and Joe Klein, "Afghanistan: A New Balance," *Swampland* blog, Time.com, October 18, 2010, http://swampland.time .com/2010/10/18/afghanistan-a-new-balance.

139 *"That's rare in a general officer":* General Jack Keane, interview by Charlie Rose, *Charlie Rose,* PBS, October 19, 2010.

140 *"In fact, the better date to think about is the end of 2014":* Warren P. Strobel, "Happy Veterans Day," *Nukes & Spooks* blog, November 11, 2010, http://blogs.mcclatchydc.com/ nationalsecurity/2010/11/index.html.

140 *Graham said that "2014 is the right date":* Lindsey Graham, interview by Christiane Amanpour, "This Week with Christiane Amanpour," ABC, November 14, 2010.

141 *Triggered by an interview Karzai gave:* Joshua Partlow, "Karzai Wants U.S. to Reduce Military Operations in Afghanistan," *Washington Post,* November 14, 2010.

CHAPTER 6: CLEAR, HOLD AND BUILD

147 *"Out here we're fighting the Taliban":* James Kitfield, "Robert Gates, David Petraeus: Partners in War," *The National Journal,* December 9, 2010.

156 *"We literally got every single thing":* Major Fernando Lujan, e-mail message to author, December 20, 2010.

161 *Karzai reported in mid-January:* Taimoor Shah and Rod Nordland, "Afghan Panel and U.S. Dispute War's Toll on Property," *New York Times,* January 13, 2011.

162 *Petraeus ordered up a "constant drumbeat":* General David H. Petraeus, morning stand-up briefing, January 12, 2011.

162 *revisited Flynn's decision in October:* Joshua Foust, "The Unforgivable Horror of Village Razing," Registan.net, January 13, 2011, www.registan.net/index.php/2011/01/13/the -unforgivable-horror-of-village-razing.

162 *the inaccurate* Daily Mail *story:* Pendlebury and Wiseman, "Dicing Death."

162 *He argued that bombing villages:* Joshua Foust, "The Battalion Commander Debates the Blogger (II): Foust Responds to Flynn," Tom Ricks, *The Best Defense* blog, January 21, 2011, http://ricks.foreignpolicy.com/posts/2011/01/21/the_battalion_commander_ debates_the_blogger_ii_foust_responds_to_flynn.

163 *"'We're doing the Taliban's work for them'":* Aikins, "The Master of Spin Boldak."

CHAPTER 7: LINES OF OPERATION

184 *"Counterinsurgency is that kind of fight":* Major Fernando Lujan, e-mail message to author, January 7, 2011.

185 *"I've got plenty of stragic thinkers":* J. D. Stevens, e-mail message to author, March 8, 2011.

186 *The* Post *said that neither Petraeus's exact language:* Joshua Partlow, "Petraeus's Comments on Coalition Attack Reportedly Offend Karzai Government," *Washington Post,* February 21, 2011.

186 *"Welcome to the neighborhood":* General David H. Petraeus, interview by author, Kabul, Afghanistan, May 17, 2011.

188 *"Although they resulted in large scale property damage":* Afghanistan Independent Human Rights Commission, *Afghanistan Annual Report 2010: Protection of Civilians in Armed Conflict,* United Nations Assistance Mission in Afghanistan, March 2011.

188 *In Iraq and Afghanistan, it would take:* Atkinson, *In the Company of Soldiers,* p. 167.

189 *He wasn't casualty averse:* Ibid, p. 237.

190 *The effect of the overall de-Baathification program:* Dr. Donald P. Wright and Colonel Timothy R. Reese, *On Point II: Transition to the New Campaign: The United States Army in Operation Iraqi Freedom May 2003–January 2005* (Fort Leavenworth, KS: Combat Studies Institute Press, 2008).

195 *"change the culture of the Afghan military":* Major Fernando Lujan, e-mail message to author, March 5, 2011.

197 *Gates said he thought the United States:* Robert Burns, "U.S. Negotiating Security Deal with Afghans," *The Guardian,* March 7, 2011.

197 *"You're talking about people who have seen far worse":* Karen Parrish, "Task Force Works with Afghan Local Police," Department of Defense Releases, March 9, 2011.

198 *The* Times *described the interview with Petraeus:* Carlotta Gall, "Petraeus Says Coalition Has Stymied Taliban in Much of Afghanistan," *New York Times,* March 9, 2011.

CHAPTER 8: WASHINGTON AND BACK

222 Foreign Policy *published an article:* Thomas Johnson and Matthew DuPee, "Transition to Nowhere: the Limits of 'Afghanization,'" *Foreign Policy,* March 22, 2011.

CHAPTER 9: HIGH STAKES

233 *"But it shows that it certainly will fail":* Douglas A. Ollivant, "Afghanistan Has Three Wars at Once. Let's Fight the Right One," *Washington Post,* May 22, 2011.

251 *476 prisoners escaping through a tunnel:* Department of Defense, Pentagon briefing, Federal News Service, February 10, 2011.

CHAPTER 10: TRANSITION

257 *The Title 50 authority for this operation:* Matthew Dahl, American Bar Association Standing Committee on Law and National Security panel discussion on "The Bin Laden Operation—The Legal Framework," May 26, 2011.

260 *by the spring of 2011, 95 percent:* Defense Department report issued on April 29, 2011, "Report on Progress Toward Security and Stability in Afghanistan and United States Plan for Sustaining the Afghanistan National Security Forces."

278 *"The U.S. military will continue to hunt down terrorists":* Douglas A. Ollivant, "Let's Stop Civilizing Afghanistan," *Washington Post,* May 22, 2011.

CHAPTER 11: DRAWDOWN

291 *The workweek began with a media report:* Leslie H. Gelb, "Obama's Secret Afghan Exit Formula," *The Daily Beast* blog, June 11, 2011.

300 *Gates and Clinton reluctantly had:* Thom Shanker, "Warning Against Wars Like Iraq and Afghanistan," *New York Times,* February 25, 2011.

302 *Petraeus strongly believed that "military leaders":* General David H. Petraeus, interview by author, Washington, D.C., September 2, 2011.

CHAPTER 12: MASK OF COMMAND

324 *"It is very hard, but it is doable":* Carlotta Gall, "Petraeus Confident As He Leaves Afghanistan," *New York Times,* July 10, 2011.

324 *They performed creditably and courageously:* General David H. Petraeus, Defense Department briefing, Federal News Service, July 12, 2011.

336 *In a poem published a few years ago, a British trooper:* John Bailey, "The Volunteer." Reprinted with permission. Accessed at http://www.warpoetry.co.uk/Afghanistan_War_Poetry.html.

CHAPTER 13: STILL ALL IN

342 *enemy-initiated attacks for the period June–August 2011:* "Enemy-Initiated Attacks Nationwide Monthly Year-Over-Year Change," Afghan Mission Network Combined Information Data Network Exchange (CIDNE) Database. Data as of September 29, 2011. See appendix for more information.

342 *The command had not seen this sustained year-on-year level:* Ibid.

343 *Attacks continued to increase in the east:* "Enemy-Initiated Attacks Nationwide Monthly Year-Over-Year Change by Regional Command (January 2008–August 2011)," Afghan Mission Network Combined Information Data Network Exchange (CIDNE) Database. Data as of September 29, 2011. See appendix for more information.

INDEX

Abbottabad, 255–59
Abizaid, John, 127, 195
Abrams tanks, 318
"Accidental Statesman: General Petraeus and the City of Mosul, Iraq, The," 192–93
Aceves, Omar, 180
Adamski, Frank, 229
Afghan Air Force (AAF), 183
Afghan Border Police (ABP), 93, 95, 96–97, 244, 269
Afghan CAAT (A-CAAT), 155–57, 183–86, 195–96, 222–23, 264–67, 283–85, 320–23, 351
Afghan Hands, 155–56, 183–86, 265, 288, 319–23
Afghanistan Independent Human Rights Commission, 187
Afghanistan Peace and Reintegration Program (APRP), 44
Afghanistan War:
  Afghan military forces in, 20, 24, 25, 31–32, 42–43, 46–47, 49, 54, 75, 84, 116, 119, 134, 141–43, 181, 207–8, 211, 215, 221–22, 227, 235, 248, 266, 279, 282, 300, 307–8, 314, 315–16, 318, 320–21, 325, 330, 341–42, 343, 345, 346–49; see also specific forces
  Afghan public support for, 260, 269–70, 308, 328–29
  agriculture affected by, 99, 153, 157, 159, 161, 163, 264
  air power in, 31, 53–54, 55, 57, 58, 99–100, 136, 186–88
  al-Qaeda forces in, 3, 8–9, 15, 27, 57, 62–63, 75, 113–14, 119, 147, 148, 182, 209, 212, 215, 226, 236, 252, 275, 277, 286, 299, 300, 301, 322, 323, 349
  anti-corruption efforts in, 75–82, 138, 215–16, 247, 317–18, 348–49

assassinations in, 58, 92, 99, 122–23, 131–33, 163–65, 171, 187, 262, 323, 327–28, 332
bombing strikes in, 54–55, 95–96, 136, 145, 161–63, 186–88, 196–97, 198, 226, 231, 235, 243–44, 267–69, 281–83, 285–86, 329, 351
British forces in, 49, 220–21, 266, 336, 339–40, 344, 345–46
Canadian forces in, 49–50, 344
CIA operatives in, 57, 58, 76, 131, 159
civilian casualties in, 17, 31, 49, 53–55, 58, 60, 99–100, 110, 133, 139, 163–65, 186–88, 196–97, 211, 222, 279–83, 291, 295, 315, 328–29, 344
civilian-military cooperation in, 42–48, 52, 59–62, 114–15, 132–33, 134, 138–39, 153–55, 163–65, 176–77, 233–34, 269–70, 302, 308–9, 334, 341, 346
climate in, 79, 89–90, 109, 145, 296–301
coalition forces in, 126, 166, 171–72, 181, 300–301, 332–34, 345–46; see also International Security Assistance Force (ISAF)
congressional oversight of, 78, 198, 287–88, 291, 316, 317–18
contractors in, 260, 271, 367
corruption in, 9, 15, 23, 44–45, 58, 61, 75–82, 93, 99, 123, 138, 141, 175, 176–79, 215–16, 247, 295–96, 313, 317–18, 348–49
counterinsurgency (COIN) programs in, 13–14, 16–17, 23–26, 42–43, 54–55, 58, 59–63, 76–82, 92, 100–101, 103, 109–10, 113–15, 119, 122–24, 133–40, 145–48 155–157, 166–69, 183–86, 195–96, 208, 222–23, 233–34, 248, 261–67, 271, 275, 277–78, 280–85, 289–90, 295, 300, 319–23, 324, 343, 347–48, 351–52, 365, 367
crime in, 81, 177, 270–72, 313
defense spending for, 26, 77–80, 142, 157, 200, 212–15, 262–63, 346, 347

Afghanistan War: (*cont.*)
"drawdown of forces" in, xxix, 2, 8, 9, 11–12, 14,
15–16, 20, 27, 48–49, 74–75, 117–22, 139, 140,
141–43, 156, 168, 182–83, 198, 207–8, 211–12,
221–22, 231, 248, 283, 285, 289, 291–309, 312,
313–14, 316, 330, 340, 342, 349, 356
drug trafficking in, 32, 80, 172, 177, 270–71, 352
economic conditions in, 92, 158, 183, 259,
270–72, 299, 346, 352
fighting seasons in, 296–301, 312, 340
foreign insurgents in, 111, 147, 181–82, 275, 288
governance and government in, 3–4, 9, 15, 18,
21–22, 25–26, 27, 31, 32, 41–45, 52, 57, 58, 61,
63, 75–82, 93, 99, 108, 123, 135–36, 140–42,
158, 161–63, 171–79, 182, 183, 186, 210–11, 215,
221–22, 233–34, 236, 244, 245, 247, 259,
262–63, 270–72, 277–80, 281, 282, 283, 285,
294–96, 299, 301, 308–9, 313, 316, 317–18,
323, 327–28, 332, 342, 343, 346, 347, 348–49,
352
"green zones" in, 171–72
human rights violations in, 95, 96, 161, 162–63,
186–87
improvised explosive devices (IEDs) in, 16,
18–19, 85–86, 90–91, 94–97, 100, 101, 102–3,
142, 145–47, 159, 162–63, 180, 187, 196, 206,
223, 227, 231, 266–67, 280, 291, 323, 329, 340,
344, 351
intelligence operations in, 17, 20, 21, 25, 60,
99–100, 122–24, 131–33, 137, 153, 158–59,
166–67, 223, 233, 234, 245, 271, 275, 288, 307,
318, 321, 323–24
Iraq War compared with, 20, 23–24, 26–27,
40–41, 42, 45, 57–58, 74–75, 89–90, 100, 101,
103–4, 110, 114, 118, 123, 137–39, 154, 166, 168,
203, 204–5, 247, 249, 272–73, 343, 346, 347,
352
judicial system of, 44–46, 75–76, 171–76, 251,
342, 348–49, 352
Karzai administration in, 3–4, 15, 18, 25, 31,
41–45, 61, 75–76, 79, 80, 140–42, 161, 176–79,
182, 186, 211, 221–22, 233, 247, 277–78, 281,
282, 283, 285, 294–96, 308–9, 313, 316, 317–18,
323, 327–28, 332, 346, 347, 348–49, 352
media coverage of, 1, 15–16, 21, 26–27, 31, 86,
91–92, 93, 99, 135–37, 140, 141–43, 162–63,
186–87, 198, 202, 212, 214, 221, 222, 231, 234,
248–49, 277, 284, 291, 296, 299–300, 316, 317,
322–25, 345
medivac operations in, 90–91, 226, 228, 281–82,
286
military casualties in, 10, 19, 21, 50–51, 84,
85–86, 90–91, 95, 96, 103, 109, 110, 111,
145–47, 180, 181, 212, 214–15, 226, 228, 229,
242, 243, 244, 245–46, 249, 250–51, 253, 260,
263, 280–83, 286, 319, 332–34, 344
military strategy in, 8–10, 11, 13–14, 16–21,
23–27, 30–31, 57–59, 131–40, 143, 145–48, 172,
197–98, 210, 242–46, 277–80, 288, 342

nation-building in, 57–58, 113–14, 119, 126,
152–53, 159–62, 233–34
NATO forces in, 8, 16, 21, 23, 24, 29, 30,
31–32, 42, 43, 48, 49–50, 53, 57, 61, 93, 98,
139, 140, 141, 165, 166, 168, 187, 207–8, 215,
218, 221, 222, 223, 247, 260, 264, 280, 281,
283, 287, 288–89, 296, 313, 315, 317, 335,
339, 347
night raids in, 122–23, 131–33, 136, 137, 142,
187–88, 280–83, 285, 324, 328–29, 345
Obama's policies on, 8, 11–14, 20, 27, 31, 74–75,
76, 113–22, 140, 141–43, 147–48, 181–83, 201,
207–8, 209, 211–12, 214, 217, 218–19, 251–53,
258–59, 274–77, 283, 285, 287, 291–309,
313–15, 316, 317, 318, 334, 349, 353, 356
officers in, 25, 46–47, 87–104, 122
Pakistan border conflicts in, 9, 15, 22, 32, 40, 58,
62, 111, 113–14, 119, 120–21, 135, 147, 200, 209,
224, 230, 233–36, 243–44, 246, 261–62,
267–70, 276–77, 288, 295, 313, 319, 320–21,
324, 329, 342, 348
peace talks on, 135–36, 140, 143, 209, 285, 294,
301, 346
police forces in, 25, 26, 42–45, 52, 62, 78, 92, 93,
95, 96–97, 119, 342; *see also* Afghan Local
Police (ALP); Afghan National Police (ANP)
policy reviews for, 274–77, 285, 291–303, 356
political impact of, 11–12, 27, 41–42, 57–58,
74–75, 113–22, 176–79, 221, 277–78
population figures in, 123, 134, 154, 159, 233–34,
277–78, 314
prisoners in, 46, 138, 161, 163, 171–76, 251
reconstruction programs in, 48, 76–80, 92,
123, 145, 155, 157, 160–65, 231, 251, 299,
343, 344
in rural areas, 99, 123, 153, 155, 157–59, 277–78
security and stabilization efforts in, 19–20,
42–46, 59–62, 98–100, 145–48, 153–65, 203,
204, 242–48, 259–60, 266–67, 277–78, 304–5,
312, 313–16, 322–30, 341–48, 352
Soviet conflict compared with, 17, 96, 226, 265,
329
Special Forces (SOF) in, 10, 17, 20, 21, 42, 43–44,
50, 52, 54, 57, 58, 62–63, 92, 93–97, 122–23,
129, 130–33, 136–37, 141, 154–58, 187–88, 198,
210, 222–23, 229, 230, 236, 244–45, 247,
261–67, 275, 277, 278, 284, 288, 318, 322–23,
324, 348
strategic objectives of, 8–9, 13, 30–31, 46, 48–49,
115–22, 123, 134–35, 137, 181–83, 197–98, 200,
203, 204, 218, 259–60, 262–63, 286–87,
291–303, 341–43
suicide attacks in, 243, 245, 246, 262, 280, 291,
328, 332, 343, 345
"surge" operations in, xxviii, xxix, 5, 14, 19–21,
54–55, 58, 59, 60, 89, 96, 117–22, 134, 138, 147,
168, 202, 246, 259, 272–73, 292, 300–301,
305, 306, 307, 318, 319, 330, 340, 342–43, 347,
356

Taliban insurgency in, 9–10, 15, 16–22, 31, 32, 42–45, 49–51, 57–58, 61, 62–63, 75, 78, 84–97, 99, 102, 108–15, 119, 120–24, 131–36, 138, 145–48, 155, 157, 159, 163–69, 171–76, 181–83, 186–88, 197–98, 202, 207, 208, 210, 212–13, 215, 218, 221, 222, 224, 225–36, 242–48, 251, 260–70, 271, 276–87, 300, 304–5, 313–14, 323–30, 332, 341–45

Taliban prisoners in, 138, 171–76, 251

terrain of, xxix, 16, 18, 24–25, 108–9, 123, 142, 166, 225–26, 227, 230–35, 243, 266

transfer of military power in, 141–43, 201, 202, 206–10, 211, 214–15, 221–22, 247–48, 271–72, 282, 291–303, 306–9, 341–42, 346–49

tribes in, 25–26, 47, 61, 62–63, 160, 235

U.S. military forces in, 19–20, 23, 24, 25, 26, 31–32, 58, 87–104, 113–22, 139, 141–43, 154, 202, 206–7, 221–22, 291–303, 351; see also specific units

U.S. public support for, 202, 212–15, 300–301

villages in, 42–45, 62–63, 84–85, 92, 93, 94–97, 102, 154–58, 161–65, 185, 197, 225–33, 244–45, 261–62, 277–78, 344, 351

warlords in, 44, 58, 93, 158, 270–71

Afghan Local Police (ALP), 42, 44, 52, 62, 92, 122–23, 134, 154, 157–60, 162–63, 164, 181, 185, 197, 200, 210, 236, 244–45, 247, 260, 261, 278, 284, 288, 347, 348

Afghan Military Hospital, 247

Afghan Mission Network, 344

Afghan National Army (ANA), 42–43, 46–47, 49, 84, 101–2, 111, 183–84, 195–96, 227, 249, 264–67, 304, 315–16, 322, 346–49

Afghan National Army Commandos, 94, 132–33, 230, 315–16

Afghan National Police (ANP), 42–43, 78, 158, 161, 235, 284, 304, 315–16

Afghan National Security Forces (ANSF), 42–43, 75, 137, 201, 235, 259–60, 287, 304, 305, 342, 344, 346–49

Agency for International Development, U.S. (USAID), 78, 80, 102, 157, 234

Air Force, U.S., 93–94, 108

AK-47 assault rifles, 85, 99, 158, 167, 210, 228

Allen, John, 252, 279, 299, 312, 314, 316, 323, 329, 333, 335, 337, 339, 340, 342, 344

Alokozai tribe, 160, 161

al-Qaeda, 3, 8–9, 15, 27, 57, 62–63, 75, 113–14, 119, 147, 148, 151–52, 182, 209, 212, 215, 226, 236, 252, 275, 276, 277, 286, 299, 300, 301, 322, 323, 349, 353

American Military and the Lessons of Vietnam: A Study of American Influence and the Use of Force in the Post-Vietnam Era, The (Petraeus), 69

Amor Officer Advanced Course, 65

Anaconda strategy, 137–39, 172, 210, 288, 342, 369

Andar District, 49, 99–100, 165, 167–68, 195, 314

Ansar al-Sunnah, 205

Apache helicopters, 87, 99–100, 103, 108, 188, 225, 226, 227, 228, 268–69

Arghandab River Valley, xxix, xxx, 17, 85, 87–97, 113, 145–46, 157–61, 172, 188, 197, 231–33, 250, 266, 291, 344

Aristide, Jean-Bertrand, 124, 125

Army and Vietnam, The (Krepinevich), 68

Army Corps of Engineers, U.S., 78, 319

Army School of Advanced Military Studies, 110

artillery, 89, 128, 145, 166, 206, 228, 266, 268

Assad, Bashar al-, 205

Associated Press, 120–21

Awlaki, Anwar al-, 276, 353

Axelrod, David M., 5, 118

B-1 bombers, 95–96, 145

Baath Party, 190

Babur, 92, 93, 160

Baghdad, 23, 24, 30, 40, 50, 84, 155, 188, 195, 236–38, 272, 311–12, 343

Baghdad Security Plan, 50

Baghlan Province, 133–34

Bagram Air Base, 94, 132, 226, 242, 258

Bakersfield, Battle of, 90–92, 153, 232–33

Balochistan, 348

Bamiyan Province, 222

Bankston, Ed, 227

Baqi, Abdul, 155

Barawala Kalay, 225–31, 233

Bashi, 166

Basra, 242

"Bastogne Brigade" (1st Brigade Combat Team, 101st Airborne), 83, 84, 107, 111, 225–31, 233

battlefield circulations, 242–46, 318–19

Benedict, Keith, 200

Benevolence International Foundation, 152

Best Defense, 319–20

Bickers, William, 99

Biden, Joseph, 3, 4, 12, 16, 31, 113–14, 117, 118, 119, 238, 296, 299, 316, 356–57

Bigeard, Marcel, 64

Billig, Tom, 227, 230

bin Laden, Osama, 129, 255–59, 275, 285, 293, 329, 349

biometric data, 173–74, 230, 251

Black Hawk helicopters, 16, 29, 91, 105, 108–9, 225, 233, 235

"black" operations, 131–33

Boehner, John A., 249

Bolin, Kenneth, 227

Boot, Max, 301–2

Bosnia, 39, 126, 129, 131, 148–53, 190, 213, 218, 275, 346

Bosnia Stabilization Force, 148–53

Bremer, Paul, 191

Brennan, John, 275, 292

"Bright Star" exercise, 65

Brodie, Bernard, 350

Bucknall, James, 298

Bulge, Battle of the, 83
Burgess, Bryan A., 226
Burrell, Tom, 95, 197
Bush, Barbara, 294
Bush, George H. W., 71, 294
Bush, George W., vii, 5, 6, 58, 118, 122, 143, 190, 195,
    236–37, 241, 274, 294

Caldwell, William B., 43, 183, 210, 213–14, 281, 288,
    289, 347
Cameron, David, 3–4, 220, 221
Campbell, John F., 23–24, 50–51, 109–12, 133, 147,
    166, 185, 233, 235, 242–46, 249, 263, 278, 290
Camp Lejeune, 214
Canada, 49–50, 344
Carr Center for Human Rights, 204, 205
Carstens, Roger, 284
Cartwright, James ("Hoss"), 118–19
Casey, George, 195
"cash for work" programs, 92, 153, 160–61
Cédras, Raoul, 124
Center for a New American Security (CNAS), 283,
    289–90, 321–22
Central America, 67–68, 69, 74, 348, 353
Central Command (CENTCOM), xxviii, 1–2, 5, 10,
    18, 20, 26–27, 29, 30, 39, 41, 50, 113–14, 139–
    40, 157, 193, 208, 213, 217–19, 234, 272–77,
    285, 308, 314, 319, 322, 335
Central Intelligence Agency (CIA), xxx, 57, 58, 76,
    131, 148, 150–51, 152, 159, 201–2, 214, 216, 217,
    218–19, 248–53, 255, 274, 276, 285, 289, 291,
    294, 297–98, 301–2, 322–23, 326, 335, 340,
    349, 353, 354–57
Centurions, The (Lartéguy), 64
Chambliss, Saxby, 14, 307, 308
Charqolba Olya, 157, 158, 159–63
Charqolba Sofla, 93, 95, 97
Chel Zeena Criminal Investigation Center, 46, 171,
    176
Chewning, Eric D., 24
Chiarelli, Pete, 272
Chief of Staff, U.S., 65, 147–48
China, 6, 352
Chinook helicopters, 109, 235, 267
Churchill, Ed, 267–70, 278
Churchill, Winston S., 50
Civil Operations and Revolutionary Development
    Support (CORDS), 38, 39–40
Civil War, U.S., 51, 60
Clapper, Jim, 252, 292
Clinton, Bill, 124, 125, 129, 294, 300
Clinton, Hillary, 2, 3, 5, 118, 120, 296, 297, 335
close air support, 53–54, 128
Coalition Provisional Authority (CPA), 190–92
Cohen, Eliot, 203
Cold War, 38, 58, 73, 214
Combat Infantry Badge, 99, 181
Combat Outpost Deh Yak, 100, 101
Combat Outpost Margah, 110–11

Combat Outpost Monti, 110
Combat Outpost Penich, 146–47
Combat Outpost Stout, 153
Combat Outpost Zerok, 243–44
Combined Arms Center, U.S., xxvii, 60, 195, 203–4
Combined Forces Special Operations Component
    Command—Afghanistan (CFSOCC-A),
    154–55
Combined Joint Inter-Agency Task
    Force—Shafafiyat, 77–82, 176–79, 288
Combined Joint Task Force—Kuwait, 130
Commander's Emergency Response Program
    (CERP), 157
Commander's Initiatives Group (CIG), 17–18, 41,
    113, 200–201, 220, 285, 319
Command Outpost Nolen, 91
Company C-1 "Charging Charlie" (West Point), 36
Congress, U.S., 4–16, 22, 78, 115, 117, 137–38, 198,
    200–214, 237, 285, 287–88, 291, 314–18
"Cougars" ("Bastogne Brigade"), 226–27, 228, 229
Counterinsurgency Advisory and Assistance
    Team (CAAT), 17, 23, 154–57, 183–86, 195–96,
    222–23, 264–67, 283–85, 320–23, 351
Counterinsurgency Field Manual, 6, 54–55, 58,
    59–62, 68, 114–15, 176, 203–5, 207, 271, 349,
    351–52
Crane, Conrad, 203
Creamer, Zainah C., 180
Creedence Clearwater Revival, 316
Crisis Response Unit, Afghan, 315–16
Crocker, Ryan C., 5, 42, 323, 341, 342
Cross Match Jump Kit, 173–74
"Currahees" (4th Brigade Combat Team, 101st
    Airborne), 14, 84, 98, 111–12, 267–68, 286,
    318–19

Dad, Karim, 93, 163–65
Daily Mail, 94, 162
Dari language, 17, 77, 85, 141, 155–56, 195, 196, 222,
    265, 284
Daud, Mohammed Daud, 280, 281, 282
D Company ("Currahees"), 267–68
D-Day, 83, 286
Defeat Into Victory (Slim), 7
Defense Department, U.S., 26, 78, 129, 156, 259–60
Defense Intelligence Agency, 151
Defense Ministry, Afghan, 249, 330
Defense Writers Group, 72
Deh Yak District, 165, 166, 167–68
Delta Force, 93–94, 132
Democratic Party, 14, 15, 143, 208, 213, 214, 215,
    216, 238, 288, 291, 306
Derbin, Chase M., 269
Dickinson College, 37–38
Dien Bien Phu, Battle of, 64, 188
"directed telescopes," 17, 18, 41
Do Ab District, 278–80
Donilon, Tom, 118
Dora Market, 237–38

drones, 58, 94, 117, 131, 132, 167, 230, 275, 276, 278, 318, 345, 353
Drug Enforcement Administration (DEA), U.S., 80, 270
Duarte, José Napoleón, 69
Duke Brigade (1st Infantry Division), 267

XVIII Airborne Corps, U.S., 130
82nd Airborne Division, U.S. ("Devil Brigade"), 50, 88–90 92, 98, 126–30, 145, 149, 210, 233, (504th Infantry Parachute Regiment)
Eikenberry, Karl W., 26, 29, 31, 41–42, 44–45, 76, 285, 288, 294–96, 323, 335
Eisenhower, Dwight D., 4, 36, 38, 188, 354
Elgin Air Force Base, 65
Elizabeth II, Queen of England, 221
El Salvador, 67
Emanuel, Rahm I., 5, 118

F-15 fighter jets, 146
F-16 fighter jets, 167, 318
Fallujah, 194
Faqiryar, Fazel Ahmed, 75–76
Farid, Jagaran, 265
Faulkner, Jeremy P., 226
Federal Bureau of Investigation (FBI), 152, 173, 174–76, 270
Federally Administered Tribal Areas (FATA), 288, 348
Feinstein, Dianne, 306, 308–9
Feldhaus, Dustin J., 226
Felter, Joe, 155, 156–57, 184
Fiasco (Ricks), 319
Fick, Nate, 321–22
1st Ranger Battalion, U.S., 65
Fitzgerald, F. Scott, 54
Fivecoat, David G., xxx, 48, 97–104, 107, 149, 165–69, 188, 189, 342–43
506th Infantry Regiment, 2nd Battalion, 243, 319
509th Airborne Battalion Combat Team, U.S., 63–65, 70
Flournoy, Michèle, 202, 209, 290
Flynn, David S., xxx, 87–97, 107, 145–46, 153–65, 172, 188, 197, 210, 231–33, 249–51, 253, 266, 344, 351
Foreign Affairs, 284
Foreign Ministry, Afghan, 312–13
Foreign Policy, 222
Fort Bragg, 105, 126–31
Fort Campbell, 89, 105, 153, 168, 253, 262, 350
Fort Chaffee, 73
Fort Leavenworth, xxvii, 24, 54, 60, 66, 195, 203–4, 205, 207, 236, 352
Fort Myer, 199, 252, 292, 300, 304, 354
Fort Sill, 206
Fort Stewart, 65
Forward Operating Bases (FOBs):
    Andar, 97, 102–3, 166
    Fenty, 229

Gamberi, 242, 245–46, 249
Joyce, 147
Sharana, 286, 319
Terra Nova, 160, 251
Walton, 286
Wilson, 232, 249–50
Foust, Joshua, 162–63
Fox News, 248, 316
France, 64–65, 150, 249, 284, 332–34
Frist, Bill, 105
"full-spectrum" operations, 205, 352, 355

Galvin, John R. ("Jack"), 36, 52, 65–70, 71, 121
Gamble, The (Ricks), 319
Gant, Jim, 62–63, 261–62
Gass, Simon, 341, 342
Gates, Robert, 2, 3, 4, 6, 9, 12, 20, 31, 74, 86, 114, 115, 117, 119, 120, 122, 147–48, 196–97, 201–2, 207–9, 212, 215, 219, 231, 251, 252, 279, 285, 286–87, 289, 292, 293–94, 296, 297, 300, 302, 308, 325–27
"Gators" ("Bastogne Brigade"), 227
Geneva Conventions, 96, 162–63
Gerhart, Christopher, 89
Germany, 70–71, 179, 251–52
Gerson, Michael, 117
Gfoeller, Mike, 276
Ghani, Ashraf, 141
Ghazni Province, xxx, 49, 87–104, 165–69, 180
Golden Knights, 130
Graham, Lindsey, 12, 140, 172, 215, 216, 303, 314–15, 316, 317–18
Grant, Ulysses S., 7, 51, 66, 354
Great Britain, 49, 220–21, 266, 336, 339–40, 344, 345–46
Green Berets, 130–31, 262, 284
Gregory, David, 55
Gulf War, 72, 74, 104, 129
Gunhus, Erik O., 121, 137, 252

Haass, Richard N., 15–16
Hague, William, 221
Haiti, 124–27, 153, 346, 353
Hamburger Hill, 83
Hamlet Evaluation System, 40
Haqqani network, 111, 147, 181–82, 288
Harman, Jane, 74
Harper's, 93, 163
Harvard University, xxvii, 192–93, 204, 205
Hastings, Max, 221
Hayden, Michael V., 216
Heart Beat, 91
Hellfire missiles, 94, 99–100, 167, 230, 275
Helmand Province, xxix, 10, 21, 32, 40, 49, 62, 78, 84, 86–87, 108, 111, 133, 134, 147, 165–66, 181, 198, 202, 218, 221, 224, 246–47, 264–67, 281–82, 283, 285–86, 289, 304, 305, 313, 314, 321, 322, 323, 340, 344
Herat Province, 32, 61, 222, 247

Hickman, Bill, 4, 214, 285, 333, 336
Hill, Don, 243
Hill, Marvin, 180, 249, 331
Hillah, 84, 188
Hindu Kush, xxix, 16, 22, 29, 319, 332, 336
Holbrooke, Richard, 5, 22, 31, 274, 276
Hollywood Hotel raid, 151–52
Honduras, 67
Hopkins, Stephen, 284–85, 321
Hotel International attack, 315–16, 324
House Armed Services Committee, 200, 214–17, 303, 308
Houston, Mark, 244
Howell, Edward, 34
Howell, Mark, 1, 2–3, 4, 5, 155, 199–200, 216–17
"How We Lost the War We Won" (Rosen), 99
Huntington, Samuel, 69
Hussein, Ousay, 189, 204–5, 256
Hussein, Saddam, 30, 58, 129, 130, 189, 190, 195, 204–5, 256
Hussein, Uday, 189, 204–5, 256

Ignatius, David, 137, 312
improvised explosive devices (IEDs), 16, 18–19, 85–86, 90–91, 94–97, 100, 101, 102–3, 142, 145–47, 159, 162–63, 180, 187, 196, 206, 223, 227, 231, 266–67, 280, 291, 323, 329, 340, 344, 351
Infantry magazine, 167
infiltration attacks, 243, 245, 246, 262, 280, 313, 323, 342, 345
Integrity Watch Afghanistan, 76
"Inteqal" plan, 141
International Crisis Group (ICG), 313–14, 315
International Security Assistance Force (ISAF), 8, 10, 13, 22, 24, 29, 30, 31–33, 42, 46, 50, 54–55, 59, 80, 92, 119, 122, 155, 156–57, 162, 163, 165, 177, 181, 185, 187, 198, 209, 210, 211, 220–21, 232, 233, 235, 245, 246, 247, 252, 260, 264, 266, 267, 270, 271, 278–88, 296, 299, 304, 305, 313, 314, 315, 324, 328, 329, 332–34, 335, 336, 339, 341–49
Inter-Services Intelligence (ISI), 348
Iran, 64, 65, 247, 256
Iran Hostage Rescue Mission (1979), 64, 256
Iraq Governing Council, 192
Iraq War:
    Afghanistan War compared with, 20, 23–24, 26–27, 40–41, 42, 45, 57–58, 74–75, 89–90, 100, 101, 103–4, 110, 114, 118, 123, 137–39, 154, 166, 168, 203, 204–5, 247, 249, 272–73, 343, 346, 347, 352
    al-Qaeda forces in, 138, 241
    Bush's policies on, 58, 236–37, 241
    civilian population in, 24, 238–39
    civil war in, 6, 13–14, 58, 203, 236, 242
    counterinsurgency operations in, xxviii, 13–14, 23–24, 57, 58, 60, 100, 101, 107–8, 110, 123, 154, 189–93, 236, 240

"green zones" in, 45, 171, 238
insurgency in, xxviii, 6, 137–39, 204–5, 236–42, 314
Iraqi military forces in, 237, 240, 242
military casualties in, xxviii, 238, 240–41, 242, 333–34
nation-building in, 58, 188–94
Obama's policies on, 74–75
security and stabilization issues in, 45, 154, 171–72, 203, 204, 239–42
Shia vs. Sunni populations in, xxviii, 6, 100, 138, 203, 239, 240–41, 242, 314
suicide bombings in, 237, 238, 240, 241
"surge" operations in, xxviii, 6, 13–14, 24, 30, 40–41, 50, 58, 74, 107–8, 118, 168, 236–37, 238, 240–42
troop levels in, 20, 114, 247–48, 272–73
U.S. occupation in, 6, 188–94, 239
Iron Rangers (1st Battalion, 16th Infantry Regiment, 1st Infantry Division), 261–62
ISAF Joint Command (IJC), 24, 31–33, 162, 232, 278–80, 285
ISAF Secret intelligence, 223
Italy, 64–65, 284, 289

Jamal, Hamed Abdel Rahim al-, 152–53
Jelawur, 90, 96, 161, 164
John F. Kennedy School of Government, 192–93
John F. Kennedy Special Warfare Center, 130–31
Joint Chiefs of Staff, U.S., 8, 114, 129, 147, 155, 201, 216, 285, 308
Joint Interagency Task Force—Counterterrorism, 151–52
Joint Readiness Training Center (JRTC), 74, 128
Joint Special Operations Command, U.S. (JSOC), 64, 93–94, 115, 131, 133–34, 148–53, 255–59, 272, 275, 281, 322–23
Jones, Jim, 115
Jones, Walter, 214–15

Kabul, 30–31, 32, 79, 123, 198, 199, 220–21, 222, 246, 247, 255–59, 293, 304, 305, 308, 311–37, 343
Kabul Bank, 79, 296, 317, 348
Kabul International Airport, 332–34, 336
Kandahar city, xxix, 14, 16, 17, 22, 31, 46, 84, 87, 157, 159, 316–17
Kandahar Province, 9, 25, 32, 40, 49–50, 78, 84–97, 108, 111, 113, 133, 134–35, 147, 153–65, 171, 175, 181, 187–88, 195–96, 197, 198, 202, 210, 218, 224, 232, 246–47, 249, 251, 260–61, 262, 265, 304, 305, 313, 314, 322, 323, 328, 344
kandaks (Afghan battalions), 320–21
Kandarian, Arthur, 86, 232
Karadzic, Radovan, 150
Karbala, 84, 188
Karimi, Sher Mohammad, 313
Karzai, Ahmed Wali, 327–28

Karzai, Hamid, 3–4, 15, 18, 25, 31, 41–45, 61, 76, 79, 80, 140–42, 161, 176–79, 182, 186, 211, 221–22, 233, 247, 277–78, 281, 282, 283, 285, 294–96, 308–9, 313, 316, 317–18, 323, 327–28, 332, 346, 347, 348–49, 352
Kayani, Ashfaq, 256, 277, 293, 313, 329
Keane, Jack, xxix–xxx, 18, 73–74, 104–7, 118, 130, 139, 272, 296, 300
Keating, William, 288
Kerry, John F., 291
Kerry-Lugar-Berman bill, 276–77
Kevlar body armor, 150, 227, 231, 249
Khafagi, Al-Halim Hassam, 151–52
Khan, Jalat, 171, 174, 175–76
Khan, Jan Mohammed, 332
Khan, Samir, 353
Khosrow Olya, 94–95
Khosrow Sofla, 93, 94, 95, 96, 162, 163–64
Khost, 180, 291, 304
Kilcullen, David, 81–82
kinetic operations, 129, 130–33, 138, 147
Kiowa helicopters, 87, 108, 146, 228
Kirkpatrick, Mike, 251
Klein, Joe, 137
Klemm, Hans, 45
Kneip, Markus, 280, 281
Knowlton, Peggy, 38, 253
Knowlton, William A., 8, 37, 38–40, 65, 249
Koran, 233
Korean War, 69
Korengal Valley, 244, 278
Kosovo Air Campaign, 129
Krepinevich, Andrew, 68, 69
Kunar Province, xxx, 40, 62, 107, 110, 111, 146–47, 186, 196–97, 224, 225–31, 232, 234, 235, 244–45, 261–62, 277, 278, 324
Kunduz Province, 133–34
Kuwait, 72, 74

Laghman Province, 222, 247
Lamborn, Doug, 288
Larteguy, Jean, 64
Lashkar Gah, 222, 281
Lawrence, T. E. ("Lawrence of Arabia"), 55, 62, 82, 195–96, 354
Levin, Carl, 7, 207–9, 211–12, 214, 308, 309, 315
Liberi, Dawn, 274–75
Lieberman, Joe, 140, 302, 306, 316, 317, 318
"Lifeliners" (101st Sustainment Brigade), 242, 246
Lincoln Lawyer, The, 199–200
Lindskog, Jameson, 229
Lisbon summit, 135–36, 140, 143, 209, 285, 294, 301, 346
low-intensity conflict (LIC), 126, 203
Lugar, Dick, 238–39
Lujan, Fernando, xxx, 16–17, 18, 155, 156, 184–86, 195–96, 222–23, 224, 264–67, 283–85, 288, 289–90, 320–22, 351

Lute, Douglas E., 1, 118
Lyon, Kyle, 153

M58 Mine Clearing Line Charge, 86
MacArthur, Douglas, 36
McCain, John, 7, 8, 11–12, 208–9, 212, 314, 316, 317, 318
McChrystal, Stanley A., 1–4, 5, 9, 10, 15, 17, 20, 21, 22, 23, 29, 30, 31, 32–33, 41, 43, 47, 53, 57, 59, 61, 65, 110, 113–22, 131, 136, 139–40, 187, 214, 240, 279, 282, 283, 285, 295, 319, 323, 342
McConaughey, Matthew, 199–200
McKiernan, David, 57, 114–15
McMaster, H. R., 77–82, 138, 176–79, 183, 216, 247, 270–72, 274, 288, 348
McNamara, Robert, 191
McNeill, Dan, 130
McRaven, William H., 255–56, 258, 275
Maliki, Nouri al-, 42, 44, 241, 242
maliks (village chiefs), 93, 96, 97, 155, 160, 163–65
Manarah Canal, 93
Mangwal, 62–63, 261, 262
"Man in the Arena" Theodore Roosevelt speech, 355–56
Marine Corps, U.S., 24, 84–85, 114, 203, 264, 281–82, 286, 344, 351
Marjah, 10, 21, 84, 86, 260, 264
Marshall, George C., 354
Martins, Mark S., 45–46, 138, 171–76, 183, 251, 288, 317
Mattis, James, 201, 208, 212, 255, 285, 292, 303, 308, 309, 351
Mazar-i-Sharif, 222, 282
Meese, Edwin, 149
Meese, Mike, 48, 149, 348
Meet the Press, 74
Merchant Marine, U.S., 33, 34
Mi-17 helicopters, 269
Milani, Andy, 148–52
Military Operations in Urban Terrain (MOUT), 204–5
Miller, Scott, 154–55
Mine-Resistant Ambush-Protected vehicles (MRAPs), 100, 101–2, 111, 264, 327
Ministry of the Interior, Afghan, 154–55, 162–63, 173–74, 197, 280, 316, 330, 347, 348
Mioduszewski, Christopher W., 268
Mittler, Shaun M., 50–51
Moby Group, 80
Mohammed, Haji Shah, 93
Mohammed, Issa, 160, 161, 164
Mooldyk, Evan J., 180
Moore, Benjamin G., 180
Morrison, James R., 268
mosques, 134, 155, 161, 163, 231, 232, 238, 251, 328
Mosul, 6, 85, 103, 149, 189–94, 206, 311
Mott, Kevin, 108
MoveOn.org, 241
Muhammad, Sardar, 327–28

mujahideen, 96, 265, 329
Mulholland, Sean, 150
Mullen, Michael G., 3, 4, 9, 20, 114, 115, 116, 117, 118, 119, 120, 201, 217, 285, 292, 293, 296, 297, 303, 308, 319, 335, 354–55
Multi-National Force, xxviii, 171–72
Multi-National Security Transition Command—Iraq (MNSTC-I), 193–94
Multiple-Launch Rocket System (MLRS), 93
Mumbai attacks (2008), 316
Murmansk, 34–35
Muslims, xxviii, 6, 45, 100, 138, 151, 184, 203, 204–5, 232, 233, 239, 240–41, 242, 314
My Lai massacre, 38, 39

Nad-e Ali, 264–65
Nagl, John A., 60, 203, 290, 321–22
Naim, Mohammad, 93
Najaf, 84, 188–89
Napoleon I, Emperor of France, 17
National Directorate of Security (NDS), Afghan, 166
National Military Academy, Afghan, 221
National Military Hospital, 178
National Security Agency (NSA), 132, 151
National Security Council (NSC), Afghan, 186, 187
National Security Council (NSC), U.S., 12, 124, 129, 178, 218, 274, 283, 306, 314, 323
NATO Rule of Law Field Support Mission (NROLFSM), 317
NATO Training Mission—Afghanistan (NTM-A), 347
Navy, U.S., 93–94
NDS Counter-Terrorist Pursuit Team, 304
Negron, Carlos J., 50–51
Netherlands, 34
Newsweek, 15–16
New York Times, 135, 198, 241, 300, 323
New York Times Book Review, 60
Nicholson, John (Mick), 293
Nightingale, Keith, 14–15, 64, 65, 70, 141, 219–20
NOFORN intelligence, 223
Noorafzhal, Malik, 62–63, 261, 262
Nordby, Landon, 330–31
Norgrove, Linda, 234
Noriega, Manuel, 72
North Atlantic Treaty Organization (NATO), 8, 16, 21, 23, 24, 29, 30, 31–32, 38, 41, 42, 43, 48, 49–50, 53, 57, 61, 64, 69–70, 80, 93, 98, 139, 140, 141, 147–48, 149, 165, 166, 168, 187, 207–8, 215, 218, 221, 222, 223, 247, 260, 264, 280, 281, 283, 287, 288–89, 296, 313, 315, 317, 335, 339, 347
Northern Alliance, 57
Northern Distribution Network, 273
"No Slack" battalion (2nd Battalion, 327th Infantry Regiment, 101st Airborne), xxx, 107–10, 227, 228, 230, 232, 233, 234, 262–64
Now Zad District, 281–82

nuclear weapons, 69, 70, 273, 352
Nugent, Richard, 288
Nuristan Province, 40, 165–66, 224, 278–80, 324

Obama, Barack, xxix, 1–16, 19, 20, 23, 27, 31, 48, 75, 76, 107, 113–22, 140, 141–43, 147–48, 181–83, 201, 207–8, 209, 211–12, 214, 217, 218–19, 251–53, 258–59, 274–77, 283, 285, 287, 291–309, 313–15, 316, 317, 318, 334, 349, 353, 356
Obama's Wars (Woodward), 113–14
Odierno, Raymond, 237, 239, 240
Office of Servicemember Affairs, U.S., 248
O'Hanlon, Michael, 74, 136, 238, 241
Ollivant, Douglas, 23–26, 109–10, 135, 185, 233–34, 262–63, 277–78
Omar, Mullah Mohammed, 84
101st Airborne Division, U.S. ("Screaming Eagles"), xxvii, xxx, 6, 7, 23–24, 45, 48, 50–51, 55, 74, 103–12, 124, 134, 153–65, 176, 188–94, 204–5, 209, 227, 228, 230, 232, 233, 234, 235, 256, 262–64, 311, 333–34, 354
173rd Airborne Brigade Combat Team, U.S., 181, 317
One Tribe at a Time: A Strategy for Success in Afghanistan (Gant), 62, 261
On Strategy (Summers), 68
Operational Detachment Alpha 316, U.S., 62
Operation Desert Shield, 72
Operation Desert Spring, 130
Operation Desert Storm, 72, 83–85
Operation Dragon Strike, 84–85, 86, 135
Operation Eagle Claw, 94–97
Operation Hamkari, 85, 260
Operation Iron Blade II, 167
Operation Just Cause, 71–72
Operation Moshtarak, 21, 22, 260
Operation Overlord, 243
Operation Strong Eagle I, 108–9, 110, 233
Operation Strong Eagle II, 109–10, 233
Operation Strong Eagle III, 225–31, 233, 262, 263
Ostlund, Bill, 350–51

Pace, Peter, 237
pacification programs, 38, 39–40
Pakistan, 9, 15, 22, 32, 40, 58, 62, 110, 111, 113–14, 119, 120–21, 135, 147, 200, 209, 224, 230, 233–36, 243–44, 246, 255–62, 267–70, 276–77, 288, 293, 295, 313, 319, 320–21, 324, 329, 342, 348, 353
Paktika Province, 48, 98, 111, 166, 224, 244, 246, 286, 319, 320
Palace Information Coordination Center (PICC), 186–87
Panama, 67–68, 71–72, 126, 127
Panetta, Leon E., 148, 252, 322–23
Pashto language, 77, 146, 155–56, 160, 195, 222, 265, 319
peacekeeping missions, 124–27, 129, 149–54

Pech Valley, 196–97, 226, 233–36, 244, 277, 278
Perry, Tony, 146–47
Pershing, John J., 354
Persistent Threat Detection System (PTDS), 167
Peters, Ralph, 204–5
Petit, Kevin, 127–29
Petraeus, Anne, 67, 199, 249
Petraeus, Carol, 35
Petraeus, David H.:
  advisers and aides of, 18–19, 23–24, 76–82,
    97–98, 106–7, 122, 168–69, 176–79, 183,
    200–205, 218, 350–51
  Afghanistan command of, xxix–xxx, 1–87, 107,
    121–24, 126, 131–48, 152–53 168–179,
    195–236, 242–64, 277–303, 311–37, 339, 340,
    348–49, 350, 353, 356, 365, 367, 369
  "all in" quote of, vii, 237
  background of, 4, 33–40, 294
  Baghdad operations of, 30, 40, 155, 188, 195,
    236–38, 272, 311–12, 343
  in Bosnia, 39, 126, 129, 131, 148–53, 190, 213, 218,
    275, 346
  briefings given by, 30–33, 52–53, 120, 122,
    137–39, 140, 154, 259, 279–80, 288–89, 293,
    303, 304–6, 312–13
  Bush's policies as viewed by, 58, 122, 143, 190,
    195, 236–37, 241, 274
  at Central Command (CENTCOM), xxviii, 1–2,
    5, 10, 18, 20, 26–27, 29, 30, 39, 41, 50, 113–14,
    139–40, 157, 193, 208, 213, 217–19, 234,
    272–77, 335
  CIA director appointment of, xxx, 148, 201–2,
    214, 216, 217, 218–19, 248–53, 285, 289, 291,
    294, 297–98, 301–2, 322–23, 326, 335, 340,
    349, 353, 354–57
  combat experience of, 103–7, 188–94, 203–6,
    311–12
  confirmation hearings of, 4–16, 22, 31, 291, 293,
    297–98, 301–2, 306–9, 322
  congressional testimony of, xxx, 137–38, 198,
    199–217, 220, 237, 259
  counterinsurgency doctrines of, xxvii, 5–6,
    13–14, 23–26, 38–40, 46–47, 54–55, 58, 59–
    62, 67, 74, 107–8, 113–14, 122–26, 133–40,
    145–53, 183–86, 189–92, 195–96, 203–7, 208,
    248, 271, 277–85, 319–20, 324, 347–48, 349,
    351–55, 365, 367
  criticism of, 5–6, 47, 121–22, 176–77, 241, 312,
    313–14, 349
  Croce d'Oro awarded to, 289
  Defense Distinguished Service Medal awarded
    to, 335
  doctoral dissertation of, 69, 355
  education of, 33, 35–40, 66, 69, 124, 127
  as 82nd Airborne Division ("Devil Brigade")
    commander, 126–30
  farewell message of, 331–32
  final days of command for, 311–37
  Georgetown University fellowship of, 124

  in Germany, 70–71, 179, 251–52
  Haitian task force command of, 124–27, 153,
    346, 353
  interviews given by, 74, 198, 248–49, 292, 312,
    318, 323–24, 348
  Iraq command of, xxviii, xxx, 2, 6, 7, 13–14,
    23–24, 30, 40–55, 74–76, 83–84, 103–8, 125,
    126, 131–39, 149, 152–53, 155, 176, 188–94, 195,
    203, 204–5, 206, 213, 216, 218, 236–42, 247,
    249, 256, 272, 275, 311–12, 314, 325, 335, 340,
    343, 346, 347, 350, 353, 356
  in Italy, 64–65, 289
  Kabul headquarters of, 30–31, 198, 199, 220–21,
    255–59, 293, 311–37
  Karzai's relationship with, 41–45, 52, 61,
    140–42, 176–79, 186, 196–97, 198, 273, 281,
    282, 285–86, 296, 308–9, 323, 334–35
  leadership of, xxviii, xxx–xxxi, 6–7, 13–14, 20,
    36–37, 40–55, 306, 309, 354–57
  Légion d'Honneur awarded to, 249
  "lines of operation" of, 183–86, 198, 210–11, 248,
    297
  in London, 220–21, 339–41
  Medal of Ghazi Wazir Mohammad Akbar Khan
    awarded to, 334–35
  media coverage of, 3, 15–16, 26–27, 55, 74, 86,
    113–14, 120–22, 135–37, 143, 198, 202, 214,
    216, 218, 248–49, 292, 296, 299–300, 308, 312,
    318, 323–24, 348
  as military strategist, 5–9, 13, 30–31, 46, 48–49,
    52–53, 103–7, 124–39, 172, 203–7, 210,
    223–24, 272–77, 288, 291–303, 342, 349–57
  Mosul operations of, 6, 149, 189–94, 206, 311
  NATO Meritorious Service Medal awarded to,
    335
  Obama's Afghan command appointment of,
    xxix, 1–16, 19, 23, 48, 107
  Obama's policies as viewed by, xxix, 1–16, 19,
    23, 48, 74–75, 76, 107, 113–22, 140, 141–43,
    147–48, 181–83, 201, 207–8, 209, 211–12,
    214, 217, 218–19, 251–53, 274–77, 283, 285,
    291–309, 313–15, 316, 318, 334, 349, 353,
    356
  as 101st Airborne Division commander, xxvii,
    xxx, 6, 7, 23–24, 45, 48, 50, 74, 103–7, 124, 153,
    176, 188–94, 204–5, 209, 256, 263–64, 311,
    333–34, 354
  Panama command of, 67–68, 126, 127
  parachute accident of, 130
  "Peaches" as nickname of, 37
  personal ambition and competitiveness of, xxx,
    6, 33–34, 36, 37, 71, 105–7, 121–22, 126, 217–19,
    311–12, 336–37
  physical stamina of, xxviii, 35, 51–52, 105, 130,
    179, 199, 202, 213, 220–21, 252, 253, 281, 289,
    292, 313, 334, 341
  political aspirations denied by, 55, 301–2
  Princeton graduate work of, 40, 66, 69, 127
  prostate cancer of, xxviii

Petraeus, David H.: (*cont.*)
    reputation of, 4, 5–6, 7, 71, 103–7, 120–22,
        296, 299–303, 306, 314, 325–27, 334–35,
        354–57
    resignation as viewed by, 141, 217, 296, 302, 309
    retirement of, 311–12, 325–27, 331–32, 336–37,
        339, 354
    Secretary's Distinguished Service Award
        received by, 335
    staff of, 4–5, 18, 23–24, 29–30, 40–41, 47–48,
        51–52, 55, 122, 126, 127, 199–200, 216–17, 296,
        312
    "Tell me how this ends?" quote of, 104, 188
    victory as defined by, 8–9, 13, 30–31, 46, 48–49,
        134–35, 137
    in Washington, D.C., xxx, 71–72, 129, 137–38,
        198, 199–217, 220, 237, 251–53, 259, 273–76,
        291–303
    as West Point graduate, xxvii, 7–8, 33, 35–40,
        63–64, 181, 189, 203, 354
    as West Point instructor, 66–68, 69, 184
    wounding of, 104–5
Petraeus, Hollister Knowlton ("Holly"), 2–3, 4,
    7–8, 10, 16, 30, 37–38, 66, 71, 105, 178, 180,
    199–200, 214, 220, 248, 249, 253, 300, 307,
    356
Petraeus, Miriam Howell, 34
Petraeus, Sixtus, 33–34
Petraeus, Stephen, 4, 51, 66, 180–81, 195, 215,
    248–49, 317, 333
Petrone, Adam D., 267–68
Pittman, Melissa, 91
Pittman, Robert, 91
Platt, James, 111
Pomeroy, Jason, 226
Popal, Ahmed Rateb, 78
Popal, Rashid, 78
Poppas, Andrew ("Drew"), 109, 229, 233
Powell Doctrine, 58
Powers, Josh, 101–2
Predator drones, 94, 117, 167
Priddy, Wade, 320
Protection of Civilians in Armed Conflict, 328–29
Provincial Reconstruction Team (PRT), 48, 145
Purple Heart, 99, 101, 181, 246

Radio Shariat, 230
Rafiullah (Taliban prisoner), 173–75
"Rakkasans" (3rd Battalion, 187th Infantry
    Regiment, U.S., 101st Airborne), 83–85,
    97–107, 165–69
Ramstein Air Base, 251–52
Rangers, 37, 50, 64, 65, 94, 105, 107, 132, 181, 249
Rasmussen, Anders Fogh, 3–4
Rayburn, Joel, 81
Raymond, Brendan, 250
Raziq, Abdul, 93, 95, 96–97, 163
Reed, Jack, 12
Reedy Tye, 226, 228

Regional Command East (RC East), U.S., 23–24,
    50, 51, 196, 242–46, 277–78
Regional Command South (RC South), U.S., 222,
    231, 344
Remington, Frederic, 52–53, 66
"Report on Progress Toward Security and
    Stability in Afghanistan and United States
    Plan for Sustaining the Afghanistan National
    Security Forces," 259–60
Republican Guard, 74
Republican Party, 9, 11, 14, 143, 208, 213, 214, 216,
    238, 288, 314–15
Rice, Susan, 297
Richards, David, 221, 340
Ricks, Thomas E., 120, 319–20
Ridgway, Matthew, 7, 36, 66
Riedel, Bruce, 114, 115, 274
"road to deployment," 205–6, 349–50, *371, 372*
Rockefeller, Jay, 308
rocket-propelled grenades (RPGs), 62, 99, 111, 146,
    158, 267, 278
Rodriguez, David M., xxix, 24, 31–32, 59, 185, 232,
    233, 249–50, 278–80, 285, 287, 288, 314,
    324–25
Rolling Stone, 1, 21, 31, 99, 113, 323
Roosevelt, Theodore, 10–11, 355–56
"Route Civic," 267–68, 269
Rule of Law Field Force—Afghanistan
    (ROLFF-A), 45–46, 138, 171–76, 183, 288,
    348–49
rules of engagement, 125–26, 128–29
Rumsfeld, Donald, 29, 57, 193

Sadat, Kosh, 222–23, 264
Sadat, Noorullah, 172
Sadr, Moqtada al-, 241
Sadr City, Battle of, 155, 242
Saleh, Ali Abdullah, 275–76
Salehi, Mohammed Zia, 76, 178
Samarra Mosque, 238
Sanchez, Loretta, 215–16
Sarajevo, 148–53
Sar-i-Pul Province, 289
Sarkozy, Nicolas, 332–33
Sarobi District Center, 244–45
Sarowbay, 225–31, 233
Sarposa prison, 46, 171, 251
Sayed Zada, Sayed Abdul Ghafar, 171, 173, 175
Schoomaker, Peter, 195
Schwarzkopf, Norman, 72
Schweinfurt, 70–71
Scott, Austin, 288
SEALs, 93–94, 132, 234, 255, 257–58
SEAL Team Six, 93–94, 257–58
Seaton, Jim, 319, 320
Sedwill, Mark, 29, 42, 140, 142, 339–40, 346
Senate, U.S.:
    Armed Services Committee of, 4–16, 22, 115, 117,
        137–38, 200–214, 237, 285, 314–15, 316

Foreign Relations Committee of, 291
Intelligence Committee of, 291, 292, 293
Seneca, xxx–xxxi
September 11, 2001 terrorist attacks, xxvii, 8, 10, 19, 50, 59, 107, 151, 182, 199, 212, 213, 259, 307, 311, 312, 340, 351, 352, 357
Serbia, 150, 151
Seven Pillars of Wisdom (Lawrence), 194–95
75th Ranger Regiment, U.S., 94
Shaffer, Andrew, 90, 91, 94–95
Shahzad, Faisal, 120–21
Shelton, Hugh, 121–22, 129, 152, 183
Sherman, William T., 51, 55
Shia Muslims, xxviii, 6, 100, 138, 203, 239, 240–41, 242, 314
Shiloh, Battle of, 51
Shinseki, Eric, 120
shuras (council meetings), 92, 100, 160, 163, 182, 195–96, 244, 279, 316
Silver Star, 38, 153, 232–33, 249–50, 261
Simmons, Anthony W., 51
Situational Awareness Room, 31, 255–59
60 Minutes, 244
Slim, William, 7
Smitchger, Ellen, 36
Smith, Gregory J., 29–30, 137
Soldier and the State, The (Huntington), 69
Somme, Battle of the, 350–51
Sons of Iraq, 154
South Carolina National Guard, 100, 103
Southern Command Headquarters, U.S., 67–68
Southern European Task Force, U.S., 64
Soviet Union, 17, 34–35, 38, 65, 96, 226, 265, 329
Special Forces/Special Operations Forces (SOF), 10, 17, 20, 21, 42, 43–44, 50, 52, 54, 57, 58, 62–63, 92, 93–97, 122–23, 129, 130–33, 136–37, 141, 154–58, 187–88, 198, 210, 222–23, 229, 230, 236, 240, 244–45, 247, 256, 261–67, 275, 277, 278, 284, 288, 318, 322–23, 324, 348
Special Mission Unit (SMU), 13, 148–53
Special Operations Command (SOCOM), 129, 156, 322–23
Special Operations Task Force (SOTF), 210, 261–62
Stampede by Lightning (Remington), 52–53, 66
Standard Operating Procedure 373, 282
Stansbery, Michael L., 90, 91
Starks, Donald, 111, 112
State Department, U.S., 20, 25, 26, 78, 79, 80, 129, 172, 173, 176, 270, 274, 323, 335
Stout, Kyle B., 90, 91
Strategic Implementation Plan, 115–22
"Strike" (2nd Brigade Combat Team, 101st Airborne), 84, 86, 87, 232, 249–51
Summers, Harry, 68
Sunni Muslims, xxviii, 6, 100, 138, 203, 239, 240–41, 242, 314
Supreme Headquarters Allied Powers Europe (SHAPE), 69–70

Swat Valley, 277
Sylvester, John B., 150, 151
Syria, 189–90

Tactical Directive, 25, 30–31, 53–54, 211
Tactical Driving Directive, 282
Tal Afar, 77, 79
Talbott, Strobe, 124, 125
Taliban, 9–10, 15, 16–22, 31, 32, 42–45, 49–51, 57–58, 61, 62–63, 75, 78, 84–97, 99, 102, 108–15, 119, 120–24, 131–36, 145–48, 155, 157, 159, 163–69, 174, 181–83, 186–88, 197–98, 202, 207, 208, 210, 212–13, 215, 218, 221, 222, 224, 225–36, 242–48, 251, 260–70, 271, 276–87, 300, 304–5, 313–14, 323–30, 332, 341–45
Tanzola, Rob, 184–86, 195, 223, 264, 283, 284, 285, 322
Tarok Kolache, 93–96, 145, 155, 157, 162–63, 231–33, 344
Tehrik-i-Taliban, 277
Tenet, George, 150, 306
Tennyson, Alfred Lord, v
10th Mountain Division, U.S., 180
Terry, James, 154, 155
3rd Armored Cavalry Division, U.S., 176
3rd Infantry Division, U.S., 70–71, 188, 206
3rd Platoon, 1st Battalion, 503rd Infantry 173rd Airborne Brigade Combat Team, U.S., 180–81
3rd Special Forces Group, U.S., 62
Times (London), 186
Times Square bombing attempt (2010), 120–21
Tolo TV, 79–80
"Top Guns" (1st Battalion, 320th Artillery Regiment), xxx, 172, 188, 210, 231–33, 250, 253
Transportation Command, U.S., 273
Treasury Department, U.S., 270, 274
Trinquier, Roger, 101
Turkey, 189, 190, 272
24th Infantry Division (Mechanized), U.S., 65–66, 206
24th Special Tactics Squadron, U.S., 93–94
25th Infantry Division, U.S., 88
"Twenty-Seven Articles" (Lawrence), 82
"Twenty-Eight Articles: Fundamentals of Company-Level Counterinsurgency" (Kilcullen), 82
205th National Army Corps, Afghan, 183–84, 195–96, 265
212th Military Police Detachment, U.S., 180
215th National Army Corps, Afghan, 263, 264–65

Udall, Mark, 14
Ullman, Richard, 66
"Ulysses" (Tennyson), v
"Understanding the Environment," 284
United Nations, 19, 124, 125, 187, 211, 291, 328–29

United Nations Assistance Mission in Afghanistan (UNAMA), 19, 328–29
Uzbekistan, 273

Vanderbilt University Medical Center, 105
video teleconferences (VTC), 18, 30, 47–48, 51, 200, 304, 329
Vietnam War, 19, 38–40, 60, 63, 64, 65, 67, 68, 69, 71–72, 74, 83, 95, 103, 107, 109, 191, 330, 348, 355
Village Stability Operations (VSO), 43–44, 154–58, 185, 197, 244–45, 261–62
Vines, John, 129
Vowell, J. B., xxx, 107–10, 146–47, 225–31, 233, 234–35, 236, 262–64, 278, 342–43
Vuono, Carl, 71–74, 105, 121, 124, 129

Wahidi, Haji Sayed Fazlullah, 109
Wallace, William, 203–4
Wardak, Abdul Rahim, 249
Wardak Province, 180–81, 247
war on terror, 8–9, 16, 120–21, 128, 148, 248, 275, 322–23
Washington Post, 113–14, 117, 135, 137, 141, 186, 202, 212, 277, 284, 291, 292, 312, 319

Watanwal, Mohammed Hasham, 332
Westmoreland, William, 38, 39, 40
West Point (U.S. Military Academy), xxvii, 7–8, 16–17, 20, 33, 35–40, 50, 63–68, 69, 101, 106, 118, 120, 122, 147, 181, 184, 189, 203, 207, 296, 300, 301, 304, 322, 354
White, Chris, 36, 356
WikiLeaks, 295
Wilson, Charlie, 329
Wolfowitz, Paul, 192
"Wolverines" ("Bastogne Brigade"), 227–28, 229, 230
Woodall, Rob, 288
Woodward, Bob, 113–14, 121
World War I, 350–51
World War II, 33, 38, 83, 286, 345

Yaftali, Ahmad Zia, 247
Yemen, 15, 275–76, 353

Zabul Province, 222, 264, 320
Zahir, Haji Abdul, 21–22
Zellem, Ed, 186–87
Zhari District, 84, 87, 113

PHOTO CREDITS